BENJAMIN RUSH

Benjn Rush

Benjamin Rush

PHYSICIAN AND CITIZEN

1746–1813

By

Nathan G. Goodman

UNIVERSITY OF PENNSYLVANIA PRESS

Philadelphia

1934

London

Humphrey Milford

Oxford University Press

To
JULIA
and
SUSAN

Preface

OFTEN, as I worked over material on the men and events of the period during and after the War for Independence, the name of Benjamin Rush sprang up to engage my attention. Four years ago I discovered, in preparing a newspaper article on Rush, that no biography of this most distinguished American physician existed. It seemed to me that historians and biographers had neglected an important figure in the nation's past. After examining countless letters, documents, and newspapers in evolving this full-length portrait of the only Doctor of Medicine to sign the Declaration of Independence, I found that there emerged a man vigorous in mind and body, and heroic in stature.

The helpfulness of many librarians lightened the burden of research, and I owe thanks particularly to the librarians and assistants of the following institutions: American Philosophical Society, College of Physicians (Philadelphia), Historical Society of Pennsylvania, Library Company of Philadelphia (Ridgway Branch), Library of Congress, Massachusetts Historical Society, Pierpont Morgan Library, New York Academy of Medicine, New York Historical Society, New York Public Library, Pennsylvania Hospital, Princeton University Library, Surgeon-General's Library, and the University of Pennsylvania. Through the kindness of Mr. Benjamin Rush and others, various manuscripts were made available.

For editorial suggestions and criticism of the text of several chapters I am indebted to Dr. Esther Katz Rosen, Dr. Henry J. Tumen, and Dr. Edward Weiss. I am most of all grateful to my wife, Julia N. Goodman, who assisted in research, labored over the manuscript, offered helpful criticism, and made it possible to complete the book in time for publication this year.

NATHAN G. GOODMAN

Germantown, Philadelphia
March ninth, 1934

Contents

Contents

Illustrations

I

Early Years and Medical Apprenticeship
1746–1766

PHILADELPHIA in the mid-eighteenth century, boasting something less than fifteen thousand inhabitants, chiefly Quaker and German, was the largest and most comfortable city in the American colonies. Its citizens enjoyed physical, social, and cultural advantages far beyond those offered in other cities. It was largely because of the genius of the foremost citizen among them, Benjamin Franklin, that the business of living was made a pleasant one. He had organized a street-cleaning system, a fire-fighting company, and a night watch. A circulating library and a philosophical society had come into existence under his inspiration. In his newly invented smokeless stove, fires blazed away in many homes while families regaled themselves with *Poor Richard's Almanac,* his perennial brain-child. Indeed, Philadelphia of the period was heavily indebted to Franklin, and to any boy or girl growing up in the city in those years this scientist and sage must have been among the household gods.

The capital of the Quaker province was a busy city. Ships entered and left port frequently, bound on concerns of trade and war. An adventurous youth lured by the call of the sea might have signed on the three-hundred-ton *Pandour,* Commander William Dowell, fitting out for a cruising voyage against King George II's enemies in early 1746.

Slaves and indentured servants found their place in the social structure. Although the idea of slavery was generally accepted and faithful service expected, masters often experienced trouble in keeping what they considered their rightful property. One John Howell, tanner, reported the disappearance of a servant, James Gardner by name, about thirty years of age: "He is of pretty fresh complexion, middle stature, and round and full-bodied: He had on and with him, a dark homespun coat, with flat metal buttons, a half worn hat, a worsted cap, a light coloured cloth jacket, with pewter buttons, covered with leather, new black and white stockings, good shoes, two homespun shirts, and a pair of short trousers."[1]

Runaway animals as well as servants were advertised in the lost and found columns of *The Pennsylvania Gazette*. "Came to the Sign of the Swan, on Chestnut Hill, Germantown Township, Philadelphia County, on the 26th of last Novem.," ran a typical insertion in 1745, "a white mare and colt, the mare is about 12 hands high, a natural pacer, and is branded, but unintelligible. The owner, by identifying the mare and colt and paying may have them."

From the very founding of the city in 1683 Philadelphia boasted substantial, well-built houses. A large number of William Penn's settlers were artisans who knew how to build and took pride in the careful maintenance of their homes. Anxious to patch up holes and cracks before the winter set in, the householder might have made his purchases at the Sign of the Golden Ball, opposite the end of Strawberry Alley near the Tun Tavern on Chestnut Street. Here Christopher Ball kept a stock of paints, brushes, tools, and a "variety of gums, and most sorts of varnishes and lackers, spirits of wine and turpentine, English glue, India ink, gold and silver leaf, &c. with most sorts and sizes of crown and common glass, suitable to glaze houses, ships, clocks, pictures."[2]

Philadelphia was the metropolitan center for the towns and hamlets lying within a radius of some fifteen miles. Its famous market sheds stretched westward from the Delaware River occupying a goodly portion of High (Market) Street, and for the accommodation of the southern section of the city a market place was set up on South Second Street at Cedar (South). Visitors were interested in the inns and taverns, in such spacious churches as Christ Church on Second Street, and in the imposing new State House on Chestnut Street where the provincial Assembly met. The farmers from the surrounding counties came into the city to sell their products, to buy supplies and to hear the news. To the south and west were the settlements of Chester and Darby. To the northwest lay Germantown, and northeast along the Delaware were a number of small farming communities.

Twelve miles up the river flourished Byberry, a conservative Quaker agricultural colony. Sometime during 1683, on the very heels of Penn's first settlers, an elderly dissenter and Oxfordshire yeoman, John Rush, settled on a farm here with his family, six sons and a daughter. Under Oliver Cromwell, whom he knew personally, he had served as Captain of a troop of horse, gaining for himself a worthy reputation under arms. One day, the story has come down, seeing Rush's mare come into camp without its rider, Cromwell supposed the warrior had been killed. Lamenting the loss of a brave soldier, the great leader exclaimed: "He has not left a better officer behind him!"[3]

In 1691 factional fights caused the Byberry Friends to split into two divisions, John Rush remaining with the old group led by John Hart, near whose home stood the meetinghouse and on whose property was the burial ground. Eight years later John Rush died, about eighty years of age, having outlived his eldest son, William, by three years. The family traditions were therefore, after 1699, in the hands of William's eldest son James. James's eldest son by Rachel Peart was John, born in 1712. John Rush married Susanna Harvey, daughter of Joseph Hall of Tacony. Her mother had been the widow of an extravagant and intemperate man who had died three or four years after their marriage. She bore John Rush seven children: James (1739), Rachel (1741), Rebecca (1743), Benjamin (1745), and Jacob (1747); Stephenson and John died in early childhood. Jacob was destined to become one of the judges of the Supreme Court of Pennsylvania.[4]

It was on Christmas eve, 1745, Old Style (January 4, 1746, New Style)[5] that the baby Benjamin was born on the five-hundred-acre Rush farm at Byberry, the fourth child in a family of seven. The birthplace is still standing and occupied. It is near the present Red Lion and Academy Roads, on the side of a hill within walking distance of the Torresdale Station of the Pennsylvania Railroad. The Rush estate, now called The Homestead, passed into the hands of Jonathan Parry in 1765 and has been maintained as a residence and farm by his descendants down to the present day. On several occasions supplementary rooms have been added to the original house, but the old walls, eighteen inches thick, and the thirteen-inch floor boards remain. The old rooms are eight feet two inches high. The fireplace has been so renovated that there is no evidence of its age. A hundred yards east of the residence is the old spring house, now unused. The present owners have hung in the hallway the original deed of sale of two tracts of the farm land, seventy-two and twelve acres, dated February 9, 1748. John Rush sold this land to John Hall for £450.

Benjamin's mother had been educated in a Philadelphia boarding school. As a woman she enjoyed an enviable reputation for her kindness, generosity, energy, and force of character. Benjamin's later devotion to moral and religious principles can be traced directly to his mother's training and influence. The father, who had inherited both his farm and his trade of gunsmith and blacksmith, was known to his neighbors as a meek and quiet man, so honest in his relations with others that it was said in Byberry that more could not be said of a man's integrity than that "he was as honest as John Rush." He apparently prospered, for he purchased a large tract in Warminster, several miles away, but was not to enjoy his work, his possessions, and his family for many years.[6] He died on July 26, 1751, in Philadelphia, and was buried in Christ Church Yard at Fifth and Arch Streets. Although her husband had successfully pursued the trade of gunsmith in Philadelphia and owned sizable pieces of land, Mrs. Rush did not inherit sufficient property in the city to permit her to support the family independently.

The Pennsylvania Gazette for October 24, 1751, carried the following notice: "All persons indebted to the estate of John Rush, late of this city, Gun-smith, deceased, are hereby desired to discharge the same: and all those that have any demands against said estate, are desired to bring in their accounts in order to be adjusted, by William Rush, black-smith, and Susannah Rush, Execut. There is likewise to be sold, A likely negroe woman, has had the small-pox and measles. Likewise a parcel of black-smiths and gun-smiths tools, such as are fit for rifelling, to be disposed of; and a smith's shop to be lett."

Mrs. Rush, forced to make her own way in the world, lost no time in doing so. She opened a grocery and provision store, the "Blazing Star," on the south side of Market Street about the fourth door east of Second, opposite the market sheds, later expanding the business and purchasing a house on the opposite side of the street. At one time she added to her stock a line of chinaware.[7] The young Benja-

BIRTHPLACE OF BENJAMIN RUSH

min was only six years of age at this time and more than likely was frequently under foot about the store.

Notwithstanding the difficulties encountered in establishing a paying business, Mrs. Rush found time to turn her mind to the problem of her children's education. It was not a difficult one, inasmuch as her sister, Sarah Hall, had married Rev. Samuel Finley, a schoolmaster and Presbyterian clergyman. Nothing was more natural than that Benjamin's education should be placed in his uncle's hands. The schoolmaster wielded over the lad in this formative period a profound influence that shaped and strengthened his character for the struggles he was to face.

Born in the north of Ireland in 1715, Finley came to America in 1734, studied at Log College, a Presbyterian institution in Bucks County, Pennsylvania, and obtained a preaching license in 1740. After six months in the pulpit of Philadelphia's Second Presbyterian Church, he was formally ordained and, two years later, became the pastor of the church at Nottingham, Maryland. At the same time, 1744, he founded an academy in that town, designed chiefly to prepare young men for the ministry. For seventeen years, until his election to the Presidency of the College of New Jersey, now Princeton, in 1761, he continued to train young men at Nottingham.

Almost immediately the school attained a reputation for excellence as a seat of learning, and its rolls were soon to list such distinguished names as the future Governors Henry of Maryland, and Martin of North Carolina; Dr. John Morgan, one of the founders of the Medical School of the University of Pennsylvania; Rev. Charles Cummins of South Carolina; Dr. John Archer of Maryland; Dr. Thomas Ruston; and Ebenezer Hazard, Esq., of Philadelphia, a close friend and correspondent of Rush's. The last four men were classmates of Benjamin Rush, who was sent to the academy at Nottingham with his brother Jacob, probably in 1754.

Naturally, Headmaster Finley manifested special interest in his nephews. Severe, perhaps, in the classroom, in the days when corporal punishment was the rule, Finley was kindly in his relations with the students outside of class hours. It was his practice to invite them on occasion to take dinner with distinguished visitors in whose presence they could cultivate poise and dignity. They listened to anecdotes and participated freely in general discussions. Benjamin Rush, young though he was, profited greatly from these contacts. Mrs. Finley was not only a good provider in her capacity as house-keeper, but also a pleasant and lively woman, always keeping the boys in buoyant spirits.

In the dining hall Finley encouraged gentlemanly conduct. He was able to rebuke an individual without being harsh or without engendering in the boy a sense of injustice. "His government over his boys was strict, but never severe nor arbitrary," recalled Benjamin Rush in after years. "It was always by known laws which were plain and often promulgated. . . . The instrument with which he corrected was a small switch which he broke from a tree. The part he struck was the palm of the hand and that never more than three times. The solemn forms connected with the punishment were more terrible and distressing than the punishment itself. I once saw him spend half an hour in exposing the folly and wickedness of an offense with his rod in his hand. The culprit stood all this while trembling and weeping before him. After he had ended his admonitions he lifted his rod as high as he could and then permitted it to fall gently upon his hand. The boy was surprised at this conduct. 'There, go about your business,' said the Doctor. 'I mean shame and not pain to be your punishment in the present instance.' "[8]

Benjamin Rush adjusted himself admirably to the school and the system which taught him to be orderly, diligent, and punctual. Indeed, it seems that the discipline and general spirit of the school and the character of its headmaster impressed the young student more lastingly than the chief subjects of study, Latin and Greek. He was inspired, moreover, by Finley's talks on religion and by his morning and evening interpretations of the Bible. Physically as well as mentally and morally the health of the students was considered. An interest in rural life was stimulated through a course in practical agriculture. "I bear on one of my fingers to this day," wrote Rush in his *Memorial* forty years later, "the mark of a severe cut I received in learning to reap." Here, then, the mind and body of Benjamin Rush were molded in no uncertain manner in his formative years.

When he was admitted to the Junior class of the College of New Jersey at the age of fourteen, in the spring of 1759, his native ability in composition and public speaking were at once recognized by Rev. Samuel Davies, President of the College. Few courses were offered at this time at the College at Princeton, which had been founded to educate ministers for the Presbyterian Church. Latin and Greek there were, of course, and a smattering of philosophy, literature, and mathematics, but no science. At Nottingham and Princeton Rush studied Latin for more than six years, and yet he did not grasp the language completely. His classmate, Ebenezer Hazard, a few years later suggested that they correspond in Latin, but Rush was not equal to the invitation, and confessed to Hazard: "It is so long since I learned the latin language that I am afraid I shall not be able to correspond with you in it."[9]

From Dr. Davies, Rush learned to record in a book which he called "Liber Selectorum" such passages in the classics that appealed to him as he read them. "By recording those passages," he said, "I was led afterwards to record facts and opinions. To this I owe perhaps in part the frequent use I have made of pen and ink. I have constantly associated them with every book I have read—sometimes by making extracts from them, but more frequently by making references to them in a commonplace book, or by making marks or indexes in them."[10]

Because he was an excellent public speaker at college, Rush announced to President Davies that he planned to study law. Both the President and Mrs. Rush agreed that the choice was a wise one, and plans were made to place the young man in the office of a Philadelphia lawyer. Before the step was consummated, however, fate intervened and Rush's life swung into an entirely new path. He came to his final decision against the advice of friends, who pleaded that he could not put to use his superior oratorical ability outside the legal profession. Their entreaties were made in vain, however, after his uncle and former mentor, Rev. Samuel Finley, advised definitely against the study of law.

It was on a casual visit to Maryland with a friend that Rush called at the Finley's, where discussion naturally led to the tentative plans for the boy's future. Finley declared that the practice of law was full of temptations. Though no record of the actual interview exists, one can imagine that the schoolmaster was stubborn in his refusal to be swayed in favor of law by arguments based upon Rush's aptitude for public speaking and his facility in composition. After a long and serious discussion, Finley finally suggested the possibility of medicine as a profession. The idea appealed to the boy, and medicine it was to be!

"There were periods in my life in which I regretted the choice I had made of the profession of medicine," Rush confessed in 1800, "and once, after I was thirty years of age, I made preparation for beginning the study of law. But Providence overruled my intentions. . . . I now rejoice that I followed Dr. Finley's advice. I have seen the hand of heaven clearly in it."[11]

In September 1760 Rush was granted the Bachelor of Arts degree by the College of New Jersey, and, having made his decision in favor of medicine, he applied himself to the usual task of a young man about to enter the profession—to search for an advantageous apprenticeship.

*　　*　　*　　*　　*　　*　　*

Medical apprenticeship in the eighteenth century was not the easiest of occupations. Books on medicine were few and poor, and medical students received their training largely by means of actual practice. The medical apprentice had to be something of a jack of all trades, an errand boy, a servant, an orderly who accompanied his teacher on visits to patients, a technician assisting in bloodletting operations, and a nurse.

It was in his native city of Philadelphia that Rush, upon his return from Princeton in 1760, felt he could find the greatest opportunity in the field he had chosen. The city was growing steadily, and by this time had been laid the foundations of progressive institutions of all kinds that were to flourish in the next century. The Pennsylvania Hospital, America's first public hospital, had been in operation for almost a decade. The Academy, which ultimately became the University of Pennsylvania, had opened in 1749, three years after Rush's birth. A fire insurance company was functioning and, since 1753, under Deputy Postmaster-General Franklin, letters had been delivered daily by carrier.

A weekly stage-coach line was in operation between Camden, across the Delaware from Philadelphia, and New York City, a three-day journey. The stage line was a welcome innovation, inasmuch as practically everyone traveled on horseback. In 1761 in Philadelphia there were only twenty-nine families who enjoyed the luxury of a chair, a chariot, or other carriage in which to jog through the streets of the city or out into the country.

The shops in the city were stocked with a wide assortment of goods. On Second Street near Arch, James Dundas displayed a full line of dry goods and notions. Matthias M'Combe, trunk manufacturer, celebrated the New Year, 1760, by moving to a new shop on Third Street above Walnut where he sold all manner of trunks, even portmanteau trunks containing drawers and hat boxes—the wardrobe trunk of colonial days! James Beals, net-maker on Fourth Street near Market, sold all sorts of nets: nets to protect horses from flies, nets to cover army tents, hoop nets, fowling bags, and billiard-table pockets.

By way of amusement children and adults went to see, for two shillings, a large live lion at James Rorke's house on Water Street.

In the decade and a half since Rush's birth, the Quaker City had been easily able to hold its own as a thriving metropolis and the most important city on the continent. In February 1761 the fifteen-year-old Princeton graduate apprenticed himself to a distinguished and busy Philadelphia physician, Dr. John Redman, a short, dark, animated individual who inspired confidence on first sight.[12] Redman was on the staff of the Pennsylvania Hospital, and this connection meant much to the young apprentice who was permitted to observe the work of all the physicians at the hospital.

After a few months' experience as a medical apprentice, he reflected that, although the work of a physician is necessary to the welfare of mankind, that of a clergyman is nobler. He was probably surprised at himself that he was not using his oratorical powers as a clergyman or as a lawyer. He was, indeed, somewhat envious of his classmate Enoch Green, who had entered the ministry, and to whom he wrote: "I am so very glad to hear of your welfare & am well pleased to hear you have obeyed nature's dictates in the sublime study of divinity,—doubtless you might have tho't too I was designed to fill some station wherein eloquence would have been a requisite accomplishment.—But it has happened otherwise from my aversion to the study of law & my incapacity for that of divinity—to be sure to have officiated in the sacred duty would be my most delightful employment to spend & be spent for the good of mankind is what I chiefly aim at—tho' now I pursue the study of Physick I am far from giving it any preiminence to divinity. Oh no—we are employed it's true in a necessary calling—but a calling that enforces to us the weakness & mortality of human nature—this earthly frame, a minute fabrick, a center of wonders is forever subject to diseases & death, the very air we breath too often proves noxious—our food often is armed with poison—the very elements conspire the ruin of our constitutions & death forever lies lurking to deceive us—now how inglorious must this study appear when set in composition with divinity, the one employed in advancing temporal happiness the other external,—one applying remedies to a fading, mortal body—the other imployed in healing the sickness of a soul: immortal & everlasting:—Every pursuit of life must dwindle into nought when divinity appears—What station in life is more honorable? What more agreable? than for the embassadors of heaven to enjoy the fruits of their labours—& tho alas they too often fail of success, yet to a truly generous & pious mind the attempt, & endeavour yields some comfort."

Rush confessed that he was "in a conflict," and that he still had hopes of being numbered among those who are "the heralds of the Kingdom of heaven—who knows but my heart may be sufficiently changed to enter into that holy calling."[13] As the months passed, however, he became deeply interested in medicine, and in later years his desire to preach was satisfied by the reform movements in which he participated.

Until July 1766, for five and a half years, Rush worked in Redman's "shop" and was a member of his household. During this period he was absent from work only eleven days, and on only three occasions did he spend an evening beyond the confines of his patron's house. Redman fully appreciated the work of this serious student and, so great was his confidence in his apprentice, that he frequently placed Rush, after only a year's observation and practice, in full charge of patients. The student likewise was grateful to his master.

"I have experienced kindness from Dr. Redman I had little reason to expect," he wrote Ebenezer Hazard, "and have ever found in him not only the indulgent master, but the sincere friend and tender Father. . . . There is something, methinks, pleasing in being dependent upon a man of conscience and piety, who will not only make good but more than perform his promises."[14]

The work satisfied Rush and his master inspired him. In spare hours he diligently sought to improve himself by study. In the early morning and late at night he pored over all the medical books which came within his reach. In spite of his struggles with Greek he translated the aphorisms of Hippocrates into English. Profiting by Dr. Davies' training at college, Rush recorded systematically in a notebook interesting and valuable observations; in 1762 he made extensive notes of the yellow fever epidemic which prevailed in that year in the section of Philadelphia near the river. The notebook habit was retained throughout his entire life.

By this time there was slowly coming into being a native American literature of which the young student might have tasted. It was finding its way to the shelves of the bookshops and the Library Company of Philadelphia. Colonials, busy with the concerns of making a living, subduing the forests and the Indians, and shaping a new world, hardly found time to free their minds for artistic creation of any kind. In 1760, however, George Cockings published *War*, a heroic poem inspired by the capture of Louisburg. In Philadelphia James Ralph, Thomas Godfrey, and Nathaniel Evans were writing verse, inferior though it was. Jonathan Edwards' fame as a metaphysician rests on his *Freedom of the Will*, published in 1754. The tracts against slavery by John Woolman had won some little popularity, especially in the Middle Colonies, and these Rush must have seen in view of his later stand on the question. Franklin's pen and press had been constantly busy turning out all the kinds of writing this wizard was able to produce—philosophic, scientific, witty, satiric, political, journalistic, moralistic. Whatever there was of native literature was at hand for Rush's perusal and must have taken its place in his room beside the medical books over which he burnt much midnight oil.

On November 11, 1762, Dr. William Shippen, Jr. announced in

the local newspaper his first lecture in a course in anatomy, to be delivered at six o'clock on November 16 in the State House. These lectures, the first course of anatomical lectures to be offered in America, were prepared not only for medical students but also "for the entertainment of any gentlemen who may have the curiosity to understand the anatomy of the Human Frame." A discussion of all the necessary operations in surgery was promised, as well as a course in bandaging. Benjamin Rush was one of the ten students who attended the lectures regularly. They were held subsequently in the laboratory erected for the purpose by Dr. Shippen in the rear of his father's residence on Fourth Street north of Market. The entrance was reached through an alley that ran north from Market Street west of Fourth. Angry crowds, opposed to dissection, appeared in the alleyway when this lecture hall was opened, and once the windows of the dissection room were smashed. The cadavers that were studied were frequently obtained from the graves of slaves and paupers. More than once Shippen found it necessary to hide from gatherings of outraged citizens. Andreas Vesalius had similar experiences in Paris in the sixteenth century. Shippen, too, refused to capitulate, and continued to lecture in his private rooms before the classes of the College of Philadelphia's (later the University of Pennsylvania's) medical department after its establishment in the fall of 1765, the first medical school in America. In addition to this work under Shippen, Rush pursued Dr. John Morgan's course on materia medica in the College.[15]

In this year Rush began to consider the advisability of going to Europe to study in one of the recognized medical centers. On second thought, however, he decided that he would be a better student in Europe if he had further training and practice under Redman. Because a large part of Philadelphia's population was German in origin, he also thought it wise to study German. At the same time he brushed up on his Latin and Greek by reading Horace and the Greek Testament.[16] His earliest writing, in 1764, was a eulogium on Rev. Gilbert Tennent, who for twenty years had been pastor of his church, the Second Presbyterian Church in Philadelphia.

During the last year of his apprenticeship Rush developed an interest in politics through his concern over the celebrated Stamp Act.

In November 1765, he feared daily that the stamps would actually be used in Philadelphia, and he criticised Benjamin Franklin, colonial agent in London, for his failure to denounce the Act. "Philadelphia is cursed with a sett of men," he complained to Hazard, "who seem resolved to counteract all our efforts against ye Stamp Act, and are daily endeavouring to suppress the spirit of Liberty among us. You know, I mean ye Quakers. They have openly spoke in favour of ye Act and declare it high treason to speak against ye English Parliament."[17] Soon, however, the British Parliament sensed the folly of its ways and repealed the Act, and the furor in America subsided for the moment. Rush was one patriot who did not forget, and his antagonism to the British Crown never disappeared after this event.

About this time the famous preacher, George Whitefield, was visiting the city for the second time. His sermons set Rush to examining his own religious beliefs. At school and at college the atmosphere had been strongly religious, and Rush not only participated in public worship but also derived comfort from daily private devotion. He had been baptized by the Episcopal minister, Eneas Ross, and as a child had attended services in Christ Church on Second Street. His mother, however, was a Presbyterian and, after the death of her husband, she took her children to Rev. Gilbert Tennent's church, the Second Presbyterian, then on Fourth Street. Until the 1780's Rush remained a Presbyterian; then he accepted Unitarianism, but in 1788 he was once more confirmed in St. Peter's Episcopal Church. He was, however, to shift again. "In consequence of an alteration in the forms of baptism and the communion service,— the former admitting infant regeneration, and the latter favoring transubstantiation," he explained, "I declined after a year or two communing in the church, and had my children baptized by Presbyterian ministers." Always religiously inclined, particularly in times of stress, Rush was strongly moved with a sense of the power and presence of the Divine.[18]

It was on Dr. Redman's sound advice, however, rather than by reason of divine inspiration, that Rush packed his books and belongings and left his native haunts in the late summer of 1766 for further study across the ocean.

A Student at Edinburgh
1766–1768

Two medical students were passengers on the *Friendship* when she sailed eastbound under Captain Pierce's command in August 1766. Both Benjamin Rush and Jonathan Potts were on their way to Edinburgh, which boasted the foremost medical school in Great Britain and probably in Europe. The passage was a stormy one, the ship having been all but lost off the coast of Ireland and almost wrecked at Holyhead off the coast of Wales. Laudanum brought Rush some relief from severe attacks of seasickness, but the firm planks of the Liverpool docks, reached in October, afforded the only cure. Before leaving the port town the young men rested, enjoying the hospitality of several families to whom they had letters of introduction. Proceeding northward, they reached Edinburgh about the first of November.

Potts had requested Benjamin Franklin to forward letters to his distinguished friends in the Scotch capital. The busy colonial agent at once wrote Sir Alexander Dick, eminent Edinburgh physician, requesting him to be on the lookout for the American students. "They are strongly recommended to me," he said, "by many of my acquaintances as young gentlemen of ingenuity & application & excellent morals." And "from the character they bear of ingenuity, industry, & good morals," he wrote Dr. William Cullen, esteemed professor of medicine, "I am persuaded they will improve greatly under your learned lectures & do honor to your medical school."[1]

Enrolling at the University of Edinburgh, Rush shortly began to take advantage of the courses in anatomy, chemistry, medicine, natural philosophy, and practice of infirmary, offered by the leading professors of the time: Doctors Monroe, Cullen, Black, Gregory, and Hope. On November 16, 1766, after thanking Dr. John Morgan, Professor of Medicine in the new College of Philadelphia, for his letter of introduction to Dr. Cullen, he went on to discuss the courses at Edinburgh: "According to the plan you proposed to me when I left Philadelphia I am now attending Dr. Monroes lectures upon anatomy—Dr. Black's ingenuous lectures upon chemistry—Dr. Russell's upon natural philosophy,—and the great Dr. Cullen's on the Institutions of Physic, the last of whom daily exhibits such surprising efforts of genius & learning, that I am no longer surprized that you used to call him the Boerhaave of his age, and speak of his great merit with all those emotions you were wont to do. I find it a painfull piece of labour to attend these lectures as I should do, and I am now more fully convinced than ever, how much sleep you must have sacrificed in transcribing those volumes of learning you carried with you to America."[2]

Dr. Cullen's personality immediately impressed Rush, and he noted years later, in a eulogium of the great teacher, that his constant aim was to produce in the minds of the students a change from a passive to an active state, and to force upon them such habits of thinking and observation as would enable them to teach themselves. Especially gratifying to Rush was Cullen's introduction of English into medical instruction, in place of the Latin forms and formulae. In his relations with his pupils Cullen was kind and affectionate, affable without being sociable, sociable without being familiar, and familiar without losing a particle of respect. Frequently he would invite students to dinner at his home, and "upon these occasions his social affections seemed to have an influence upon his mind."[3] That both Redman and Cullen made a deep and permanent imprint on Rush's character is evident.

No detailed knowledge of Rush's life as a student at Edinburgh has come down to us. We know that he was struck by the high moral tone of the city. There was not a sound on the streets after ten o'clock at night and on Sundays the churches were filled to capacity. Rush insists that he never saw a pack of cards in either a public or private house. Dancing was enjoyed in large gatherings; swearing and drunkenness were both rare; integrity was the dominant characteristic of all classes of people.[4]

"Edinburgh is built upon one-third less ground than Philadelphia, but contains double the number of inhabitants," observed Rush. "I think they compute eighty thousand souls in the city. The reason why they occupy so much less room is owing to the height of their houses, in each of which seven or eight families reside. There is one common pair of steps which communicate with all the rooms of the house. These steps are open and exposed, and are trod by everybody in the same manner as the public streets. Dr. Franklin called them, some years ago when in Scotland, perpendicular streets. The inhabitants, although they live together in their human hives, are entire strangers to [one] another. There is a family living above me and another immediately below me, and yet I know no more of their names or persons than you do. This way of living subjects the inhabitants to many inconveniences, for, as they have no yards or cellars, they have of course no necessary houses and all their filth of every kind is thrown out of their windows. This is done at night generally, and is carried away next morning by carts appointed for that purpose." The peculiar method of presenting the freedom of the city to strangers is described: "Unhappy they who are obliged to walk out after ten or eleven o'clock at night. It is no uncommon thing to receive what Juvenal says he did, in his first satire, from a window in Rome. This is called here being *naturalized*. As yet I have happily escaped being made a freeman of the city in this way, but my unfortunate friend Potts has gained the honour before me." The Records of the Town Council of Edinburgh indicate, without recording the reason for the action, that Rush was admitted a burgess and gild brother of the city on March 4, 1767.[5] What honor the title bore is not known.

In the spring of 1767 Richard Stockton, who nine years later became Rush's father-in-law, was visiting in England. Because he was one of the Trustees of the College of New Jersey, he was asked to notify the Rev. Dr. John Witherspoon, Presbyterian clergyman of Paisley, Scotland, of that gentleman's selection as President of the College to succeed Samuel Finley, who had recently died. When Mrs. Witherspoon heard of the prospect of moving westward she threw up her hands, protesting that she cared not to live in America. The Reverend Doctor, not wishing to displease his wife, declined the proffered post at Princeton.[6]

Young Rush was apparently instructed to see whether or not he could persuade the Witherspoons to change their minds. He visited them in the summer. His mission was successful, for he was a convincing pleader; Mrs. Witherspoon withdrew her objections. On April 9, 1767, Dr. John Redman wrote Rush: "I find by your last letter we are likely to get Dr. Weatherspoon for which I greatly rejoice and hope yet again to see Nassau Hall flourish and triumph over all its enemies." Four months elapsed before Rush was able to notify Redman that Witherspoon had finally agreed to accept the Presidency, and the Trustees proceeded to elect him once more.[7]

Through Rush's exhortation there came to Princeton this able scholar whose influence in the college was strongly felt. Immediately he improved the curriculum by adding new courses and giving life to the old ones. Later he became active in the Revolutionary cause, serving in the Continental Congress and signing the Declaration of Independence.

In June 1768 Benjamin Rush received the degree of Doctor of Medicine, after having presented to the faculty of Edinburgh University a thesis on the digestion of food in the stomach, *De Coctione Ciborum in Ventriculo,* written in classical Latin. This study, according to Dr. John Coakley Lettsom, celebrated London physician, was "a performance so accurate, and so ingenious and lucid in diction, as to have placed him [Rush] in a prominent and honourable point of estimation in that celebrated school, which a Munro raised, and a Cullen supported and dignified."[8] In commenting on the thesis Dr. David Ramsay of South Carolina said: "The eagerness of its author to acquire professional knowledge, induced him to test a medical opinion in a way against which a less ardent student would have revolted. To ascertain whether fermentation had any agency in digestion he made three unpleasant experiments on his own stomach." He used an emetic three hours after dinner and examined the ejected contents of the stomach. "By taking five grains of an alkaline salt, he first destroyed any acid that might be accidentally in it [the stomach], and immediately afterwards dined on beef, peas, bread, and beer. Three hours after dinner, he took an emetic of two grains of emetic tartar." The contents of his stomach proved to be acidic. Then he tried veal instead of beef, and water instead of beer, and the result was the same. For the third test he used chicken instead of beef or veal, and cabbage instead of peas, and unleavened bread instead of the bread in common use. The result was unchanged. "From these facts, thrice repeated, an inference was drawn, that the aliment in the human stomach, in the course of three hours after deglutition, underwent the acetetous fermentation."[9]

At last he was Doctor Benjamin Rush! More than seven years of apprenticeship and formal study had been necessary before this goal was attained. After graduation the Doctor remained in Edinburgh for the summer, attending special lectures on the practice of physic. He admitted later that the two years' stay in Scotland had profoundly influenced his character and future conduct. Contact with the leaders of medical thought threw within his reach fresh and new ideas on medicine, politics, education, and social questions. A certain John Bostock turned his mind into the realm of republican ideas. Rush became convinced that the theory of hereditary power was inherently wrong, and he began to doubt the prerogatives of the all-powerful royal heads of Europe. It was not long before he concluded that the consent of the governed should be the basic factor in any modern government. During this period of ceaseless mental activity, doubt was his watchword in all fields of thought, and more than likely at this time there were sown the seeds of his later liberal beliefs on education, penology, slavery, temperance, and government.[10]

At the end of the summer Rush turned southward, arriving in London in late September. He found rooms at the Widow Jeffries' in the Haymarket before registering for study at St. Thomas Hospital and for a course of Dr. William Hunter's lectures. Much was to be learned not only from the variety of diseases treated at St. Thomas, but also from the weekly medical meetings at the home of Dr. Huck, who introduced the young American to Sir John Pringle, Court physician. He too invited Rush to attend informal weekly medical meetings at his home. In the company of the great physician and the distinguished Dr. John Fothergill, the young American enjoyed many discussions over the breakfast table. Out on Tottenham Court Road he visited Preacher Whitefield, who had inspired him years before. In town he called on the arch foe of the royalists, John Wilkes. "His books," observed Rush, "consisted chiefly of histories and commonplace literature from which I formed an indifferent opinion of his taste and judgment. A man's pictures and books are generally pretty copies of the intellectual and moral qualities of his mind."[11]

Rush wrote Hazard in late October that his time was employed in attending lectures, visiting hospitals, and sight-seeing about London, but nothing was said of the illustrious persons who entertained him.[12] Years later, however, he recalled that he had spent many agreeable evenings with the painter, Benjamin West, who introduced him to several celebrated artists of the Royal Academy, including Sir Joshua Reynolds. There was at least one red-letter day for Rush. Reynolds invited him to dine with Dr. Samuel Johnson and Oliver Goldsmith. "Soon after the company met, it was remarked to one of them (Goldsmith) that the reviewers had been very severe upon a work he had lately published. 'What then,—said Dr. Johnson to the gentleman,—where is the advantage of having a great deal of money, but that the loss of a little will not hurt you, in like manner where is the advantage of having a great deal of reputation but that the loss of a little will not hurt you, you can bear the censures of the reviewers.' " Not long after this meeting, the young medico dined with Goldsmith in his rooms in the Temple. He also engaged frequently in literary gossip with Edward and Charles Dilly, London publishers.[13] For public amusements Rush had little taste and, while in London, he went to the theatre only three or four times. On one of these occasions he saw David Garrick.

Benjamin Franklin was, of course, the friend of every American in England. Before Rush left London for Paris, in February 1769, Franklin gave him a letter of credit on a Paris banker for two to three hundred guineas. Rush actually drew thirty guineas on Franklin's account, repaying Mrs. Franklin in Philadelphia out of the first money he earned after his arrival home.[14]

Armed with letters of introduction from Franklin and other friends to Parisian celebrities, Rush booked a seat in the coach which left London on February 16, arriving in Dover on the same evening. He crossed the English Channel at night, landing at Calais on the next morning. From the coast he traveled to Paris in company with two gentlemen, but found little excitement during the journey except for the quarrels with tavern keepers about bills and the crowds

of beggars to be seen in every village. The countryside he found
extremely beautiful, green in many places even in mid-February.
"Few countys in England exceed Picardy (the only Province over
which I travelled, & which I am informed is one of the poorest in
France)," he recorded. "It wants nothing but a greater plenty of
water to afford the richest prospects in nature."

He was charmed with the castle of Chantilly, its mirroring ponds
and the romantic forests. In the account of his sojourn in France
he tried consciously to be impartial in his judgments of the country
and its people, philosophizing that "National prejudices are of such
a nature, that it is seldom they are entirely overcome. We are very
apt to imagine everything we see in our country to be the standard
of what is Right in Taste, Politeness, Customs, Language &c. and
therefore we condemn everything which differs from [them]. This
is a fruitful source of error in the opinion we form of different
stations." All countries, decided Rush, including France, have different customs, some good, some bad.

He was disinclined to accept the prevailing estimate that Paris
was one-third smaller than London in size and population. "Considering the more oval figure of Paris, it appears to cover as much
ground as London, which is rather of an elliptical form and considering the greater height, and compactness of their houses, together
with the narrowness of their streets, I am apt to think it contains as
many inhabitants as London (about 800,000) especially when you
exclude from the latter, the vast number of seamen, that daily
crowd the streets, who belong to other countries, and who are by no
means to be rated among the inhabitants of London." Paris was far
more beautiful architecturally: "Their palaces more in number, and
more magnificent in their appearance than any buildings perhaps in
the whole world. Their churches impress the mind with a sublime
kind of solemnity, which is easier to be conceived than described.
The richness of their altars—the grandeur of their images, and the
beauty of their paintings made a stranger imagine he is walking in
the temple of Solomon itself." The art treasures in and about Paris
afforded the highest entertainment to a man of taste. "Here is everything that is instructing in *portraiture, history, poetry,* and *religion*
represented to the very life." This was Paris in 1769. Philadelphia,

however, had no palaces of which to boast, no medieval church structures with stained-glass windows, no museums, no art galleries. All the things which contributed to a richer and fuller life Americans found in Paris.

Especially noteworthy to Rush were the charitable institutions for the relief of the poor and sick. On a single day twenty children were received at the Foundling Hospital where, it was supposed, one-eighth of the children born in Paris were brought. "One reason why it is so much crowded is, that if a woman brings forth a dead child, without first declaring her pregnancy, she is burnt alive; this puts an entire stop to child murther, and every poor child of course that is born in Paris, is naturally sent to this hospital."[15] Near the door of the hospital, which was always open, rested a basket made like a cradle and in this basket the infants were placed. The person who brought the infant then rang a bell and disappeared.[16]

The French stage, in Rush's estimation, was inferior to the London theatre. If he saw as few plays in Paris as he saw in London, however, he based his opinion upon rather slender evidence. In general the Parisian ladies struck him as being very beautiful even if their loveliness was derived from a generous use of cosmetics. "The French nation are particularly fond of *painting*," he commented. "This is a custom which prevails chiefly among savages. Among these it was introduced partly to defend the face from the inclemency of the weather, and partly to add to its beauty. It is used among the French people chiefly to answer the latter purpose . . . no one will pretend to say that the works of nature are so perfect as to be incapable of receiving any improvement from Arts. . . . Painting the cheeks therefore with vermilion is only imitating nature, and notwithstanding all that has been said against it, adds much to its beauty. . . . There is as much real virtue among the Ladies of France as among the women of any other country in the world." At one of the weekly salons at the home of the Marquis de Mirabeau, Rush, fascinated by the behavior of the ladies, observed that "they were umpires of all disputes. To them all the conversation was addressed, and a gentleman was listened to with more or less pleasure, according as he seemed to entertain them."

In the chapel at the Palace of Versailles Rush caught a chance glimpse of King Louis XV who was so youthful in his appearance that "no one would take him to be above 45," although he was fifty-nine. On one occasion, when Rush was present while the royal family dined in public, he noticed that the Dauphin took a piece of meat which he had been chewing in his mouth and, after examining it minutely in the presence of the hundred spectators, threw it under the table.[17]

Rush was entertained from time to time by Franklin's friend, Dr. Barbeu Dubourg; by LeRoy, an academician; Sue, the anatomist; Abbé Nollet, lecturer on natural philosophy; and Diderot, French philosopher and friend of Voltaire's.

After a lapse of thirty years, recalling his visit to Paris, Rush wrote: "In contemplating the French character, concentrated as it was in Paris, I was struck with its immense difference from that which I had observed in the character of the English nation. There appeared to me to be but *one* Frenchman in Paris. There was no variety in their manners. The same taste in dress pervades all classes from the nobleman to the beggar. The same phraseology was heard in their language. 'Honor' and 'pleasure' were the hackneyed words that composed a material part of it. The subjects of conversation, except among literary men, had no variety. Amusements and anecdotes of the court formed a principal part of them. The King was at this time the idol of the nation. He was called 'Lewis the well beloved.' The extent of the attachment of the nation to him and the principles of the French monarchy may be best conceived by the following anecdote. I heard Mr. Wilkes say on the day I dined with him at Newgate,[18] that he once dined with twelve gentlemen in Paris, eleven of whom declared they should think it their duty to surrender up their wives to the King if he desired it."[19]

After a stay of a few weeks in Paris, Rush concluded that there was little chance of adding much of value to the sum of his medical knowledge because the science of medicine was not highly developed in France.

Sailing across the Channel again on March 25 he spent the next two months in the British capital. On May 24 he saw London for the last time. He embarked on the good ship *Edward*, Captain Salmon commanding, and tried to calm his restless mind and body during the Atlantic crossing by constant reading. The fact that he read Blackstone and Forster's *Crown Law* on this voyage is evidence that he still retained his earlier interest in the law. From a fellow passenger he borrowed a German grammar, dictionary, and Bible, and proceeded to study German as he had planned to do four years before. The Captain loaned him a novel in Italian, which he also read.

Although not actually seasick, Rush never felt perfectly fit during the crossing. On July 14, after a voyage of seven weeks, the ship anchored in New York, where Ebenezer Hazard was on hand to greet his classmate. Three things caught the attention of the returning physician as he surveyed the people on the streets of New York: "1st. They had less color. 2nd. They walked less erect, and 3dly. They moved with a less quick step than the citizens of London. This difference in the complexion and manner of walking in the two countries ceased to attract my attention after I had been a few weeks in America. The evening, and day after my arrival, I felt an uncommon depression of spirits, the usual effect of a high tide of joy upon the system. I now believe the accounts which have been published, of melancholy and even suicide following similar emotions of the mind."[20]

Leaving New York, the young M.D. reached Philadelphia by coach on the evening of July 18, 1769. His brother met him at Bristol; his mother, sisters, and friends accorded him a hearty welcome in the city, and for several days he did nothing but receive friends and return visits.

He lost no time, however, in locating adequate quarters, agreeing to share a house on Arch Street between Front and Second with his brother Jacob, now a practising attorney. A sister, who had experienced an unfortunate marriage, kept house for the professional brothers. After a few months on Arch Street, however, the Doctor moved to Front Street near Walnut, where he lived for twelve years.

Exuberance, gaiety, and the carefree spirit of youth is totally lacking from the picture we reconstruct of the young Benjamin Rush. Physically he was well built, vigorous, attractive, and dignified in his bearing—a young man whose appearance and manner were bound to inspire confidence in those to whom he would minister. Mentally, he was alert, intelligent, ever curious and diligent in seeking out facts and adding to his store of knowledge. He was endowed with what we have come to call a scientific mind, meticulous about detail, keen in powers of observation, anxious to experiment and to trace cause and effect. Emotionally the young man was restrained, sober, and serious, but was not blessed with a sense of humor. Impressed with the importance of his profession, he placed it before all other concerns in his scheme of life. One is struck in his early letters, especially in those from abroad, with the objectivity of his observations, his purely scientific attitude of mind carrying over into his scrutiny of men and manners. Nowhere does he reveal himself as highly introspective. The letters and notes which remain from this period of his life point to few close friendships. Ebenezer Hazard is the one regular correspondent of whom we have certain knowledge. Although he was fond of his mother and brothers and sisters, he mentions them seldom in the letters that are extant. The contacts he made abroad were with men of high intellectual attainments, whose companionship he definitely sought and keenly enjoyed. Of young women, love affairs, or youthful frolics, he makes no mention. Life was too serious a business for him to indulge in its frivolities. Whether or not the inclination to occasional levity was strong within him, we cannot know. It does not seem so.

This was the twenty-three-year-old man who in 1769 was ready and, for his day, well prepared to practise medicine in his native city.

III

Building a Practice
1769–1775

In 1769 Rush again returned to his native city after the completion
of another step in his education and, after careful consideration, he
decided upon Philadelphia as the city offering the widest opportunity
for a medical practice. Besides being the largest city, and wealthy by
reason of flourishing trade, it supported the first medical school in
the colonies, established in 1765. The eyes of physicians throughout
the colonies were on Philadelphia. Then, too, the city was an important clearing house for the growing anti-British feeling.

There were new people, new homes, and new shops here and
there in the town when Dr. Rush returned. From the residence in
Arch Street his sister might have walked around the corner to Joseph
Stansbury's shop to buy her kitchenware. He sold every imaginable
kind of pots and pans and crockery. Down the street and around the
corner on Front Street was the City Vendue Store where weekly
auctions were held. Close by, too, was the tobacco shop of Jacob
Renno. He also carried a stock of distilled spirits, oils, and waters,
such as: "Mint oil, penny-royal oil, rose and mint, flour of teleca,
lilly, sweet margerum, sage, lavender, parsley . . . and several other
distilled waters too tedious to mention. Likewise the spirit of elder-
berries, excellent for sweating, wormwood extract, and an excellent
salve for any kind of wounds." Renno's customers were "assured of
being used well, and at the lowest rates."[1]

A line of wall paper and mirrors was on display in the wood-carv-
ing and gilding shop of one James Reynolds on Front Street, and a
general assortment of East Indian goods found its way into a Market Street hardware store. In fact all the luxuries and refinements
of a typical eighteenth-century colonial home could be bought in the
Philadelphia stores along with the necessities every housewife shopped
and bargained for.

Slaves, of course, were still being sold. By inquiring at the office of *The Pennsylvania Gazette* one could have examined a negro, twenty-one years of age, able to drive a carriage and trim horses, a sober fellow who had never given any cause to suspect his honesty. A healthy mulatto girl of the same age, who had already had the smallpox and was used to country as well as city work, was also offered for sale.

There were frequent calls for wet nurses. One advertisement sought "A wet nurse, with a good breast of young milk, a sober, honest discreet woman, who can be well recommended; such a person may hear of a good place, by applying to the Printers;" but warning was given that "none but such as is described need apply."[2]

Rush, desirous of attaining some fluency in foreign languages before his practice engaged all his attention, possibly read with interest the advertisement of Emanuel Lyon, who "late from London, acquaints the public, that he intends to teach a few gentlemen the Hebrew language, in its purity, either at his lodgings, at Mr. John Taylor's in Front Street, at the corner of Race Street, or at their respective houses. As it is a Mother tongue, very necessary to be understood by the studious, he hopes to meet with encouragement, he will do his utmost endeavour to merit it. Mr. Lyon will translate the Hebrew into English, or Dutch, to the general satisfaction of those gentlemen who are judges."[3]

The thickly populated portion of the city proper at this time stretched from the Delaware River front to Sixth Street, and from Vine on the north approximately to Cedar (now South) on the south, covering a little over one square mile.

When Rush set up his "business," medical quacks flourished as well as qualified physicians. Indeed, competition between them was keen, the quack profiting by newspaper advertising. Sure cures for every conceivable type of disease were promised in the columns of the local newspapers, and not only city but also country patients flocked to the offices of the advertising medicasters. Naturally the legitimate practices of the graduate physicians were seriously impaired by the large number of charlatans.

One Thomas Anderton, a glazier by trade, decided to expand his business in 1772 by fitting up his residence adjoining his store on Market Street as an office for the treatment and cure of venereal diseases. Dr. Anderton stated that he need hardly "suggest to the public the usefulness of such an undertaking." He promised "a sound and lasting cure" to those who encouraged his project, and further guaranteed secrecy and suitable accommodation during their short stay. He gave advice and "chirurgical assistance" gratis daily from ten in the morning till two, and from four in the afternoon, till nine at night. He sold Sanxay's medicines, "the first ever offered in the world, that will effectually and radically cure every symptom of the venereal disease, without pain or sickness, or any confinement whatever. Salivation is wholly by them rendered unnecessary, and they will undoubtedly cure when that fails. They are taken by the most delicate of both sexes, at all seasons of the year, and by fishermen in water, without any hurt to the constitution; for they improve and invigorate the whole nervous system."

"Gleets and seminal weaknesses, in both sexes, impotency, fistulas, and obstructions in the urinary passage, cured on moderate terms," Anderton's advertisement continued. He also sold prepared medicines:—Turlington's balsam of life, or the true American balsam; Daffy's elixir; Stoughton's bitters; Anderson's Scotch pills; Baron Van Swieten's worm plumbs, for grown persons or children; *Pro bono publico*, a cure for the piles; Dr. Stork's tincture for the toothache; and a fine water for sore eyes.[4] Undoubtedly Philadelphians visited Dr. Anderton and his colleagues and bought these remedies; the number of cures that were effected, however, can hardly be determined.

A year after the glazier Anderton set up his medical practice, Dr. Day arrived from London ready to cure those suffering from stone in the bladder. "The medicines he administers are very good to take, and gives no uneasiness, but works off gently by urine: He also sells a bottle and a box for a dollar each, that infallibly cures the worst of fevers and agues, or the worst rheumatisms: He greatly assists the eyes in both young and old. Any gentleman that hath occasion for a private lodging in any difficult disorder, may be accommodated at the Doctor's in Vine-street, near Fourth street. He hath his name over the door in brass letters."[5]

Dr. Anthony Yeldall sought patients "in any case of Physic or Surgery." "Those who may please to apply," he advertised, "may be assured they will never be encouraged in any disorder but where there is probability of success. The Doctor omits saying anything of his abilities in practice, his well-known travels for these five years past through different parts of this continent, and the many surprising cures that, under God, have been performed by him, both in physic and surgery, speak more powerfully than anything that can be here inserted; and as it has been found of the greatest inconveniency to some, and rendered impossible to others to obtain his advice and medicines by reason of his not attending anywhere but at his house, in order to render himself as useful to his fellow creatures as possible, he will, for the future attend at the houses of such patients as are not able to attend on him, either in town or country, and that in as regular a manner, and allowing the same credit for his attendance and medicines as is usual, and hopes by his assiduity, care and moderate charge to merit what he most regards, the love and esteem of the public." The Doctor also advised the public that he stocked most of the patent medicines in general use, and "those that live in the country may, by sending an account of their disorder, have advice and medicines as the nature of their case may require."[6]

All families were advised to keep on hand a supply of Dr. Ryan's incomparable "worm destroying sugar plumbs," at seven shillings, six pence, for a box of a dozen. These "plumbs" allegedly struck at the very source of many ailments in men, women, and children. "They are one of the best purges in the world for gross bodied children that are apt to breed worms, and have large bellies; their operation is mild, safe and pleasant; they wonderfully cleanse the bowels of all stiff and clammy humours, which stop up the parts, and prevent the juice of food being conveyed to the liver and make blood, which is often the case with children, and is attended with a hard belly, stinking breath, frequent fevers, rickets, and a decay of strength in the lower parts: Likewise settled aches and pains in the head, swellings, old sores, scabs, tetters or breakings out, will be perfectly cured, and the blood and skin restored to its original purity and smoothness; they purge by urine, and bring away the gravel, and effectually cure all obstructions of the urine, or ulcers in the kidnies. They at once strike at the true cause of the scurvy and entirely destroy it, and all scorbutic humours and effects, root and branch, so as never to return again; and what makes them more commendable is, they are fully as agreeable to both taste and sight, as loaf-sugar; and in their operation as innocent as new milk."[7] Certainly no medicine chest could be without such a marvelous cure-all; not even for a single day!

With this type of competition the medical profession had to contend. Super-salesmanship on the part of the quacks had to be met by super-training on the part of the physician. The mediocre physician had no place in this scheme of things unless he went over to quackery.

In order to enhance his reputation at the very outset of his career as a practitioner, Benjamin Rush, even while he was still studying in Edinburgh, was on the lookout for an opening on the faculty of the medical department of the College of Philadelphia. The appointment of John Morgan as professor of the theory and practice of medicine, on May 3, 1765, paved the way for the organization of this first medical school in America. On September 17, 1765, William Shippen, Jr. was chosen professor of anatomy, surgery, and midwifery. Both Morgan and Shippen, incidentally, had attended Finley's school at Nottingham.[8]

As early as January 20, 1768, Rush wrote Morgan from Edinburgh thanking him for the pains he had taken to hold open the professorship of chemistry until his return to Philadelphia. Rush felt that he was capable of teaching that science, after having attended Dr. Black's lectures for two years; and that he could demonstrate its application to medicine and philosophy. "I should likewise be able more fully," added Rush, "from having a seat in the College, to cooperate with you in advancing the medical sciences generally."[9]

Cullen, in a letter of congratulation to Morgan on the work of the new medical school, suggested that Rush would be a valuable addition to the faculty: "He has indeed applied to every branch of study with great diligence and success, but chemistry has always been a principal object and I am persuaded he may make a figure in that profession much to the credit of your college."[10] By October Rush must have felt confident of his election to the faculty, for he wrote Morgan: "I am much obliged to you for continuing to read lectures on chemistry. I hope to be in Philadelphia in May or June next, so that I shall relieve you from the task the ensuing winter. Is it necessary for me to deliver publickly an Inaugural Oration?"[11]

The matter was not settled, however, and was not to be decided for almost a year. On May 12, 1768, Redman had acquainted Rush with the state of affairs concerning the professorship of chemistry: "It would not have been proper, nor would the Trustees choose to deprive themselves of the liberty of election so long before the qualifications of a person would be certainly determined; as your friends could not expect this, neither would they ask it, knowing that they could easily prevent either the application or election of another, until your return. Thus matters stand at present; nor has the person you might suspect (or any other) applied, well knowing from proper points what he might expect if he had. Those trustees who are not medical think little about it, and those who are, with the professors, are carefully silent about it, so that I believe you need not fear but it will be vacant till you return, nor less so of your election upon proper application, and bringing sufficient testimonials of your diligent attendance to that branch of medical science and art and your qualifications therein, which I advise, as it will be to your credit as well as to that of our College to be so certified of your abilities."[12]

Just before Rush left London for Philadelphia in the spring of 1769, Dr. Fothergill suggested to Thomas Penn, Proprietor of the Province of Pennsylvania, that he recommend Rush to the Trustees of the College of Philadelphia as professor of chemistry, and that the young doctor deliver to the College a chemical apparatus which Penn was about to send over as a gift. Penn agreed; Rush packed the apparatus in his trunk and Penn wrote the Trustees in May: "Dr. Rush having been recommended to me by Dr. Fothergill as a very expert Chymist, and the Doctor having further recommended to me a chymical apparatus as a thing of great use, particularly in the tryal of ores, I send you such as Dr. Fothergill thought necessary, under the care of Dr. Rush, which I desire your acceptance of. I recommend Dr. Rush to your Notice."[13]

On July 23 the letter was read to the assembled Board of Trustees and a reply was sent on August 1, reading in part: "We have likewise the pleasure to acknowledge a fresh instance of your benevolence in sending us a chemical apparatus under the care of Dr.

Rush, who will meet with all the encouragement from us due to your recommendation and his own good character."[14]

The day before, Rush had presented his formal application to the Trustees: "As the Professorship of Chemistry, which Dr. Morgan hath some time supplied, is vacant, I beg to offer myself as a candidate for it. Should you think proper to honor me with the Chair, you may depend upon my doing anything that lies within my power to discharge the duties of a Professor, and to promote the reputation and interest of your College."[15] On August 1 he was elected Professor of Chemistry, the fifth member of the faculty and the youngest, and the first formal professor of chemistry in America. He joined Morgan and Shippen, Adam Kuhn, professor of materia medica and botany, and Thomas Bond, professor of clinical medicine.

The College grew slowly. During the first decade of the medical school's existence, the bachelor's degree was granted to twenty-eight graduates, four of whom presented theses in 1771 and received the M.D. degree. After 1789 the bachelor's degree was no longer granted in medicine, the M.D. degree being the only one recognized by the University of Pennsylvania, successor to the College of Philadelphia. Since 1812 American medical schools have granted only the M.D. degree to their graduates.[16]

This appointment to the College enhanced Rush's reputation at the very outset of his career as a practitioner; it also gave him a small but certain income which he needed at this time, the expense of his study abroad having been substantial. He attracted attention in 1770 by publishing a *Syllabus of A Course of Lectures on Chemistry,* the first textual contribution in chemistry to be written by an American.

Informed Philadelphians respected any physician who had received his training at Edinburgh, because in the last half of the eighteenth century the great Scottish medical school enjoyed the highest rating. Each of the first six professors on the staff of the College of Philadelphia had taken an M.D. degree at Edinburgh. They had also been influenced by the London leaders of the profession: Dr. Fothergill, who was kept busy with one of the largest practices in London; John Coakley Lettsom, a close friend and colleague of Fothergill's, and the Pennsylvania Hospital's agent for the purchase of medical books in England. These men in particular, and Sir John Pringle, the pioneer military hygienist, taught and entertained the American medical students in Edinburgh and London.

Rush's appointment to the College faculty was concrete recognition of his professional ability. It remained for him to win the favor of the citizens at large in order to establish a satisfactory practice. There were four ways open to attract patients. The patronage of a great man was the quickest and most certain, but from this quarter Rush could count on no assistance. Secondly, he had no hope of obtaining patients through the influence of extensive and powerful family connections. Inasmuch as he belonged to the Presbyterian Church, not at that time powerful in the city, he could not win favor through the patronage of a dominant religious sect. The only means left was to concentrate his practice among the poor.[17] Indeed, Rush's early practice actually comprised, for the most part, poor patients from whom trifling fees were collected.

Rush further cut himself off from the possibility of waiting upon the more affluent citizens when, during the controversy over American Independence, his sympathy with the rebels was disclosed. The wealthier inhabitants were largely loyalists and naturally refused to consult a rebel physician, his professional ability notwithstanding.

From the fall of 1769 until 1776 the Doctor toiled throughout the day often until midnight, and then read until two or three o'clock in the morning. His "shop" was crowded every morning and at mealtime with poor patients. In the course of a day he visited patients in almost every street and alley in the city. "There are few old huts now standing," he recalled in 1800, "in the ancient parts of the city in which I have not attended sick people. Often have I ascended the upper story of these huts by a ladder and many hundred times have I been obliged to rest my weary limbs upon the bedside of the sick, from want of chairs, where I was sure I risqued, not only taking their disease but being infected with vermin. More than once did I suffer from the latter."[18] During the first five years of his practice he could not possibly have found time for recreation, relaxation, or the pleasant diversion of social intercourse.

A man who sacrifices friendships, social contacts, and all amuse-

SYLLABUS

Of a COURSE

OF

LECTURES

ON

CHEMISTRY.

By
Benjamin Rush M.D.
1770

PHILADELPHIA: Printed 1770.

TITLE PAGE OF RUSH'S CHEMISTRY TEXT

ment must find for these things compensations within himself. The young physician withdrew into his work, from the world of men and things, and was apparently unaware of his loss. He took himself very seriously and confidently believed that his practice had grown so quickly not only because of his connection with the College, but chiefly because of the skillful treatment and the faithful service he rendered even to patients who could pay no fees. A sober and earnest young man, handsome in appearance, dignified in bearing, and obviously certain of his ability, he developed a professional and bedside manner that immediately inspired in his patients the absolute confidence every physician craves.

To his introduction of the Suttonian System of inoculating against smallpox he also attributed an enlargement of his practice. "The mode of infecting the arm by a small puncture, instead of a long incision was a very popular one, and brought me many patients, some of whom continued to employ me in other diseases," said Rush. "I had learned likewise from my master Dr. Cullen to give but few medicines in diseases, and to rely more upon diet and drinks than had been common in Philadelphia. This likewise helped to introduce me into business."[19]

Habits of diet and clothing, and the diseases prevalent among the inhabitants of Philadelphia at this period are revealed, from a physician's point of view, in Rush's observations covering nearly a half century. Meat was the most important food, being eaten in all families twice and in some three times daily. About an hour before dinner it was the custom to eat a "relish" consisting of a slice of ham, a piece of salted fish, occasionally a steak, and always plenty of punch or toddy. Tea was sipped sometime between dinner and supper, and in many families wine and bitters were served just before dinner. Frequent banquets were held in taverns and clubs. Although business men met at the taverns every evening to drink beer, drunkenness was rare at these places. It was common, however, among all classes throughout the city.

Men dressed in woolens in winter, and in silk or thin woolens in summer. Wigs were not worn after middle life except by the Friends. Women's dresses were made of silk and calico.

What might have been a happy combination of diversion and the fulfillment of the demands of personal hygiene was attempted when, in 1761, Dr. Lauchlin McClen conceived the idea of an establishment akin to the old Roman baths. He suggested the erection near the center of the city of warm and cold baths in conjunction with a hippodrome. The project, as one might expect, was immediately frowned upon as "unfriendly to morals" by the religious societies and the city fathers who went so far as to petition the governor of the province to prevent the execution of the plan. Dr. McClen soon left the city, no doubt to lay his project before more liberal men.[20]

Of the diseases which prevailed, cholera morbus occurred frequently during the summer months, and an intermitting fever in August and in the fall. Cases of dysentery were treated from time to time, and in the fall of the year in the thickly settled sections of the city there were many cases of a slow chronic fever, called at that time the nervous fever. In 1762 yellow fever appeared in the neighborhood of Spruce Street wharf; in the spring of the previous year there had been an epidemic of influenza. The mortality rate from smallpox was uniformly high. Inasmuch as no dentist had yet appeared on the medical horizon, diseases originating from decayed teeth were common. During the winter and spring, physicians saw many cases of pneumonia, rheumatism, sore throat, and catarrh.

The system of Hermann Boerhaave, who flourished as a clinical teacher in Holland until his death in 1738, governed the practice of almost every physician in Philadelphia through the 1760's. Because, according to this theory, diseases in general were ascribed to what were termed "morbid acrimonies, and other matters in the blood," the physician attempted, by various remedies, to thin the blood. He was constantly on the lookout for the discharge from the system of the morbid cause of the fevers. "This matter was looked for chiefly in the urine, and glasses to retain it were a necessary part of the furniture of every sick room. To ensure the discharge of the supposed morbid matter of fevers through the pores, patients were confined to their beds" in sick-rooms from which all fresh air was excluded. Spirit of sweet niter was a specific in general use, and, in dangerous cases, Virginia snakeroot was added. In cases of pleurisy and rheumatism bloodletting was the usual remedy, although it was resorted to only sparingly in other diseases. "Purges or vomits began the cure of all febrile diseases, but as the principal dependence was placed upon sweating medicines, those powerful remedies were seldom repeated in the subsequent stages of fevers." Opium was used primarily to mitigate pain. Dr. Thomas Bond was responsible for the introduction of mercury into general use; he prescribed it in all diseases which resisted the common remedies, and he even tried it, though unsuccessfully, in pulmonary tuberculosis. In only a few cases were warm and cold baths prescribed.[21]

Almost as soon as he opened his office, in 1769, Rush set about to abandon the medical system of Boerhaave in vogue in Philadelphia, adhering instead to the system of Dr. Cullen, his teacher at Edinburgh. Boerhaave, chief exponent of the humoral school, maintained that there were salt, putrid, and oily temperaments representing what is today called diatheses, or constitutional predispositions. The oily temperament, arthritism, is a condition in which the organism functions imperfectly. Boerhaave prescribed such depleting and debilitating remedies as purgatives and bloodletting. Rush, however, declared this theory, which located diseases in the fluids of the body, to be entirely incorrect. Cullen's system to which Rush subscribed located the cause of disease in the solids.

Cullen claimed that fever is caused by "sedative powers," which produce a general weakness of the body by diminishing the energy of the brain. To restore the energy of the brain, the heart and larger arteries, the physician must seek to increase their activity.

Rush, always hot-headed and stubborn, was far from tactful in opposing the system used by nearly all his colleagues in Philadelphia. He publicly attacked it, bringing upon his head a mountain of criticism and denunciation. On the other hand, Cullen's system, which Rush was supporting so vigorously, was likewise openly condemned in the newspapers. As a result of the controversy, the young medico alienated himself from many of his colleagues with dire consequences to his private practice. During the first seven years "in business" not a single physician referred a patient to him.[22]

The young man had returned from Edinburgh, medical center of the world, eager to pursue his profession and deeply impressed with a sense of his importance. Physicians with his training were few and far between, and the place he was to fill in the community was to be one of dignity and authority. His technical education had embraced the latest theories and, at the age of twenty-three, he had obtained an appointment to the faculty of the first medical school in the colonies.

A cocksure and self-confident young man and an individualist in all circumstances, he soon found himself embroiled in bitter controversies with older men who, quite justly, were indignant over the tactics of this mere youngster. The firmer his belief in the truth and the justice of his ideas, the more indiscreet and tactless he became in their defense. To the end of his life Rush was conscious of the undying resentment his early conduct had engendered in the minds of his colleagues.

His convictions, even outside the realm of medicine, commendable though they were, helped to impair his practice. In 1772, one of the first Philadelphians to champion the cause, he published a pamphlet against slavery, drawing toward himself the enmity of the slaveholders.

Notwithstanding the strong feeling harbored against him personally by a large number of wealthy and influential citizens, his practice grew and by 1775 his annual income amounted to £900, a substantial amount.[23] In July 1772 he was appointed one of the physicians of the House of Employment, the almshouse (later the Philadelphia General Hospital).[24] His lectures at the College of Philadelphia kept his name before the public and at the June 1773 commencement he delivered the oration to the graduates in medicine.[25] In January 1774 he offered a course of eight public lectures in chemistry, the price of the subscription being one guinea. This attempt to popularize science consisted in a discussion of the "parts of chemistry as abound with the greatest variety of the most useful and entertaining facts." The lectures embraced such varied subjects as the effect of heat on liquids and solids, the history of cold, the structure of thermometers, climate, the laws of chemical attraction, chemical apparatus, the methods of manufacturing saltpeter and gunpowder, mineral waters, principles of agriculture, and the causes of volcanoes.[26]

In 1772 there appeared a delightful, popularly written paper called *Sermons to Gentlemen Upon Temperance and Exercise*, still interesting a century and a half later. Rush admonished the reader that the more simple our food, the better; that both meat and vegetables should be included in a well-balanced diet; and that vegetables should predominate especially in warm seasons and in warm climates. He believed that most people eat too much, and advised only one "hearty" meal daily, suggesting that "food . . . may be said to be taken in too large a quantity, when we do not feel light and cheerful after it." The principal meal should be eaten in the evening, followed by a short rest which aids digestion.

The most modern section of the *Sermon* discusses exercise. Writing in a period in which little attention was given to the need of formal exercise and athletics in daily life, Rush claimed that exercise is necessary to preserve not only one's physical health but also one's mental vigor. In his list of "active" exercises he included walking, running, dancing, fencing, swimming, skating, jumping, and golf. Walking he described as a "gentle species" of active exercise: "It promotes perspiration, and if not continued too long, invigorates and strengthens the system." Running, on the other hand, is too violent for frequent or continuous indulgence. Dancing is recommended as a most salutary exercise: "By its mechanical effects on the body, it inspires the mind with cheerfulness, and this, when well founded, and properly restrained, is another name for religion." But one should not dance more than once a week, or expose one's self to cold air after dancing. Fencing not only exercises most of the muscles but also stimulates the brain. Swimming, as Benjamin Franklin also found, is highly beneficial. Not only does it exercise the limbs but it also "serves to wash away the dust which is apt to mix itself with the sweat of our bodies in warm weather."

Rush's note on golf, a game then hardly known, is amusing: "Golf is an exercise which is much used by the Gentlemen in Scotland. A large common in which there are several little holes is chosen for the purpose. It is played with little leather balls stuffed with feathers; and sticks made somewhat in the form of a bandy-wicket. He who puts a ball into a given number of holes, with the fewest strokes, gets the game. The late Dr. McKenzie, author of the essay on Health and Long Life, used to say, that a man would live ten years the longer for using this exercise once or twice a week."

The "passive" exercises Rush designated for "valetudinarians." Of these, sailing brings into play every muscle during the effort one makes to keep from falling. Carriage riding is recommended only for those unable to ride a horse or walk. Horseback riding is set down as the most manly and useful type of exercise for men, being especially salutary for the nervous system.

The proper time for exercise, Rush believed, is between five and seven o'clock in the morning, but never after a heavy meal.

The few hours the busy physician could snatch from his patients, his lectures, and study, he spent in the company of intellectually stimulating friends. He was fortunate enough to be a frequent guest at the salons held at the home of Dr. Thomas Graeme. The society of the Graemes was pleasing and satisfying to Rush's serious temper. Later Dr. Graeme and his daughter, Elizabeth, after Mrs. Graeme's death, oecupied one of the show-places of the city, in the spacious home surrounded by a beautiful garden, on the north side of Chestnut Street above Sixth, and at this house every distinguished visitor to the city was entertained. The versatile and brilliant Elizabeth Graeme presided at the Saturday evening gatherings. Contrary to European convention, salons in America were usually attended only by men. To the Graeme salon, however, ladies as well as gentlemen were invited.[27]

In 1773, when Rush was twenty-seven, he met Sarah Eve. She was an attractive young woman of twenty-three, the daughter of Oswald Eve, a sea captain. Her red hair was always becomingly arranged, her dresses the last word in fashion, and her bearing stately. She lived about two miles from Rush's residence on a farm located at what is now about Fifth Street and Thompson. The Eve and the Rush families were on visiting terms and, in the journal Sarah kept, are recorded many of the family calls. Dr. Rush always managed to be present whenever Sarah dropped in to take tea with his mother. Occasionally she dined with Mrs. Rush and once stayed over night. Late in the spring, when the weather turned mild and pleasant, the handsome young doctor stole an hour or so from his work to stroll with the lovely young girl to the mineral spring at Sixth and Chestnut Streets where it was the fashion at this time to drink the water despite its excessively disagreeable taste. Throughout the summer Sarah's visits continued, though it is conceivable that her attentions to Mrs. Rush were inspired in part by the attractiveness of the son. Nor was the doctor insensible to the young girl's charm. Early in September he called at the Eve farm. Later in the month, upon one of his visits, he was distressed to find both Sarah and her mother ill. Next day he rode out to the farm twice to offer professional advice and several days later braved a September northeaster to satisfy himself that his patients had fully recovered.

Rush carried on his courtship during the following year until the love affair promised a happy consummation. The wedding date was set for late December 1774. The marriage, however, was destined never to take place. Sarah fell into a lingering illness that neither she, with hope of future joy, nor Rush, with all his knowledge, skill, and devotion had power to combat. Three weeks before she was to be married, Sarah died. She was buried on December 4.[28]

The tragedy affected Rush deeply. Under the stress of his emotion he was moved to write a eulogy upon her. It appeared, unsigned, in the *Pennsylvania Packet* on December 12, 1774, under the title, "A Female Character." "Her understanding was strong," it reads, "her imagination brilliant, and her taste correct. These were improved by an intimate acquaintance with some of the best poetical and prose writers in the English language. Her disposition was amiable; a person who had lived with her from a child, declared that she had never once seen her angry, or heard a hasty word from her lips. Her manners were polished. They were not put on, and laid aside, like a part of a dress; she was always alike captivating, even in her most careless moments, and in the society of her most intimate friends. Her person was elegant, her face had a happy mixture of the happy and beautiful in it; her voice was soft, and her elocution was flowing. Her sentiments were often original, and always just; it was impossible for her to speak upon any subject without gaining the attention of company. Such were her unaffected displays of good sense, modesty, and good humour, that no one, I believe, ever left her without emotions of love, esteem, or admiration."

Strangely enough, Rush fails to mention the name of Sarah Eve in the sketch of his life which he wrote in 1800, a quarter of a century after her death. Perhaps the tragic love affair formed an episode in his life which he definitely chose to close forever. His love for Sarah was sealed with the eulogy, and the sad memory of her was soon drowned in worldly pursuits. Indeed, it was not many months before Rush had formed a new attachment, this time one which was to bring him lasting happiness.

In August 1775 he journeyed to Princeton where he visited Richard Stockton and Dr. Witherspoon, whom he had persuaded, while in Scotland eight years before, to become President of what is now Princeton University. Rush was a guest for several days at "Morven," the Stockton estate in Princeton. He was not too preoccupied, however, with his serious conversations with Stockton and Witherspoon to notice the eldest daughter of the Stocktons, Julia, then only sixteen years of age. Captivated by her engaging manner and her scintillating conversation, he came to the almost immediate decision that this was the girl he must marry. Born at "Morven" on March 2, 1759, Julia Stockton was only a child of four when, one evening following commencement in 1763, young Rush had carried her in his arms from the college hall to her father's house.[29]

Back in Philadelphia Rush was more certain than ever that he was in love with her, and shortly after his return wrote to her mother, Annis Boudinot Stockton, begging permission to visit Julia. The girl, besides being attracted to the handsome young man, must have been flattered by the attention of the serious, respected, and successful physician. Rush journeyed to Princeton several times and, finally, after a courtship that seems to have been more formal than romantic, the date was set for the wedding.

On January 11, 1776, Rev. Dr. Witherspoon officiated at the marriage ceremony at "Morven." Only the briefest announcement appeared in the Philadelphia newspaper: "Married, At Princeton, Doctor Benjamin Rush, of this city, to Miss Julia Stockton, daughter of the Honourable Richard Stockton, Esq."[30] Seven months later both Stockton and Rush were to sign the Declaration of Independence.

Rush more or less unromantically explained to a friend in Scot-

MRS. BENJAMIN RUSH

land that Julia was generally admired for her beauty, which he describes vividly, but that he had lost his heart to her because of her temper, prudence, understanding, and unusual accomplishments. "Figure to yourself a woman of your own size, brown hair, dark eyes, a complexion composed of white and red, a countenance at the same time soft and animated, a voice mild and musical and a pronunciation accompanied with a little lisp and you will then have an idea of the person and manner of my dear Mrs. Rush. . . . Think only what the friend, companion, wife, in the full meaning of each of those words, should be and you will then have a just idea of my happiness."[31] And after a quarter century, in 1800, he was still singing her praises in his matter-of-fact way: "Let me here bear testimony to the worth of this excellent woman. She fulfilled every duty as a wife, mother, and mistress with fidelity and integrity. To me she was always a sincere and honest friend. Had I yielded to her advice upon many occasions, I should have known less distress from various causes in my journey through life."[32] Mrs. Rush lived until 1848, to the age of ninety.

Dr. and Mrs. Rush had thirteen children of whom only nine reached maturity, a telling commentary, perhaps, upon child rearing in those days, even in families possessed of whatever medical knowledge was available. The eldest son, John, became a lieutenant in the United States Navy. James, following in the footsteps of his father, studied medicine at Edinburgh. He married Ann Ridgway, the belle of Philadelphia society, and on his death, in 1869, endowed the Ridgway Library in Philadelphia. William was also a physician. Richard, however, was the most distinguished son. Born August 29, 1780, and admitted to the bar twenty years later, he received wide recognition before he was thirty years of age. At various times he was Attorney-General of his state and the nation, Comptroller of the United States Treasury, Secretary of State, Minister to England, Secretary of the Treasury, and Minister to France.

Rush's marriage was one of the fortunate circumstances in his life. His wife and children were a constant source of comfort to him, in the hectic days of the Revolution, during the frightful epidemics of yellow fever, and throughout several bitter personal controversies. After the outbreak of hostilities in 1776, he took an active part in the work of Congress and in the medical division of the army. Many times the resourcefulness and patient understanding of Mrs. Rush were taxed to the utmost in calming her strong-willed and often obstinate husband. Conflicts with colleagues and officials, though entered into in the name of patriotism or firm personal conviction, reveal Rush's inability to work harmoniously with other men.

His character was laid upon foundations of integrity and service, and once he was sure within himself of the soundness and morality of his stand, he resolutely refused to compromise. He would not yield an inch even to gain a foot; and therefore he was doomed to meet defeat and condemnation many times when he deserved better. Furthermore, his candid self-righteousness only aggravated his adversaries and made him deaf to reason as well. It was a tragic contradiction of Rush's life that his stubborn individualism obscured the originality of his mind, the attractiveness of his personality, and the honesty of his motives.

IV

Rebel and Patriot

1776–1789

THE Philadelphia which welcomed the First Continental Congress in September of 1774 was a gay city. There were 24,000 people living within its limits and it was recognized as the first city in colonial America. Quaker influences were not powerful enough to frown down entirely the colorful attire and the lively spirit of the day. Up and down Market Street the townspeople were constantly passing. Most of them were going busily about in their workaday clothes. Some well-to-do gentlemen sauntered along proudly parading their cocked hats, satin breeches, silk hose, gold-headed canes, and huge ornamental shoe buckles, their white jackets and scarlet ones. One Timothy Matlack, known about town as the "fighting Quaker," strode past in his accustomed fierce temper, rattling the mighty sword which he carried morning, noon, and night.

The dignified brick houses with their graceful doorways lent an air of solidity and permanence to the town. The American Philosophical Society, the College, and the Library gave evidence of its interest in things cultural; the well-kept and beautiful gardens expressed its artistic sense and a love of nature. On the outskirts of the city were the splendid country homesteads of the wealthier among the Revolutionary fathers. Nine miles to the north Judge Chew lived on his spacious and dignified estate, "Cliveden," an example of Colonial architecture at its best. James Logan, secretary to William Penn, had established his homestead with its famous garden about four miles north of the city. The house still stands in a park at what is now Seventeenth and Courtland Streets. Robert Morris enjoyed a broad view of the Schuylkill River and the rolling country behind it from his mansion, "The Hills," on Lemon Hill three miles from the State House. In a new world these men had quickly amassed wealth through commerce, agriculture, trading with the Indians, and land speculation.

Class distinctions were strongly marked. Although more than ninety per cent of the people throughout the colonies were engaged in agriculture, Philadelphia was definitely a commercial city, crowded with shop-keepers, artisans, traders, importers, and tavern-keepers. They lived in small brick or stone houses built in solid rows and set close to the narrow streets and alleys near the river. Thus, by virtue of slender means and different background, they formed a class totally distinct from that of the aristocratic merchants and land owners, who gave gay balls in their beautiful Georgian homes and rode to church in their fine carriages.

Rich and poor alike, Philadelphians of 1774 paused in their daily pursuits to pick up the latest gossip and to scan the current newspapers for accounts of the demonstrations against the British Crown, particularly in New England. The year before, the ill-advised cabinet ministers in London had decided to help the East India Company out of its financial straits by dumping upon the colonies some of the seventeen million pounds of tea held for duty in England. The plan was extremely distasteful to the Americans. When, therefore, shiploads of tea began to reach American ports late in 1773, resistance was the order of the day. In New York and Philadelphia the ships were not permitted to land. Bostonians, unable to restrain their ire, turned the arrival of the ships into a veritable drama. On the evening of December 16, masked as Indians, a group of patriots raided the tea ships along the river front and threw more than 300 chests of tea into the harbor. Naturally the British Parliament in its turn was aroused, and passed measures, called by Americans "Intolerable Acts," aimed directly at punishing Massachusetts. The British lion proved to be a poor disciplinarian, for the Acts only fanned the flame higher throughout the colonies.

From the very moment the colonies became conscious that the chastisement of Massachusetts was a challenge to all, to be answered by united action, the British Empire in America was doomed. Town meetings and committees of correspondence agreed upon a general assembly of representatives of the thirteen colonies. The First Continental Congress, the immediate result of this protest movement, met in Philadelphia and boasted a membership of fifty-five distinguished Americans, including George Washington, Richard Henry

Lee, Patrick Henry, John Dickinson, John Jay, Samuel Adams, and John Adams. All of these men Benjamin Rush was to meet in Philadelphia.

Rush for several years had followed closely the progress of the struggle of the colonists for constitutional rights. He had become convinced that the imposition of taxes by the Crown without representation was unjust and, over several pseudonyms, he had published in the newspapers a number of articles defending the professed rights of the colonists. By the time Congress assembled he had gained more than a passing knowledge of the problems and issues facing the colonies.

On August 29, 1774, preparations were made by Philadelphians to greet the New England delegates to the Assembly which was to go down in history as the First Continental Congress. A committee met these distinguished gentlemen at Frankford, on the outskirts of the city, and rode into town with them. In the coach with John Adams and Robert Treat Paine rode Benjamin Rush. They asked him many questions about the temper of public opinion and the character of the men active in the anti-British movement. The young doctor of twenty-eight swelled with pride at the important rôle he was fulfilling.

A master of the social graces, Rush could be a delightful host. He entertained many of the members of Congress. For a time John and Samuel Adams were house guests in his home in Front Street, and from the guest room on the second story they enjoyed the panorama of the Delaware River and New Jersey beyond it.[1] Rush and John Adams soon cemented a friendship that was to last many years. One day Patrick Henry came to Dr. Rush to be inoculated against the smallpox. George Washington records in his diary that on October 18 he dined at the physician's home before spending the evening at the new City Tavern.

Rush enjoyed meeting and mixing with these men. He was inspired by their unselfish spirit, their earnestness, and their honesty. One evening Rush, Washington, General Mifflin, the two Adamses, and General Lee had foregathered for sociability. They could not long avoid the subject closest to their hearts. John Adams raised his glass and offered a toast: "Cash and gunpowder to the Yankies."

The inevitable war, he said, would be started by these same Yankees, sturdy New Englanders who were thus dubbed both by their friends and enemies.[2]

On the evening after its adjournment the members of Congress gave a gay supper at the City Tavern. Rush, as one of the Philadelphians who had entertained the members, was proud to be included. He could count himself among the patriots.

With the departure of the delegates from the city, Rush became, for the most part, a mere spectator of the rapidly moving events. After blood had been shed at Lexington and Concord in April 1775, however, he took an active part in an undertaking directly related to the revolutionary movement. Industries had to be organized for war immediately, and one of the first to take the step was the cotton industry. A joint stock company, the United Company for Promoting American Manufactures, was formed for the manufacture of cotton in Philadelphia. The first general meeting of this organization was held on February 22, 1775, and three weeks later, on March 16, Rush was elected president at a meeting of all the subscribers. A house was shortly leased on Market Street and by the fall of the year 400 women were employed. This company, which operated for three years, introduced the first spinning jenny into this country and was the first to attempt the manufacture of cotton cloth. As president of the organization, at the meeting on March 16 in Carpenters' Hall, Rush delivered a lengthy address on its urgency, its objects, and its plans. He pointed out that, inasmuch as Congress had placed an embargo on the importation of British goods, of which woolens, cottons, and linens comprised a considerable part, it was absolutely necessary that Americans establish woolen, cotton, and linen factories of their own. He believed that as long as the arbitrary ministers continued in power, no change in British policy was to be expected. An economic blockade, however, would bring the London officials to terms. Continue the embargo, he pleaded, and foster home industries!

The success of the cloth industries was certain, Rush insisted. Already a large number of families in Pennsylvania were manufacturing all the woolens and linens used by them in their own homes. If special pains were taken in breeding and caring for the sheep, American wool would soon be as fine in quality as the English, and within five years there would be wool enough in Pennsylvania to clothe all its inhabitants. Cotton could be imported from the West Indies and southern states upon such terms as would enable the Philadelphia manufacturer to undersell British cotton cloth. Because cotton cloth was worn so extensively by Americans, the encouragement of the cotton industry seemed to Rush to be an object of the utmost consequence. At the same time this commercial intercourse between the northern and southern colonies would strengthen their political union.

The subscribers were caught by Rush's analysis of the advantages of the new cloth industry to Pennsylvanians themselves. He calculated the population of the province at 100,000, and assuming that 50,000 inhabitants spent five pounds sterling annually on British clothing, Pennsylvania would keep within its own borders a total of £250,000 after the establishment of the new industry. And is not industry, next to agriculture, the basis of national wealth? he asked. The new business would employ a large number of poor persons in Philadelphia, and much of the work could be done in their own homes. European industrial workers would be encouraged to settle in America, and this immigration would add to the nation's strength by creating wealth. And lastly, by establishing our own industries we should at once erect an additional barrier against the encroachment of tyranny, because we should no longer be dependent upon foreigners for clothing and should, therefore, feel less subject to them.[3] These proposals and practical suggestions were made by Rush with the possibility of American independence in mind.

From this time Rush was to bear a definite share of the duties and burdens of the approaching revolution. When the Second Continental Congress met in May 1775, having established himself already as a patriot and advocate of independence, he spent most of his time in company and conference with those members who cherished the idea of complete separation from England. Together with such men as Benjamin Franklin and Thomas Jefferson, he attended the dinner on the banks of the Schuylkill given by a party of delegates in honor of George Washington immediately after his appointment in mid-June as commander-in-chief of the Continental armies. Rush records that after the General had responded to a toast, a silence ensued "as if every heart was penetrated with the awful, but great events which were to follow the use of the sword of liberty. . . ." Patrick Henry told Rush that, when he spoke to Washington, the General confessed that he was unequal to the post in which his country had placed him, and added with tears in his eyes: "Remember Mr. Henry what I now tell you—from the day I enter upon the command of the American armies, I date my fall and the ruin of my reputation."[4] Events were to disprove Washington's own prophecy of his future.

After Congress organized the American armies with Washington as head, Pennsylvania set about to provide for itself stronger local protection. On July 3, 1775, the Pennsylvania Committee of Public Safety, presided over by Franklin, decided to build a fleet of gunboats with which to protect the Delaware River entrance to the city. By mid-September thirteen of these small boats, built at a cost of £550 each, were afloat, parading such names as *Bulldog*, *Experiment*, and *Liberty*. Several of the ships had been built in three weeks. They were propelled by oars, like galleys, and each vessel, carrying two howitzers, besides swivels, and muskets, was manned by fifty-three sailors and several. officers. Rush accepted a commission as fleet surgeon, a post which he held for ten months. His salary and the exact nature of his work with the Pennsylvania navy are difficult to determine. In August 1776, when he learned that the Council of Safety had received some money from Congress, he wrote Owen Biddle to lay his account before the Council. "I hope you will not forget," he said, "the extraordinary services to the artillery company &c not mentioned in the vote of the last committee of Safety respecting our salery. You will find the day we left off attending the boats by looking for the date of Dr. Dunlap (the present surgeon's) appointment."[5] Rush was anxious to obtain his full salary, whatever it may have been.

Saltpeter was badly needed for the manufacture of domestic gunpowder. A premium was offered by Congress for this compound and instructions were published in regard to the methods of manufacturing it. Rush was a member of a committee appointed to superintend the Philadelphia saltpeter factory on Market Street.

Less direct but more important than his work in these posts was the part that Rush played in bringing about the publication of Thomas Paine's *Common Sense* which, more than any other single publication, caused Americans in large numbers to embrace the patriot cause and openly to favor complete separation from England.

Thomas Paine came to Philadelphia from England in November 1774, ostensibly to give private lessons in geography or to teach in one of the schools. While searching for employment he occasionally wandered into Robert Aitken's bookstore on the site of the present 110 Market Street. Here the English Bible was first published in America, and here could be found one of the most extensive collections of books in the province. Aitken's attention was attracted to a man who on several occasions had browsed about the shop, picking up and examining book after book. One morning the bookseller opened a conversation with him. His name was Thomas Paine. Paine soon found himself employed by Aitken, and for several months he conducted for him the *Pennsylvania Magazine, or American Museum*. Rush dropped in at the Aitken shop one day late in February 1775, to buy a few books, as he was wont to do, and was introduced to Paine. They conversed for only a few minutes, but long enough to discover comrades in each other. Immediately thereafter, when Rush learned that an antislavery article in the local newspaper had been written by Paine, his fellow feeling for the young Englishman was complete, because he had already allied himself with the very young antislavery movement.

At this time American opinion generally favored arbitration of the current disputes with the mother country and opposed the very thought of independence. Rush's attitude, however, was not conciliatory. For some months he had been gathering material for a propaganda pamphlet on the necessity for American independence and, although he planned to distribute it throughout the colonies, it seems that, on second thought, he was afraid to go through with the project. Philadelphia was still largely a Tory city and Rush feared that his practice would be ruined if his attack on the British Crown were to appear. Furthermore, he had fallen in love and was contemplating marriage. Thus he was under obligations to provide a living for his wife even at the sacrifice of his convictions to economic necessity. Frankly, he feared the personal consequences of this proposed stroke and lacked the courage to act. Certain it is that, in publishing the pamphlet, he would have cast himself headlong into fire. Instead, he took a safer course. He invited Paine to his home. In the course of a discussion on the state of political affairs he asked Paine pointblank to write an appeal for complete American independence, convincing him that, inasmuch as he had not yet developed strong connections in Philadelphia, he had nothing to fear from the opposition that the address would arouse in conservative circles. Paine agreed, and immediately set about the task. He had already quietly been gathering arguments against the British overlordship.[6]

From time to time, as chapters were written, he read them to Rush; otherwise, he seems to have had no assistance. In October, Franklin offered such materials as he possessed on the history of the transactions looking toward independence, and expressed a desire that a volume on this subject be published in the spring of 1776. Paine politely refused the kind offer inasmuch as his pamphlet had already been completely outlined and the first half of it practically finished. He decided to surprise Franklin by publishing a pamphlet on the subject long before spring, and he whipped the manuscript into shape as quickly as possible.[7]

After the last line had been written there arose the questions of title and publisher. Paine was partial to "Plain Truth" as an appropriate and fetching title, but he accepted Rush's suggestion of "Common Sense." A political paper called "Common Sense" had been printed in London in 1739, and a pamphlet bearing the same title in 1775.[8] Whether or not Rush was acquainted with these London publications is not known.

It was not easy to find a publisher brave enough to print this treasonous dissertation. At length, however, Rush offered the manuscript to Robert Bell, a well-known Scotch bookseller on Third Street, a fearless Whig and an avowed friend of the colonial cause. He was excited over the material, and so Rush hurried Paine to his office to make the necessary arrangements. No time was lost and in a few weeks, on January 10, 1776, the pamphlet appeared, published anonymously, and priced at two shillings. It was addressed to the "inhabitants of North America."

The afterclap of *Common Sense* was immediate and far sounding.

The paper found its way into countless homes and provided a subject of discussion in clubs and inns for the rest of the winter; it was recited in the schools and preached from the pulpit. It carried the controversy over independence into all the newspapers throughout the colonies and brought the subject to the attention of every thinking citizen. Before the end of the spring season, more than 120,000 copies were sold in the colonies, and an untold number of colonists became potential rebels thereby. To approximate a circulation in proportion to today's population, *Common Sense* would have to go into editions totaling 4,000,000 copies. An obstinate attachment to Great Britain was shattered in many homes by this arsenal of arguments which tore away all the reserves which had safeguarded the Tory position. "By referrng the matter from arguments to arms," wrote Paine, "a new era for politics is struck. . . . As Europe is our market for trade, we ought to form no partial connexion with any part of it. It is the true interest of America to steer clear of European contentions, which she never can do while, by her dependence on Britain, she is made the make-weight in the scale of British politics." And was it not absurd, he asked, for an island to govern a continent? He ridiculed George III and the very idea of divine right, assuring the Americans that it was the heathen who had introduced government by kings.

Common Sense, though crude in parts, is a vigorous production, noteworthy chiefly for the immediate result it accomplished in stirring up active enthusiasm for independence. In the spring of 1775 Washington had avoided a definite statement on the question of complete independence, but on April 1, 1776, he wrote: "My countrymen, I know, from their form of government and steady attachment heretofore to royalty, will come reluctantly into the idea of independence, but time and persecution bring many wonderful things to pass; and by private letters, which I have lately received from Virginia, I find *Common Sense* is working a powerful change in the minds of men."

Rush was proudly conscious of his influence in instigating the writing of the document which worked such "a powerful change" in the American mind, and which ushered in the birth of a new nation with greater rapidity than the most optimistic of separatists could have expected. Through the physician Paine met many of the leading men. "Your Mr. Payne din'd with me yesterday," wrote Major General Charles Lee from New York in late February. "I am much oblig'd to you for the introduction—He has a genius in his eyes—his conversation has much life—I hope he will continue cramming down the throats of squeamish mortals his wholesome truths. . . ."[9]

During the spring of 1776 Rush mingled constantly with the radical members of Congress. He spent many hours arguing, in his most sober manner, with conservatives on the revolutionary steps which he believed should be taken. Strangely enough, there was little violence in Philadelphia compared with other cities and towns. The members of Congress, living in the city as honored guests, were dined and wined; and although they had little time for direct contact with the mass of people, their political judgments must certainly have been affected by local opinion. The Pennsylvania Assembly, legislative body of the Province, meeting in the city at the same time, was a conservative group of men. Suffrage was restricted in the colony and consequently the Tory element held the upper hand. Indeed, three months before the Declaration of Independence was presented, the Assembly was gallantly attempting to prevent an open break with King and Parliament. The Assembly met in the Judges' Room on the west side of the State House on Chestnut Street. They had moved over from their regular meeting room on the east side of the building to make way for the Continental Congress. These two groups on either side the State House were pulling the ship in opposite directions. The election of 1776 returned a conservative majority to the Assembly, but, as later events were to prove, this majority did not truly represent the will of the people.

On May 10, Congress recommended that the provinces draw up constitutions, and that the old British charters be displaced by separate state governments. This direct blow against Great Britain led the revolutionary group in Philadelphia to agitate against the aristocrats in the Pennsylvania Assembly who were blocking all moves for independence. To some extent, however, the Assembly had broken with England inasmuch as, for many months, it had refused to submit laws to the Governor and carried on the government of the province by means of resolutions and a Committee of Safety. Such conservatives as Dickinson, Wilson, Robert Morris, and Mifflin felt, therefore, that a new constitution, as recommended by the Congress, was not necessary.

The populace at large thought otherwise and, on May 20, an immense crowd, six or seven thousand, met in the State House yard, and resolved that the Assembly was incompetent to rule because its members were elected largely by adherents of the Crown, while many "worthy inhabitants" were excluded from the franchise. The crowds came early and stayed late; their temper was an angry one. Finally, they were satisfied to put their faith in the hands of a Committee of patriots under the chairmanship of Thomas McKean, who was to report next day. After brief deliberation the Committee concluded that the Assembly did not possess the confidence of the people and that it was high time to elect an Assembly of men who would definitely support the movement for independence. A conference was arranged to determine the time and method of calling a convention to draw up a state constitution. Word was already going around the city that Virginia's delegates in Congress had received instructions to propose independence by congressional resolution. High tension and excitement followed and events began to move forward rapidly.

June had come, and with it warm weather. The heart of the embryonic nation was already throbbing. Radical Philadelphians were beginning to question the Americanism of their fellow citizens, particularly of the conservative elements opposing independence; and this wave of suspicion led to street brawls in which Tories were often maltreated at the hands of too ardent Whigs.

The city was the center for supplies for the recruiting Continental armies. The Commissary-General, Joseph Trumbull, in his Philadelphia office received bids and samples and made purchases. On June 18, he spent $60,000 for flour alone. With war in the air conservation of food was one of the first problems. When Congress learned that great quantities of salted beef and pork had been purchased by individuals for exportation, it was feared that the army's supply was endangered, and immediately a resolution was passed prohibiting the exportation of these meats.

Finally, a definite resolution of independence was introduced by Richard Henry Lee for the Virginia delegation on June 7, and the following days found Thomas Jefferson hard at work couching in strong yet simple words a declaration of independence. The Pennsylvania delegates in Congress had voted five to two against Lee's resolution the day after its introduction. This action was too much for the revolutionary Philadelphians; the Whig members bolted the provincial Assembly which, left without a quorum, adjourned never to function again.

On June 18 the Conference, called as a result of the citizens' mass meeting of May 20, met at Carpenters' Hall, presided over by Thomas McKean. This revolutionary assembly, expressing the popular will, immediately assumed control of Pennsylvania. The legal Assembly was vigorously denounced, the franchise liberalized, a new oath of allegiance, omitting the name of George III, endorsed, and the old order battered to bits. Rush, now in the thick of the fight, participated in the conference which issued a call for a convention to meet in a month. On June 23, he offered a motion to draft an address in favor of American independence and was immediately made chairman of the Committee appointed for the task. The subsequent report, adopted by the Conference on the 24th and submitted to Congress on the 25th, foreshadowed many of the salient points to be set forth in the Declaration of Independence, and even much of its phraseology anticipated the immortal document proclaimed by Congress on July 4.[10] If one is to accept as official the action of this illegally elected Conference, Pennsylvania actually declared for independence on June 24 through the report of Rush's committee. On the next day the members of the Conference, in high spirits, banqueted at the Indian Queen Tavern in Fourth Street and toasted "the free and independent States of America." Ten days later Congress proclaimed to the world the independence of the American colonies. The goal for which Rush and the liberals had been laboring was at last history. Open war against a foreign country supplanted armed resistance of outraged colonies against an uncompromising King. The American farmer, tradesman, or artisan found in the Declaration a cause to which his fighting spirit could cling.

On July 15 the Convention met as arranged, chose Franklin president, appointed a new council of safety as the executive head of the state government, and proceeded to frame a state constitution. It was completed on September 28 and went into effect on November 1. This constitution, which was not submitted to the people, and which drove many of the wealthy Quakers into the Tory ranks, provided for a single legislative body elected annually and a supreme executive council, of twelve members, whose president had practically no power. Most peculiar was a council of censors, whose duty it was to decide whether or not the constitution was being observed and the laws duly executed. The Convention elected Benjamin Rush among its nine delegates to Congress, turning out all those who had not supported independence.

Rush's election to Congress was particularly gratifying to him, inasmuch as it gave him the enviable opportunity of signing the Declaration of Independence with the other members, in August. His neat signature stands between those of Benjamin Franklin and Robert Morris.

Rush was conscious of the dynamic force of the Declaration. "The declaration of independence," he commented in the spring of 1777, "was said to have decided & weakened the colonies. The contrary of this was the case. Nothing but the signing, & recognizing of the declaration of independence preserved the congress from a dissolution in December 1776 when Howe marched to the Delaware. . . . But further the declaration of independence produced a secession of tories—timid—moderate & double minded men from the counsels of America in consequence of which the congress as well as each of the States have possessed two times the vigor and strength they had formerly."[11]

His inherent interest in men and their habits of mind provoked his thoughtful comment upon "the strength, and weakness of the human understanding and the extent of human virtue, & folly" as displayed in the national legislature. "Time will ameliorate us," he wrote a friend in Richmond. "A few more misfortunes will teach us wisdom & humility and inspire us with true benevolence. The

republican soil is broke up—but we have still many monarchical &
aristocratical weeds to pluck up from it. . . . We have knocked up
the substance of royalty but now then we worship the shadow."[12]

He took his seat in the Continental Congress on July 20 and
served for nine months. On August 6 Congress resolved that one
member be added to the committee already appointed to investigate
and to remedy the defects of the powder made at the mills, and
Rush was called upon. On the next day Congress resolved further
that his name be added to the committee for procuring medicines.
On September 24 he was made chairman of a committee of five
appointed to devise ways and means of furnishing the northern army
with provisions, medicines, and general supplies. Two weeks later
he was made a member of a committee on the condition of prisoners
of war; and on October 17 he was made chairman of a committee
to select authentic accounts of the condition of the army and navy
to be published by Congress.[13]

Although Rush sat on various committees, took part in debates,
and performed the routine tasks assigned to him during his nine
months of service, it cannot be said that he was a leading figure in
Congress. He lacked the qualities which made men follow with unquestioning confidence the brilliant and powerful statesmen who
were building a nation. Although these active committees made constant demands on his time, they offered Rush an opportunity for
close association with these same great leaders, and for intimate
examination of the problems facing them.

The task before Congress was a gigantic one. Already, in the
summer of 1776, the British troops, outnumbering the Americans
two to one, had driven Washington out of the city of New York
and across New Jersey. Disheartened by the course of military events,
thousands of Continentals deserted; many others were captured by
the British; and, as a result, Washington found himself with less
than 5,000 soldiers primed for action. Fortunately the Commander-
in-Chief, manifesting his dauntless character in this trying situation,
gathered loose ends. On Christmas night he crossed the Delaware
in the face of a driving sleet storm, pounced on the Hessians at
Trenton, causing them to surrender, and then dashed forward to
Princeton where three British regiments were forced to beat a hasty

retreat. After this performance, brilliant and daring, the atmosphere in Congress cleared, and it went ahead more hopefully with its job of fashioning and defending a government.

With unselfish devotion to the cause of independence, Rush was not content to spend his entire time in Congress. Driven to more active participation in the actual business of fighting, he conferred directly with Washington and later volunteered his medical services on the battlefield at Princeton.

Congress was hard at work on a plan of confederation. The knotty question of representation particularly engaged Rush's attention and he participated in the debates on the subject. The small states favored a system by which each state would have the same voting strength in Congress; the large states, however, contributors of the bulk of the man power as well as the financial power of the revolutionary movement, demanded that the representation in Congress be based directly on the population of the respective states. Rush joined Franklin in espousing the cause of the large states. On August 1 he delivered a speech marked by patriotic fervor, and recalling the forceful oratory of his college days. In it he referred to himself as "a citizen of America." He attributed the decline of the Dutch Republic to three factors: First, that the consent of every state was required in all legislative matters; second, that the legislators were obliged to consult their constituents on all occasions; and third, that they voted by provinces, thus destroying the equality of representation. Rush held that if this method of voting by states were introduced in the American confederation, colonial distinctions would be maintained, factions fostered in Congress, and freedom crushed. On the other hand, if representation were based on population, liberty would always be safe, the larger colonies being so situated as to render visionary every fear of their combining. "Massachusetts is contiguous to two small colonies, Rhode Island and New Hampshire; Pennsylvania is near New Jersey and Delaware; Virginia is between Maryland and North Carolina. We have been too free with the word independence; we are dependent on each other, not totally independent states. . . . I would not have it understood that I am pleading the cause of Pennsylvania. When I entered that door, I considered myself a citizen of America." Provincialism, exclaimed Rush, must give way to Americanism! That was the key-note of his plea. The more a man aims at serving America, the more he serves his colony. Further, this passionate opponent of slavery did not fail to point out that representation based on the number of free inhabitants would have the excellent effect of inducing the states to discourage slavery and to encourage, instead, the increase of their free inhabitants.[14] In spite of Rush's argument, the Articles of Confederation provided for equal state representation regardless of population.

To what extent could a state act independently of the central government? This question arose in late December 1776, when in Providence, Rhode Island, a conference of deputies of four New England states—New Hampshire, Massachusetts, Rhode Island and Connecticut—agreed to regulate the price of food and dry goods. In Congress it was asked if this conference was a proper one, and if its validity did not depend upon congressional approval. Rush, ready with his pointed and forceful arguments, took the floor again to sway his audience with his brilliant oratory. "The desire of independence is natural not only to individuals but to communities," he insisted. "There was a time . . . when it was wrong to say a word agst the dependence of the colonies upon Great Britain—a time came when it was equally criminal to enforce that dependence. The time may come & probably will come, when it will be the interest of the United States to be independent of each other, but I can conceive of no temporal punishment to be severe eno' for that man who attempts to dissolve, or weaken the union for a century or two to come. I admire the proceedings of the committee assembled at Providence. They are full of political virtue and wisdom, and I think the other states will act wisely & virtuously in proportion as they resemble them. But I think the meeting is full of great & interesting consequences, and should be regarded with a serious & jealous eye. Their business is chiefly continental, and therefore they usurped the houses of Congress as much as four counties would usurp the powers of legislation in a state, shd they attempt to tax themselves . . . tho' the meeting was necessary and no injustice intended or done by it to any state, yet it becomes us to remember that arbitrary power has often originated in justice & necessity."[15] From one who a few months before was extolling the glories and urging the necessity of united action, this view is more liberal than one might have expected.

A perplexing problem from the very outbreak of hostilities was that of increasing commodity prices. Shoes, which had been sold in the spring of 1776 for $1.75, were priced at $3.75 in September. Butter doubled in price to fifty cents a pound. The steady rise in prices, of course, affected Philadelphia, which had been known throughout the colonies for its low-priced and excellent markets. In May of 1776, the price of fine salt was fixed at $1.87 a bushel, and in the fall it reached the unheard-of price of $6.25, and even at that exorbitant figure it was difficult to get. Rev. Henry Muhlenberg noted in his diary that "the people push and jostle one another wherever there is the smallest quantity to be found about town. The country people complain bitterly because they suppose there are hidden stores in Philadelphia." Attempts were made, though unsuccessfully, to extract salt from the sea water off the coast of New Jersey.

The question as to whether or not Congress should recommend that the states adopt the plan of the Providence conference to reduce and regulate the price of labor, manufactures, and provisions, precipitated a debate on February 14, 1777. Rush was among those who vigorously opposed the regulation of prices by the government, claiming that Congress would be able to enforce its decrees only temporarily, and that the open violation and circumvention of such a law would lead to a general disregard of the supremacy of Congress in legislative matters. A century and a half later the nation was to experience an outbreak of lawlessness caused in part by the inability of the government to enforce its liquor prohibition laws.

In opposing this resolution, Rush attacked all unenforceable regulations. "The wisdom & power of government have been employed in all ages to regulate the price of necessaries to no purpose," he said. "The Congress with all its authority have failed in a former instance of regulating the price of goods. . . . The committee of Philad^a limited the price of West India goods about a year ago— but what was the consequence? The merchants it is true sold their rum, sugar & molasses at the price limited by the committee, but they charged a heavy profit upon the barrel or the paper which contained the rum or the sugar. Consider, sir, the danger of failing in this experiment. The salvation of this continent depends upon the authority of this Congress being held as sacred as the cause of liberty itself. Suppose we should fail of producing the effects we wish for by the resolution before you. Have we any character to spare? Have we committed no mistakes in the management of the public affairs of America? We have, sir! It becomes us therefore, to be careful of the remains of our Authority & character. . . . We estimate our virtue by a false barometer, when we measure it by the price of goods. The extortion we complain of arises only from the excessive quantity of our money. Now, sir, a failure in this attempt to regulate the price of goods will increase the clamors against the rapacity of dealers, and thus depreciate our public virtue. . . . The price of goods may be compared to a number of light substances in a bason of water. The hand may keep them down for a while, but nothing can detain them on the bottom of the bason but an abstraction of water. The continent labours under a universal malady. From the crown of her head to the soal of her feet she is full of disorders. She requires the most powerful tonic medicines. The resolution before you is nothing but an opiate. It may compose the continent for a night, but she will soon awaken again to a fresh sense of her pain & misery."

John Adams, James Wilson, Dr. Witherspoon and others supported Rush in his opposition, and the original resolution to recommend the price-fixing plan to the states was defeated; the plan was, instead, only referred to the states to act upon as they deemed proper.[16]

While in Congress Rush appointed himself watchdog of its powers, believing that the assemblage in Philadelphia should be the final arbiter in all matters pertaining to national questions. When it was proposed that the question of the appointment of three major generals be referred to the general officers of the army, he saw nothing but mischief in the motion, and in no uncertain terms expressed his convictions on the floor of Congress on February 19, 1777. Should Congress surrender to Washington the power of appointing his general officers? "One of the most powerful & happy commonwealths in the world, Rome, called her general officers from the plough &

paid no regard to rank, service or seniority," he said. "We have of late been successful it is true, but I despair of our country being saved till the instrumentality of military wisdom & virtue are employed for that purpose, and these can never be had till we use a sovereign power in calling them forth where ever we find them. It is to no purpose to talk of the practice of despotic princes. They promote according to seniority it is true, but they possess an absolute power of recalling, disgracing, or breaking the general officers as soon as they make them, and we find they are fond of exercising this power upon the least neglect, inattention, or want of success. The case is different with us. A general may lose a battle or a province, and we possess no power to recall or to displace him. If the motion is passed, I shall move immediately afterwards that all the civil power of the continent may be transferred from our hands into the hands of the army, & that they may be proclaimed the highest power of the people."[17] If the army could choose its own officers, what hold would Congress have over the personnel of the military establishment? Rush's objection was most certainly in order; decentralization of power and authority would lead only to disorganization and ruin.

In the debates in Congress Rush was constantly on the alert with objections to any move which he believed might weaken or hinder the progress of the Continental forces. He was entirely out of sympathy with any suggestions for peace at this time; they were in his opinion premature and tended only to break down the morale. The conference to discuss a possible peace, held on Staten Island in September 1776, between Richard, Lord Howe and a committee of Congress was futile. On February 20, 1777, Congress received a letter from General Charles Lee, then a prisoner in the British lines in New York, stating that Lord Howe desired to discuss matters of great importance to America with two or three congressmen. Rush joined John Adams in denouncing another conference with Lord Howe. He had, in fact, opposed the Staten Island conference in September. "General Lee with all his great qualities, possesses the weakness of being easily imposed upon," he explained. "His characters of men are dictated by caprice or passion. I have seldom known him give a true character of any man. He is fond of negociations &

conferences. . . . I believe Genl Lee to be honest & sincerely attached to our cause, but some people suppose he threw himself in the way of being taken prisoner. Considering all these things, I maintain that a compliance with the general's request would be impolitic, & highly dangerous to the union & safety of the united states."[18] There was much truth in this frank analysis of Lee's suggestion, and its open presentation before Congress indicates the sincerity of Rush's stand. Even at the risk of alienating friends, he would fight for what he conceived to be right for the common good.

He was aroused to action and eloquence by those Americans who had developed a veritable lust for piratical gold. Many of the Continental soldiers waited impatiently for the expiration of their enlistments so that they could rush off to sea to share in the spoils of the pirate raids in the West Indies. Men were badly needed by Washington and his aides, and Rush believed that the nation had the right to demand their services and their blood. "We must have an Army," he wrote Richard Henry Lee; "the fate of America must be decided by an Army. It must consist of seventy or eighty thousand men. and they must all be fit for the field before the first day of May next."[19]

His constant and characteristic attention to duty in the halls of Congress, his conscientious and successful endeavors to concentrate power in the hands of Congress in order to strengthen the military establishment, were not appreciated, however, by the Pennsylvania Assembly when it again chose its delegates to Congress in February 1777. When the new delegates presented their credentials, on March 12, Rush was not among them. His opposition to the unicameral legislature, and his search for a system of checks and balances in the government led to defeat. Disgusted with the manner in which the government of Pennsylvania was functioning, he wrote Anthony Wayne that the constitution of 1776 was intolerable because "it has substituted mob government for one of the happiest governments in the world. . . . A single legislature is big with tyranny. I had rather live under the government of one man than of seventy-two." In the spring of 1777 he complained again to Wayne of the sorry state of politics in Pennsylvania. Later, he wrote that, although the government of Pennsylvania was not operating efficiently, some encouragement was to be had from the conduct and spirit of the Pennsylvania troops.[20]

So interested was Rush in the problem of ameliorating the defects of Pennsylvania's constitution that he took to his study and read Montesquieu, Bolingbroke, and other authorities on political thought. He searched deeply for a solution, and at length published, in 1777, his "Observations upon the present Government of Pennsylvania in Four Letters to the People of Pennsylvania." In this pamphlet he set forth the theory that the framework of every government should consist of a bill of rights, a constitution, and general laws; but that the existing Pennsylvania constitution included clauses which should have been placed in either the bill of rights, or in the laws. It jumbled the departments in a most unsystematic manner. Rush called on the people to unite and form a more effectual and more practicable form of government. Again declaring the one-house legislature dangerous, he added that "all governments are dangerous and tyrannical in proportion as they approach to simplicity." He pleaded for a second legislative house, "inasmuch as each body possesses a free and independent power, so that they mutually check ambition and usurpation in each other." Naturally, after he had denounced his state government as "a tyranny," he could hardly expect the Assembly to return him to Congress. To Rush, however, that seat in Congress was less important than the honest expression of his opinion. Two years later he went so far as to organize the Republican Society, the object of which was the revision of the state constitution.

One might easily disagree with Rush's opinions on public questions, but no one could question his integrity or the ardor of his patriotism. His actions outside as well as inside the halls of Congress were governed by the needs of his country. After Washington had been driven out of New York in late August 1776, it was feared that the British would follow the retreating army and occupy Philadelphia. Congress, therefore, adjourned to meet temporarily in Baltimore. Rush sent his family to the home of a relative, Elihu Hall, at Mount Welcome, Cecil County, Maryland, and moved some of his furniture and his books to a friend's house in Darby, a few miles southwest of the city. Strangely enough, Sir William Howe later made his headquarters in this house on one of his excursions from Philadelphia, and used one of Rush's tea tables as a desk.

Rush was resolved to stand or fall with his country. Having settled his family, he immediately joined the Philadelphia militia on the way to reinforce Washington's retreating army and to prevent the occupation of the capital. He accompanied the militia to Bristol where, without a commission, he volunteered to supervise the medical section. In December he visited Washington at the General's quarters about ten miles above Bristol. "He appeared much depressed and lamented the ragged state of his army in affecting terms," runs Rush's account of his interview with the Commander. "I gave him assurances of the disposition of Congress to support him, under his present difficulties and distresses. While I was talking to him I observed him to play with his pen and ink upon several small pieces of paper. One of them by accident fell upon the floor near my feet. I was struck with the inscription upon it. It was 'victory or death.' " A few days later Washington crossed the Delaware and surrounded the Hessians at Trenton. "I had reason to believe . . .," recalled Rush, "that in my interview with General Washington he had probably been meditating upon his attack upon the Hessians at their posts on the Jersey side of the Delaware at the time of my interview with him, for I found that the countersign of his troops at the surprize of Trenton was, 'Victory or Death.' "

After the battle Rush also proceeded to Trenton and, when Washington's council of officers was unable to agree on the steps that should be taken with regard to a march on Princeton, he was called into the council at which Washington outlined the situation. Asked for his advice, Rush replied that he could not be a judge of the questions before the council, but that he could state with assurance that the Philadelphia militia would be happy to obey a summons to Trenton. Next day the Americans were on their way to Princeton again to defeat the enemy. It was at this time that Rush went into action, treating the wounded on the battlefield at Princeton. He treated among others the American General Mercer and a British officer, a Captain McPherson. He directed leg amputations of four British soldiers and watched over their recovery. As soon as the wounded patients were out of danger, Rush set off to attend once more the sessions of Congress, already discussed. This short experience gave him a close-up view of conditions in the army, invaluable in his work in Congress.[21]

In April 1777, after his term in Congress had expired, Rush accepted a commission in the medical department of the army. After only nine months in the service, however, he resigned because of his disapproval of the management of the military hospitals. Here again he displayed his characteristic inability to work harmoniously with men whose opinions differed from his own. This controversy will be treated in a subsequent chapter.

Rush resigned his army post on January 30, 1778, but did not return directly to Philadelphia to reëstablish his private practice. He would hardly have been favorably received, as the city had been in the hands of the British for the past four months. Early in the previous September General Howe and Admiral Howe moved up the Chesapeake Bay, with 250 ships, landed their forces at the head of the Elk River, advanced northward on the heels of the fleeing inhabitants, and defeated Washington's army at Chadd's Ford on the Brandywine Creek, September 11. Howe might have broken the American army then and there, but, as at Long Island a year before, he wasted time, and the opportunity slipped through his fingers. Nevertheless he pushed forward toward Philadelphia, and, before the equinoctial storm unloosed its torrent of rain, redcoats were parading the streets of the capital. Members of Congress took flight and found their way to Lancaster and York by circuitous routes. When the capital fell, the French philosopher Voltaire exclaimed: "The troops of Doctor Franklin have been beaten by those of the King of England. Alas! Philosophers are being beaten everywhere. Reason and liberty are unwelcome in this world."

Voltaire's pessimism was premature. It is true that Washington failed to dislodge Howe in the battle of Germantown on October 4, but along the Hudson Valley between Albany and Saratoga General Gates, with 20,000 brave soldiers, was ready to strike at the British under General Burgoyne. The blow was finally struck on October 17, at Saratoga where Gates trounced the Britishers, capturing 5,000 of them. The victory was a decisive one and marked the turning point of the war. The loss of one of the British armies not only buoyed the American spirit but also convinced the French ministers that American success was a certainty. The French alliance was the result.

After the battle of Germantown, Washington and his troops withdrew to Valley Forge where, throughout months of want and starvation, they hibernated. Sir William Howe, on the other hand, enjoyed the winter of 1777–78 in the capital where balls and parties supplanted serious military conferences. These months of gayety tended to weaken the British morale and ultimately helped the American cause.

The capital was not evacuated by the British until the end of May 1778. Meanwhile Rush had been wandering through Pennsylvania, visiting camps and discussing the state of affairs with friends. In February 1778 he spent some time at Reading, Allentown, and Bethlehem, and then rested for three weeks at the Stocktons in Princeton. In mid-March he journeyed to Valley Forge and saw with his own eyes the distressing conditions. For the next two months he traveled—to Mount Welcome, again to Princeton, and to Wilmington. It was not until June 21 that he saw the familiar scenes of his city once more. He considered it a treat to be in Philadelphia after months of traveling, for stagecoaches were stuffy and uncomfortable, and the roads were remembered largely because of their ruts.[22]

Early in August Rush brought his wife back to Philadelphia. With her was their year-old son, John, born on July 17, 1777, at Elihu Hall's home in Maryland. He was destined to become an officer in the United States Navy. On January 1, 1779, a second child, Anne Emily, was born in Philadelphia, and the parents again were jubilant. Both the Doctor and his wife were fond of children. After the arrival of the daughter he wrote General Gates: "I now live wholly for the benefit of an amiable wife—and two children—and of my patients."[23]

He needed a complete rest from the trials of public life. His family proved to be a tonic. However, an extraordinarily burdensome and strenuous year caused Rush to break down, worn out from work and worry. On September 12, 1778, he was seized with a "malignant bilious fever" and for days his condition was critical. "My physicians Redman, Kuhn & Morgan shook their heads as they went out of my room," he recalled two months later. "My friends could do little more than weep at my bedside. I made my will and took leave of life, but in the extremity of my danger it pleased God to break the violence of my disease."[24]

General Charles Lee, who had at one time been a butt of Rush's ridicule in Congress, was delighted to learn of his recovery. "Nothing cou'd have more seriously alarm'd me than the accounts I have lately receiv'd of the dangerous situation so valuable a friend as you are has been in, and I most sincerely congratulate myself and all your acquaintances on your recovery," he wrote.[25]

By November Rush had regained his health, and on the last Tuesday afternoon of the month at three o'clock he inaugurated his new course of lectures in chemistry at the medical school of the College of Philadelphia. Rush had been appointed Professor of Chemistry in the medical school in 1769 but, before the first Continental Congress had assembled in the fall of 1774, the medical lectures had been discontinued because of the disturbed condition of public affairs. Several of the professors of the college and many of the students joined the army and, on June 30, 1777, the institution closed its doors. For over a year not even the trustees of the institution were able to get together, for the British occupied the city from September 1777, until June 1778. After the outbreak of open hostilities, in the summer of 1776, the college buildings were frequently used as military barracks, notwithstanding the protests of the faculty to the Council of Safety. In the fall of the next year much of the college equipment was removed from the city to save it from possible damage or theft at the hands of the British garrison. In the fall of 1778 Provost Smith returned to the city after an absence of a year and a half; and on September 25 the medical school reopened.

The College of Philadelphia had now been in existence for more than twenty years. It was in 1749 that Benjamin Franklin organized "The Academy and Charitable School," and in 1751 the building on Fourth Street near Arch was occupied by students. Four years later the Proprietors of the Province of Pennsylvania granted an additional charter and changed the name to "The College, Academy and Charitable School of Philadelphia." In 1762 an additional building was erected. On May 3, 1765, with no further enlargement of the physical equipment of the institution, the trustees adopted Dr. John Morgan's plan to organize a medical department, and on June 21, 1768, the first commencement of medical school graduates in America was celebrated.

After the College had reopened in 1778, the political leaders in control of the state government began to interfere in the affairs of the College, charging that it had not been reorganized by the trustees in keeping with the new republican principles of government, that it had become sectarian in its management, and that several of the trustees had joined the enemy. In February 1779 the Assembly passed a resolution calling for an investigation of the affairs of the College, and in November it abrogated the charter of the College of Philadelphia, dissolved the Board of Trustees, and set up a new institution, the University of the State of Pennsylvania, which took over all the property of the College. On December 8 the trustees of the new institution appointed a committee to "enquire into the state of the late Medical School," and to study medical courses in foreign institutions, and in the meantime to invite the former professors to continue their work. The new provost, Rev. Dr. John Ewing, experienced great difficulty in reorganizing the medical department because, of the professors in the former college, only Dr. Shippen accepted an appointment in the new university.

Rush had more than a passing interest in the situation. A professorship in the medical school brought with it not only prestige but also profitable consultations. Although he desired the connection, he was openly antagonistic to Dr. Shippen, whose conduct as director-general of the Medical Department of the army he had attacked. A version of the story of Rush's appointment appeared several years later, in 1785, in a letter to the local newspaper. The correspondent stated that when the question of appointments came up, at the close of 1779, Rush believed that if he and Dr. Morgan would notify the trustees of their unwillingness to accept posts on the staff if Shippen were also elected, the trustees would rather lose one man than two. Rush and Morgan so advised the trustees, who, however, did not act as the two had anticipated. They elected Shippen but neither Rush nor Morgan. Matters rested here for several months until Rush, becoming restive, appealed to several persons connected with the University to have him elected to the staff. The correspondent went on to explain that Rush, after disclaiming the original letter to the Board, was duly elected. In his answer to the unknown correspondent, Rush insisted that he had been elected a professor in the new institution without any solicitation whatsoever on his part.[26]

The actual details of the election and the preliminary disputes over it are unknown, but we do know that Rush delivered the introductory lecture of his course in chemistry at the University at noon on Monday, November 20, 1780. The following year his course in chemistry and the practice of physic opened on November 19.[27]

This teaching position, an extensive practice, and various interests of a public nature more than filled Rush's days. He had been critically ill in the fall of 1778 and again he was forced to bed for a time in the fall of 1780. To assist him in his medical practice he engaged one of his former students, Dr. James Hall, who had just returned from studying in the London clinics. This assistance was absolutely necessary to Rush at this time, suffering as he was from a pulmonary infection which made it dangerous for him to go out at night or in bad weather.

He actually needed more freedom from work. Several of his rival physicians, however, read into Rush's employment of an assistant a certain indication that his practice was declining and that he was getting ready to withdraw gradually from medicine in order to devote his life exclusively to public affairs. Strangely enough Rush's practice did soon begin to decline, so that he found himself able to get along without an assistant. In 1785, therefore, Hall left Philadelphia to settle in York, Pennsylvania. Nevertheless, Dr. Rush's practice continued to be extensive enough to prove lucrative. "I got a pretty little fortune with Mrs. Rush," he wrote in the spring of 1784, "and have added to it from the income of my business so as to produce an estate which if thrown into cash would yield about £300 a year sterling," a tidy income in the post-war years when few Americans enjoyed financial independence.[28]

After withdrawing from the army in 1778, Rush continued to follow closely the military operations of the next few years. The

American victory at Saratoga and the subsequent French alliance bolstered up the flimsy Continental structure for a short period. Then, to cause consternation among the revolutionists, in the winter of 1779–1780, the British transferred their active military operations to the South, where they erroneously anticipated a wholesale enlistment of Tories under the British flag. They were, nevertheless, victorious in several battles.

The setback in the South notwithstanding, the situation appeared hopeful even to the critical Rush, who wrote John Adams, April 28, 1780: "Our affairs wear their usual checkered aspect. Our governments are daily acquiring new strength. Our army, which I saw a few weeks ago at Morristown, has improved greatly in discipline since our former correspondence in economy and healthiness. The number of our soldiers is small, occasioned not by a decay of military or whiggish spirit among us, but by the want of money to purchase recruits."[29] When in June a $300,000 fund was raised to support the credit of a bank organized to furnish supplies of provisions for the armies Rush subscribed $2,000.[30]

Rush's optimism was justified in the fall. On October 7, 1780, the British advance in the South was checked at King's Mountain, resulting in an outburst of patriotic enthusiasm throughout the Carolinas. Lord Cornwallis was unable to break through the lines drawn by Nathanael Greene and Daniel Morgan.

Cause for rejoicing was, however, short-lived. Discouraging events occurred in the year 1781. Benedict Arnold's treason shocked the patriots; the complete collapse of the continental currency disheartened them; and the lack of response to the calls for volunteers led Washington to doubt if he could gather a fighting unit for an actual campaign. But somehow the indomitable spirit of General Washington kept the disorganized machine running. In Philadelphia Rush was going about urging the citizens to strike manfully against monarchy in order to secure republican institutions. "A citizen of ye United States who dares to acknowledge himself a friend to monarchy (under any name or shape) is a traitor in the worst sense of the words," he declared in the summer of 1781. A few months later he was exclaiming that even more heinous than treason, in the eyes of many, was the belief in republicanism. "There is a greater crime in the eyes of some people than treason—it is republicanism," he wrote General Gates. "It will require half a century to cure us of all our monarchical habits & prejudices. At present we are Roman Catholics in government. A pope in religion, and a king in power are equally necessary articles with many people. Let us have patience. Our republican forms of government will in time beget republican opinions & manners. All will end well."[31] Down with monarchism, was his battle cry.

Six weeks after this letter was written, the struggle was over, and monarchism in the colonies perished. After confusing the British by a false march toward New York, Washington hastened into Virginia in order to trap Cornwallis. In the meantime, answering Washington's appeal for coöperation, Admiral DeGrasse moved northward from the West Indies with the French fleet, and early in September appeared at the mouth of the Chesapeake Bay. The British fleet sailed out of New York harbor with reinforcements for Cornwallis but, finding the Chesapeake blocked by the French squadron, returned to its base. This was the beginning of the end. The American and French armies—some 15,000 men—under Washington and Rochambeau, moved closer and closer to Yorktown. Cornwallis, encircled, was unable to get help from the outside. Finally, on October 19, Cornwallis, appreciating the hopelessness of his situation, drew down the British flag, and surrendered his army of 7,000 men.

The sun had set on the British empire south of the Great Lakes, and the memorable pronouncement of July 4, 1776, was a fact. The United States of America had become an entity.

"How is the mighty fallen!" wrote Rush when news of the collapse of British arms reached Philadelphia. "Cornwallis the ravager (for he never conquered) of the South—the pride of Britain—and the pillar of all her hopes in America is fallen—fallen—fallen! How honourable is the glorious event to the combined arms of France and America! How honourable to our illustrious General! and how important will be its consequence in the great republic of Europe!"[32]

George III, on the other hand, blindly stubborn as usual, was not ready to admit defeat; he saw no reason for believing that the British hope of success had disappeared with Cornwallis' surrender.

In the spring of the following year, however, the parliamentary opposition to the King's design of renewing the war became openly defiant; the Tory ministry was forced to resign; and negotiations for peace with the new nation were inaugurated. A preliminary treaty of peace was signed by England and the United States of America on November 30, 1782; it was finally sealed nine months later.

*   *   *   *   *   *   *

For several years following the cessation of hostilities the situation in America was uncertain. First of all the new nation was practically bankrupt, and Congress had power neither to raise money by taxation nor to demand that the states contribute to the federal treasury. The war forced the states to coöperate in the common cause, but immediately after its close they began to assert local rights, and the federal Congress, under the Articles of Confederation, had practically no effective jurisdiction of a completely national character. The 1780's have most appropriately been called the critical period of American history.

At this period Rush lived in a spacious three-story house with a beautiful garden on Second Street between Chestnut and Walnut, at the northwest corner of Gothic. During these years he kept in close touch with the management of public affairs and with public problems. In the fall of 1782, at a general meeting of the holders of loan-office certificates in the Philadelphia district, he was one of five citizens appointed to a committee whose duty it was to petition Congress to pay the interest on loan-office certificates issued since 1778, and to make provision for a sinking fund so as to pay the principal in due course.[33] It was impossible, however, for Congress to meet its obligations after its credit had become exhausted.

The Pennsylvania Test Law attracted Rush's critical attention after the close of the war. This act, passed on June 13, 1777, provided that all male white inhabitants must take an oath of allegiance to the state by a specified date, otherwise they would be deprived of a citizen's rights. One clause in the oath required the deponent to swear that he had not in any manner given aid to Great Britain since July 4, 1776. Rush was finally moved to write and publish an essay, frankly propaganda, denouncing the law and demanding its repeal. It seemed to him that the law represented "an extreme degree of folly," and that it was strange to keep such an act on the lawbooks two years after the treaty confirming American liberties as well as independence. He objected that the law was unconstitutional, that it was contrary to the principles of free government, because the men who were disfranchised by the law were, in fact, reduced to a condition of servitude. The oath itself was both impolitic and tyrannical, and the limitation in the time provided for taking it was wholly unjust because many people did not even know about the Act. How, he asked, can the State expect the non-jurors, disfranchised men, to pay taxes if they are not represented in the Legislature? Was this not one of the principles on which the Revolutionary Fathers presented the case for American independence? "The non-jurors of Pennsylvania," Rush demonstrated, "are in general an industrious, frugal, temperate body of people. Whatever their political principles may be, they are for the most part genuine republicans in dress and manners. If they have erred—nay more, if they have sinned during the late war, we shall consult the freedom and prosperity of the state by forgiving them. If we are wise, we shall do more—we shall protect and cherish them, as the surest resources of the wealth and independence of the state."[34] Here one finds Rush in his natural rôles, defender of the weak or the oppressed, and exponent of republican liberties for the individual citizen. His pamphlet was addressed to the legislature as well as to the freemen of the state and called for immediate repeal of the obnoxious Act.

The propaganda brought results. In the third week of April 1786, Rush wrote delightedly to his London friend, Rev. Dr. Richard Price: "I am very happy in being able to inform you that the test law was so far repealed a few weeks ago in Pennsylvania as to confer equal priviledges upon every citizen of the State. The success of the friends of humanity in this business should encourage them to persevere in their attempts to enlighten and reform the world."[35]

Americans could hardly, however, at this time hope to enlighten and reform the world in the field of government. The Articles of Confederation had led to discontent and tendencies toward disunion.

For a time, in 1786, the American scene was ominously dark; thunderclouds hovered overhead, and a disastrous storm was brewing. Reform was needed at home, sorely and quickly. Unable to see a way out of the dilemma, a few leaders were turning over in their minds plans for peaceful disunion. "Some of our enlightened men who begin to despair of a more complete union of the States in Congress have secretly proposed an Eastern, Middle, and Southern Confederacy, to be united by an alliance offensive and defensive," Rush reported. "These Confederacies, they say, will be united by nature, by interest, and by manners, and consequently they will be safe, agreeable, and durable. The first will include the four New England States [New Hampshire, Massachusetts, Rhode Island, Connecticut] and New York. The second will include New Jersey, Pennsylvania, Delaware, and Maryland; and the last Virginia, North and South Carolina, and Georgia. The foreign and domestic debt of the United States they say shall be divided justly between each of the new confederations. This plan of a new Continental Government is at present a mere speculation. Perhaps necessity, or rather Divine Providence, may drive us to it."[36] Disunion was prevented, in fact, only by the timely realization on the part of the political leaders that the Articles of Confederation had to be scrapped completely and a new constitutional structure built.

In the first number of the *American Museum*, issued in January 1787, Rush listed the defects of the Articles in an "Address to the People of the United States." He pointed out the weakness of Congress and the lack of executive authority, and the folly of not giving Congress exclusive power to issue paper money and regulate commerce. He held that the sovereign power of the United States should not be vested in a one-house legislature, nor should the members of this legislature be elected too frequently. Rush showed that as soon as legislators and men in the government service had become expert in their work, they were usually turned out in the frequent elections, and the government, therefore, could never have many trained workers. "Government is a science," he wrote, "and can never be perfect in America, until we encourage men to devote not only three years, but their whole lives to it. I believe the principal reason why so many men of abilities object to serving in Congress, is owing to their not thinking it worth while to spend three years in acquiring a profession which their country immediately forbids them to follow."

Rush also urged the individual states to surrender their power to issue money in order to bring about a uniform currency which would facilitate trade and help to keep the states together. Further, he insisted that no single state as such has any claim to independence, but that "she is independent only in a union with her sister states in congress."

If the American nation was to survive, the structure of its government had of necessity to be remodeled. Constitutional change was Rush's chief public concern in 1786 and 1787. He harped upon the subject in speech and writing. The theme of his Fourth of July address in Philadelphia in 1787 sounded the warning that the revolution in government was by no means over and, in fact, must continue. "There is nothing more common than to confound the terms of American Revolution with those of the late American war," he said. "The American war is over; but this is far from being the case with the American Revolution. On the contrary, nothing but the first act of the great drama is closed. It remains yet to establish and perfect our new forms of Government; and to prepare the principles, morals and manners of our citizens for these forms of Government after they are established and brought to perfection. The Confederation, together with most of our State Constitutions, were formed under very unfavorable circumstances. We had just emerged from a corrupted monarchy. Although we understood perfectly the principles of liberty, yet most of us were ignorant of the forms and combinations of power in republics. . . . In our opposition to monarchy, we forgot that the temple of tyranny has two doors. We bolted one of them by proper restraints; but we left the other open, by neglecting to guard against the effects of our own ignorance and licentiousness."[37]

When this address was delivered, delegates from all the states except Rhode Island had already been meeting in Philadelphia for six weeks in a convention called by Congress for the purpose of "amending" the Articles of Confederation. In reality, however, the fifty-five delegates who met on May 25 proceeded very wisely not to amend the old, but rather to frame an entirely new constitution.

Within a week after the convention had opened, Governor Randolph of Virginia presented the complete plan of a new system. This Virginia Plan provided for three distinct departments, legislative, executive and judicial, with the federal government deriving its power from the people of the nation rather than from the several state legislatures. The small states immediately opposed the Virginia Plan providing for the election of representatives in proportion to population and, ultimately, a compromise was reached by which the lower house was elected on the basis of population, while in the upper house each state was equally represented. The disputes over this and other technical questions led the pessimists to predict that the convention would fail and the government collapse.

Rush, however, was optimistic. He believed that all obstacles would be surmounted. "You must not be surprised if you should hear of our new system of Government meeting with some opposition," he assured Richard Price. "There are in all our states little characters whom a great and respectable Government will sink into insignificance. These men will excite factions among us, but they will be of temporary duration. Time, necessity, and the gradual operation of reason will carry it down, and if these fail, force will not be wanting to carry it into execution; for not only all the wealth, but all the military men of our country (associated with the Society of the Cincinnati) are in favor of a wise and efficient Government. The order of nature is the same in the political as it is in the natural world—good is derived chiefly from evil. We are traveling fast into order and National happiness. The same enthusiasm now pervades all classes in favor of *Government* that actuated us in favor of *liberty* in the years 1774 and 1775, with this difference, that we are more *united* in the former than we were in the latter pursuit. When our enemies triumph in our mistakes and follies, tell them that we are *men*, that we walk upon two legs, that we possess reason, passions, and senses, and that under these circumstances, it is as absurd to expect the ordinary times of the rising and setting of the sun will be altered, so as to suppose we shall not *finally* compose and adopt a suitable form of Government and be happy in the blessings which are usually connected with it."[38]

His prediction was to prove correct. The "little characters" were crushed, and section by section the new constitution was finally accepted by the distinguished delegates in the convention. By the end of August, with success assured, Rush was able to visualize a wise and effectual government. "The new federal government like a new Continental waggon will overset our State dung cart, [Pennsylvania's Constitution] with all its dirty contents (reverend and irreverend) and thereby restore order and happiness to Pennsylvania," he wrote Timothy Pickering. "From the conversations of the members of the Convention, there is reason to believe the Federal Constitution will be wise, vigorous, safe, free, and full of dignity. General Washington, it is said, will be placed at the head of the new Government, or in the stile of my simile, will drive the new waggon."[39]

After bitter and long debates, reports, and discussions, the Constitution was at length whipped into shape. Adopted on September 17, 1787, it was immediately submitted to the states for ratification. In the list of notable men who participated in the Convention one finds the names of George Washington, James Madison, Edmund Randolph, George Mason, Benjamin Franklin, Gouverneur Morris, James Wilson, Elbridge Gerry, Roger Sherman, John Rutledge, John Dickinson, and Alexander Hamilton. It was a brilliant assemblage, and the form of government which these men constructed was without question infinitely superior to the Articles of Confederation.

The pathway to ratification was a thorny one. In the State conventions, called specifically for the purpose, the fight waxed hot and furious. The voters had had no share in the election of the Convention delegates, who had been appointed by the legislatures. This was one reason why the public at large were by no means eager to accept the Constitution this body of men had framed, and were holding up its ratification in nine of the thirteen states.

Advocates of a stable government, seeking immediate ratification, conducted campaigns of education in their respective states. Rush was most active in Pennsylvania; he served on various committees and contributed articles to the newspapers over several pen names. In his address at a meeting of the citizens of Philadelphia in the State House, in early October, he rehearsed the calamitous state of affairs under the Articles; he enumerated the advantages which would grow out of the adoption of the new Constitution: namely, the advancement of commerce, agriculture, industry, the arts and sciences, and the abolition of paper money. He concluded with a ringing appeal, that were this the last moment of his life, his dying request and injunction to his fellow citizens would be to accept and support the new Constitution.[40]

On November 3, at a meeting of the freemen of the city, he was one of five men chosen to represent Philadelphia at the state convention summoned to consider ratification of the Constitution. In the very first meeting of the Pennsylvania convention, November 21, Rush moved that a minister of the gospel open the convention on the following day. Several members believed that this procedure was unnecessary, and that it would be difficult to select a clergyman who would satisfy all. Rush hoped that there was sufficient liberality in the convention to unite in prayer for the blessing of Heaven upon the proceedings, without considering the sect of the officiating minister. He observed, furthermore, that the convention which framed the Pennsylvania constitution of 1776 had not prefaced its business with prayer, and this was probably why the state had been so disorganized! However, final consideration of Rush's motion was postponed. On November 22 he was assigned to the committee on Rules and Regulations.[41]

When discussion of the Constitution actually opened, Rush played no minor part. Here was ample opportunity to display the oratorical talents which had drawn the admiration of his classmates and teachers. He was an out-and-out advocate of immediate ratification. When it was objected that a Bill of Rights should have been included in the Constitution, Rush, facile and eloquent in argument, demonstrated that clauses definitely guaranteeing the rights of citizens were not needed, because the new system of representation and the legislative system of checks and balances provided adequate safeguards. "I consider it as an honor to the late convention," he asserted, "that this system has not been disgraced with a bill of rights. Would it not be absurd to frame a formal declaration that our natural rights are acquired from ourselves." Never was a Bill of Rights made which was not broken, he said, citing Magna Carta as an example. "In truth, then, there is no security but in a pure and adequate representation; the checks and all the other desiderata of government are nothing but political error without it, and with it, liberty can never be endangered."[42] Ultimately, however, a Bill of Rights, the first ten amendments, demanded by several of the States as the basis of ratification, was drawn up by Congress and became a part of the Constitution in the fall of 1791.

For the most part, the delegates in the convention from the western part of Pennsylvania were opposed to ratification, and Rush exerted much effort in winning over these members to the federalist viewpoint. When the argument was advanced that the new government would abridge the sovereignty of the respective States, Rush recalled in the Convention, on December 1, that this passion for separate sovereignty, had destroyed the Greek world. This plurality of sovereignty, he maintained, is in politics what plurality of gods is in religion—the idolatry, the heathenism of government. He took occasion to point out that, under the new constitution, all citizens would have an immediate voice in the election of members of Congress, that worthless paper currency would be eliminated, that religious tests would be abolished, and that commerce would flourish by reason of uniform regulations. Rush concluded his speech by affirming his faith in the new Constitution which, he was certain, would endow the nation with freedom, knowledge, and religion.[43]

On the last day of the Convention, December 12, Rush made one more eloquent and stirring plea for ratification; indeed, he went so far as to beg that the Constitution be accepted unanimously. The *Pennsylvania Packet* reported that Rush "entered into a metaphysical argument, to prove that the morals of the people had been corrupted by the imperfections of the government; and while he ascribed all our vices and distresses to the existing system, he predicted a millennium of virtue and happiness as the necessary consequence of the proposed Constitution. To illustrate the depraved state of society, he remarked, among other things, the disregard which was notorious in matters of religion, so that between the congregation and the minister scarcely any communication or respect remained. . . . Doctor Rush then proceeded to consider the origin of the proposed system, and fairly deduced it from heaven, asserting that he as much believed the hand of God was employed in this work, as that God had divided the Red Sea to give a passage to the children of Israel."

It was not unusual for Rush to offer with sincerity and conviction a religious interpretation of public as well as private events. Just what effect his quasi-religious oration had on the minds of those who originally opposed ratification cannot be determined. However, ratification was carried by a forty-six to twenty-three vote. Before the celebration of the twelfth anniversary of the Declaration of Independence eight states had joined Pennsylvania, and the Constitution became the fundamental law for those states.

Rush was jubilant. He visualized nothing but progress and steady development for the nation, under the guidance and protection of the Constitution. He had taken part in the work of overthrowing the Articles and of setting up a new system because his sense of patriotic duty moved him deeply. Now that the federal government was in no further danger, he planned to devote his time to scientific pursuits and to withdraw from public life.

Often he sang the praises of the great instrument of government he had so faithfully supported. If the new Constitution promised no other advantages than exemption from paper money it would be enough to recommend it to honest men, he assured Rev. Jeremy Belknap, the eminent Boston divine. "To look up to a government that encourages virtue, establishes justice, insures order, secures property, and protects from every species of violence," he said, "affords a pleasure that can only be exceeded by looking up in all circumstances to a General Providence. Such a pleasure, I hope, is before us & our posterity under the influence of the new government." To Rush life in America promised the felicity and serenity of Paradise, and he hoped to enjoy long life therein. "I pant for the time," he wrote, "when the establishment of the new government, and the safety to individuals which shall arise from it, shall excuse men who like myself wish only to be passengers from performing the duty of sailors on board the political ship in which ou[r all] is embarked. I have yielded to a deep sense of [the ex]treme danger of my country, in quitting the [cabin?] for a station at the pump. As soon as the storm is over, and our bark safely moored, the first wish of my heart will be to devote the whole of my life to the peaceable pursuits of science, and to the pleasures of social and domestic life."[44]

There was still one uncompleted campaign in which Rush had been a soldier for many years—the fight to overthrow the Pennsylvania Constitution of 1776 with its unicameral legislative body. He had railed against its defects ever since the instrument was framed in the fall of 1776, and had not been returned to Congress in March 1777, chiefly because of this opposition. Finally, the turn came. On September 15, 1789, a resolution was passed by the Legislature calling for a convention to alter the state constitution. According to Rush, the movement which led directly to this resolution had originated in his house in the spring when several leaders were discussing the subject in the course of a social evening. Benjamin Rush was, in fact, one of the signers of the circular letters which urged that petitions be drawn up demanding that the legislature call a convention.[45]

On November 24, 1789, the convention met and, after prolonged meetings and debates, agreed on a two-house legislature and a single executive with veto power. On September 2, 1790, the new Pennsylvania Constitution was proclaimed, and Rush could once again sit back and reflect that another fight had been won. His strong pride in personal achievement gave added satisfaction to his conviction that Right had triumphed. Two weeks after the new constitution went into effect Rush and eight other citizens published a letter in *The Pennsylvania Gazette* asking for the support of Arthur St. Clair for governor. In the subsequent election, however, St. Clair was defeated and Thomas Mifflin became the first chief magistrate of the state under the new constitution.

At the age of forty-four Rush now retired from active participation in public affairs; he believed that the critical years of the nation's formative period had passed. The incentive which had moved him to fight for American liberty and then for her solidarity was gone; the United States of America was at last functioning under an adequate constitution.

For almost twenty years Rush had given generously of his time, thought, and energy to public causes, to say nothing of the sacrifice of income during that time. When the First Continental Congress

met in 1774, young and inexperienced, he had entertained many of
its members, intelligently discussing weighty problems with them.
In order to insure some measure of industrial independence he had
been instrumental in organizing a company to manufacture cotton
and woolen cloth. Then, after the clash of arms at Lexington and
Concord, engaging actively in the struggle for American independence, he had served as fleet surgeon in the Pennsylvania navy. He
had been largely responsible for the publication of Thomas Paine's
dynamic pamphlet, *Common Sense*. He had sat as a member of the
Provincial Conference which called the convention to frame Pennsylvania's first state constitution and, as a member of the Continental
Congress at the age of thirty, had signed the Declaration of Independence. After the close of the war he had fought successfully for
the repeal of Pennsylvania's Test Act, and the revision of the state
constitution. He had exerted his influence and eloquence against the
Articles of Confederation, and vigorously urged the Pennsylvania
convention, of which he was a member, to ratify the new federal
constitution. Rush could look back with just pride upon nearly two
decades of public service although the controversies into which he
was drawn, spectacular as they were, did not always enhance his
reputation. The years had been painful, trying, and many times
tragic, and his course had been a stormy one beset by violent squalls
and frequent storms, but nothing could deprive him of the deep
and abiding satisfaction that comes to those who do not doubt the
rightness of their acts.

V

The Army Medical Department
1776–1781

By 1776, when the colonies were breaking away from the absentee overlords in London, medical science on this side of the Atlantic could boast no original discoveries; it merely reflected the theory and practice taught and used in the British medical schools and hospitals where the most distinguished of the colonial physicians were trained. A large number of the physicians in the colonies obtained their medical education solely through a system of apprenticeship lasting from three to seven years. The colonists could boast of only two medical colleges of their own, one in Philadelphia, founded in 1765, and the other in New York, organized in 1768. There was but one state medical society, that of New Jersey, founded in 1766, but no American medical journal at all until 1797, when the *Medical Repository* of New York appeared.

Medical practice consisted largely in prescribing great quantities of strong drugs. Surgery had made little progress since the foundations of modern technique were laid by the two army surgeons of the sixteenth century, Ambroise Paré of Paris and Felix Würtz of Basel. The only major operations were amputations; the great cavities of the human frame were rarely touched. Seventy years were to elapse before Dr. William Thomas Morton, at the Massachusetts General Hospital, conquered the pain of surgical operations by the use of ether.

The gathering of pus was anticipated in all cuts and bruises. Aseptic treatment was still far in the future. Much reliance was placed on therapeutics, even in surgical cases, in the years before the medical scientist had begun to conquer local infections. A big dose of medicine was the chief stock in trade of the physician. The ever-ready medicine chest contained a copious supply of cathartics, emetics, opium, and barks. Then, too, resort was had to bloodletting and blisters upon the least provocation. The physician, to be sure, had few tools and little certain scientific knowledge which could be used in his practice. The efficacy of vaccination was not proclaimed by Jenner until 1798. The all-important stethoscope was not invented by Laennec until 1819, and it was not until the middle of the nineteenth century that thermometry was recognized in clinical diagnosis, following the observations of temperature in disease made by Carl R. A. Wunderlich of Württemberg. The alkaloids and a thousand and one other drug preparations of our own day were beyond the conception of the Revolutionary physician. The same can be said of the hypodermic syringe.

The surgeons attached to the Continental Army, handicapped by lack of funds, had even fewer instruments and drugs than the physicians in private practice; and, outside of the permanent hospital in Philadelphia and the one in New York, there were few institutions to which the army surgeon could send a disabled soldier for special attention and treatment. The army hospitals, as we shall see, were so crowded and so inadequately equipped that the death rate increased shockingly rather than decreased after they began to function.[1]

The Continental Congress recognized the need of military hospitals a few weeks after Washington's appointment as commander-in-chief of the Continental Army. On July 17, 1775, it adopted a hospital plan designed for an army of 20,000 men, providing for a director-general and chief physician whose pay was four dollars a day; four surgeons; one apothecary; twenty surgeon's mates; two storekeepers; and one nurse to every ten patients. A year later it provided one surgeon and five mates for each 1,000 men.

The first director-general was the distinguished Boston physician and patriot, Benjamin Church, who served, however, for only a few months when he was found guilty of treasonous correspondence with the enemy. On October 16, 1775, Dr. John Morgan succeeded Church. He was the principal founder of the first medical school in America, in 1765, and was the first professor of medicine in this department of the College of Philadelphia. Learned, energetic, honest, and thoroughly competent, he nevertheless found the task of organizing and directing the medical department of the army an almost impossible one, in the face of a dearth of supplies and of the petty politics in Congress. In October 1776 Congress hit upon the indefensible plan of dividing the executive authority of the army medical department, placing Morgan in control of the hospitals east of the Hudson River, and Dr. William Shippen, Jr. in charge of the hospitals west. Without one actual head, confusion and failure were the only possible results. The plan was probably nothing but a scheme to eliminate Morgan and install Shippen, and this is exactly what happened. In January 1777, without consulting the Commander-in-Chief and without holding hearings, Congress passed a resolution calling for the dismissal of Morgan, who had served diligently and faithfully. The doctor was outraged and for two years he continued to demand a hearing. When, after disheartening delays, it was finally granted, complete vindication followed.

On April 11, 1777, the entire medical department was reorganized, and Dr. Shippen was appointed director-general. The post of surgeon-general of the Middle Department was accepted by Benjamin Rush, who had already seen service as a volunteer at Trenton and Princeton. In July his title was changed to physician-general of the Middle Department.

Not only had Rush had practical experience with the army's sick and wounded on the battlefield, but he also had observed the administration of the medical department as chairman of the Medical Committee of Congress. He was particularly interested in preventing smallpox in the army by inoculation. Here was an infectious disease which the Continental physician could fight with some success. The mortality rate from natural smallpox was over fifteen per cent, whereas the mortality rate from the disease produced by inoculation was less than one per cent. When recruits were inoculated under proper conditions before going to the front, not more than one in three or four hundred died, and the army as a whole benefited from the consequent immunity.

In the early months of the war, although Congress took no definite stand on inoculation, this protective measure was generally applied. It was not until February 1777 that the Medical Committee was directed to discuss with Washington the expediency of inoculating those soldiers who had not previously suffered from smallpox. As Chairman of the Committee Rush wrote General Washington from Baltimore on February 13:

"The Congress apprehending that the Small Pox may greatly endanger the lives of our fellow citizens who compose the army under your Excellency's command, and also very much embarrass the military operations, have directed their Medical Committee to request your Excellency to give orders that all who have not had that disease may be inoculated, if your Excellency shall be of opinion that it can be done without prejudice to your operations.

"Some battalions from Virginia are now on their march to join you, and are ordered to take the upper rout, in order to avoid Philadelphia where the infection now prevails. It is submitted to your Excellency whether they ought not to stop somewhere to undergo inoculation. . . .

"We beg leave to remind you that the Southern troops are greatly alarmed at the Small Pox, and that it very often proves fatal to them in the natural way. This suggestion we doubt not will, with regard to this object, draw your particular attention to the troops who may be ordered to join you from those States. We hope Sir this attention may prevent the danger and inconvenience apprehended by Congress and we have the most perfect reliance on your Excellency's well known humanity. . . ."[2]

Whether or not Washington took immediate action we do not know; but on April 23 Congress ordered Dr. James Tilton to proceed to Dumfries, Virginia, to take charge of all Continental soldiers who were to be inoculated. Later in the month Congress directed Major General Schuyler to hasten the march of the Continental troops from the Carolinas, and to direct them to halt at Dumfries, Colchester, and Alexandria in Virginia for inoculation.

The virus used was removed from young and healthy subjects on the twelfth or thirteenth day, probably from the milder cases. Dried scabs, having lost some of their virulence, were also used. The subjects were prepared for the inoculation with a cathartic; the doctor's kit contained calomel, jalap, nitre, Peruvian bark, and snakeroot.[3]

Smallpox was definitely controlled by means of inoculation, but camp fever or putrid fever and dysentery played havoc with the soldiers. Dysentery, which was almost universal, was described by Surgeon Tilton in his *Economical Observations in Military Hospitals*: "The putrid diarrhoea was generally the result of dregs of other camp and hospital disease; and was the most intractable disorder of any we had to deal with. The patient would often be able to move about, with little or no fever, his skin remarkably dry and dusky, and constant drain from bowels. Various attempts have been made to force the skin by warm bathing, Ipecac mixed with opium, &c., and by that means to divert the current of humours from the bowels; but all to no purpose." Some success, it seems, was had with an astringent composed of a mixture of equal parts of Tincture Huxham and Tincture Japonica given in doses of two teaspoons twice daily. "But," said Tilton, "while the patients remained about the hospital, nothing appeared to have more than a palliative effect. Multitudes melted away, as it were, of this miserable complaint, and died. The only expedient I ever found effective for their relief was to billet them in the country, where they could enjoy pure air and a milk diet; or to furlough them to their own homes, if within reach."

Putrid fever, including typhoid, known also as jail fever, camp fever, or hospital fever, was feared above all other diseases. In these cases, although recourse was also had to Peruvian bark, tartar emetic, laxative salts, opium, blisters and bloodletting, wine was considered a capital remedy. It was Rush's opinion that men who came into the army hospitals with pleurisies or rheumatism soon contacted the more serious typhus; and that, furthermore, fever was carried from the hospitals to the camps by blankets and clothing. The mortality rate was higher among the negroes than the whites. Rush also observed that typhus was not universal throughout the Continental armies until the troops of the eastern, middle, and southern states met in New York in 1776.[4]

He found more sickness among the soldiers when they were in tents than when they were in the open. He also discovered that they were healthier when on the march than when in camp. Men under twenty years of age were most subject to the camp diseases while men over thirty years of age were the hardiest in the army. His records indicated further that the native Americans were more sickly than the Europeans who served in the Continental army, and that those officers who wore flannel shirts usually avoided the fevers. Those soldiers who were billeted in private houses generally escaped typhus and typhoid, and recovered more rapidly from other diseases than the soldiers in barracks. His observations indicated that the spread of disease was shocking in the military hospitals which, in many cases, were built of coarse logs, with fireplaces in the center of earthen floors, and with holes in the roof for the discharge of smoke.

Rush was outraged at the condition and administration of the military hospitals. His fearless criticism, which gave rise to heated disputes with the higher-ups, eventually led to his resignation. "Hospitals are the sinks of human life in an army," he recalled years after the war. "They robbed the United States of more citizens than the sword. Humanity, economy, and philosophy, all concur in giving a preference to the conveniences and wholesome air of private houses; and should war continue to be the absurd and unchristian mode of deciding national disputes, it is to be hoped that the progress of science will so far mitigate its greatest calamities, as to produce an abolition of hospitals for acute diseases. Perhaps there are no cases of sickness in which reason and religion do not forbid the seclusion of our fellow creatures from the offices of humanity in private families, except where they labour under the calamities of madness and the venereal disease, or where they are the subjects of some of the operations of surgery."[5]

At the improvised hospital in Wilmington, Delaware, in September 1777, at Princeton nine months earlier, and at several other battle fronts, Rush reached the conclusion that the army hospitals afforded far from adequate care for the sick and wounded. Nor was he alone in holding this opinion. Surgeon Tilton was early convinced that as few of the sick as possible should be sent to the general hospitals. "It would be shocking to humanity to relate the history of our general hospital, in the years 1777 and 1778," he admitted, "when it swallowed up at least one half of our army, owing to a fatal tendency in the system to throw all the sick of the army into the general hospital; whence crowds, infection and consequent mortality too affecting to mention."[6]

Surgeon Waldo's picture of a hospital scene is harrowing. "I am prodigious sick and cannot get anything comfortable—" he recorded in his diary. "What in the name of Providence can I do with a fit of sickness in this place where nothing appears pleasing to the sickn'd eye and nauseating stomach. . . . I cannot eat beef if I starve—for my stomach positively refuses such company. . . . I am sick—discontented—and out of humour. Poor food—hard lodging—cold weather—fatigue—nasty cloaths—nasty cookery—vomit half my time—smoak'd out of my senses—the Devil's in't—I can't endure it—why are we sent here to starve and freeze—what sweet filicities have I left at home; a charming wife—pretty children—good beds—good food—good cookery—all agreeable—all harmonious. Here, all confusion—smoke, cold—hunger and filthyness—a pox on my bad luck. Here comes a bowl of beef soup—full of burnt leaves and dirt, sickness enough to make a hector spue—Away with it Boys—I'll live like a cameleon upon air."[7]

Only by making broad allowance for the crudeness of the medical practices of the period and the abnormal conditions of war, is it possible to take a charitable view of the revolting story of the hospital service. Of untrained men employed in the capacity of physicians there were many, but of honest-to-goodness surgeons there were but few. Even though a board of examiners had set up a series of tests for candidates for positions as surgeons and assistants, many utterly incompetent men managed to obtain commissions. The paucity of competent physicians, and the lack of beds, medicines, and blankets, caused the loss of more lives, in the opinion of some contemporary observers, than the swords and guns of the enemy. Almost always the medical quarters were cramped, located as they were in huts hastily constructed in an inconvenient section of the barracks, or in inns or school buildings unsuited for hospital purposes, and with a water supply that fell far short of the bare needs of the sick and wounded.

By the fall of 1777 the sorry plight of the medical organization was more than Rush could bear, and he unburdened himself to John Adams who was already working overtime in and out of Congress with a hundred and one army problems. It was, of course, unfortunate that Washington's forces were cut to pieces at Brandywine in September 1777, but the inability of the military forces to cope with a superior body of redcoats was no excuse, Rush believed, for the confusion and disorder in the hospital department, "eno' to sink our country without the weights which oppress it from other quarters." He hinted that the system was organized for the benefit not of the sick and wounded but for Director-General Shippen. He denounced the unlimited powers, with no checks, given Shippen. "The sick suffer, but no redress can be had for them," he wrote Adams on October 1, 1777. "Upwards of 100 of them were drunk last night," he reported, and complained because there were no military police to prevent this evil, whereas in the British army a captain's guard was assigned to every 200 sick, chiefly to keep up the military spirit. "One month in our hospitals would undo all the discipline of a year," Rush conjectured, "provided our soldiers brought it with them from the army. . . . The present management of our army would depopulate America if men grew among us as speedily & spontaneously as blades of grass. The 'wealth of worlds' could not support the expense of the medical department above two or three years."[8] On casual reading, the prophecy appears to be exaggerated and far-fetched, but on second thought one can sympathize with the strength of Rush's assertion, upon realizing the fact that thousands of soldiers were needlessly sacrificed to the frightful conditions and the unforgivably inefficient management of the hospitals.

The hospital affairs were the object of further denunciation in Rush's letter of October 21 to John Adams, written at Reading, Pennsylvania. Claiming that it was growing worse and worse, Rush pointed out that several hundred wounded soldiers would have died had they not been assisted by the contributions of charitable private citizens. Grievous fault was found not only with the organization itself but also with Director-General Shippen, who was accused of both ignorance and negligence. According to Rush, he never even put his foot inside a hospital. "My heart is almost broken," Rush declared, "at seeing the distresses of my countrymen without a power to remedy them." He was quite sincere in his protestations, and signified for the first time in this letter that if the hospital department was not reformed he would resign. "If it cannot be altered," he said, "& that soon I shall trouble you with my resignation & my reasons shall be given to the public for it." He suggested that the British system, if put into operation, would save men and money.[9]

Again he wrote Adams, in the same tone, from Bethlehem, Pennsylvania, ten days later, October 31. He reiterated his plea that the

British system be adopted if the desired results were to be effected. "While I am writing these few lines," he went on, "there are several brave fellows expiring within fifty yards of me from being confined in a hospital whose air has been rendered putrid by the sick & wounded being crowded together." He proposed that, inasmuch as the physicians on duty in the hospitals understood the local situation, they should be independent of the orders of the directors who were, indeed, far removed from the actual suffering. "We see, we feel the distresses of the sick," he defended himself and colleagues, "and therefore are better capable of directing everything necessary for their convenience than men who never go into a hospital but who govern them by proxy as Genl. Schuyler commanded Ticonderoga at Albany." As a direct slap at Director-General Shippen, Rush offered the following proposals to remedy abuses:

"1. Resolved, that the Director & Ass. Director furnish the Physician & Surgeons General & Senior Surgeons with such medicines, stores & accomodations as they shall require. The requisition to be made in writing & to be used afterwards as a voucher for the expenditures of the D. General.

"2. That all the Accts. of the D. General for medicines, wines, stores, &c. be certified by the Phy. or Surgeons General before they are passed. This resolution is of the utmost importance, and I have good reason to say will save thousands to the continent.

"3. That all returns of sick, wounded, & of officers of the hospital be delivered to the Medical Committee by the Phy. or Surgeons General. The reason of this is plain. They can have no interest in making out false returns and the returns from them will always be a check upon the expenditures of the Director General."[10]

Was this another way of accusing Dr. Shippen of graft in connection with the purchase and supply of medical stores and of tampering with the census of sick and wounded as reported to Congress? It was, indeed, just this.

The needless suffering, the continued failure of the Director-General to provide adequate supplies, and the growing disregard for discipline within the hospitals, bore heavily on Rush's sensitive nature. On the second day of December 1777, from Princeton he appealed directly to Shippen to put an officer in command of the place. "A hospital cannot be governed without one," he urged. "Besides, the discipline of a whole year is lost in one month by the total neglect of it which prevails in our hospitals. An officer of rank & reputation is always stationed near the hospitals in the British army." He suggested, further, that stores be purchased at once for the coming year because of the increasing scarcity of commodities and the steady rise in prices. On the same day he also requested Major General Greene to detail several officers to the hospital at Princeton in order to restore some respect for military authority. "We have in the hospital of this place," he wrote Greene, "near 500 sick and wounded soldiers many of whom have complaints so trifling that they do not prevent their committing daily a hundred irregularities of all kinds. The physicians & surgeons of the hospital possess no power to prevent or punish them."[11]

Day after day, as he made his rounds in the hospitals, Rush knew that the conditions, already deplorable, were becoming worse and worse. John Adams was too busy to take into the halls of Congress his friend's complaints, addressed to him in personal letters; and Director-General Shippen either did not care to coöperate or believed that the grievances were exaggerated. One evening at Princeton, while worrying over the dreadful state of affairs, Rush decided to bring the matter to the attention of Congressman William Duer. In a lengthy letter, December 8, 1777, every point of dissatisfaction was noted, and again the conclusion was drawn that the hospital would be a more serviceable institution if Congress were to remodel it after the British system. He outlined this system, proposing an inspector-general and chief physician whose sole duty would be to examine the hospital units, the quantity and quality of medicines and stores, and the instruments, and to receive and deliver reports to the commander-in-chief on the number of sick and wounded. Secondly, he proposed a purveyor-general to provide hospital buildings, medicines, stores, beds, blankets, and other supplies, having, however, no direct connection with the actual care of the sick. Thirdly, physicians and surgeons-general were to administer the stores provided by the purveyor-general and to attend the sick; but the purveyor was always to be subject to their written orders, which served as expense vouchers. They were to be required also to counter-sign all of his accounts.

This system seemed to Rush to be the most admirable in use any-where throughout the world. In the American system the director-general was a czar possessing all the powers of the several heads in the British organization. Because all reports came through his hands, he could tamper with the recorded numbers of dead and wounded so as not to alarm Congress. His accounts were not certified by the physicians and surgeons-general and, as a result, Rush believed that "the sick have no security for the stores and medicine intended for them." There was, apparently, no check at all on the director-general's power to purchase and to distribute supplies. "These ample & *incompatible* powers thus lodged in the hands of *one* man," con-tinued Rush, "appear to be as absurd as if General Washington had been made Quartermaster—Commissary—& Adjutant General of your whole army. And your having invested him with a power to direct the physicians & surgeons in anything while he acts as pur-veyor is as absurd as it would be to give the commissary general power to command your commander in chief. To do the duty of Purveyor General only requires a share of industry, & a capacity for business which falls to the lot of few men in the world. What can be expected then from one who added to that office is responsible for every life in the army?"

For the moment Rush absolved Shippen from personal blame, and told Duer that much of the misery and general corruption could be traced to the very nature of the medical establishment.

It was bruited about that Rush had been complaining merely to obtain Shippen's dismissal in order to have the post for himself. Rush, however, advised Duer that he would not be director-general "for the riches of India," and that he had decided to resign as soon as the campaign closed, since, as he wrote: "I cannot act agreeable to the dictates of my conscience and judgement."[12]

"For God's sake do not forget to take the medical system under your consideration," exclaimed Rush in a second letter to Duer on December 13, 1777. "It is a mass of corruption & tyranny, and has wholly disappointed the benevolence & munificence of the Congress." Corruption and tyranny are strong words; they were used by Rush after he had found 5,000 soldiers in a hospital with supplies for 1,500 and, in another hospital, 600 patients without a single officer to punish irregularities. Convalescence was prolonged; new diseases were contracted; clothes were traded for liquor; and petty thievery was general. When Rush advised Director-General Shippen of the extraordinary conditions, the answer was that he (Shippen) was the only judge of hospital affairs, and Rush's only duty was to treat all patients sent to him.[13]

The evidence that we have seems to indicate that there was no selfish motive behind the presentation of Rush's grievances. It is possible, of course, that he enjoyed the publicity which he received during the controversy. One might also guess that he was jealous of Shippen's rise to power. In any case Rush, a reformer by nature, derived a measure of satisfaction in fighting for righteous causes. Actual conditions justified the complaints; and Rush, sensitive and conscientious, could hardly have stood by without waging a valiant battle for the sufferers. It was, as far as we can judge, a purely unselfish fight.

Revolving in his mind the observations made in the army hospitals during the year, Rush turned from destructive to constructive criticism and wrote a thoroughly worthwhile pamphlet called "Directions for Preserving the Health of Soldiers." These recommendations were first printed in the *Pennsylvania Packet* and were later published by order of the Board of War. The art of preserving the health of a soldier, the pamphlet maintained, consists in careful attention to dress, diet, sanitation, encampments, and exercise.

As to dress, Rush was satisfied that linen was worn too extensively. Perspiration is absorbed by the linen and, when rain falls on it, the resulting miasmata produce fever. He suggested that flannel shirts be worn. He recommended that the soldier comb his hair daily and keep it thin because "the hair, by being long uncombed, is apt to accumulate the perspiration of the head, which by becoming putrid sometimes produces diseases."

Army diet should consist largely of well-cooked vegetables. Warning was given that rum be used only on rare occasions because, by gradually wearing away the strength of the body, it lays the foundation for fevers and most of the diseases which are found in the military hospitals.

The problem of sanitation was attacked from many angles. Rush urged that the soldier wash his hands and face daily and take a bath two or three times a week, change his clothes frequently, and expose his blanket to the sun daily. The importance of keeping kitchen utensils clean, and the environs of the tents free from filth, was also stressed. Attention was called to the bad habit of resting or sleeping in wet clothes.

Although unaware of the danger of swamp lands as breeding places for specific disease germs and carriers, Rush nevertheless warned against the construction of encampments near marshes and ponds; he also suggested that camp sites be changed frequently. In camp, provision for regular physical exercise at stated periods was advised.[14]

The pamphlet was received favorably by military men here and abroad, and even today its general suggestions are sound and practical.

The problem that the American army faced demanded immediate solution, and mere approval of Rush's pamphlet would not bring it to pass. On the morning after Christmas 1777 Rush, after surveying the entire situation again, decided to complain directly to the Commander-in-Chief, who was at this time fighting desperately against cold and hunger on the hills at Valley Forge. Washington was so preoccupied with the tragedy before his own eyes that he did not reply to Rush until January 12. He agreed that, if the medical department was as bad as pictured, it should be reformed without delay, and that the men on service in the hospitals should be asked to point out the defects of the system. "We might do much better," wrote Washington, "if more order and discipline is observed by the patients." Lax discipline was one of the causes of Rush's earliest complaints, and now Washington, agreeing with him, wrote that he had appointed a field officer to visit the principal hospitals to set up disciplinary regulations. Supporting the request for reforms in the hospital management, Washington concluded: "I shall always be ready to contribute all in my power towards rendering the situation of these unhappy people who are under the necessity of becoming the inhabitants of them as comfortable as possible."[15]

Washington's letter was coöperative in tone, but it reached Rush after he had decided to resign from the army, and after he had made ready for a journey to York, where Congress was then sitting.

Rush and Shippen were both summoned to appear before Congress to answer questions relating to the charges made against the management of the hospitals. Upon his arrival at York, Rush found a general disposition among the members of Congress to reform the system and, so encouraged was he by their attitude, that for a few days he gave up the thought of resigning. "It will be a disagreeable task to accuse him [Shippen] publicly of ignorance & negligence of his duty," wrote Rush in a self-righteous mood, to his wife, "but the obligations I owe to my country preclude all other ties. I shall act strictly to the dictates of my conscience & if the system is altered and Dr. Shippen can be restrained by proper checks from plundering the sick I shall not resign my commission."[16]

On the evening of January 26 and again on the morning of the next day the Congressional committee, under the chairmanship of John Witherspoon, listened to the arguments on both sides.[17] Some promise of change was apparently made because, two days after the testimony was heard, Rush wrote a friend in Reading that he had decided to remain in the hospital service now that the abuses complained of were going to be removed. He wrote with pleasure that Congress had altered the regulations in an effort to mitigate the distress and to reduce the high mortality rate in every encampment in New Jersey and Pennsylvania. "In consequence of these new regulations," he decided, " I shall remain for some time longer in the hospital where I shall now be able by a free and independent exercise of my own judgment to do some good to my suffering countrymen."[18]

From the old family homestead in Braintree, Massachusetts, John Adams hurried a plea to Rush "by all the tyes of friendship to your country" to remain in the service. "Men who are sensible of the evils in the hospital department are the most likely to point them out to others, and to suggest remedies. Patience! Patience! Patience!

The first, the last, and the middle virtue of a Politician," exclaimed Adams.[19] This appeal arrived too late, however, for something had happened before the sun had set on the 30th of January, which caused Rush to make his final decision. He was, of course, disgruntled because Shippen was not being forced out of office; and he was not able to visualize any marked reforms as long as Shippen directed the work of the department. On the other hand, it seems that Shippen on his side refused to serve further with Rush. He signified that, unless Rush resigned, he would demand that the entire organization be investigated. The Congressional committee feared skeletons in the closet and, having no desire to encourage the controversy between Rush and Shippen, kept hands off.

Through Congressman Witherspoon, Rush presented his resignation, dated January 30: "Finding it impossible to do my duty any longer in the department you have assigned me in your hospitals in the manner I would wish, I beg the favor of you to accept the resignation of my Commission."[20] The resignation was accepted at once "without a word said by any person upon the subject." "I am sorry for the necessity of the measure," explained Witherspoon, "and yet I question whether you could have done anything more proper for Dr. Shippen was fully determined to bring the matter to a contest between you, refusing positively to serve with you which would have occasioned an examination and judgement troublesome to us hurtful probably to both of you and uncertain in its issue."[21] In apprising the Philadelphia patriot, Robert Morris, of Rush's resignation, Richard Peters, Secretary to the Board of War, approached the truth when he wrote: "There is so much said on both sides that I fancy both were wrong at least in some degree."[22]

Even after the interval of many months Rush was unable to speak calmly about his experiences in the military hospitals. A lengthy letter, undated, to Dr. John Morgan, who had been retired in favor of Dr. Shippen in January 1777, marshals the details of the whole affair and, because of its importance, calls for extensive quotation. Rush explained that when he first entered the office of physician-general, believing the abuses to be the result of the system, he spoke about them quietly to John Adams and other members of Congress. This busy assembly had, of course, a hundred and one serious prob-

lems with which to grapple and could hardly take up Rush's grievances on the instant. Nevertheless Rush soon decided that it was his
duty as a citizen to complain publicly to Congress. "I charged the
extraordinary sickness mortality & waste of public stores chiefly upon
the lax nature of our hospital system—a system which had been
fabricated by Dr. Shippen—and which tempted to fraud almost beyond the possibility of detection," Rush recalled in this letter to Dr.
Morgan. "The Congress instead of ordering a committee of their
body to repair to the hospitals to enquire into the truth of the facts
I had commanded to them, summoned Dr. Shippen & myself to
appear before them on January 26, 1778 at Yorktown," he continued. "A committee . . . was appointed to hear us. I complained
of the abuses that existed in the hospitals—I informed them that our
sick suffered & died from the want of air—clean linnen—blankets—
and proper food—that the hospitals were crowded, and that a putrid
fever had been generated in most of them which had proved fatal
to many hundred of our soldiers in the last month—that our hospitals were without guards which rendered it impossible to govern the
convalescents, or prevent their relapsing when cured—that I had
demanded all the above necessaries for the sick over and over but
without obtaining them. I then objected to the hospital system that it
invested the purveying & directing business in the same hands which
was as absurd as if the commissary general & the supreme command
of our army should be united in the same person—that Dr. Shippen
required no vouchers for the expenditure of hospital stores which
gave the commissaries & stewards of the hospital most unlimited op-
portunities to defraud the public—that there was nothing to prevent
the Director General from converting all the stores of the hospital
to his own use—that while our sick were suffering from the want
of madeira wine at Reading he had sold six pipes upon his own account which he had transported thither among hospital stores in public waggons. I concluded my complaints by declaring that I was not
actuated by the least personal resentment against Dr. Shippen. That
my complaints arose from the purest affection to my country—and
that while some members of congress affected to ascribe all the
abuses and distress of the hospital to a want of harmony between
Dr. S & myself, I had only to beg the public's pardon that I had lived

so long in harmony with him—and that to have harmonized any longer with him would have been high treason against my country. The Doctor replied to most of these complaints by denying them. . . ."

When Chairman Witherspoon asked for proofs of the charges against Shippen, Rush replied that he would produce them only if Congress appointed a court of inquiry. This maneuver to force Congress into an investigation was not, however, successful.

After the committee had listened to both Rush and Shippen, the latter declared to several members of Congress that he could not serve any longer with Rush. Witherspoon then advised Rush as to what was going on, and asked if he intended to resign. "I told him no," reads Rush's relation to Morgan, "that Genl Roberdeau had told me that the system was to be altered, & that the purveying business would be taken out of Dr. S hands. He then told me that it was necessary that either I resign or I should leave the hospitals for that we never would be happy together. I told him I would answer for myself—that I should never have another contradiction with him provided the sick were removed by a change in the system beyond the possibility of being injured by him. He then repeated a second time that one of us must leave the department, that I had made myself many enemies in congress by complaining of Dr. Shippen, & that I had better resign." But when Rush refused to resign because of incompatibility with Shippen, Witherspoon changed his tactics and stated that no material changes were contemplated in the medical department and that the purveying business would not be removed from Shippen's hands. Then, inasmuch as he saw no prospect of serving in a reformed system, he resigned an hour after the conversation with Witherspoon.[23]

It is true that the hospitals were badly managed by Shippen, but it is also true that definite reforms might have been obtained with Rush's assistance, had he not resigned so hastily, and had he placed the matter in an official way before John Adams and other friends in Congress.

Rush, now definitely out of the army, never reëntered the service. Nevertheless he persisted in his attacks upon Shippen and the medical department in general. In letters of self-defense, written to friends and officials immediately after he had resigned, he reviewed the complaints against Shippen.

As soon as his affairs had been wound up, Rush left York. On February 4, while in Lancaster, he wrote his friend Major General Gates, then President of the Board of War, in an angry tone: "As I have constantly acted from motives of the most republican nature since I came into public life I am neither disgusted nor distressed with that partiality in some of our superiors which made the resignation of my commission a necessary step to restore (not order—oconomy—or discipline) but, harmony to the medical department. As there is a union in politicks which is often fatal to liberty, so there is a harmony in the operations of war which is fatal to victory." If the compulsion of patriotism were by any chance urged upon him, he was justified in his belief that it is hardly patriotic to coöperate with those who are responsible for the death of thousands of fellow citizens. "To harmonize with ignorance—negligence—and prodigality of the property and blood of freeman," was, in Rush's opinion, high treason. If ever he should bring himself to live in harmony with such vices, he prayed: "May the delightful words of freedom and independence cease to excite music on the strings of my heart! My country—in which I include the people at large & posterity, is dearer to me than war, and while there are 500 men in America in arms I shall not withhold from it the humble mite of my labours & life."[24]

When he returned to Princeton in late February, Rush felt that it was his duty to acquaint General Washington with the facts which prompted his resignation. He offered details of the evidence in support of his charges and complaints. The madeira wine used at the Bethlehem hospital, he pointed out in his letter of February 25, was so adulterated as to be useless for medicinal purposes, and the commissary-general was in the habit of reducing by one-third requisitions for wine and other stores ordered for the sick by the surgeons. Although the commissary department purchased quantities of poultry, it was never served unless patients themselves bought it. Notwithstanding the fact that the hospital at Bethlehem was badly in need of blankets, shirts, straw, and other supplies for the sick, Shippen visited the institution only once in six weeks. More serious than the charge of lack of attention to this particular hospital was the direct statement that Shippen sent Congress incorrect reports of mortality in the army hospitals in order to present a rosy picture of conditions. Furthermore, there was downright graft. "While our brave countrymen were languishing and dying from the *total* want, or scanty allowance of hospital stores," wrote Rush, "I am sorry to add that the director General was employed in a manner wholly unbecoming the dignity of his office, and the liberality of his profession in selling large quantities of madeira wine, brown & loaf sugar &c &c. which had been transported through the country in hospital waggons, & secured as hospital stores under the name of private property."[25]

During the month of February Rush was in a continual rage. He was too excited to survey logically and calmly in his own mind the real state of affairs. Always impulsive, he insisted on fighting the battle immediately, although he knew that Shippen had relatives and close friends in Congress, and attacks on him at this particular stage would, therefore, be unavailing. The letter of February 25 to Washington, with its heinous charges against Shippen, was destined to do its writer more harm than good. Washington was just barely surviving a terrible winter at Valley Forge and it was unfair of Rush to expect the Commander-in-Chief, himself in a critical position, to jump into the Rush-Shippen melée as referee. In reporting the matter to Congress, Washington implied that the Committee at York had already disposed of the complaint and that, therefore, it might be dismissed entirely. Patriotic fervor aside, Rush did not deserve special attention from Washington at this critical moment. Uppermost in his mind was the desire to have Shippen court-martialed, but Washington wisely would not allow himself to be drawn into this course of procedure. He merely placed before Congress in late March the Rush letter containing "charges of a very heinous nature against the Director-General, Doctor Shippen, for mal-practices and neglect in his department" in the nature of a "public accusation." "I have showed it to Doctor Shippen," continued Washington, "that he may be prepared to vindicate his character if called upon. He tells me, that Doctor Rush made charges of a similar nature before a committee of Congress, appointed to hear them, which he could not support. If so, Congress will not further occasion to trouble themselves in the matter."[26]

Congress, still sitting at York because Howe and his redcoats had not yet been driven out of Philadelphia, pigeonholed the matter by handing Washington's letter to a committee which in turn wrote Rush: "We wish to proceed in this business, so as to obtain the most perfect information of the mal-practices, if there are any, of the Director-General; & to this end, we desire that you will be pleased to ascertain with precision, & transmit to us, the charges, & upon oath the evidence you have, or can procure, against him; also, the names of the witnesses, & places of their residence."[27] But Congress did not honestly wish "to proceed in this business," and Rush, unwilling to appear before another Congressional committee, asked for a military court. He insisted that Shippen was attached to the army and should, therefore, be tried by court-martial. If the committee should seek direct evidence against Shippen the whole medical department would be temporarily crippled because, as Rush explained: "Should the evidences be collected at Yorktown the sick in the hospitals would suffer from the want of surgeons to attend them, for there are nearly as many witnesses against him as there are surgeons in the hospitals."[28] Rush's request for an army court, with himself as prosecutor, evaporated into thin air once it reached the halls of Congress. Shippen continued to go about his business as he pleased, while Rush retired in deep disgust.

It was a bitter pill for Rush to swallow. He, the accuser, was forced to make his exit from the public stage while the man whom he accused of fraud, neglect of duty, falsification of records, and speculation in hospital stores, continued in the limelight, pursuing his regular line of duty with the tacit approval of Congress. Even a less sensitive soul than Rush would have found the situation unbearable. The wound was all the deeper because Rush viewed the entire affair from the standpoint of his patriotic duty. He complained about the hospital department, he said, because of purely patriotic motives, and now he felt that he had been humiliated and penalized for being loyal to his country.

Finding Congress deaf to his complaints and demands, Rush finally retired to his father-in-law's home at Princeton, where his life was both inactive and unhappy. The prospect of building up a practice in Princeton was unpromising and, furthermore, he had no desire to set up a practice in the rural districts. Low in spirit, in the spring of 1778, he went so far as to decide to study law, ultimately to practice in New Jersey, backed by his father-in-law's influence. Just as he was preparing to start work on his studies, however, news came that the British army had evacuated Philadelphia, and the idea of entering the legal profession was thrown overboard immediately.

The news from Philadelphia seemed to give Rush a new lease on life. His spirit rose almost over night, and as soon as he returned to the city on July 21, 1778, he went about rebuilding his practice with freshness and gusto. According to Rush his practice became both extensive and profitable almost at once, largely because the British had left the city in such a filthy condition that there was an abnormal number of sick persons.[29]

The blaze of the medical department investigation, however, had not been completely extinguished, and Rush was ever ready to feed the flames with more fuel. On June 13, 1779, after a delay of two years, the Medical Committee of Congress finally brought in its report on Dr. John Morgan's dismissal in 1777, and Congress passed a resolution vindicating completely the heartbroken physician. Three days after this vindication Morgan sent a letter to Congress charging Shippen with malpractice and misconduct, and offering to produce the necessary evidence. Learning of the charges, Shippen immediately asked Washington to have the matter sifted by a court-martial. Meanwhile, Morgan requested Rush to give him an outline of the testimony he could produce regarding the misconduct of Shippen. On July 17, 1779, Rush replied that he was ready to testify against Shippen; that his (Shippen's) ignorance appeared in every aspect of his work, especially in the manner in which public money was spent; that he was negligent and failed to heed requests for sick-room needs with resulting loss of life; that "he traded largely in hospital stores"; that he deceived Congress with false reports of the number of sick and wounded.[30]

At length Shippen was court-martialed at Morristown, New Jersay, March 15, 1780, where, after some delay, the trial continued throughout April, May, and June. The proceedings were marked by extraordinary excitement and intense bitterness. Attacks and counter-attacks, full of personal venom, were made day after day. Finally, finding the charges not clearly proven, the court-martial acquitted Shippen. On August 18, 1780, Congress discharged Shippen without, however, confirming the acquittal by the court. Congress probably considered Shippen reprehensible in his management of supplies, but the policy of delay until the evidence had lost its force, together with Shippen's strong political support, probably saved him from the just consequences of his misconduct.[31]

On October 6, 1780, Congress reorganized the medical department and again appointed Shippen Medical Director. He was shortly ordered to report to headquarters and to put himself under the orders of the Commander-in-Chief.

The fact that Shippen was not dishonorably discharged by Congress in the summer of 1780, and that he was again appointed Chief in the newly organized medical department was too much for Rush to bear, and he immediately and vehemently expressed his anger in the press. On November 18 the *Pennsylvania Packet* carried a letter addressed to Shippen. "Your injured country," Rush wrote, "which you have robbed of above a thousand of its citizens by your negligence and inhumanity; the parents and children of those men whom you suffered to perish without honour or benefit of their country in your hospitals; and the graveyards of Bethlehem, Reading, Lancaster, Princeton, and Philadelphia, all of which you have crowded with the bodies of your countrymen; cry aloud for your dismission from office. You have become the butt of the camp, the jest of taverns, and the contempt of the coffee-house. Women bedew the papers that contain the tales of your cruelties to the sick with their tears; and children who hear them read, ask if you are made and look like other men."

Rush's hatred for Shippen approached a mania. The letter goes on to say that, although Shippen's crimes can be matched in other countries, the condonation of them—never! "But your reappointment to your present high and important office, after the crimes you have committed, is a new Phoenomenon in the history of mankind. It will serve like a high water mark to shew posterity the degrees of corruption that marked the present stage of the American revolution." According to another Rush "Letter To The Public," which the *Packet* ran on November 18, many members of Congress actually opposed Shippen's reappointment as director-general, but Pennsylvania made a state issue of supporting its son and carried his nomination.

A few weeks later Rush again wrote the newspaper, this time declaring that the whole American experiment would fail if Shippen were to continue in office. Unless Shippen is dismissed, exclaimed Rush, "then let the sons and daughters of freedom lament over the blood and treasure they have wasted in our glorious cause; let the devout patriot, and minister of the gospel, cease to pray for the successful issue of the war. Let Virtue hide her head, and let Liberty (celestial maid), wave her hand and tell, in her flight from this new world, that a resting place could not be found for her on the surface of the globe. If Shippen triumphs one day longer, then is virtue a shadow, and liberty only a name in the United States."[32]

On January 3, 1781, Shippen finally resigned his commission, and liberty could raise its head once more! For Rush the ultimate safety of the Continental government was assured, even though the fate of the American cause was still uncertain—Yorktown was still ten months in the future. The erstwhile arch-critic of the army medical department could now withdraw and devote his energies entirely to his private practice in Philadelphia.

It must be admitted that much of Rush's criticism was just. The hospitals were miserably managed and in them many soldiers died needlessly; individuals undoubtedly profited from the purchase of supplies. Except in Philadelphia and New York there were no public hospitals, and in the improvised military hospitals the paucity of medical supplies was appalling. Petty politics, exemplified in the unfair dismissal of Dr. Morgan as head of the hospitals in January 1777, were responsible for much of the dissension and inefficiency. Rush was probably correct in stating that Shippen's political friendships kept him in power even after the lax methods of his department had been laid bare. By directing his criticism more definitely against Shippen himself than against the system, Rush materially weakened the effectiveness of his attack.

That Rush was in a position to stand in judgment goes without saying. At Trenton and Princeton he had seen service for some time before being formally commissioned in the Medical Department, in the spring of 1777. As chairman of the Medical Committee of Congress he had been particularly interested in the prevention of smallpox by inoculation.

Actual conditions, which he saw with his own eyes, led to his fearless criticism which probably began with a letter to John Adams on October 1, 1777. Later he complained directly to Dr. Shippen, to William Duer, and to General Washington. At length he appeared before a committee of Congress at York in late January, 1778, but was unable to bring about the dismissal of Shippen. Finally, when serious charges were revived by Dr. Morgan, Shippen was acquitted, by a narrow margin of doubt, by court-martial, but Congress was dubious in seconding the court's action in bringing in a verdict of not guilty. Shippen's friends in Congress came to his rescue once more and he was able to resign voluntarily. Rush's charges, however, have never been entirely disproved. He was single-minded and fearless enough to fight for truth against the heavy odds of political influence.

VI

A Quarrel with Washington

In the midst of the lamentable wrangling in the Army Medical Department, Rush further embroiled himself through his denunciation of the Commander-in-Chief of the Army for his refusal to deal directly with the crying needs of the hospitals. With his usual boldness, coupled with his accustomed lack of tact, Rush did not hesitate to attack Washington, thereby earning for himself the strong condemnation of many of his contemporaries as well as of posterity.

On the other hand, Rush was not the only man who dared to utter criticism against the tactics of General Washington. In fact, off and on during the early years of the war, the Commander-in-Chief was forced to bear personally the brunt of misfortunes arising from circumstances far beyond his control. Then again he would surprise his fellow men by a skillful and effective maneuver that would change the whole face of affairs.

With a poorly equipped army Washington was unable to defend New York City, in the summer of 1776, against the well-trained British regulars under General Howe. The superior British forces, outnumbering the Americans by two to one, drove Washington out of Manhattan and across New Jersey into Pennsylvania, and all hope for the American cause vanished. Then followed a bold stroke, ably and courageously executed. On Christmas night, with less than 3,000 men in his camp, Washington recrossed the Delaware, surprised the Hessians at Trenton, and pressed on to Princeton, where the British regiments were forced to beat a panicky retreat. Complete annihilation of the Continentals and consequent failure of the War for Independence at its very outset were thus avoided by Washington's astute and masterly stroke at this critical juncture.

The next summer, 1777, Howe decided to move some of his troops by sea from New York to the head of the Chesapeake Bay, preliminary to an attack on Philadelphia. When news of this plan reached American headquarters, Washington hastened across New Jersey into Pennsylvania to prevent Howe from capturing the

American capital. The opposing forces met on the Brandywine Creek near Wilmington, Delaware, where Washington's army was severely defeated and driven northward on September 11. A few weeks later, October 4, the British again succeeded in defeating Washington at Germantown. The Americans then retired to Valley Forge and General Howe occupied Philadelphia.

His failure to protect Philadelphia brought down on Washington's head a flood of criticism, much of it unjustified. Many of the obstacles in Washington's way were nearly insurmountable: raw troops, desertions, few trained officers, lack of equipment and supplies, and petty politics in Congress. What had put Washington in an unfavorable light in the fall of 1777 was the contrast between his position and that of General Gates in New York. Supported by Schuyler, Arnold, and Morgan, Gates had dealt a crushing blow to the British under General Burgoyne at Saratoga on October 17, where 5,000 red jackets surrendered. It was a signal victory, breaking up the British plan to separate New England from the Middle Colonies, and leading directly to an alliance with France.

If Gates could win a victory of such consequence, why must Washington miss the mark at Brandywine and Germantown? His critics seized upon these failures to add weight to their censure. Claiming that Washington had opposed his promotion in the army, Thomas Conway, an Irishman who had come to America for adventure, used his talents to build up a faction—the Conway Cabal—to oppose the Commander-in-Chief. He gathered to his side General Gates, General Charles Lee, Thomas Mifflin (Quartermaster-General), and other army officers and members of Congress. It was after the unfortunate defeats suffered by Washington's armies at Brandywine and Germantown, and the glorious victory of Gates at Saratoga, that the Conway Cabal began to operate in earnest. It denounced Washington for incompetence and claimed that the appointments he was making were not based on merit. In October 1777 these accusations found many ears ready to believe them and many tongues eager to repeat them. So influential did the Cabal become that in November, when the Board of War was reorganized, Mifflin was made a member of it and Gates its president. On several occasions Washington found himself in the anomalous position of being forced to recognize Gates as his superior. To add further insult to injury Congress appointed Conway inspector-general of the army with the rank of major general. By appointing Washington's personal enemies to positions of high command, was Congress trying to press him to resign?

Those members of Congress who were prompted by such motives were doomed to disappointment and embarrassment. There fell into Washington's hands a letter, the contents of which crystallized definitely the plot against him. It was written by Conway to Gates and mentioned among other things "a weak General and bad Counsellors." When news of the letter leaked through to the public, Washington's position was materially strengthened by this flagrant breach of etiquette. Even Conway's friends, fearing the results of the blunder, rushed for the Washington band-wagon. Conway himself was soon forced out of the army and the Cabal became an inglorious page in history.

The name of Benjamin Rush has usually been linked to the Conway Cabal. It is doubtful, however, that the Doctor was definitely connected with any concerted effort to remove Washington as commander-in-chief of the Continental Army, although it is true that he was friendly with many of those who were associated with Conway in his schemes. He was outspoken in his criticism of Washington's methods in letters to John Adams in October 1777. His disapprobation was based, not on any personal hatred for Washington, but rather on his desire as a patriot to strengthen the army by pointing out weak spots observed in his line of duty. He was a bitter critic, but he was also a patriot, and never a conspirator. It cannot be said that his denunciation of Washington was motivated by self-interest. He aimed only at victory for the American armies and achievement of independence. The manner in which he censured the Commander, however, is justly open to review. That his attack was made anonymously carries the imputation of cowardice, of which weakness, however, one can hardly accuse a signer of the Declaration of Independence. In fact, unsigned letters of criticism and denunciation were common. To condemn Rush merely because he tried to place the blame for inefficiency in the army is to place a premium on sentimental hero-worship. And to call him a conspirator is to read something into the story which has not been found in the available documentary sources.

Rush had questioned Washington's competency before Gates's victory at Saratoga gave strength to the Conway Cabal. Indeed, while he was a member of Congress, before March 1777, he was doubtful as to the probable length of Washington's service as Commander. He recorded in his notebook this interesting observation: "I think it more than probable that general Washington will not close the present war with G Britain 1) Because in ordinary revolutions different characters appear in their first and last stages. 2) Because his talents are better fitted to unite the people of America into one body than to give them afterwards a national complexion. 3) Because his talents are unequal to those degrees of discipline, and decision which alone can render an army finally successful. 4) Because he is idolized by the people of America, and is tho't to be absolutely necessary for us to enable us to carry on the war."[1] This prophecy was made a half year before the battles of Brandywine and Germantown.

Rush remained on cordial terms with Washington. In a letter written to him in late August, requesting a parole for a British officer wounded at Princeton, Rush worded the closing paragraph: "I beg leave to assure your Excellency of the great respect and esteem in which I have the honor to be your

Most Obedient
Humble Servant."[2]

On October 10, 1777, a week after the defeat at Germantown, he dined with the distracted General but made no mention in his diary of any hostile feeling toward him. He merely recorded: "Dined with the commander in chief of American army—no wine—only grog—knives & forks eno' for only half the company—one half the company eat after the other had dined at the same table. The General gave the head of his table to one of his aids-de-camp, and sat 2d or 3rd from him on his left side."[3] Not a single word of blame appears in this entry, and Rush was not the man to miss a chance to scold.

At the same time Rush saw things in the camps which needed correction. He believed that if he wrote confidentially to John

Adams, the faults would be corrected in due time without making the remonstrances public. He hesitated to make his objections public lest Washington be subjected to uninformed, popular clamor. His object was to improve the army discipline and not merely to present strictures against the Commander.

On October 1, 1777, Rush wrote Adams from Trenton about conditions in the army. "In my way to this place," he observed, "I passed thro' Genl. Washington's army. To my great mortification I arrived at the Head Quarters of a general of an outpost without being challenged by a single sentry. I saw soldiers straggling from our lines in every quarter without an officer, exposed every moment to be picked up by the enemy's light horse. I heard of 2,000 who sneaked off with the baggage of the army to Bethlehem. I was told by a Captain in our army that they would not be missed in the returns, for as these were made out only by Sargeants they would be returned on parade, and that from the proper officers neglecting to make out or examine returns Genl. Washington never knew within 3,000 men what his real numbers were. I saw nothing but confidence about Head Quarters, and languor in all the branches & extremities of the army." These charges were serious, indeed, and John Adams as one of the Congressional leaders ought certainly to have known about the state of affairs.

Apparently Rush felt that Washington was holding himself aloof from the bureaus and divisions of the army not under his immediate command, and that he was, therefore, unaware of the conduct and methods of his commanding officers. "A general should see everything with his own eyes, & hear everything with his own ears," he claimed in the letter to Adams. "He should understand & even practice at times all the duties of the soldier—the officer—the Quarter Master—the Commissary—& the Adjutant General."

Conditions pointed to catastrophe, to collapse of the patriot cause. "I am distressed to see the minions of a tyrant more devoted to his will, than we are to a cause in which the whole world is interested," he suggested further to Adams. "New measures and new men alone can save us. The American mind cannot long support the present complexion of affairs. Let our army be reformed. Let our general officers be chosen annually. The breaking of 40 regiments, and the dismission of one field officer from every regiment & of one subaltern from every company will save many millions to the continent. Your army by these means may be made respectable & useful. But you must not expect to fill it with soldiers for 3 years, or during the war. The genius of America rebels against the scheme. Good General Officers would make an army of six months men an army of heroes. Wolfe's army that conquered Canada was only 3 months old. Stark's militia who have cast a shade on everything that has been done by regulars since the beginning of the war shew us what wonderful qualities are to be called forth from our country men by an active & enterprising commander. The militia began, & I sincerely hope the militia will end the present war."[3a] Only a change in men and management could alter the distressing picture.

The defeat of Washington's forces at Germantown on October 4, 1777, was proof for Rush that his criticism of the army was justifiable. In great excitement he wrote John Adams again, on October 13, denouncing the weakness of the army's discipline and, incidentally, praising General Conway of the Cabal fame. The outcome of the battle of Germantown disgusted him. "We lost a city, a victory, a campaign by that want of discipline & system which pervades every part of the army," he complained. "General Conway wept for joy," he continued, "when he saw the ardor with which our troops pushed the enemy from hill to hill, and pronounced our country free from that auspicious sight. But when he saw an officer low in command give counter orders to the Commander in chief, and the comr. in chief passive under that circumstance, his distress and resentment exceeded all bounds. For God's sake do not suffer him [Conway] to resign. He seems to possess Lee's [General Charles Lee] knowledge & experience without any of his oddities or vices. He is moreover the idol of the whole army. Make him a major-general if nothing else will detain him in your service. He is entitled to most of the glory our arms acquired in the late battle. But his bravery and skill in war are not his only military qualifications. He is exact in his discipline, and understands every part of the detail of an army. Besides this, he is an enthusiast in our cause. Some people blame him for calling some of our generals fools, cowards & drunkards in public company. But these things are proof of his integrity, and should raise him in the opinion of every friend of America. Be not deceived my dear friend. Our army is better than it was two years ago. The spirit of our men is good. Our officers are equal, nay, superior to Howe's. A few able Major Generals would make them a terror to the whole power of Britain."[4]

From this letter it is obvious that Rush was campaigning for Conway, whom he honestly believed competent. In Conway's elevation Rush saw an improvement in the discipline and field activities of the army, and he was interested above all else in improving the army. There was certainly no conspiracy against Washington in mere suggestions to a member of Congress.

Before his next letter was written to Adams, October 21, Rush had received news of Gates's glorious victory at Saratoga, and he seized the opportunity to speak his mind. Gates's army was compared to a well-regulated family, Washington's to an unorganized mob. "Look at the character of both!" exclaimed Rush. "The one on the pinnacle of military glory—exulting in the success of schemes planned with wisdom, & executed with vigor and bravery—and above all see a country saved by their exertions. See the other outgeneraled and twice beated [Brandywine and Germantown] . . . forced to give up a city the capital of a state. . . ." How can Congress let these events pass by without an investigation? asked Rush. It was a natural question after seeing success of one army in New York and utter defeat of another in Pennsylvania, a question posed by a patriot, not a conspirator.

Listing specific complaints in his recital to Adams, he noted that in the British army pickets were relieved once or twice every day and guards every two hours, whereas pickets in Washington's army were known to have remained on duty five days and guards an entire day without relief, "and destitute at the same time of provisions except such as they plunder or buy with their own money. This negligence is a fruitful source of diseases in our army." It was also hinted by Rush that there were "nearly as many officers as men in our army."[5]

These critical suggestions, based on actual contact with conditions in the camps, were not acted upon by Adams or by Congress as a body. That censure was deserved is evident in the military histories of the War, even though it must be recognized that the Continental Army and its staff were faced with innumerable, gigantic obstacles. It was, in fact, a remarkable feat on Washington's part that he held the army together at all. Rush, on his side, was not merely captious. His open dispraise of the Commander arose from sincere patriotic fervor and sympathy with his suffering fellow men. Both Rush and Washington were sacrificing themselves to the same cause—American independence—but the clash came over an issue which, to one man, called for instant action, whereas, to the other man, it was only one of countless grave and pressing problems.

Rush has unfortunately called down calumny upon himself largely because of a single letter which he addressed to Patrick Henry, January 12, 1778, one in which he praised the Northern and Southern armies, but for the Middle army under Washington's direct command he had no good word. It was, indeed, needless for Rush to dispatch this letter anonymously. When it was discovered that he was the writer, he immediately found himself in a most unpleasant position. Never before had he attempted to hide his identity in his criticism of men or things, and in doing so on this occasion he foolishly jumped into a thorn bush.

The unsigned letter to Henry declared that "The Northern Army has shown us what Americans are capable of doing with a General at their head. The spirit of the Southern Army is in no ways inferior to the spirit of the Northern. A Gates, a Lee, or a Conway, would in a few weeks render them an irresistible body of men. The last of the above officers has accepted the new office of Inspector-General of our army, in order to reform abuses; but the remedy is only a palliative one. In one of his letters to a friend he says, 'A great and good God hath decreed America to be free, or the General and weak counsellors would have ruined her long ago.' "

These were sharp words, indeed, and, believing that the Commander-in-Chief should see them, Henry finally dispatched the letter to him. Washington, whose officers and men were just squeezing through a terrific winter at Valley Forge, was outraged. On March 28, 1778, he replied to Henry: "The anonymous letter with which you were pleased to favor me, was written by Dr. Rush, so far as I can judge from a similitude of hands. This man has been elaborate and studied in his professions of regard for me; and long since the letter to you. My caution, to avoid anything, which could injure the service, prevented me from communicating, but to a very few of my friends, the intrigues of a faction, which I know was formed against me, since it might serve to publish our internal dissentions; but their own restless zeal to advance their views has too clearly betrayed them, and made concealment on my part fruitless. I cannot precisely mark the extent of their views, but it appeared in general, that General Gates was to be exalted on the ruin of my reputation and influence. This I am authorized to say, from undeniable facts in my own possession, from publications, the evident scope of which could not be mistaken, and from private detractions industriously circulated. General Mifflin, it is commonly supposed, bore the second part in the cabal; and General Conway, I know, was a very active and malignant partisan; but I have good reason to believe that their machinations recoiled most sensibly upon themselves."[6] Of course Washington was bitter against Rush, but nowhere in this letter does he connect the Doctor with the Cabal. It is hardly commendable to write anonymous letters of denunciation, but it is a far graver offense to be implicated in a vicious conspiracy. Rush was guilty of the first, but there is no evidence to link his name in any way with the second.

After Rush was recognized as the author of the anonymous letter, Washington's full coöperation with him in his charges against Dr. Shippen and the Medical Department could hardly have been expected. It is possible that, in Rush's attack on Shippen, the Commander was sensible of a roundabout scheme of firing at him. The controversy had become too bitter and too involved, and the military demands were too pressing to permit of attempts at reconciliation at this time, so the cloud continued to hover over the army headquarters. Rush retired temporarily from the scene.

In June 1778 General Clinton, having evacuated Philadelphia, fell back toward New York City, and in the course of the journey he was met by an American force at Monmouth, New Jersey. Victory for the Americans appeared certain when General Charles Lee of the Cabal ordered a retreat, the necessity for which, it was later claimed, was doubtful. Washington arrived in time to rally the

Americans; Clinton decamped during the night. The Commander, incensed at Lee's action, ordered him to stand trial before a court-martial, and on August 12 he was found guilty of treason.

Lee's disgraceful retirement did not please Rush, who wrote John Adams on October 27, 1778: "Characters appear in one age and are only to be known in another. General Conway who was the nerves —Mifflin who was the spirit, & Lee who was the soul of our army have all been banished from Head Quarters. The last has been most unjustly condemned by a court martial for saving our army at Monmouth on the 28 of June last. Genl. Washington was his accusor." A week later he wrote Dr. David Ramsay: "Conway— Mifflin—& Lee were sacrificed to the excessive influence of ONE MAN. They were the first characters in the army and all honest men."[7] Lee, in turn, praised Rush: "You appear to me to be one of the very few mortals who from the beginning and through the whole course of the contest, have acted from the pure unadulterated principles of liberty and republicanism, uninfluenc'd by any views of avarice or ambition—every days acquaintance has improve'd your character in my opinion. . . ."[8]

After he returned to Philadelphia to his practice, which grew appreciably in the 1780's, the bitter controversies of the war period were slowly forgotten. The past was history and Rush spent his spare time in new fights, against slavery, intemperance, and an antiquated penal system. He concerned himself, too, with establishing a college at Carlisle. A quarter century after the controversies with Shippen and Washington, he destroyed what concrete reminders he still held in his possession of this unhappy season of his life. John Adams deplored the destruction of Rush's letters and papers. "I am extreamly sorry you relinquished your design of writing Memoirs of the American Revolution," he scolded Rush. "The burning of your documents was, let me tell you, a very rash action, and by no means justifiable upon good principles. Truth, justice and humanity are of eternal obligation, and we ought to preserve the evidence, which can alone support them." And later he added that he was "half inclined to be very angry" because of the destruction of anecdotes and documents which would have told the complete story of Rush's personal battles during the war.[9]

Rush's animosity toward Washington gradually waned and eventually gave way to a warm regard for him. When Washington came to Philadelphia to attend the Constitutional Convention in 1787, and later, when he came as President, Rush was on most cordial terms with him, entertaining him, favoring him with gifts, and discussing with him subjects of mutual interest. In one of his small pocket notebooks one finds a reference made by Rush to Washington as the Gustavus of America. This was in 1784. The exact entry, being a copy of a portion of a letter to Granville Sharp, reads: "Mr. Washington formerly the commander in chief of our armies has assumed the dress & manners of a Virginia planter. On his way home after delivering his Country he was caught in a shower of rain between Philadelphia and Baltimore. To screen himself from it, he dismounted his horse, & took a seat in a common stage waggon. When the waggon stopt at a tavern the innkeeper who knew the rank & character of his illustrious guest invited him into a private chamber, & offered to prepare a dinner for him & his two friends by themselves,—'no—no' said our hero—'it is customary for the people who travel in this stage always to eat together. I will not desert my companions.' Upon which he sat down & dined with a large company in a common room in a country inn. Some of the company were persons of great obscurity & by no means qualified for such a companion as the Gustavus of America."[10] The last trace of discord had disappeared; Rush saw the hero in the man he had bitterly denounced.

The two men saw each other during the sessions of the Constitutional Convention, and immediately thereafter Rush supported Washington for the Presidency. On June 24, 1787, Washington made this significant entry in his diary: "In Convention. Dined at Mr. Morris's, drank Tea, by appointment and partr. Invitation at Doctr. Rush's."[11] On April 14 of the following year Rush sent the future President "a print of the celebrated Mr. Napier, which was committed to the Doctor's care, for the General, from the Right Honble the Earl of Buchan of Scotland."[12] Two weeks later, appreciating Washington's deep interest in agriculture, Rush sent him a package of rare seeds with a most cordial note: "I received a small quantity of the mangel wurgel or scarcity root seeds a few days ago from Dr. Lettsom of London. In distributing these seeds among the friends of agriculture in this country, I should have been deficient in duty, and patriotism to have neglected to send a small portion of them to your Excellency. The pamphlet which accompanies the seeds will furnish your Excellency with a particular account of the method of cultivating—as also—of the great encrease, & useful qualities of this extraordinary vegetable. From an accurate examination of the plant, the botanists have agreed in its being a mongrel species of the beet. Dr. Lettsom has called it the 'Beta hebrida.' " And the friendly closing: "With respectful compliments to Mrs. Washington in which Mrs. Rush joins, & sincere wishes for your Excellency's health & happiness, I have the honor to be your most obedient servant. . . ."[13]

As the years passed Rush deeply regretted the necessity which had aligned him with Washington's enemies, even though he had no cause to reproach himself for being involved in any unsavory plot. When, in 1804, he heard that John Marshall's biography of Washington was about to be published, he sought to have deleted from the book the anonymous letter of January 12, 1778, to Patrick Henry, and Washington's letter of March 28 to Henry. He pleaded with Bushrod Washington, the President's nephew, to strike out the objectionable passages, offering a defense and explanation of his own conduct. The letters to Bushrod Washington are self-explanatory and are printed herewith in their entirety.

The first letter in this correspondence, dated August 24, 1804, reads:

"I have this day learned that a letter from me to Governor Henry of Virginia which was sent by him to General Washington with the General's answer to it are to be printed in the history of his life. It is foreign to my wishes to hint at the state of the public mind towards the close of the year 1777, and which events subsequent to that year altered in his favor. I shall mention one passage only in his letter (dated March 28, 1778) to Mr. Henry in which there is an evident mistake. 'This man' (alluding to me) 'has been elaborate, and studious in his professions of regard for me, and that long since his letter to you.' The letter written to Mr. Henry by Rush was dated on the 12th of January, 1778. I resigned my charge of the military hospitals on the 30th of the same month. All official intercourse ceased from that day between General Washington and me. I retired to private life remote from the army immediately afterwards nor did I see General Washington until fourteen months after the date of my letter to Mr. Henry, and then first at Morristown in New Jersey.

"In the month of December, 1777, I addressed two letters to the General as Commander in Chief of the Army, dated from Princeton. The first stating the errors, abuses and distresses which prevailed in the military hospitals, the second containing complaints of the administration of the hospitals by the Director General. Both of these letters were written in the customary stile of respect to persons of high stations, but though written before the 12th of January, 1778, contained no expressions that could convey the ideas before mentioned in the General's letter to Mr. Henry. An attested copy of the first of the letters shall be sent to you if required—the second is mislaid. The originals of both were sent by the General to Congress & I suppose are still on their files.

"The mistake on the part of General Washington in the reference to the time in which those letters were received & of their contents is a natural one, especially by a person daily occupied in receiving and writing letters.

"After this statement of facts I submit it to your judgment whether it would not be proper not to publish the letters alluded to or to erase the passage objected to in General Washington's letter to Gov. Henry as well as the inference he has drawn from it."

Rush's second plea to Bushrod Washington was made on September 13 and reads:

"I am much obliged by your polite and friendly letter which I have just now received. I answer it thus promptly, to request the favor of you immediately to write to Mr. Wayne to suppress the letter alluded to, to Govr Henry, or at least the two paragraphs in it in which I am accused of having acted an insincere and inconsistent part towards the General. I mentioned the reasons formerly why it cannot be correct.

"To vindicate myself from the reflections thrown upon me by Gen'l Washington would compel me to do great violence to my

present feelings to his name and character. It would compel me
further to mention several private military anecdotes communicated
to me by persons of great respectability who were never suspected
of being unfriendly to him. One of those persons Govr Henry; two
others of them were members of his family in the years 1776 &
1777. It has been my constant wish and intention that those anecdotes should descend to the grave with me. Part of the gentlemen
who mentioned them, died in habits of respect for the General.
The survivors venerate his memory.

"In suppressing the letter, or passages alluded to, you will prevent
a great deal of pain to a large family of children, some of whom
are now reading with great pleasure, the history of the General's
life.

"By writing to Mr. Wayne and also to Mr. Sam Bradford to
whose friendship I am indebted for the knowledge of the above
letter, you will much oblige, Dear Sir,

"Your sincere friend and most obedient servant."

In order to clarify misunderstood points of his request, Rush
wrote again on September 21 as follows:

"You have indeed misapprehended me in supposing I intended
publicly to defend myself against the charges contained in General
Washington's letter to Governor Henry. Far, far from it. I had
determined to submit to them in silence. To my family and friends
only I had intended to justify myself. Now this would have been
painful for in doing so I should not only have done violence to my
present feelings but to the habitual respect I have uniformly done to
his illustrious character. Of this there are some proofs on record in
our public papers during the last political acts of my life in the
years of the formation of the new Constitution and of the General's
election to the chair of the U. States.

"I neglected to mention formerly that my first interview with the
General in Morris County after the date of my letter to Mr. Henry
took place in consequence of an unexpected card to dine with him
before I had waited upon him. This generous act induced me to
believe he had dismissed the remembrance of my letter from his
mind, and led me constantly to pay my respects to him every time

he came to Philada. afterwards. I was confirmed still more in that belief by the honor of an afternoon's visit to my family during the time he presided in the national convention [1787].

"Of how few events, public men or even friends do we think alike in different periods of our lives!

"For your kindness in this business, accept my sincere thanks. To a man disgusted, as I have long been, with public pursuits and anxious for retirement, and wishing to pass the small remnant of my days unnoticed by the world, the favor will be remembered with the most grateful emotions."

When the objectionable letters in their entirety were set in type through an error, Rush hurriedly requested Bushrod Washington to have the key sentences removed.

"My son called at Mr. Wayne's immediately after my receiving your last letter, but did not see him till the next day," he wrote on September 24. "He told me the letter you kindly consented to suppress had been struck off in its original state. Upon being told by my son, that I would chearfully defray the expenses of reprinting the sheet that contained it, he said he would wait till you came to Philada in order to be supplied with some matter to occupy the blank made by the abstraction of the letter. As this may not be practicable and as the journey to Philada may be delayed, I take the liberty of suggesting to you that the erasure of the two sentences formerly mentioned that reflect upon me will be satisfactory. I wish it to be done so as not to leave a suspicion of a chasm in the letter in the public mind. As the erasures will not make more than 10 or 12 lines, the new sheet may be so composed, as that those erasures will not be perceived.

"I have only to request one more favor & that is that your instructions to Mr. Wayne be of a positive nature.

"Did you know the distress which this business has given to me and to those branches of my family who are acquainted with it, you would excuse the solicitude I have discovered to leave nothing to accident in it."

A postscript followed: "I will thank you to accompany your letter to Mr. Wayne by a letter to my son Richd Rush, Attorney-at-law,

Philada. informing him of your instructions to Mr. Wayne. When I have the pleasure of seeing you in Philada I will give you my reasons for this request."[14]

Rush was never comfortable about what had happened during the war. The unpleasant memory haunted him all his life. Only a year before his death, in a long and detailed letter to John Adams, written on February 12, 1812, he attempted once more to defend his conduct. Since it was written more than thirty years after the war, time and a desire to forget must have blunted many sharp thrusts. Always meticulous, however, about the truth, the Doctor prepared the letter carefully, writing several drafts before he was satisfied to dispatch it to Adams. It is about two thousand words in length and deserves close examination.

"I forgot in the enumeration of the hatreds with which I have contended," it reads, "to mention not only the 'odium nigro-tyrannum' [opposition to his early abolition essays] but the 'odium Washingtonium.' It was of a violent and of a chronic nature. I will give you a history of its cause in as few words as possible. For its not being perpetuated in the history of his life, I am indebted to the goodness of his nephew, Judge [Bushrod] Washington.

"In the year 1774 I published the note from Mr. Davies' sermon in which he destined Major Washington at a future day to perform some great services to his country.

"During the sessions of Congress in the year 1774 in Philadelphia I met Colonel Washington at the coffee house at the time he was generally spoken of as Commander in Chief of the American Army, and informed him that his appointment would give universal satisfaction to the citizens of Pennsylvania and hoped he would not decline it. I had reason to believe that he considered this opinion as an expression of attachment to his military character never to be cancelled, and that a subsequent change of that opinion was an evidence of insincerity. The sequel of this letter will show that I was not singular in this respect.

"In the summer of 1776, or thereabouts I dined in a select company with General, then Colonel Stevens, on his way from Virginia to the Camp. I sat next to him. He asked me who constituted General Washington's military family. I said 'two of them were Colonel

Jos. Reed and Major Thomas Mifflin.' 'Are they men of talents?' said he. 'Yes,' said I. 'I am glad to hear it (said the Colonel) for General Washington will require such men about him. He is a weak man. I know him well. I served with him in the last French war in America.'

"After the defeats and retreats of our army in 1776 I went out as a volunteer physician to General Cadwallader's corps of Philadelphia militia. During this excursion I rode with Col. J. Reed from Bristol to the camp on the Delaware nearly opposite Trenton. On our way he mentioned many instances of General Washington's want of military skill, and ascribed most of the calamaties of the campaign to it. He concluded by saying he 'was only fit to command a regiment.' General Gates informed me in March, 1777, that Patrick Henry had said the same thing of him when he was appointed Commander-in-Chief.

"A little later than this time General Mifflin told me that 'he was totally unfit for his situation, that he was fit only to be the head clerk of a London Compting house,' and as a proof of his assertion mentioned the time he wasted with his pen and particularly noticed his having once transcribed a letter to Congress of three sheets of paper only because there was two or three erasures on the original.

"The brilliant affair at Trenton in January, 1777, dissipated all the impressions which these opinions and anecdotes of General Washington had excited in my mind.

"In April or May, 1777, I accepted of the appointment of physician-general of the military hospitals of the United States under the direction of Dr. Shippen. Here I saw scenes of distress touching to humanity, and disgraceful to a civilized country. I can never forget them. I still see the sons of our yeomanry brought up in the lap of plenty and domestic comforts, shivering with cold upon the bare floors without a blanket to cover them, calling for fire, for water, for suitable food, for medicines and calling in vain. I hear the complaints they utter against their country,—I hear their sighs for their fathers' firesides,—I hear their groans,—I see them expire,—while hundreds of the flower of their youth were dying under such accumulated sufferings, Dr. Shippen was feasting with the general officers at the camp, or bargaining with tavern keepers in Jersey and

Pennsylvania for the sale of madeira wine from our hospital stores, bought for the use of the sick. Nor was this all. No officer was ever sent to command or preserve discipline in our hospital (a practice universal in European armies) in consequence of which our soldiers sold their blankets, muskets, and even clothing for the necessaries of life or for ardent spirits. In this situation of our hospital I addressed two letters to General Washington, the one complaining of the above abuses and pointing out their remedies,—the other complaining of Dr. Shippen for mal-practices. I expected that a court would be ordered to inquire into Dr. Shippen's conduct in consequence of my second letter. In this I was disappointed. Both my letters were sent to Congress, and a committee appointed to hear my complaints against the Director-General. On my way to Yorktown where the Congress then sat, I passed through the army at Valley Forge where I saw similar marks of filth, waste of public property and want of discipline which I had recently witnessed in the hospitals. General Sullivan (at whose quarters I breakfasted) said to me, 'Sir, this is not an army, it is a mob.' Here a new source of distress was awakened in my mind. I now felt for the safety and independence of my country as well as for the sufferings of the sick under my care. In Yorktown I found alarm and discontent among many members of Congress. While there I wrote a short account of the state of our hospitals and army to Patrick Henry and concluded my letter by quoting a speech of General Conway's, unfriendly to the talents of the Commander-in-Chief. This letter Patrick Henry transmitted to General Washington and hence the cause and only cause of his hostility to me.

"Dr. Shippen was acquitted by the Committee of Congress of which Dr. Witherspoon was chairman. The Dr. had witnessed the sufferings of the sick soldiers at Princeton, but he was, notwithstanding, the friend of Dr. Shippen upon this occasion. Disgusted with the issue of this business, I resigned my commission, and returned to private life.

"In the year 1779 Dr. Morgan dragged Dr. Shippen before a court-martial at Morristown where I was summoned as a witness. During the trial several members of the court-martial were changed, a thing I believe never done in such courts, nor in juries except in case of sickness or death. The Doctor was acquitted, but without honor, and by a majority of a single vote. Soon after this cold and bare acquittal he resigned. Gen. Washington gave him a certificate approving of his conduct while Director-General of the hospitals, and saying that the distress of the sick arose from a state of things inseparable from the new and peculiar situation of our country.

"The change which took place in the army by the appointment of Baron Steuben, Inspector General, Mr. [Robert] Morris, Financier, and Colonel [Alexander] Hamilton, a member of George Washington's family, restored him to the universal confidence of his country. You may easily conceive the nature of this change when I add that Baron Steuben said the cloaths, destroyed by our army, would cloathe the largest army in Europe (previously to his appointment) and of course that an immense saving of money and health and lives was the consequence of the economy he introduced into the army in that article alone; also, that Mr. Morris informed me that the expenses of the hospital department alone after he took charge of the finances were reduced from five million to one million of dollars in one year, estimating the value of paper money in gold and silver coin in both years.

"Feeling no unkindness to General Washington during the years of the war after 1777, and after its close, I joined in all the marks of gratitude and respect showed to him from time to time by the citizens of Philadelphia. I first pointed him out as the future President of the United States in all our newspapers while the Convention was sitting which formed the new Constitution, in the same publication in which I mentioned your name as Vice-President. These acts were the effects of a belief that the councils of Steuben, Green[e] and Hamilton aided by his own experience had qualified him for his station. I rejoiced in cherishing this belief, for I had no doubt of his always acting honestly and faithfully for the benefit of our country. I entertained him while he presided in the Convention and treated him whenever I met him with uniform respect while he was President of the United States.

"From the statement I have given you, I hope you are convinced that the epithet he applied to me as far [as] it related to my conduct to him, was not merited. He cherished in his family and honoured

with his confidence several persons who treated his character with a
disrespect very different from that which was conveyed by my quoting a speech of General Conway's [in the letter to Patrick Henry]
concerning him. Your son-in-law, Colonel [William Stephens]
Smith, informed me that he had heard one of his Secretaries call
him 'a d—d fool.' I have heard an officer who often did business at
headquarters, say 'he was a greater imposter than Mahomet.' A gentleman of high rank who traveled thro' the United States soon after
the conclusion of the war, informed me that he had heard General
Hamilton say 'that he had no heart, that he was a stone, that he was
no general and that he had never read anything upon the art of war
except Sims' Military Guide.' I have heard Major Edwards say that
he has heard General Green[e] (to whom the Major was aid-de-
camp) say 'that the world was deceived in his character—that' but
eno', eno' of this hateful subject. Help me to blot the knowledge
and recollection of such speeches from my memory.

"The Venerable Charles Thomson,[15] now 81 years of age, now
and then visits me. I once suggested to him to write 'secret memoirs
of the Revolution.' 'No, no,' said he, 'I will not. I could not tell the
truth without giving great offense. Let the world admire our patriots and heroes. Their supposed talents and virtues by commanding
imitation will serve the cause of patriotism and of our country.' I
concur in this sentiment and therefore I earnestly request that you
would destroy this letter as soon as you have read it. I do not even
wish to make it known that General Washington was deficient in
that mark of true greatness that characterized Caesar, Henry the
Eighth and Frederick the Second, the ability to forgive.

"I thank God my destiny in the world of spirits to which I am
hastening is not to be determined by slaveholders, old tories, Latin
and Greek schoolmasters, Judges who defend capital punishment,
Philadelphia physicians, persecuting clergymen nor yet by General
Washington. All of whom I have offended only by attempting to
lessen the misery and ignorance of my fellow men.

"When Calvin heard that Luther had called him 'a child of the
devil,' he cooly replied, 'Luther is the servant of the most high God.'
In answer to the epithet which General Washington has applied to
me, I will as cooly reply: 'He was the highly favoured instrument

whose patriotism and name contributed greatly to the establishment of the independence of the United States.' "[16]

His defense was eloquent. His protestations, however, should never have been necessary, because except for his friendliness toward Gates and Conway, there is no evidence upon which to convict him of conspiracy in the Conway Cabal. His greatest crime was indiscretion. He was brusque and outspoken in passing censure on Washington and the management of the army; he was ruthless in condemning Shippen and the administration of the medical department; he was imprudent in stooping to anonymity in his personal attack. Bold, uncompromising, a crusader in spirit, he allowed impulse to overrule prudence and self-possession and even the fact that most of the criticism was justified did not save him from obloquy.

VII

Teacher and Physician

As a teacher, Rush exerted more influence on the medical profession in America than any other one person during the quarter century following the War for Independence. His students practised throughout the country from Massachusetts to Georgia and kept in touch with his medical ideas through correspondence and through his published writings. As a physician, he outranked the members of his profession in Philadelphia, the largest and most important city in the new nation, and was used as a consultant by physicians in all parts of the country. For a time he was easily one of the most prominent physicians in America and certainly the busiest in his native city. Boasting the first medical school in America, Philadelphia remained the medical center of the nation for over a century.

After his return from Edinburgh in 1769, Rush had been elected professor of chemistry in the College of Philadelphia where he continued to lecture year after year. Beginning in February 1774, as one of the physicians of the Society for Inoculating the Poor Gratis, every Tuesday morning in a room in the State House (Independence Hall), he inoculated patients against smallpox. His formal lectures on chemistry were, however, interrupted during the British occupancy of Philadelphia, when the College was closed and Rush was out of the city. Upon the reopening of the College, he resumed the lectures on chemistry and continued to offer them regularly until 1779. In November of that year, because of a political controversy in the State, the Legislature suspended the charter of the College of Philadelphia and set up a new institution in its stead, the University of the State of Pennsylvania. On December 8, 1779, the trustees of the new institution appointed a committee to "enquire into the state of the late Medical School," and, in the meantime, to invite the professors to continue their work in the new University. At first, as a protest against the action of the Legislature, none of the professors except Dr. Shippen would accept a post in the new institution.

It took more than a year for Rush's wrath to subside, but he finally capitulated and on November 14, 1781, *The Pennsylvania Gazette* announced that his lectures on chemistry and the practice of physic would begin in the new University on the following Monday at three o'clock in the afternoon. By 1783 practically all of the old professors were in harness once more. In 1786 Rush's lectures were advertised as embracing medicine as well as chemistry.

At about the time the new federal government under the Constitution was getting under way, the Pennsylvania Legislature repealed the Act of 1779, and returned to the old College of Philadelphia its original powers and property. Three days after the passage of the Act, March 6, 1789, members of the Board of the College as of 1779 held the first of several reorganization meetings at the home of Benjamin Franklin; and, in a few months, the College of Philadelphia again opened its doors. Shippen, Kuhn, and Rush accepted appointments to the posts held by them in the medical school before its dissolution in 1779. When Dr. Morgan died in the fall of 1789, the Trustees, on October 24, elected Rush to the chair of the theory and practice of medicine, Dr. Caspar Wistar being chosen to succeed Rush as professor of chemistry. Not being fully prepared to assume the new post, Rush found it necessary to devote considerable time and energy to the preparation of lectures for the new course.[1]

The College of Philadelphia and the University of the State of Pennsylvania could not progress as separate institutions and, in the fall of 1791, they merged, operating under the name of the University of Pennsylvania. On January 23, 1792, Rush was elected professor of the institutes of medicine and clinical medicine in the new University, of which John Ewing was the provost. On the resignation of Dr. Adam Kuhn, in 1796, Rush received an additional appointment, that of professor of the practice of physic. Until his death he lectured on the institutes and practice and supervised the medical clinics, the three posts making considerable demands on his time. Immediately after the merger in 1791 Rush spoke of "the arduous business" assigned to him in the new arrangement of professorships, "to teach the institutes of medicine and to illustrate them by clinical lectures upon such diseases as may occur in the Pennsylvania Hospital during the winter." The increased burdens notwithstanding, Rush was pleased with the merging of the schools and he expressed his satisfaction to the students in his first introductory lecture in the new University of Pennsylvania, in November 1791: "I should do violence to my feelings should I proceed to the subjects of the ensuing course of lectures, without first congratulating you upon the union of the two medical schools of Philadelphia, under a Charter founded upon the most liberal concessions by the gentlemen who projected it, and upon the purest principles of patriotism in the Legislature of our State. By means of this event, the ancient harmony of the different professors of medicine will be restored, and their united efforts will be devoted, with accumulated force, towards the advancement of our science."[2]

Rush took infinite pains in preparing his lectures. Seated, he read them to his classes, rising occasionally to stress a particular point. The fact in itself that he taught more students than any contemporary American professor of medicine testifies to his outstanding position as a teacher. A keen observer and inveterate note-taker, he also sprinkled his lectures with entertaining as well as instructive anecdotes. An especially well-read man, he had at his command more than a working knowledge of history and literature. A convincing speaker, he inspired confidence by reason of his personal honesty and the fearless attitude he assumed in expressing what he believed to be truthful, though often unpopular, opinions. The students knew that Rush worked incessantly and diligently, that his opinions had foundation, that he took his lectures most seriously. For these students he was, therefore, a teacher to be honored and respected.

One Charles Caldwell, a member of one of Rush's classes in 1792, said of his teacher: "He was one of the best public readers I have ever heard. As a mere colloquist, moreover, having cultivated, with great attention and care, the art of conversation, he was uncommonly eloquent, correct, and interesting. In his lectures, and other public discourses, which he sometimes pronounced, he never attempted to be, in delivery lofty, exciting, and impressive, except by reading." He referred to Rush's introductory lecture of 1792 as "a performance of high order," and continued: "In matter it was instructive, in style and manner interesting and attractive; it was elegantly recited, or rather read, and its general tone, and the adroitly

Americanized spirit of it were judiciously fitted to give it favor and popularity with an American audience."[3]

In lecturing, "Dr. Rush mingled the most abstruse investigation with the most agreeable eloquence—the sprightliest sallies of imagination with the most profound disquisitions; and the whole was enlivened with anecdotes, both pleasant and instructive," said Dr. David Ramsay. "His language was simple and always intelligible, and his method so judicious, that a consistent view of the subject was communicated, and the recollection of the whole rendered easy. His lectures were originally written on leaves alternately blank. On the blank side he entered, from time to time, every new fact, idea, anecdote, or illustration, that he became possessed of, from any source whatever."[4]

Dr. Charles D. Meigs recalled that immediately upon entering Rush's lecture room in the University of Pennsylvania on Ninth Street he was captivated by the lecturer. "I was enrapt," recalled Meigs in later years, "his voice sweeter than any flute, fell on my ears like droppings from a sanctuary, and the spectacle of his beautiful radiant countenance, with his earnest, most sincere, most persuasive accents, sunk so deep into my heart that neither time nor change could eradicate them from where they are at this hour freshly remembered."[5]

Some students were impressed with the deep religious spirit which pervaded Rush's teaching. Thomas E. Bond expressed his appreciation of this phase of Rush's power as a teacher in a letter to his master: "While you have instructed me in the principles of medicine you have not neglected a much more important and essential concern—I mean the nature and truth of the Christian religion with the relative duties it injoins.—You have taught me by word and by example that great talents and eruditions are not inimical to the Christian faith. You have encouraged me to espouse religious principles and practice religious duties in despite of all the sophistical arguments of infidels, and have abundantly contributed to confirm my faith in that holy religion, which affords the only solid basis of human happiness, without which life would be a burden and death the most fearful of events."[6]

Before 1790 the number of students in Rush's classes varied between sixteen and forty-five annually. In 1779 there were eighteen students registered in his course, thirty-two in the following year, twenty-eight in both 1785 and 1786, thirty-eight in 1789, and forty-five in 1790. After the latter year the enrollment increased considerably and rapidly. The following summary, in the handwriting of Rush's son, James, is in the Ridgway Branch of the Library Company of Philadelphia:

1790	45	1802	91
1791	72	1803	125
1792	119	1804	153
1793	76	1805	189
1794	105	1806	231
1796	93	1807	260
1797	81	1808	276
1798	90	1809	307
1799	105	1810	369
1800	105	1811	348
1801	128	1812	332

According to James Rush's figures, 2872 students were registered in his father's medical classes between 1779 and 1812. They paid fees totalling $69,030, about $24 per student.

In addition to the students regularly matriculated at the College and the University, Rush also had some private students under his wing. One of these was James McHenry, who worked with Rush before the War for Independence, and later became secretary of war under President Washington. Dr. David Ramsay, who knew Rush for thirty-five years, said that in the last nine years of Rush's life the total number of his private students was not more than fifty, although this figure was mere conjecture on Ramsay's part.[7]

It was, naturally, a special privilege for a private student to pursue his medical apprenticeship in the office of the distinguished Dr. Rush. Applications came from far and wide, and in the 1790's, when he lived at Fourth and Walnut Streets, he maintained six apprentices and, in order not to increase that number, he charged them a high fee. "Any person connected in any way with, or recommended by you, cannot fail of commanding my disposition to serve him," Rush wrote John Dickinson, October 4, 1791. But, he went on to explain: "My usual fee with an apprentice is £100 cash. I have in many instances lately, objected to reducing this sum, chiefly with a design to reduce the number of my apprentices. At present I have six in my shop—one of whom will leave me in a few months. If under the above circumstances, your friend insists upon coming to me, I can make no objection to him."[8] In 1807 one A. M. Lane, of Wilmington, Delaware, sent Rush a check on the Bank of the United States for $266.67, covering the Doctor's fee for a three-year term for Lane's son, one of the apprentices.[9]

Among the list of Rush's apprentices one finds such names as James McHenry (1771), John Rodgers (1775), James Mease (1788), John Redman Coxe (1791), and James Rush (1805).[10] Chandler Peyton, Robert Carter, James Jones of Amelia, Robert Burton, and Elisha Dick, all eminent Virginia physicians, studied under Rush.[11] Sixty of the members of the South Carolina Medical Society had been taught by him. This number comprised more than half the membership of the Society.[12]

Rush entertained definite ideas as to the proper curriculum and methods of instruction which should prevail in medical schools. He was very exacting, for instance, about the legibility of handwriting appearing on prescriptions and in letters containing medical advice. Therefore, he stressed penmanship. "Considering how often we are obliged to convey our advice to patients by means of letters; and how many medicines we prescribe in words which are not in common use: considering likewise how injurious a mistake in a single word or letter, or even the neglect of our prescriptions," he remarked to his class in November 1792, "from an inability to read them, may be, in their consequences, to the health and life of a patient; the writing a fair and legible hand should be considered as part, not only of learning, but of the morality of a physician." The Doctor then went on, as an expert penman, to offer directions for acquiring a fair hand. Then he turned to arithmetic which, he said, is to the eyes and ears, what the sense of touch is to the whole body; it serves to correct mistakes. As part of his general training the medical student should also make a study of climate, weather conditions, soils, and the foods, manners, and medicines of different countries, he insisted. Latin and Greek are not absolutely necessary, but French, German, and Spanish are valuable. History and literature should be included in the curriculum because they enlarge his "sphere of social intercourse." Extemporaneous speaking in societies "will exercise his active faculties," while a knowledge of drawing helps a physician to keep accurate records. It was, of course, natural for the meticulous Rush to demand that students follow in his footsteps.[13]

In the manuscript of his lectures on the practice of physic, now preserved in the University of Pennsylvania Library, one finds further suggestions for students on the method of acquiring medical knowledge: "There are three ways of acquiring medical knowledge, reading books, hearing lectures, observing diseases as they occur. Practical books should not be read by students before they have an opportunity of observing practice. The best method is to read as cases occur. Ears are sometimes more retentive than eyes. Dr. Franklin could never recollect his acquaintainces untill they spoke. In attending lectures in the first place be punctual in attendance, secondly do not copy your notes during the lectures as your time may be better employed, thirdly do not attend many courses in one season, as they will confuse you; when you retire from the lecture, converse on it, you cannot call it your own till you have communicated it. Pay great attention to nature—more attention is necessary in the United States of America as our diseases differ much from those of Europe. . . . Diseases [are] much more instructing than books: as well might a man attempt to swim by reading, as practice medicine from books."

Economy of time is vitally important to any student. Time spent on useless studies is an absolute waste. "As a means of retaining the strength and activity of the intellectual faculties," he wrote, "no portion of them should be wasted upon unprofitable studies. We hear much of oeconomy in the expenditure of money and time, but few people think of the precious nature of this excellent virtue as applied to the expenditure of intellect. The attention which is employed in reading novels, plays, and in idle conversation, carries away with it a portion of the excitability of the intellectual faculties, which can never be recovered; and thus deducts from that vigor which might have been profitably employed upon useful subjects."[14]

Rush advised his students to rely neither on experience nor on observation separately, but to combine the two in treating patients. In one of his introductory lectures, in November 1791, "On the Necessary Connection Between Observation and Reasoning in Medicine," he stated that physicians were divided into empirics and dogmatists; the former guided by experience and the latter by reasoning alone, and that it is not possible for a physician to rely exclusively on his own experience because the longest life is not long enough to acquire a correct and perfect knowledge of all diseases. "Neither can the defect of experience, nor the decay, or weakness of the memory in one physician," Rush claimed, "be supplied by the experience and observation of others. Few men see the same objects through the same medium." Further, he continued: "To observe is to think, and to think is to reason in medicine. Hence we find theories in the writings of the most celebrated practical physicians. . . . I believe no empiric ever gave a medicine without cherishing a theoretical indication of cure in his mind." At the same time there are objections to the exclusive reliance upon theory because, Rush insisted, in the first place our knowledge of the structure of the human body is imperfect; secondly, the mind "acquires truth too slowly to act with effect, in the numerous and rapid exigencies of diseases." The good physician, therefore, combines "observation and reasoning" in his practice.[15]

Believing that many useful remedies for human ailments have been discovered by observing their salutary effects upon domestic animals, Rush suggested, in a lecture to his students in November 1807, the advisability of including a course in veterinary science in the curriculum of every medical school. As a matter of fact, it had not yet been taught as a formal course anywhere in this country. In the lecture "On the Duty and Advantages of Studying the Diseases of Domestic Animals, And the Remedies Proper to Remove Them," Rush suggested: "By extending our knowledge of the causes and cure of the diseases of domestic animals, we may add greatly to the certainty and usefulness of the profession of medicine, as far as it relates to the human species. The organization of their bodies, the principles of animal life, and the manner in which the remote and proximate causes of diseases produce their morbid effects, are the same as in the human body; and most of the medicines produce in them, and in us, nearly a similar operation. Their acute diseases are the same as ours. . . . In short, when we except the diseases which are the effects of certain trades and professions, of intemperance, of the operations of the mind, and of a peculiar function in the female body, there is scarcely a form of disease mentioned in our systems of nosology, but what is to be met with in domestic animals. To encourage us to extend to them the benefits of medicine, let us attend to the light and knowledge which several branches of our science have derived from them."[16] Thus Rush set himself down as the earliest proponent of the study of veterinary science in America. Thirty years were to pass before Rush's suggestion was to assume practical form when the first veterinary school in America was founded in Boston. No courses in veterinary medicine were given in Rush's own college, the University of Pennsylvania, until the opening of its veterinary school in October 1884, over seventy-five years later.

Two years after the appeal was made for veterinary medicine, Rush asked that a special course in natural philosophy be offered the students in the medical school of the University of Pennsylvania. Both proposals are unique in connection with the formal curriculum in our early medical schools. The plea for a course in natural philosophy, in a letter to George Clymer, Jr. under date of November 25, 1809, pointed out that during the first years of the medical school of the College of Philadelphia, all students who had not previously been graduated from a college were required to attend a course of lectures on natural philosophy before graduation from medical school. Although the rule had been neglected for several years, "to the great injury of our medical school, and of medical science in our country," as Rush expressed it, he still deemed the course highly important for members of the medical profession. "Permit me to suggest to you," the letter continued, "the necessity of appointing a professor of natural philosophy for the express purpose of teaching that important branch of science to students of medicine in the extensive way in which it is taught in European universities. Such a course of lectures will not interfere with the instruction in natural philosophy given to candidates for degrees in the arts by the Provost of the University. They will be addressed to persons of a most advanced age, and will embrace many objects especially necessary and useful to students of medicine. Should such a professorship be instituted, there will be no difficulty in filling it. Mr. Robert Hare's[17] extensive knowledge in natural philosophy, and all its collateral subjects points him out as a most suitable person for that purpose. His splendid talents and ardor in scientific pursuits I have no doubt would add greatly to the reputation of our medical school, and to the honor of our city, and state. Should you think proper to propose the professorship I have mentioned, suppose you add to it at the same time a professorship of rural oeconomy?"[18]

Rush was interested in the young men he taught not only as students but also as physicians. What are the rules of success in the medical profession? How should the young physician proceed in setting up a medical practice? Having learned many simple rules in years of experience as a busy physician, Rush formulated codes of professional ethics, which he presented to the students from time to time within and without the lecture hall.

When he drew up the list of "Duties of A Physician," more than nine-tenths of the population of the United States lived on farms or in rural communities, and it is easy to understand, therefore, the place of importance which he assigned to the farm. He advised every young physician to go to the country and settle on a farm, to convince the farmers that he assumed "no superiority over them" because of his education. On a farm the physician might promote scientific improvements in agriculture and keep his mind occupied and his body in condition in the healthy seasons of the year. The income derived from the farm would enable him to pursue his practice with greater dignity by reason of financial independence. Occasionally patients could pay their bills by working on the farm or by substituting farm stock for money. Furthermore, "the resources of a farm will prevent your cherishing, for a moment, an impious wish for the prevalence of sickness in your neighbourhood."

The physician was warned, in "Duties of A Physician," to dress plainly and to avoid eccentricities in manner. It is important in visiting the sick never to appear in a hurry or to talk of unrelated matters before having made the necessary inquiries into the patient's symptoms. The physician must not make light of any case, or object unnecessarily to the simple prescriptions of the patient; at the same time he must be inflexible in essential directions. Preserve a cheerful countenance in the sick room, Rush warned, and inspire as much hope of a recovery as the case merits consistent with truth. "Make it a rule never to be angry at anything a sick man says or does to you. Sickness often adds to the natural irritability of the temper. We are, therefore, to bear the reproaches of our patients with meekness and silence." The physician must never give up hope: "Avoid giving a patient over in an acute disease. It is impossible to tell in such cases where life ends, and where death begins. Hundreds of patients have recovered, who have been pronounced incurable, to the great disgrace of our profession."

The question of fees was as troublesome then as it is today. Although medical education is costly and although the busy physician must make many sacrifices of personal comfort, nevertheless, said Rush, sickness reduces the patient's capacity to earn, and high professional charges drive patients from reputable physicians into the hands of quacks. "Let the number and the time of your visits, the nature of your patient's disease, and his rank in his family or society," Rush pleaded, "determine the figures in your accounts." He claimed it fair to charge more for risking your life in the treatment of a contagious disease than in a trifling non-contagious ailment; and that "you have a right likewise to be paid for your anxiety."

It is the duty of the young graduate, Rush maintained, to try to improve medical science by studying and experimenting continuously. When there is no objection, autopsies should be performed. Careful records should be kept, especially of chronic cases and epidemics. At a time when practically no attention was given to the mental aspect of illness, Rush warned his students that there is a "reciprocal influence of the body and mind on each other." He also suggested that they talk to persons, who have recovered from ailments without the aid of a physician. Nurses and elderly women frequently have valuable suggestions to offer.

There are foul as well as fair means used in making a medical practice productive, as Rush pointed out in the first lecture of the academic year, in November 1807: "On the Means of Acquiring

Business and the Causes Which Prevent the Acquisition, And Occasion the Loss of It, In the Profession of Medicine."[19] Honorable methods of acquiring a practice include the following: Great application to study in order to sharpen the powers of observation, punctuality in visiting patients, politeness, sympathy with the sick, attendance upon the poor, regard to simplicity in dress, "cures performed of difficult diseases," and the publication of a popular and worthwhile book. Of the artificial and accidental means of building up a practice, Rush called to mind the following: Patronage of a great man, a society leader, or an influential family; patronage of a political party; patronage of a religious organization; patronage of an elderly, well-known physician; connections formed while serving in the medical department of an army; popular humanitarian activities; facility in speaking a number of languages; eccentricity of manners and conduct; particular minuteness in inquiring into the symptoms of diseases; "an affectation of a sudden and intuitive knowledge of a patient's case by feeling but a few strokes of his pulse, or by barely inspecting his countenance"; an accidental cure or a chance correct opinion on the nature of a disease; the introduction of a new and pleasant medicine into practice or new and safer methods in surgical operations; and, lastly, an attractive appearance. Rush was speaking for the future as well as for his own day and age.

To the following "dishonourable" methods Rush called attention: Opposing the principles and questioning the character of fellow physicians, traducing new and popular remedies, "performing great and sudden cures by some of those remedies in a disguised form," taking undue advantage of fellow physicians in consultations, publishing reports of mythical cases and of cures that have never been performed, and fixing fees so low as to lure patients from their regular physicians.

The second section of this lecture "On the Means of Acquiring Business . . .," deals with the causes which militate against a physician's success and lead to the loss of his practice. Rush considered the following causes "just": "Ignorance of medicine inferred from an ignorance of other things—a physician of a London hospital lost all his business by misspelling the name of his patient's disease on the board which was placed over his bed," inattention to the history of tedious cases, careless or superficial examination of patients, indelicate conduct and brutal manners, "an unfavourable prognostic of the issue of a disease, especially if it be delivered in an abrupt and unfeeling manner," refusing to answer night calls, deserting old patients in epidemics, trifling medical publications, and high and exorbitant charges.

There are other reasons for the falling off of practice wherein the physician is not necessarily at fault. Some of these are: Failing to recognize a disease immediately, making light of a disease which a patient incorrectly believes serious, prescribing medicine which brings no relief, the lack of engaging manners even if one's medical knowledge is sound, the rise of persons from humble to high positions in society causing them to change physicians, personal illness of a physician or failure to reach him while on vacation, and unpopular religious or political opinions. "I have heard of a physician," said Rush, "who lost the attendance upon two families in this city in consequence of the offensive noise made by his shoes in ascending their stairs, and entering their sick rooms."

In one of his lectures Rush discussed professional etiquette and the cultivation of an engaging bedside manner. It was urged that servants be treated as politely as their masters, that the physician remove his hat on entering a patient's house, and that "if you be conducted by a Lady to your patient upstairs remember always to go before her but come down hindmost." Uneasiness on the patient's part is avoided if the physician gives some sign of his arrival. If there be two physicians, the younger should enter first, and in consultations the consultant should not visit the patient without the attending physician and "he ought by no means to prescribe." The physician is warned not to frighten the patient by proceeding immediately to feel his pulse upon entering the room. "Never wait till a chair be handed you, always make it a rule to sit down on the bed side of your patient," and never discuss topics of the day until an examination has been made—"let your patient ask for news, if he does it is a good sign."

It was further suggested in the "Form on Visiting Patients" that physicians refrain from visiting patients very early or very late or at meal times. "Send your medicines as soon as prescribed. Let your directions be written in a legible hand. Students should not think hard of serving some time as apothecaries to their teachers. Tis as necessary for a student to be an apothecary as for a General to be a soldier. I would not trust a physician who was not so much an apothecary as to know the composition of the medicines he prescribed. . . . No patriotism, pleasure or any duties whatever should detain you from visiting your patients. . . . Let your conversation always inspire hope."[20]

Furthermore, Rush attempted the unusual in formulating a definite code of medical ethics concerned with the relationship of patient to physician thereby sparing the physician embarrassment and the patient an unwitting breach of etiquette. In November 1808, the subject of his introductory lecture at the beginning of the college year was: "On the Duties of Patients to their Physicians."[21] He asked that patients seek medical advice only from trained physicians, giving preference to a physician "whose habits of life are perfectly regular," but that only one physician be consulted, and that he be called even in cases of the most trifling nature. The patient is urged to be faithful in communicating to his physician the history of his ailment without obtruding details of his business or family concerns. He should obey the physician's orders promptly and strictly, should not take medicine unless directed to do so, and should notify the physician of any change in his condition. He should never call a consultant without the consent of the attending physician, and if he wishes to dismiss his physician, he should give reasons for the action. And, not to miss a very obvious detail, Rush noted that "the last duty which a patient owes to his physician is to remunerate him for his services."

* * * * * * *

Rush was, indeed, qualified by broad training and experience, to compile this exhaustive list of do's and don't's for physicians and patients. He was looked up to by many of his contemporaries as the most distinguished physician in America. Dr. John Coakley Lettsom, celebrated British physician, called him the "Sydenham of America," and others referred to him as the "Fothergill of America," "The American Hypocrates," and the "Sydenham of Columbia."

His former students, practising in all parts of the country, recognizing him as the leader of the profession, wrote to him continually, seeking advice on cases.

"He was a physician of no common cast," eulogized Dr. David Ramsay. "His prescriptions were not confined to doses of medicine, but to the regulation of the diet, air, dress, exercise, and mental action of his patients, so as to prevent disease, and to make healthy men and women from invalids. . . . In attendance upon patients, Dr. Rush's manner was so gentle and sympathizing, that pain and distress were less poignant in his presence. On all occasions he exhibited the manners of a gentleman, and his conversation was sprightly, pleasant and instructive."[22] Rev. Manasseh Cutler, agent of the Ohio Company, visited Philadelphia in April 1787, and recorded in his diary: "The Doctor is a complete gentleman, and one of the first literary characters in America." After calling at the Pennsylvania Hospital, where he observed him at work, Cutler noted: "Dr. Rush makes his visits with a great deal of formality. He is attended by the attending Physician, who gives him an account of every thing material since he saw them last, and by the Apothecary of the Hospital, who minutes his prescriptions. In every case worthy of notice, he addresses the young physicians, points out its nature, the probable tendency, and the reason for the mode of treatment which he pursues."[23]

In the course of a letter to Rush, detailing his aches and pains, James Taliaferro of Richmond wrote: "Being under the impression that you are the greatest physician in the United States; and thinking that I have contracted a nervous complaint; excites me to take the liberty of writing you by way of stating my case."[24] Reference to Rush as the "greatest physician" is found again and again. The reputation lasted throughout the century and, in 1888, seventy-five years after his death, Dr. J. H. Musser, himself an eminent physician of his own time, said of Rush that "he exhibited the highest type of a physician" and that in his work and methods one could see "the forerunner of the present plan of treatment of disease . . . by a study into the relations of things, the environment of the patient, and of the multiplex causes, and hence an adaptation of conditions of life to extraneous conditions."[25]

PENNSYLVANIA HOSPITAL

In his extensive practice, probably at its height in the late 1780's and early 1790's, he was assisted for a time by six apprentices. He called on and saw patients in his office from early morning until after sundown, and then retired to read and study. His case records, carefully checked, required considerable time. It must also be noted that physicians, with the assistance of their apprentices, dispensed whatever medicines they prescribed. Most of the drugs used by Rush in his practice were imported by him from London. The strain of a full life at times bore heavily on this "greatest physician." "My business continues to be extensive," he wrote in 1789, "but my health is so precious that I know not how long it will continue so. Severe study in early life, and constant public & private pursuits, since the year 1774, have nearly worn me out."[26]

Rush claimed that his consultations began to decline around 1789 because, at that time, he propagated some of his own medical theories which angered other local physicians. Then, too, most of the physicians in Philadelphia were loyalists and objected to Rush's display of patriotism during and after the War for Independence. Regardless of the antagonism of fellow physicians and the consequent loss of consultation practice, he was bent on simplifying medicine by introducing his own methods and by rejecting many drugs as useless. At this time, 1789, he withdrew from many public activities and rarely dined out or spent an evening away from home or his work. Between 1789 and 1793 his general practice, regardless of obstacles, increased in extent largely among the newcomers in the city. After the epidemic of 1793, and until 1797, it remained stationary, and then declined. "I had no new families except foreigners added to the list of my patients and many of my old patients deserted me," he recalled regretfully.[27]

It is in Rush's private correspondence, in his notebooks, and in the letters and papers of his patients and friends, that we find the busy physician pictured. On April 17, 1795, Elizabeth Drinker jotted down in her diary: "Dr. Rush here—we had some discourse relating to a particular religious tenet, deemed by many erroneous. He promised to lend me a volume on the subject." A week later he was back to inoculate two members of the household.[28]

When the Doctor came downstairs in the morning, he not infrequently found notes left under his door during the night by patients. Here is a typical request: "11 o'clock at night—Will Doctor Rush be so obliging as to call on Thos. O. Irving, tomorrow, at No. 348 South Front, who is laboring, under a paroxism of the gout, sufficient almost to drive him to the horrid act of suicide."[29] Of appreciative letters there were many. "I know not how far I shall act in conformity to established usage," wrote one patient, "when I venture to make an estimate of professional services, rendered me, at different intervals, by you. The many instances of kindness & friendship, for which I am indebted to yourself & family, I can only appreciate, not requite. I often reproach myself with unjustifiable negligence, in having so long delayed to acknowledge my obligations, and I beg you Sir, to consider the enclosed, in the light of an offering of diffidence at the shrine of indulgence."[30]

Rush always listened with interest and respect to any layman's suggestions of treatments and remedies, and he not infrequently jotted them down in the notebook he always carried in his coat pocket. One of these small notebooks, called by him the Quack Recipe Book, now preserved in the Ridgway Branch of the Library Company of Philadelphia, is chock-full of home remedies. Hiccoughs can be cured by taking from six to ten drops of the oil of amber on a piece of sugar. For a sore under the eye, of seven years' standing, one Mrs. Clymer used common salt in spirit applied seven or eight times a day. The preparation, it was suggested, should be carried in a small vial in the pocket. A woman across the Schuylkill recommended an eye salve: "Equal parts of fresh butter, without salt and calamine stone in fine powder mixed intimately together, a small quantity to be rubbed on every night in those cases where the eyelids stick together in the night, or where there is an unusual dryness of the eyes from excessive heat, or riding in the wind." To eliminate warts a Captain McPherson suggested that salt be dissolved in vinegar and the affected parts of the skin washed frequently. Further on we find Rush's own prescription for worms: A dose of jalap with five or six grains of calomel according to the age of the patient—the dose of jalap for an adult is half a drachm, for all children above two years of age, from fifteen to twenty-five grains; below two years of age "it may be a good rule to give nearly the same number of grains of rhubarb, and jalap as the children have lived months." On the next page is his prescription for toothache: "If evulsion cannot be practised take laudanum in doses of thirty drops till the pain is relieved, and apply a blister behind the ear nearest the part effected." A quack in North Carolina had an idea that cancer could be cured by arsenic followed by poultices of roasted onions "to digest away the escar."

From time to time cancer remedies came to Rush's attention. The arsenic-onion cure was one of many. In 1784 occurred the death of one Hugh Martin, a surgeon in one of the Pennsylvania regiments of the Revolutionary War and one of Rush's former students. While practising in Philadelphia after the war, he had advertised that he could cure cancer with a powder he had discovered in the woods in the neighborhood of Fort Pitt. After his death one of the executors of the estate gave Rush some of this powder, which was carefully examined and found to contain some arsenic. Rush believed that arsenic was the most efficacious caustic then used in the treatment of cancer, but warned that it should be used carefully. "Dr. Martin's composition was happily calculated for this purpose," said Rush. "It gave less pain than the common or lunar caustic. It excited a moderate inflammation, which separated the morbid from the sound parts, and promoted a plentiful afflux of humours to the sore during its application. It seldom produced a scar; hence it insinuated itself into the deepest recesses of the cancers, and frequently separated these fibres in an unbroken state which are generally called the roots of the cancer." In an ulcerated cancer Rush preferred this remedy to the knife. He found that Dr. Martin used pure white arsenic mixed in a vegetable powder in the proportion of one to forty. "It remains yet to discover a cure for cancers that taint the fluids or infect the whole lymphatic system," said Rush. "This cure I apprehend must be sought for in diet, or in the long use of some internal medicine."[31] He suggested the possibility of using Dr. Martin's cancer powder, in 1789, in treating George Washington's mother, whose case was called to his attention by his kinsman, Dr. Elisha Hall of Fredericksburg, Virginia. To his inquiries Rush replied: "The respectable age & character of your venerable patient, lead me to regret that it is not in my power to suggest a remedy for the cure of the disorder you have described in her breast. I know nothing of the root you mention is found in Carolina & Georgia, but from a variety of inquiries & experiments, I am disposed to believe that there do not exist in the vegetable kingdom an antidote to cancers. All the supposed vegetable remedies I have heard off, are compounds of some mineral caustics. The arsenic is the most powerful of any of them. It is the basis of Dr. Martin's powder. I have used it in many cases with success, but have failed in some. From your acct. of Mrs. Washington's breast, I am afraid no great good can be expected from the use of it. Perhaps it may cleanse it, and thereby retard it spreading. You may try it, diluted in water. Continue the application of opium & camphor, and wash it frequently with a decoction of seed clover. Give anodynes when necessary, & support the system with bark & wine. Under this treatment she may live comfortably many years, & finally die of old age."[32]

Twenty years later, in 1810, Rush still had faith in arsenic as the basic cancer powder, although he believed most cancer doctors and cancer cures to be fakes. In advising a physician in that year on cancer cures, he expressed his professional attitude concerning the danger of proposing doubtful cures. "Since my settlement in Philadelphia," he wrote, "I have known a great number of cancer doctors, who have for a while succeeded in curing cancerous sores, but who have uniformly depreciated in character and fortune from their various failures or from a return of the sores which are said to have been cured by them. I have observed further that most of the cancer doctors pretend to have obtained their remedies from the Indians of our country and that they consist wholly of vegetables. The improbability of this being the case appears from cancers being unknown among the Indians and from so small a number of vegetables retaining a strongly irritating power when they are dry. I suspect arsenic to be the basis of all the cancer powders which do not destroy sound as well as morbid flesh. . . . Should you succeed in the cure of cancer from the remedy you have mentioned, you would derive but a small profit from your labors, for a majority of the persons inflicted with it are poor people. Should you fail in all or most cases, you would loose [sic] the fair and respectable character

you have gained by your extensive education and honorable graduation in medicine."[33]

Rush carried on an extensive correspondence with physicians who
wrote him for advice, from all parts of the country. Individual
patients also sought counsel by mail, sending the Doctor a statement
of symptoms. This medical mail-order consultation practice became
large and profitable, and fulfilled a definite need in a sparsely populated country.

A clergyman, the Rev. John M. Crery, who had been suffering
for twenty years, finally asked the advice of Dr. Rush. He wrote:
"About twenty years since, I was distressed by a complaint in the
small of the back, which was generally supposed to be the stone or
gravel in the kidney, for which I applied to several physicians in
Philadelphia and was treated with great kindness by the gentlemen
of the healing art. The pain in the region of the kidneys gradually
decreased; but I was affected with frequent chills, coldness in the
feet especially attended with a pain in the small of the back, which
at times would seem to creep up to the shoulders and make me
stomach sick. My common remedy then was, to strip my feet and
warm them well with fire, sometimes bath[e] them in warm water.
Thus I struggled on with tolerable ease, for sixteen or seventeen
years, and exercised a great deal in the business of my office both
summer and winter; perhaps too much. About the beginning of
March last, I was suddenly seized with a pain in the left side, which
gradually increased 'till in the space of three or four hours it became violent, affected the stomach and occasioned a puking, which
immediately removed the pain; but was preceded by a chill and a
fever which continued for some days.

"In September last, the complaint returned, but in the right side,
increased and passed away in the same manner by puking; then in a
month; then in two or three weeks, and so the intervals decreased
until I would have a return of the pain three or four times in a
week and always in the right side, succeeded by a fever . . . which
in the beginning of December last confined me to the house.

"I was directed to use laudanum and apply warm bladders to the
part affected, which, tho' the pain frequently returns, has hitherto

prevented its becoming violent. At present, and during two months past, have had a pain not only in the right, but also in the left side and frequently in the small of the back and at the shoulders. So that I have wearisome nights, having no place to lie upon without pain. All these complaints, are frequently very tolerable, but there is a constant uneasiness; and the least cold excites the pain in my right side. I am almost wholly unable to read or write, or even to think with attention of mind upon any subjects. Reading or writing greatly increaseth the uneasiness in the small of my back. With much difficulty I write this short state of my case."[34]

Unfortunately Rush's reply is not extant.

A relative in Newark sent Rush a summary of his symptoms. The Doctor, diagnosing the case as gout, forwarded the treatment:

1 The tap of 12 ounces of blood, if your pulse be full or tense. if it be not

2 a purge, once a week of 20 grains of jalap & five of calomel. —on the intermediate days, take

3 From 10 to 15 grains of nitre, three times a day in a little sugar & water.

4 Your legs should be rubbed for half an hour every morning (never at night) and upwards only—never downwards.—

5 Wear a tight bandage round your feet & legs made of flannel, under your stockings. lay aside garters.

6 If your pulse be full & tense, live abstemiously, but if it be weak, live generously, & take a little red wine with your meals.

7 Go to bed early, & rise at 7 o'clock every morning.

8 Avoid sitting long, or standing long at a time.

9 Use moderate exercise, especially in walking, but never till you are fatigued. . . .[35]

A gentleman in New York City, who had been bled by his physicians to the extent of ninety ounces without obtaining relief, wrote Rush that he had been "reduced to the most distressing state of debility & weakness." He asked whether or not Rush would recommend a trip to Europe, adding "that my state is direct debility, brought on by loss of blood, and too great a drain by blisters kept open for 8 months." Six weeks later he again wrote: "I am much subject to palpitation at the heart, & a beating of the arteries which seems to strike audably upon my ear, particularly when lying in bed. I one night lately took a drink of porter & water going to bed, & all these affections subsided immediately." He went on to say that he was somewhat afraid of porter because of Rush's averseness to its use, evidently expressed in a previous long-distance consultation.[36]

To a Miss Elizabeth Micklin, complaining of sore throat, Rush suggested a simple remedy:

1 Gargle it two or three times a day with a little weak salt water.
2 Apply to the outside of it a small blister, etc.
3 Take a teaspoonful of the powder of bark every day either early in the morning, or about 11 o'clock in any thing agreable to you.
4 Protect your whole body, and particularly your feet from the cold.
5 Avoid, and prevent costiveness.

Six months later the same patient complained of "giddiness." "To prevent its increasing, and to obviate any bad effects from it," Rush advised, "please to continue to live abstemiously as to the fat of meats, butter, coffee, and strong tea. Take gently opening physic once or twice a week, & lose blood when the disease is unusually distressing. A Burgundy pitch plaster worn between the shoulders, has done good in similar cases. Gentle exercise should not be omitted. Avoid sleeping the same side constantly, and never sleep upon your back. Your shoulders as well as your head should be gently elevated in bed."[37]

In Petersburg, Virginia, John W. Campbell, having suffered from severe headaches for seven years finally wrote to Rush for professional advice:

"Calculating upon your charity, I avail myself of this method of stating to you my case, & desiring, if consistent with the numerous calls on your attention, to give me your counsel upon a matter as important as human life. My distant situation & some other considerations preclude me the extreme satisfaction of seeing & conversing with the learned & reputable physicians of Philadelphia—but I have been too long acquainted with your tenderness of heart & too often heard of your attention to the afflictions of your fellow creatures, to doubt your readiness to give me your advice and direction.

"I have been for about seven years afflicted by a continual headache, which came on gradually & which I believe is caused by a determination of the humours to the head—I am inclined to think so for the following reasons—First—the pain is always worst in the morning, or after being in a horizontal posture—Secondly—the vessels of the head appear distended & discover every mark of a plethora in the brain—thirdly—when the pain is greatest & the head overcharged with blood the extremities become cold & blue by the want of vigor in circulation.

"I have been under the ablest physician in this state without success—I have tried all the mineral waters & cold, warm & hot baths—I have tried electricity—bleeding—emetics &c. . . .

"I have for two years remained hopeless & waited with the fortitude that Christianity inspires for the hour of my dissolution—but after the return of my dear Aunt Carter & her family from Philadelphia I resolved to make you acquainted with my case & trust to your wisdom & benevolence for an answer."[38]

A skin condition worried one David Howell of Providence, Rhode Island, who began to think that he was suffering from cancer. Many remedies brought no relief, and advice from Philadelphia's great physician was at length sought. Having nothing to work on except Howell's description of the scales on his face, Rush suggested a treatment:

"SCALES, such as you have described, on your face, often occur between the ages of 60 and 70. They rarely end in cancers, and never, except when they are neglected, or treated with improper remedies.

"A plaster made of equal parts of tar and bees' wax should be spread on a piece of BLACK SILK OR LEATHER, and worn constantly upon the affected parts. It will do most service when applied immediately after the falling of the scab. If this application does not cure the sores in five or six weeks, apply to them a little white arsenic three or four times at intervals of three or four days, still covering it with the plaster of wax and oil. This remedy is so effectual in removing the disease for which I have presented it, that it will be unnecessary to mention any others.

"Your diet should by no means be abstemious. You may eat eggs, oysters, fish, and a little animal food daily, with safety and advantage. The sores on your face are of a local nature. Your blood is not in the least tainted with any humor connected with them. A little wine may be taken with the above food.

"I shall NOT name a CANCER DOCTOR to you, for YOU ARE IN NO MORE DANGER OF THAT DISEASE FROM YOUR PRESENT TRIFLING & SUPERFICIAL COMPLAINT THAN YOU ARE OF DROPSY, OR PULMONARY CONSUMPTION.

"Dr. Physick concurs with me in the above advice. No internal medicines of any kind are indicated in your case."[39]

Rheumatism was causing Timothy Pickering, once Secretary of State in Washington's administration, no end of pain, and so he detailed the nature of his ailment in letters to Rush. The Doctor, concerned over his friend's condition, suggested a treatment: "If your rheumatism be attended with a full or tense pulse," he wrote, "first lose ten ounces of blood, and the day afterwards, take a smart purge. If your pulse be not preternaturally excited, take the purge only. It may be an ounce of salts or fifteen grains of jalap & ten of calomel. The day after taking the purge, begin and bathe the parts affected with equal parts of sweet oil and the spirit of turpentine every morning and evening. Lessen the proportion of sweet oil gradually, so as finally to bathe the parts only with the turpentine. Should it inflame the skin so as to render its application painful, leave it off for a few days. Take at the same time from ten to twenty drops of the spirit of turpentine (encreasing them gradually) every morning and evening in a little molasses or sugar & water. If you are not relieved by these remedies in a few days, try a plentiful sweat. Bring it on by hot drinks & warm bed clothes. . . ."[40]

Bleeding and purging were advised in the majority of cases.

The correspondence between Rush and other physicians, especially former students, was very heavy. When a young graduate was confronted with a disease he did not recognize, he wrote Rush. When, in a far-off county, a patient asked for another physician's advice, very often a letter was dispatched to the dean of Philadelphia's medicos.

One Dr. Samuel Agnew, a young graduate, practising in Gettysburg, Pennsylvania, in 1803, wrote his former master frequently, admitting that because of his youth and narrow practice, the patients requested that Rush be consulted. In very serious cases Agnew asked Rush to consult Dr. Physick also, another famous Philadelphia physician of the period. After discussing the symptoms of one of his patients in a lengthy letter to Rush on April 14, 1803, and asking for an opinion, Agnew went on: "I am happy in making this request to you, as I shall be a participator in the satisfactory result. As his [the patient's] situation is peculiarly strange and dangerous, as well as his mind uneasy & anxious, I hope you will gratify the sufferer & myself, by transmitting with your own opinion, that of some experienced & celebrated surgeon, as Doctr. Physick, advising of the nature of the disease, the most suitable & efficacious remedies, & the probable issue of the same."[41]

Dr. Archibald Alexander, of Charlotte Court House, Virginia, wrote Rush for advice in connection with a case of "a very violent uterine hemorrhage." Dr. Ashton Alexander, of Baltimore, sent him a patient who had been suffering from gout for many years. Dr. Stephen Alexander, of Harford County, Maryland, requested instructions for treating hydrophobia, and Dr. J. Alexander, of Camden, South Carolina, sent a patient suffering from "mental derangement." Two years after his graduation from Rush's course, Dr. Edward Gantt, practising in far-off Maryville, Tennessee, sought advice from his "father in medicine" for several of his patients. Dr. Samuel Garland, whose office was just a half mile from Rush's in Philadelphia, sent him a note requesting assistance in "a case of inflammatory intermitting fever of fourteen months standing that has baffled every method of cure." To Rush, Dr. John Gibbons, of Laurel, Delaware, turned "for salutary advice" on a patient suffering from inflammatory rheumatism.[42]

Naturally information of a very personal and confidential nature was unfolded in some of the letters which Rush received. Former students, especially, laid before him their domestic problems and financial difficulties. Some correspondents discussed their love affairs in tearful letters such as this: "I am now in a most dreadfull dilemma, will you be so favourable as to give me your ingenious observations on the passion of love, it will tend to extricate me from the dreadfull situation—To love & be disappointed most unhappy dreadfull state! advise how to forget a lady whom for years (think it not recent for it has subsisted four years) I had the most ardent passion, & enjoyed every promise & privilege, save only I can say we were not united.—Teach me the noble science to forget? Teach me how to conduct myself when frequently in her company, she appearing to triumph at my mortification."[43]

Rush's name was given as reference by hundreds of his students and he was constantly writing letters of recommendation. "Dr. George Cheyne Shattuck," reads one of these notes, "attended all the medical lectures given in the University of Pennsylvania in the year 1807 with diligence & punctuality, and afterwards graduated with honor to himself, and to the entire satisfaction of the Professors of the University. I believe him to be amply qualified for any medical situation in which talents, knowledge and industry are required."[44]

As one of the senior physicians on the staff of the Pennsylvania Hospital, from 1783 to 1813, Rush was actively interested in efforts to provide hospital care for the deserving poor. The number of ward patients admitted was, of course, limited. Many physicians appealed to Rush to intercede for persons who needed hospital care and might not otherwise be admitted to the Pennsylvania Hospital. Admission blanks, with Rush's approval written thereon, still exist, and in Independence Hall can be seen one of these Pennsylvania Hospital forms, signed by Rush, stating that one Samuel Purviance is afflicted with "madness," and that a David Conyngham has agreed to provide clothing for the patient and to pay six dollars weekly for board.

It seems that it was the Hospital's custom to require in advance from every free patient a deposit for possible interment, in case of death. This custom is mentioned in the following letter from Rush to a clergyman seeking the admission of a poor patient: "As it is not my time of attendance in the hospital, I cannot tell whether there is a vacancy for a poor patient in it. Tomorrow is the public admission day. Please to send your poor neighbour to the hospital about 11 o'clock, or a little before that hour. I will attend there, & plead his cause (with your note in my hand) with the managers. If he should be admitted without pay, it will only be necessary for a friend to give an obligation for five dollars to defray the expenses of his interment in case of his death. From the report of one of my pupils of the hospital being less filled than usual with patients, I think it highly probable there will be little or no difficulty in getting your neighbour admitted."[45]

After close association with the work of the Pennsylvania Hospital for twenty years, Rush took as the subject of his introductory lecture at the opening of the academic year, in November, 1802, "Construction and Management of Hospitals."[46] There were only a handful of hospitals in the United States at that time and many physicians had no contact at all with them.

A hospital, Rush told the students, should be located at some distance from the city so as to get the benefit of pure air and of a current of winds from every quarter. It must, however, be in the vicinity of a good water supply, but should be kept away from factories. The front of the building should enjoy a southern exposure, and the ceilings should be not less than fifteen feet in height. A hospital should have large wards and a few private rooms, and also dark rooms for eye patients. Each ward should be designed definitely to meet the needs of particular diseases. Those for the use of patients suffering from pulmonary tuberculosis should be warmed in winter by means of stoves so regulated "as to cause the heat to resemble the temperature of those climates which are most favourable to the diseases of the breast." Earthen floors were suggested for the "fever" wards.

As for windows, Rush believed that hospitals should have large ones but not too many, and that shutters should be attached to them, to regulate the intensity of daylight in the rooms. As to ventilation Rush was certainly ahead of his times: "In every ward there should be a ventilator communicating with the external air to carry off the foul air in cool and cold weather."

Every hospital should provide space for an apothecary's supply shop, an amphitheatre for surgical operations, a gymnasium, a museum, a kitchen, a laundry, a morgue, a sun porch for convalescents, a small library for the patients, and special rooms for members of the staff; many of these ideas have been realized. Furthermore, the insane should be separated entirely from the other patients—a bold proposal for the year 1802.

Stray bills that have been unearthed, covering a period of over thirty-five years, since they fail to indicate the number of visits, give only a general idea of Rush's charges. From what evidence there is, the assumption may be made that his fees, including charges for drugs, were ample. Then too he was at the top of his profession, in a position to set his own price if he cared to. On the other hand it must be borne in mind that Rush treated hundreds of poor patients absolutely free.

One bill, dated November 15, 1776, to a Mr. Shaw for services and medicines for his child in August 1775, notes a charge of £2 2s. In January 1776, fifteen shillings was charged for attention to Mrs. Shaw and four months later £5 was listed "to inoculating his two children for the smallpox." Observe that the bill was for services rendered fifteen months previously, and that the cost of inoculation was high. In 1782 Lambert Wilmer paid Rush £6 for inoculating his two children. Oliver Pollock, a wealthy merchant, was charged £15 "To advice to himself in his own case, and to medical attendance to his negro man in October and in October and March 1783—also to medicine for child in Feb 1782."

Clergymen, it seems, were as a rule treated gratis by Rush. Rev. John Coleman's letter of May 6, 1782, is self-explanatory: "I must beg leave to thank you for your benevolence. It seems your affection for the preachers of the Gospel will not suffer you to receive any pecuniary satisfaction for your services—may Heaven reward your kindness & generosity! I esteem, and hope to remember you as one of my benefactors—Your letter was so kind, and full of so good wishes, that I cannot leave the city contented without expressing my fervent desire for your health, spiritual and temporal."

Rush evidently did not present his bills at fixed times. In 1795, for instance, we find him sending a bill of £8 10s. to Maria Benezet, covering the years 1790–1791–1793–1794. At the same time he forwarded a bill of £58 5s. to Rev. Dr. Blackwell covering attention to his family and servants during the three-year period 1792–

1795. Occasionally a patient did not care to wait months and months for a bill. Such a one was Henry Clymer, who wrote the Doctor in December 1795: "The enclosed is a check on the Bank of the United States for one hundred dollars which I beg your acceptance of as a small consideration for the important services rendered me during the last autumn."

After the attacks made on Rush by fellow physicians during the epidemics of 1793–1797 his income along with his practice decreased materially, and it was necessary for him to become more insistent that his bills be paid when submitted. One John Lawlis paid £4 10s. for professional services during March and February 1797. Apparently, however, many of the mail-consultation patients in distant communities were not strictly conscientious about their indebtedness. Postage being collected on delivery, Rush found himself not only giving advice to these patients but also paying the postage on their requests. In 1798 he decided on a cash payment plan for professional attention by mail. He explained to one correspondent in that year: "So much of my time has lately been taken up in answering letters for advice for which I have received no compensation, and for which I am obliged to pay the postage, that I have been compelled to resolve to reply to no letter for advice which is not accompanied with a fee, unless it comes from persons who acknowledge themselves to be poor. You will not I hope complain of this conduct when I add that my business in Philadelphia has been nearly ruined by the public and private persecution to which my principles & practice in medicine have exposed me—that I have a large family and that I do not think it just to work for nothing for those who are able to pay for my services." In 1801, in replying to an inquiry for medical advice, Rush said that his regular charge for such letters was ten dollars.

The estate of George Roberts paid Rush £17 15s. for services during the four years 1798–1801. At the close of the year 1804 the Doctor was delighted to receive £52 12s. from George Willing for services to the Willing family during 1802, 1803, and 1804, including "visits in the night in consultation with Dr. Physick" and for vaccinating the son and daughter. The charge for each vaccination was £3.

In 1808 Dr. Ashton Alexander wrote Rush for an opinion, the charge for which was ten dollars. In December of the same year he received the large sum of £85 from the estate of John Beekley covering his services to the Beekley family. Realizing the unfairness of expecting free medical advice by letter, Joseph Coppinger wrote Rush from Baltimore in July 1809: "I perfectly agree with you in the propriety as well as prudence of your determination in withholding your opinion on any written case until you had first been paid your fee."

James S. Guignard, a gentleman in Columbia, South Carolina, had a relative in the insane department of the Pennsylvania Hospital and in 1810–1811–1812 he sent Rush three fifty-dollar notes covering three years' attendance to his kinsman. It was customary in sending money through the mail to cut each note in half, each piece being sent by separate post, since one half of the bill was worthless without the other. Guignard remitted his fee in this manner as bank bills were frequently stolen, or lost in the mail.

It is safe to assume that the meticulous Rush kept careful records of his accounts, although they have not been uncovered. It is not possible, therefore, to arrive at an estimate of his annual income. Certain it is, however, that it was far above that of the average physician. Because of the paucity of records, comparative costs are also difficult to calculate. In his study of *Medicine in Virginia in the Eighteenth Century* Wyndham B. Blanton illustrates the cost of living by citing a few prices. We are told that a horse cost only from £2 to £3, while a feather bed cost from £1 to £3. A coat and waistcoat cost £2. Preachers and physicians frequently received tobacco in payment of their services. Dr. John Bowman presented a bill of 120 pounds of tobacco to one patient, and Dr. Johue Fry received 2,000 pounds of tobacco for salivating a negro. His usual charge was 10 shillings for a single visit. Dr. William Cabell received from £1 to £5 a visit, depending on the distance, and £7 10s. for amputating an arm or leg. A traveler in Virginia reported: "I have heard physicians declare that they do not annually receive one third of what is due to them for their attendance; that they have some of these debts of five and twenty years' standing; that their claims are frequently denied, and that in order to recover payment they are obliged to send, write, carry on lawsuits, etc." Rush's percentage of collections was probably higher than that of physicians in the country.

Material reward was not Rush's sole concern. Fundamentally an idealist, he was interested in serving his fellow men, especially the poor. The Philadelphia Dispensary for the poor, the first free dispensary in America, was organized after Rush had carried on a campaign in which he pointed out the dire need for such an institution in a city. At length he prevailed upon a blind scientist, Dr. Moyes, to give a public lecture, the proceeds to start a fund for the dispensary. The lecture not only provided some money for organization, but also stimulated public interest in the proposal and immediately brought in private contributions. Early in 1786 Rush went ahead with the plans. A room was fitted out on Strawberry Alley, on the east side of Fifth Street below Chestnut, and was opened to the public on April 12. The opening of this first free dispensary was announced in the *Pennsylvania Packet* on that day: "The Philadelphia Dispensary for the medical relief of the poor will be opened this day, at twelve o'clock in Strawberry Alley—Two of the physicians will attend at the Dispensary, on Mondays, Wednesdays, and Fridays, from twelve till one o'clock, to receive applications from the sick. Those who are prevented by the nature of their diseases, from attending at the above hour, are desired to leave their names and places of abode (after being properly recommended by a contributor) with the apothecary of the dispensary, at any time, and they will attend at their own houses." This example of a gracious, charitable spirit on the part of Rush and his colleagues was followed later in other cities.

As one of the consulting physicians, Rush contributed his services to the institution for many years. During the first eight months of its operation, from April 12 to December 12, 1786, 719 patients were treated without charge. During its first five years, 7613 patients received attention. During the twelve-month period, December 1, 1789 to December 1, 1790, the number of patients admitted to treatment totaled 1796, and of these 1578 were cured, 63 died, and the remainder were either somewhat relieved or sent to the hospital.[47]

Although Rush's private practice was necessarily reduced by one-fourth, according to his estimate, through the activities of the Dispensary, he viewed the success of this pet project with delight. Indeed, so unselfish was he that he wished to expand the scope of its work. He opposed the organization of a maternity hospital because he believed that the Dispensary could adequately care for obstetrical cases. "I do not think we are as yet ripe eno' in vice or poverty for a lying in hospital in any part of this country," he wrote Rev. Jeremy Belknap. "An attempt was made to establish one in this city last year, but without success. Our Dispensary supplies the necessity of such an institution at a 10th part of the expense that would attend it, and in a manner more consistent with the female delicacy and the secrecy that is injoined by the gospel in the acts of charity."[48]

Another institution of which Rush was one of the founders is the College of Physicians in Philadelphia. He realized the need for a society where physicians could exchange views; and for several years before the College of Physicians was actually established he was casting about for ideas for such a group. Nothing could be done, however, during the war. On November 15, 1783, Rush wrote Dr. Lettsom in London: "I approve of your plan for instituting a Medical Society in Philadelphia, and am not without hopes of seeing it carried into execution, as soon as the minds of our literati are more perfectly detached from the political subjects that have swallowed up all the ingenuity and industry of our country."[49] According to the first city directory, printed in 1785, there were in Philadelphia forty-five physicians and surgeons from whom the society could draw its membership.

It was not until September 1786 that a few of the leading physicians got together and gave serious consideration to the subject of a medical society. Rush was one of these founders, and his name appears in the list of twelve senior fellows, published in the *Pennsylvania Packet*, February 1, 1787, a month after the actual organization of the College of Physicians, of which Dr. John Redman was the first president. Meetings of the College were held in the rooms of the University on Fourth Street below Arch on the first Tuesday of the month at four o'clock in the afternoon from October until March, and at five o'clock from April until September. Twenty-nine physicians were admitted to membership during the first year. The entrance fee was three pounds, Pennsylvania currency—equal to $8.00; and the annual dues were fixed at 15s.—equal to $2.00. Rush was elected one of the four censors, or directors.

At one of the first meetings of the College, February 6, 1787, Rush read a paper "On the Means of Promoting Medical Knowledge," in which he set forth the purpose of the new institution and indicated that it was the intention of the founders to organize a medical library in order "to diffuse knowledge among us on easy terms." In June 1788 a committee was appointed to draw up plans for a library, and it was resolved that "the several members of the college be requested to send to the secretary such books as they mean to present to the college." The first contributions to the library were made by Dr. John Morgan. Rush was one of the early contributors. Today the library of the College is second only to the medical library of the Surgeon-General in Washington.

Although he was one of the founders and a very active member of the College during the first six years of its existence, he resigned on November 5, 1793, angered by the manner in which several prominent members of the College had opposed the methods used by him in combating the yellow fever epidemic in the fall of that year. Accompanying his letter of resignation he sent with his compliments a copy of Wallis' edition of the *Works of Dr. Sydenham.* "I intended, by present of Dr. Sydenham's works," he explained, "to convey to the College a defence of the principles which had regulated my practice in the yellow fever, and a rebuke of the ignorance of many of the members of the College of the most common laws of epidemics, which are recorded in almost every page of that author."[50] This was his answer to what he felt was the abuse and persecution he had suffered at the hands of the College during the epidemic. A few years later, when the Philadelphia Medical Society was organized, with a meeting hall at the southwest corner of Fifth Street and Arch, Rush served as president for many years. The controversy with the College in 1793, however, in no way mars the honor attached to his name as one of the founders of this internationally famous institution.

In spite of the unhappiness and chagrin Rush suffered throughout the controversy over his treatment of yellow fever, he derived, during those same years, deep satisfaction in watching the growth of his pet institutions, the Dispensary, first free clinic in America, and the Philadelphia College of Physicians. He was gratified, too, at the progress of worthy causes he espoused, such as penal reform and antislavery. In 1803, after more than thirty years of practice, he could speak to his students with authority "On the Pains and Pleasures of A Medical Life."[51]

The "pains" he divided into three sections: vexation, distress, and solicitude. Vexation was the result of the ignorance of mankind in general and of the nature of medicine itself, which leads to credulity and superstition, and the resort to quacks. It is disheartening to a physician to hear about or to see people who rely on spells and charms to cure disease. A piece of stolen butcher's meat, for example, rubbed upon warts, and afterwards buried in the earth, had long been a popular remedy. A physician is often vexed by seeing mediocre medical men, who have by some chance or fortune won popular favor, build up an enviable practice. He is vexed by attacks made on him in his attempts to introduce new cures; by the intolerant attitude of people who disagree with his ideas; by public ingratitude; and by the failure of attendants and nurses properly to carry out his orders. He feels distressed occasionally because his contact with people is confined largely to the times in which they are unhappy by reason of their ailments; and at other times because his remedies fail to effect a cure. A physician's solicitude "includes all those painful feelings which are excited by doubts of the nature of our patient's diseases," by the anxious inquiries of the friends of the sick, and by the physician's constant fear that he is not doing enough for the patient.

But there are "pleasures," also, both intellectual and moral, in the medical life. The wonders of nature are unfolded before the inquisitive mind of the physician while examining the various organs of the body. The study of chemistry, by disclosing the fascinating effects of the elements on one another, is a continuous source of pleasure. So too is "the study of the laws of animal economy in health, of their derangements in diseases, and of the cure of those diseases." The physician who discovers a new medical truth is infinitely happy. There are, too, said Rush, moral pleasures such as the gratification that comes in relieving sufferers of pain, the possible confidence and respect of patients and even of whole communities.

On the whole, Rush concluded, "by discharging all the duties to our profession and to our patients, which have been enumerated, with integrity and diligence, the sum of our pleasures will far exceed our pains, in the course of our lives."

His own life as a physician had been for the most part a successful one, not merely by reason of the profitable practice which he built up, but also because of the unselfish service which he rendered his fellow men, of the great adventure involved in advancing new medical theories, and of the respect of foe as well as friend, which a courageous life brought him. In his prime, between forty and fifty years of age, he was undoubtedly the foremost physician in America. As he grew older he felt keenly the competition in the profession as the number of physicians rapidly increased. When, in 1812, a young physician asked for advice as to where to settle, Rush replied: "The facility with which a medical education is acquired in our country has multiplied physicians to such a degree, that I do not know of a spot in the United States in which you could fix yourself with more advantage to yourself than in the one you now occupy. Competition and slow pay are now the conditions of a medical life everywhere. My advice to you is to remain where you are. You will grow with the growth of the settlement. Purchase if possible, and upon credit, a small farm. A little debt will make you industrious and furnish you with an excuse to send in your bills as soon as your patients recover. Employ the leisure which a healthy season will give you, in agricultural labor; the more you obtain in this way, the more independent you will be of your patients, and of course the more you will be courted by them."[52]

The American physician of the next generation was one of a crop of young men, for the most part, trained in formal medical schools in this country, according to a prescribed course. When Rush embarked on his career, most of the physicians in the towns throughout the colonies were trained either as apprentices in a physician's office or in the British universities. Formal education was fast supplanting the older system of medical apprenticeship, and Rush himself was the most distinguished teacher in America, having taught more than

3,000 medical students in forty years. This record was not surpassed by any professor in any medical school in this country at that period, 1770–1813. Furthermore, he exerted a profound influence on the students who came in contact with him, and his medical theories must, consequently, have been adopted by many of them. His own extraordinary zest for learning, his unusual capacity for work, and his personal magnetism pervaded the classroom, ultimately to influence the professional lives of many of his students.

Rush's theories and methods were discussed and adopted by physicians throughout the country, and his professional advice was sought by patients and physicians in every state in the Union. His reputation was nation-wide, while across the seas he was known as the "Sydenham of America," a significant title. To his own patients he was a humane, courteous, careful, honest, and charitable physician.

VIII

The Yellow Fever Epidemic

1793

Busy and lively the city always had been, but in 1790, as the capital, it took on added color in spite of Quaker influence and closed Sundays. Newspaper advertisements of the day attest to the flourishing trade of the town and the varied occupations and amusements of the people. Slaves were still being bought and sold; small shops were expanding into stores which carried a general line of merchandise that might stock a small department store of today. In Water Street, below Market, Vanuxem and Lombaert sold everything from chintz to chalk, from pins by the pound to "elegant marble chimney pieces." Many of the trinkets and jewels worn by the ladies at the Presidential levees were purchased from the shop of one Joseph Anthony. He called attention to new and original patterns he could offer in buckles, earrings, chains, and snuff boxes. He sold steel or gilt knee, hat, and shoe buckles, inlaid mahogany knife cases and snuff boxes which were a part of every well-dressed gentleman's wardrobe.

From the shelves of the bookstore of one Enoch Pratt on Second Street near Arch one could have formed a general estimate of the literary taste of the day. For a shilling there was offered: "Patrick in Prussia, or Love in a Camp: A Comic Opera (Being the Second Part to the Poor Soldier), also, the Poor Soldier." Encyclopedias, geographies, dictionaries, histories, Bible commentaries and sermons found their way to the book auctions held from time to time. Among the most useful of books was the handy letter-writer, published in the city by one William Spotswood, *The New Complete American Letter Writer, or the Art of Correspondence: Containing Letters on the most important subjects, viz.: business, friendship, love and marriage, courtship, politeness, economy, affectation, amusement, duty, advice, religion, &c.* Theatre-goers rejoiced at the opening of the New Theatre on Chestnut Street west of Sixth, in February 1793, with a seating capacity of two thousand. Here one could see such famous English actors as James Fennell in *King Lear*, John Bernard in *The School for Scandal*, and Mrs. Merry in *Othello*.

Medical quacks still flourished throughout the city, luring patients from the legitimate practitioner, with promises of quick, easy, and miraculous cures for every ailment. Countless persons received their medical advice only through the mails, slow and uncertain as they were, meager and inexact as the instructions must have been. At the corner of Pewter Platter Alley in Front Street near Market one Dr. Amos Gregg hung out his shingle and opened his apothecary shop. From London he received his shipments of opium, red and common Jesuits' bark, cream of tartar, jalap, ipecacuanha, camphor, rhubarb, manna, as well as the patent medicines then in use. Not only did he solicit the drug trade of medical practitioners, captains of vessels, and the citizenry of the town, but he also offered, in the capacity of physician, to accompany the drugs with "suitable directions if desired."[1] The out-and-out charlatans still specialized in the treatment of painful and incurable ailments, winning over to their quackery patients whom Rush and other recognized physicians with the limited information of that day were unable to aid.

Although Rush had withdrawn from active participation in politics soon after the adoption of the Federal Constitution, he was none the less interested in the proceedings of the Congress. Furthermore, he was able to keep up the contacts he enjoyed so much with the leaders in the government. Rush's social life, however, had never been extensive; thus he hardly cared to enter into the gay whirl of the capital. Among his intimate friends were the Drinker family, who often entertained the Doctor at their home in Front Street below Race. Elizabeth Drinker recorded many of these visits in her journal.[2] At this time Rush was tremendously busy. He was occupied with his large private practice, medical lectures at the University of Pennsylvania, clinics at the Pennsylvania Hospital and Philadelphia Dispensary, and his own writing.

Pressure of work and weak lungs, an unhappy combination, sapped his strength. In February 1791 he suffered from an old weakness in his chest and was unable, even had he been so inclined, to enjoy any of the festivities during the session of Congress. At the beginning of March he had barely enough strength to attend his patients.[3] A month later, when the birds were coming back and the maples and chestnuts along the streets were budding, he felt more cheerful. "My breast is much mended," he wrote Jeremy Belknap, "I thank you for your prescription of a ride to the pines of New Hampshire, but I thank God such an excursion will not now be necessary. I consider long journies to new or distant countries as nearly the only radical cure for pulmonic complaints."[4] The medical profession was not yet aware that for such condition high country is more important than a new or distant one.

The following spring, 1792, Rush was happy, healthy, and hard at work. In March the lower branch of the Pennsylvania Legislature passed a bill appropriating $15,000 for the erection of a separate building for the insane at the Pennsylvania Hospital. Early in 1791 Rush had addressed an appeal to the newspapers for this building. He was pleased when the Legislature took steps in the same session to establish free schools, which he had strongly advocated in the 1780's. Rush's satisfaction in these triumphs was marred, however, by the failure of Governor Thomas Mifflin to renew his appointment as one of the port physicians. The post had been worth about twenty pounds annually to him for the past ten years. His failure to retain the office caused him to speculate that one should not trust to the gratitude of one's country for services to it.

Turning to the commonplace book in which Rush recorded notes on what he did, where he went, and what he thought, one finds that one day in the spring of 1792, accompanied by his wife and children he went to see a fierce two-year-old lion on exhibition in Race Street. "His keeper told me that he ate twelve pounds of flesh and drank three quarts of water every day, that he endured the cold of the last winter perfectly well; that he would play with a puppy but would always tear a dog to pieces."[5]

The same commonplace book was also the vehicle for stray bits of sermonizing during these years when he became sharply critical of men and their manners. One finds, for instance, a memorandum written in July 1792, asserting that the term "gentleman" was being grossly abused. "A man who has been bred a gentleman cannot work, dig he cannot and he will not ask for charity, for to beg he is ashamed, and therefore he lives by borrowing without intending to pay, or upon the public or his friends. A gentleman cannot wait upon himself and therefore his hands and his legs are often as useless to him as if they were paralytic. If a merchant be a gentleman he would sooner lose fifty customers than be seen to carry a piece of goods across a street. If a doctor should chance to be a gentleman he would rather let a patient die than assist in giving him a glyster or in bleeding him; if a parson he loses all his zeal; if a tradesman should happen to be a gentleman he is undone forever,—by entertaining company, by a country-seat, or by wishing to secure the good-will and society of gentlemen by trusting them. In a word, to be a gentleman subjects one to the necessity of resenting injuries, fighting duels, and the like, and takes away all disgrace in swearing, getting drunk, running in debt, getting bastards, etc., it makes nothing infamous but giving or taking the lie, for however much gentlemen pretend to be men of their word they are the greatest liars in the world, they lie to their creditors, to their mistresses, to their fathers, or wives, or to the public.

"The Indian savages oblige their women only to work; among civilized nations the women obliged the men only to work, the men among the former and the women among the latter consider the opposite sex made only to administer to their comfort without any coöperation on their part; both are wrong, men and women were made to work together in different ways."[6]

It is well that the Doctor took time to record his thoughts in the summer of 1792, for in August of the next year Philadelphia was virtually crippled by a violent yellow fever epidemic and there was no time to indulge in philosophic contemplation.

The city had experienced similar epidemics several times in its history. When William Penn sailed up to the city the first week in December 1699, on his second visit, the citizens gladly welcomed an occasion for celebration because the yellow fever, which had been playing havoc with young and old during the fall, was finally disappearing. Again, in 1741, the fever raged from June to September.

When the fever broke out in the city in 1762, young Benjamin Rush was a medical apprentice in Dr. Redman's "shop." The fever, first observed during August of an unusually hot summer, lasted until December. At the height of the epidemic upwards of twenty persons died daily. According to the notes taken by Rush at the time, "The patients were generally seized with rigors, which were succeeded with a violent fever, and pains in the head and back. The pulse was full, and sometimes irregular. The eyes were inflamed, and had a yellowish cast, and a vomiting almost always attended. . . . An excessive heat, and burning about the region of the liver, with cold extremities, portended death to be at hand."[7]

Rush, now a practising physician, again experienced a yellow fever epidemic in the summer and fall of 1780. In mid-August, bad news from the battle-front as well as the horror of disease within the city caused Philadelphians intense worry and strain. General Washington had sent General Gates with a few regiments to assist the militias of Virginia and the Carolinas in blocking the advance of the British under Cornwallis through the South. Gates, however, was unsuccessful at Camden, South Carolina, and the halls of Congress in Philadelphia were anything but cheerful at the news. Then the epidemic struck, first along the Delaware River front, spreading to all parts of the city. Young and old were stricken. A sore throat was the commonest symptom, although many patients first became faint and dizzy. Severe pains in the head, back, and limbs were general. On the first suspicion of the fever, Rush prescribed tartar emetic. If it continued beyond the third or fourth day without breaking, he resorted to blisters: "Those which were applied to the neck, and behind the ears, produced the most immediate good effects." Opium was also prescribed "judiciously."[8] Fortunately, the epidemic of 1780 did not reach the gigantic proportions of the outbreak that was to paralyze the city thirteen years later.

During the 1780's it was gossiped abroad that Pennsylvania had grown "more sickly" and that fevers were appearing in high as well as in low places. If this was the true state of affairs, Rush wondered why it was so. First of all, he said, the erection of dams for mill ponds leads to an increase of intermittent fevers. Second, when forests are cut down, the way is open for the "propagation of marsh effluvia"; to be healthful, lands should be drained and cultivated. Thirdly, when the spring floods recede, an extensive area of moist ground is exposed to the sun, resulting in the "generation and exhalation of febrile miasmata." All this could be prevented if trees were planted around mill ponds as close as possible in order to shelter the ponds from the action of the sun. Rush further advised that cultivation keep pace with the clearing of forests; that areas from which trees had been cut be drained and planted.

He also gave general directions as to how to root out intermitting fevers. He suggested that fire (smoke or heat) destroys the effects of marsh miasmata upon the human body and it is for this very reason that cities are healthier than the country! This was long before the days of smoking chimneys atop industrial plants.[9]

Rush was obliged to put to use all his previous experience and to test out his views on the subject of yellow and other fevers when, in the late summer and autumn of 1793, he was called upon to lead the fight against the worst epidemic in the history of the city. In January and February of that year he attended an unusual number of patients suffering from mumps. Then, too, there appeared many cases of catarrh and scarlatina. The latter was especially prevalent in April, May, and June, but otherwise the city was healthy. Noah Webster, omniscient lexicographer that he was, calls influenza, scarlatina, and mild bilious remittents "the most certain and immediate precursors of pestilence in this country; and the influenza seems to be so, in all countries."[10]

In early July the weather was warm, as usual. Cases of scarlatina, severe ones, appeared during the early part of the month. After the third week of July the weather became hot and a few bilious remitting fevers appeared. The weather during the first two or three weeks in August, however, was surprisingly temperate. Nevertheless, cholera morbus and remitting fevers were now common.

Immediately after the arrival in the city of a boatload of distressed refugees from St. Domingo, influenza appeared, and spread rapidly throughout the city; scarlatina was still prevalent among children. Although these diseases had become widespread, few deaths occurred. Then came the August drought. Even the duck ponds in the center of the city became dry. There were ponds in the rear of Christ Church on Second Street, at Eighth and Arch Streets, at Fifth and Locust Streets, and at Fifth and Market Streets, the favorite pond for skaters in winter.

Doctor Rush made his rounds as usual from one end of the city to the other, his horse and buggy kicking up dust along all the streets and alleys. Since 1791 he had been living at 83 Walnut Street, the first house adjoining the northwest corner of Third Street. The versatile Judge Richard Peters was Rush's nearest neighbor.

It was on the fifth day of August that Rush learned that the child of a Dr. Hodge was ill with a bilious fever; shortly her skin turned yellow, and on August 7 she died. Twenty-four hours earlier Rush had sent a patient, Mrs. Thomas Bradford, to bed with the symptoms of a bilious remittent fever; ordering two bleedings, then a dose of calomel. She recovered. On the same day a young man named M'Nair was suddenly seized with pains, and manifested all the symptoms of a bilious fever. Although he was bled and purged, he died a week later. On August 14 a Mrs. Thomas Leaming developed yellow fever symptoms. She was bled and purged with calomel and, although she recovered, she was yellow for many days. Early in the morning of August 18 Dr. Rush hurried up to Vine Street where one Peter Aston was suffering from an acute bilious fever, and for a few days, until his death, his face was of a yellowish color.[11] These cases, though markedly similar, made no special impression on the Doctor; they were merely cases treated along with the others in the course of his day's work.

On August 19 Rush walked to Water Street above Arch to examine one Mrs. Peter LeMaigre in consultation with Drs. Foulke and Hodge. He found her in the last stage of a severe bilious fever. She vomited constantly and complained of great heat and burning in the stomach. She died on August 20.

As he was leaving Mrs. LeMaigre's room something clicked in his mind. Rush remarked to the attending physicians that he had seen an unusual number of bilious fevers, all accompanied with symptoms of uncommon malignity. He immediately grew suspicious that the state of the city's health was not normal. Dr. Hodge volunteered the information that several persons in the vicinity of the LeMaigre residence, a hundred yards from the docks, had succumbed to a malignant fever.

This hint was enough for Rush. Dr. Foulke had also told him about a quantity of damaged coffee which had been dumped on

Ball's wharf and on the adjoining dock, on July 24, nearly directly east of the LeMaigre house. This coffee had putrefied to the great annoyance of the entire neighborhood. Was this the source of the fever? Rush believed so and in his own mind traced cases which he had treated earlier in the month to this source. Dr. Hodge lived just a few doors north of the LeMaigre's; Mrs. Bradford had spent an afternoon close to the wharf; and Mrs. Leaming, her sister, had visited her. Furthermore, young M'Nair had spent several days in a shipping office near the wharf where the coffee was exposed, and he had said that the offensive smell made him ill.

Then and there Rush decided that the bilious remitting yellow fever, which he considered highly contagious and which he had seen as an apprentice in 1762, was definitely spreading along the river front. Most of the physicians, however, denied the existence of the fever in the city, and Rush's conclusions were treated with ridicule or contempt by his fellow physicians and citizens.

He was ready for trouble. The day after Mrs. LeMaigre died, he wrote his wife at Princeton: "As yet it [yellow fever] has not spread thro' any parts of the city which are beyond the reach of the putrid exhalation which first produced it. If it should, I shall give you notice, that you may remain where you are till you receive further advice and information from me. The influenza continues to spread, and with more violent symptoms than when it made its first appearance. I did more business in 1780 than I do at present, but with much less anxiety, for few of the diseases of that year were attended with any danger, whereas now, most of the cases I attend are acute and alarming, and require an uncommon degree of vigilance and attention." When he wrote her again four days later, August 25, the situation had already taken a serious turn. "The fever has assumed a most alarming appearance," he reported. "It not only mocks in most instances the power of medicine, but it has spread thro' several parts of the city remote from the spot where it originated." In one house on Water Street he had lost two patients the night before, a merchant and his only child. "His wife is frantic this evening with grief. Five other persons died in the neighborhood yesterday afternoon and four more last night at Kensington." On August 27 he wrote that "the disease spreads, and a most alarming apathy as to exertion prevails among our citizens," and on the 29th: "The disease has raged with great virulence this day."[12]

Rush's conclusions were bruited throughout the city with amazing rapidity and, although official and public opinion were not in agreement, everyone begged for immediate action. The *American Daily Advertiser* called upon every citizen "to contribute all in his power to prevent the spreading of disorders." The editorial even suggested that "the Fire Companies would render essential service upon this occasion if they would cause their engines to be exercised daily, until rain shall fall, in wetting the streets. Which at the same time would prevent their getting out of order for want of use."[13] But Matthew Clarkson, mayor of the city, apparently took no official steps and the volunteer fighters were not yet ready to act.

Governor Mifflin thought the situation serious enough to order Dr. James Hutchinson, port physician, to determine whether or not a contagious disease was prevalent in the city. On August 24 Hutchinson asked Rush to offer suggestions, and he replied at once: "A malignant fever has lately appeared in our city, originating I believe from some damaged coffee, which putrified on a wharf near Arch-street. This fever was confined for a while to Water-street, between Race and Arch-streets; but I have lately met with it in Second-street, and in Kensington; but whether propagated by contagion, or by the original exhalation, I cannot tell. The disease puts on all the immediate forms of a mild remittent, and a typhus gravior. I have not seen a fever of so much malignity, so general, since the year 1762."[14]

The *Advertiser* published, on August 28, the report made by Hutchinson to the health officer of the Port of Philadelphia, stating that he was convinced that "a malignant fever has lately made its appearance in Water Street and in Kensington" and is spreading. If Dr. Say was correct, however, in reporting the existence of cases in Kensington before those in Water Street, observed Hutchinson, then the disease was not caused by damaged coffee and other putrefied animal and vegetable substances on the docks. The disease seemed to be confined principally to Water Street, and Hutchinson added: "It does not appear to be an imported disease; for I have heard of no

foreigners or sailors that have hitherto been infected." Such was the
first official report. There was no organized health department, however, to follow up its findings. The first public health department in
America was established by the Legislature at its first session after
the epidemic.

In the market sheds in Market Street, men and women talked
little else but yellow fever. It was the topic of discussion in the inns
and taverns. Before long almost everybody in the city was intensely
nervous, fearfully looking for the dreaded symptoms each day. The
least blotch on the skin, weary eyes or limbs, caused one to crawl
immediately into bed or to hurry to the doctor's. The busiest office
in the city was Dr. Rush's.

Rush was unable to describe the symptoms of the disease with
precision. The symptoms made their appearance differently in different persons. The warning signs were a dull pain in the right side,
poor appetite, "flatulency, perverted taste, heat in the stomach, giddiness, or pain in the head, a dull—watery—brilliant, yellow or red
eye, dim and imperfect vision, a hoarseness, or slight sore throat, low
spirits, or unusual vivacity, a moisture on the hands, a disposition to
sweat at nights, or after moderate exercise, or a sudden suppression
of night sweats." In some cases the eyes were so inflamed as to resemble two balls of fire. In others "the whole countenance was
downcast and clouded."

The pulse was slow and intermitting, caused, Rush believed, by
"a spasmodic affection, accompanied with preternatural dilation or
contraction of the heart." The disposition to sigh "can be explained
upon no other principle than inflammation, spasm, dilation, or congestion in the heart." Cool weather caused this sulky pulse to be
"succeeded by a pulse, full, tense, quick, and as frequent as in pleurisy or rheumatism." There were hemorrhages in various organs,
and many patients seemed to die of "sudden effusions of blood or
serum in the lungs." Although the liver was usually not affected, the
brain suffered from congestion, and Rush believed that this congestion was responsible for the majority of deaths in cases of bilious
fever. The stomach and bowels were also usually affected in many
ways by this fever; nausea, vomiting, and mucous or bloody dis-
charges were common. There was an abnormal secretion and excre-

tion of large quantities of bile "of very different qualities and colours." Toward the end of the disease, a large black streak appeared in the middle of the tongue and extended to every part of it. Few patients recovered once this streak appeared. Deafness and dimness of sight were common symptoms, and the sense of touch was also affected. As for the skin, a yellow color was not universal and, in fact, appeared seldom where purges had been given in large doses. "The yellowness was in all cases the effect of an absorption and mixture of bile with the blood."[15]

Dr. William Currie, another Philadelphia physician, observed in most cases, after a spell of chills, a quick, tense pulse, hot skin, pains in the head, back, and limbs, a flushed face, inflamed eyes, moist tongue, soreness in the stomach, and vomiting. These symptoms continued for one to five days and if they did not then subside, the physician looked for nasal hemorrhages, bleeding gums, and a yellowish purple color over the entire body. The critical period fell between the fifth and eighth days.[16]

These were the symptoms everyone dreaded. As the number of cases increased sharply during the last week of August, Mayor Clarkson bent every effort to prevent the spread of the dread disease. He called upon the College of Physicians for advice, and the doctors in assembly drew up a list of suggestions which the Mayor published in the newspapers on August 27. The College recommended that unnecessary intercourse with infected persons be avoided; that a sign be placed upon the door of such houses as have infected persons in them; that the sick be placed in large, clean, airy rooms; that a large hospital be provided for the poor; that the custom of tolling bells on the death of a citizen be stopped; that burials be private; that the streets and wharves be kept as clean as possible; and that fatigue of mind and body as well as intemperance be avoided.[17]

Official notices in the newspapers concerning the fever were frightening to all. The printed page played it up as the most important news of the year as, indeed, it proved to be. In the last week of August the public mind had become so terrified that scores of families packed up their belongings and hastened into the country—anywhere as long as they were out of range. For some weeks, almost every hour in the day, carts, wagons, coaches, and horses could be seen transporting families and their furniture to the suburbs. Many houses were closed up entirely; others were maintained by servants left behind for the purpose. Business in the city was soon at a standstill, and artisans were thrown out of work. Few people appeared on the streets, and those who did went about with gloomy faces.

In late October, President Washington moved to Germantown where he occupied the spacious residence still standing at 5442 Germantown Avenue. Cabinet meetings were held around the corner at 130 West School House Lane. Government officials rented quarters in the neighborhood of the temporary White House.

Fearing infection from his clothes, the Doctor sent his sons off to join their mother, who was sojourning at Princeton. The father, his passion for self-improvement still burning, requested that the boys read something worth while every day during their absence from the city. He dreaded that they might develop idle habits.[18]

By the time September rolled around, the influenza, the mild bilious remittent fever, and scarlatina, which prevailed in the city before the yellow fever was recognized, disappeared almost entirely, appearing now and then with the yellow fever, so that after the first week of September yellow fever was the solitary epidemic.

A special committee of citizens appointed by the Mayor decided, on August 31, to take over "Bush Hill," the vast estate of William Hamilton, centering around Eighteenth and Buttonwood Streets. Hamilton was abroad and his mansion, barn, and stables became the emergency city hospital for epidemic sufferers, inasmuch as the directors of the Almshouse had resolved not to admit new patients into that institution during the epidemic. A few weeks later two wealthy merchants, Stephen Girard and Peter Helm, volunteered to act as superintendents of the emergency hospital, and the services they rendered were nothing short of heroic.[19]

The modes of treatment in use at the city hospital and those prescribed by individual physicians varied. At first Rush prescribed gentle purges, but by August 20 he had decided that they were ineffectual, and so he experimented with bark in its various forms and with wine, brandy, and aromatics. He also applied blisters to the limbs, neck, and head, but this treatment was not successful. Then he tried wrapping the whole body in blankets dipped in warm vinegar, and rubbing the sides with a mercurial ointment so as to stimulate the system through the liver. Again the patients failed to react favorably, and Rush was in a quandary. Believing that he might get some ideas from Dr. Stevens, a physician from St. Croix who happened to be in the city, Rush arranged an interview, and learned that the cold bath and bark were often beneficial. On the next day he ordered buckets of cold water to be thrown frequently on his patients. Three out of four patients who received this treatment died!

One night in his study, too tired to sleep after a trying day, while rummaging through a package of old papers, he came upon a lengthy report on the epidemics of yellow fever in Virginia in 1737, 1741, and 1743, by a Dr. John Mitchell, who included case histories of patients treated by him. Mitchell was a Scotch physician who came to America about 1700. His paper on yellow fever, written in 1744, had been sent to Benjamin Franklin to be read before the American Philosophical Society in Philadelphia. According to the society's custom, Mitchell's paper was referred to Dr. Cadwallader Colden of Albany for criticism, and later it came into Rush's hands. Here it was before him in August 1793. He had read it years before, but now he read it again with excited curiosity and intense interest.

Anxiously fingering the pages, he came upon Mitchell's remark: "That evacuation by purges was more necessary in this than in most other fevers, and that an ill-timed scrupulousness about the weakness of the body was of bad consequence in these urging circumstances." Mitchell went on to say that he gave purges to yellow fever patients when the pulse was so low that it could hardly be felt, and that it was restored by them. These suggestions awakened a new train of thought in Rush's mind and provided the groundwork for his subsequent treatment of the fever. His fear of copious evacuations was dissipated by Mitchell's report, the theory and practice of which he proceeded to adopt immediately. It remained only to fix upon a suitable purge.

He recalled that he had seen Dr. Thomas Young, one of the senior surgeons in the military hospitals of the Revolution, use ten grains of calomel plus ten grains of jalap as a purge. This prescription was generally referred to as "ten and ten." Upon mature deliberation he decided to use it. Frequently, however, he added five more grains of jalap. So successful did he consider the prescription, after the first experiments, that he stopped other physicians, whom he met on the street, to tell them about it, and on September 3 gave the prescription to the College of Physicians. At the same time he prescribed bloodletting, cool air, cool drinks, a light diet, and applications of cold water to the body.[20]

By the second week in September Rush was treating scores of patients daily. Although his sister and two others were kept busy mixing the purging powders, he was unable to meet the numerous demands made upon him for them; and being unable to see all the patients who sent for him he distributed copies of the prescription to the apothecaries around the city with instructions as to treatment.

He felt that he could reach the greatest number of sufferers through the newspapers and, therefore, in the *American Daily Advertiser*, September 13, he offered directions for the prevention and cure of the fever. If you feel sick in the stomach, chilly or feverish, or develop a pain in the head or back, Rush advised that one of the powders, ten grains of calomel and fifteen grains of jalap for an adult, be taken in a little sugar and water every six hours, until four or five evacuations result. Drink plenty of barley water or chicken broth to assist the operation of the physic, he directed. "After the bowels are thoroughly cleansed," he said further, "if the pulse be full or tense, eight or ten ounces of blood should be taken from the arm, and more, if the tension or fullness of the pulse should continue. Balm tea, toast and water, lemonade, tamarind water, weak camomile tea, or barley water should be drank during this state of the disorder; and the bowels should be kept constantly open, either by another powder, or by small doses of cremor tartar, or cooling salts. . . . The food should consist of gruel, sago, tapioca, tea, coffee, weak chocolate, wine whey, chicken broth, and the white meats, according to the weak or active state of the system. The fruits of the season may be eaten with advantage at all times." It was suggested, further, that the floor be sprinkled occasionally with vinegar. To avoid the fever Rush advised a temperate diet, consisting chiefly of vegetables, only moderate exercise of the mind as well as the body, warm clothing, cleanliness, and normal bowel movements.

Requests for medical attention and advice poured in. Samuel

Powell, who was mayor of the city between 1775 and 1789, asked if the situation was sufficiently critical to cause the Legislature to adjourn, and Rush wrote at the bottom of the inquiry: "I know of but one certain preventative of the disorder, and that is to keep at a distance from infected persons and places."[21]

His labors were made unduly difficult by the failure of most of the local physicians to coöperate. Several of them moved out of the city altogether in order to avoid risking their lives. Others believed that excess bleeding and purging were responsible for many deaths, and Rush was therefore openly attacked. On September 12, there appeared in the *Federal Gazette* an open letter to the College of Physicians in defense of his methods. Rush lamented the difference of opinion among the members of the College. "I have bled twice in many, and in one acute case, four times, with the happiest effects," he said. "I consider intrepidity in the use of the lancet at present to be as necessary, as it is in the use of mercury and jalap, in this insidious and ferocious disease." On September 16, through the newspapers, he advised persons in contact with yellow fever patients to live on a milk and vegetable diet and to take purges once or twice a week.

On September 17 the *Federal Gazette* published an attack on Rush by Dr. William Currie, who bitterly denounced bloodletting and even questioned the very existence of yellow fever in the city: "The disease, which Dr. Rush calls the yellow fever, and of which Dr. R says he has cured such numbers by the new method, is only the fall fever, operating on persons who have been previously affected by the influenza. It is time the veil should be withdrawn from your eyes, my fellow citizens." There was nothing extraordinary about a public attack on a fellow physician.

Rush could not let the matter rest a moment. On the very next day his reply to Currie was printed. He held that no two epidemics of unequal force can exist long together in the same place and that all the fevers then existing in the city were from one cause. He pointed out that he himself had lately suffered from an attack of the epidemic fever and his recovery was due to two copious bleedings and two doses of mercurial medicine in two days. There were other physicians, however, who sided with Currie, claiming that two fevers were prevalent and not only yellow fever.

Two weeks passed. Currie and his disciples were going their own way. The epidemic was at its very height. Then, quite unexpectedly, on October 2, Currie retracted some of his previous statements, and admitted that most of the physicians in the city now agreed with Rush that bloodletting and purging were the proper remedies. Dr. Adam Kuhn was one of Rush's bitterest foes in this war of the medicos. In the newspapers he proposed his own treatment, the use of bark, camomile tea, cold baths, and wine.

One after the other Rush ordered patients to be bled and purged. He would not listen to the criticism of fellow physicians, for he had decided in his own mind that bleeding was a successful method of treatment. Every day during September and October Rush and his assistants plied the lancet. S. Weir Mitchell paints the picture in *The Red City:* "In an hour came Dr. Rush, with his quiet manner and thin intellectual face. Like most of those of his profession, the death of some of whom in this battle with disease a tablet in the College of Physicians records today, he failed of no duty to rich or poor. But for those who disputed his views of practice he had only the most virulent abuse. A firm friend, an unpardoning hater, and in some ways far ahead of his time, was the man who now sat down as he said: 'I must bleed him at once. Calomel and bloodletting are the only safety, sir. I bled Dr. Griffith seventy-five ounces today. He will get well.' The doctor bled everybody, and over and over."

Physicians continued to argue about the merits of their respective treatments, and criticized each other harshly, but all of them fought heroically to bring comfort to the suffering and order out of chaos. Distressing conditions obtruded themselves in every street and alley. "Thirty-eight persons have died in eleven families in nine days in Water Street, and many more in different parts of the city," Rush reported to his wife on September 1. "It is indeed truly affecting to see a solitary corpse, on the shafts and wheels of a chair, conducted thro' our streets without a single attendant in some cases, and with only 8 or 10 in any instance, and they at a small distance from it on the foot pavement."[22]

During the first three or four weeks of the epidemic Rush seldom went into a house the first time without meeting the families of the sick in tears. Many wept and screamed in his office while waiting for advice for their sick at home. After a time, Rush observed that the outward manifestations of grief were less noticeable. Anguish had "descended below weeping, and I was much struck," he said, "in observing that many persons submitted to the loss of relations and friends without shedding a tear, or manifesting any other of the common signs of grief." For six weeks a cheerful countenance was scarcely to be seen. Sorrow gnawed at every heart. More than one-half the houses were tightly shut up, although not more than one-third of the inhabitants had fled into the country. On the streets were few persons except those in quest of physician, nurse, bleeder, or men to bury the dead. The hearse alone kept up the remembrance of the noise of carriages or carts in the streets. There were no formal funeral processions. A black man, leading, or driving a horse, with a corpse on a pair of chair wheels, with now and then half a dozen relations or friends following at a distance from it constituted a funeral. They passed in most of the streets of the city every hour of the day, while the noise of the same wheels passing slowly over the pavements kept alive anguish and fear in the sick and well, every hour of the night.[23]

By the time the sun rose Rush was up and out. During the night anxious relatives pushed notes under his door asking that he call to see their sick. The following are typical calls which the Doctor found when he unlocked his front door at the break of day. "Jacob Blackwell presents his respects to Doctr. Rush and informs him that he still has that fever hanging on him and begs the farther attention of the Doctr." This one was left by Mayor Clarkson: "Mrs. Clarkson was seized this morning early with a chilliness & is now very unwell, I request you will call immediately & see her." One John Hart reported that he was feeling better: "I may inform thee I feel stronger and not much pain. I have drank the diluting drinks as directed. The root of my tongue I think is affected with the mercury." "Please to come & see my daughter," wrote one William Innes. "She was taken this morning with a headach & sick stomach there is no person to bleed her." This earnest plea reveals one of innumerable tragedies: "Will the humane Doctor Rush condescend to step to the house of mourning—another of my family is ill & I have not a person to send out—my afflicted sister requiring two women to be constantly with her." Another patient, one B. W. Morris, took one powder at three A.M. which had no effect and at six o'clock his nurse wrote asking if it would be proper to give another if "he has had no return of sickness."[24]

If he attempted to keep a record of his patients during these trying weeks, Rush's task must have been an almost impossible one. He seems to have visited at least half the houses of the city, large as well as small. Jacob Hiltzheimer, wealthy merchant, noted in his diary that, on the morning of September 12, Rush called to see his daughter, Betsey, whose illness was diagnosed as yellow fever. The Doctor ordered eight ounces of blood to be drawn from her, and left some powders. Five days later she was strong enough to come downstairs, apparently well. "My youngest son Saml is ill," wrote one Samuel Coates, "and has had 2 of Rush's calomel doses with rhubarb viz: 3 grains calomel and 10 of rhub & 3 oz. of blood are ordered. It is not by any means clear to me that the disorder abates much, at least the mortality continues great."[25]

From these and similar documents it is apparent that the fever affected persons of all ages. Rush calculated that persons between fourteen and forty were more subject to it than others, and that men were more subject to the disease than women. At first he entertained the belief that negroes would escape the fever and, early in September, he inserted a note in the *American Daily Advertiser* suggesting that negroes be employed to nurse and to attend the sick. As a result of this letter the African Society undertook to provide nurses, but before long Rush discovered that he had been mistaken, though he still believed that the disease did not attack the negroes as severely as the whites. Negro servants suffered greatly as the epidemic progressed because they attended the sick in their households and in so doing received "large quantities of contagion into their bodies."[26]

By September 12 conditions in the thickly populated sections of the city had become so bad that the Mayor appointed a committee of ten citizens to assist the poor. A special committee reported on the next day that conditions at Bush Hill, the city hospital, were intolerable. They set out to borrow money to provide food, clothing, and medicines for the poor and to look after the children orphaned during the epidemic. On September 15 Stephen Girard and Peter Helm took charge of Bush Hill. Dr. Deveze, a French physician in the city from Cape François, and Dr. Benjamin Duffield also joined the staff of volunteers. On October 3 the Mayor's committee fitted up the Loganian Library as a home for children whose parents had succumbed to the fever.

It seems that the death rate in families living in frame houses was high. Rush could not say definitely whether this was the result of the small size of the houses, of the insanitary conditions existing therein, of the contagion adhering to the wood, or perhaps of a combination of these causes. "Several families who shut up their front and back doors and windows, and avoided going out of their houses except to procure provisions, escaped the disorder." The narrower the street so much greater was the chance of infection. The spread of the disease was supposedly favored by atmospheric conditions in September and during the first two weeks of October. During this period there was little wind and mosquitoes were especially numerous—an important observation! Except for showers on two days there was practically no rain between August 25 and October 15.[27]

The whole situation was aggravated by the fact that in some households where whole families were ill, there was no one at hand to prepare food, and administer medicinal care, for there was a great shortage of nurses and many of those on duty were untrained and incompetent. There was likewise a dearth of physicians caused not only by the desertion of a few from the city but also by the sickness and death of many who served heroically. "At one time," according to Rush, "there were only three physicians who were able to do business out of their houses, and at this time, there were probably not less than 6,000 persons ill with the fever."[28] The law of supply and demand caused a sharp rise in the cost of medical care. "There is little credit given now for anything," Rush wrote Elias Boudinot on October 2. "Every service to the sick is purchased at a most extravagant price. The price of bleeding is 7/6, and nurses wages are 3, and 3½ dollars per day."[29] Naturally Rush was offered extravagant sums for special attention, but characteristically he refused. Acceptance of any extra remuneration on his part would have been entirely inconsistent with his rigid code of personal and professional ethics. His strength to fight and his fearlessness to face the dread disease he interpreted as a token of divine recognition of his unselfishness. "I was favored," he wrote in his own account of the epidemic, "with an exemption from the fear of death in proportion as I subdued every selfish feeling, and laboured exclusively for the benefit of others."

Everyone was tense and despondent; many were terror-stricken. After the middle of September, the atmosphere of the whole city was funereal. People resorted to the most fantastic measures to ward off the disease. Mathew Carey, publisher, and member of the Mayor's Committee, observed: "The smoke of tobacco being regarded as preventative, many persons, even women and small boys, had segars constantly in their mouths. Others placing full confidence in garlic, chewed it almost the whole day; some kept it in their shoes. Many were afraid to allow the barbers or hair-dressers to come near them, as instances had occurred of some of them having shaved the dead—and many of them had engaged as bleeders. Some houses were hardly a moment in the day free from the smell of gunpowder, burned tobacco, nitre, sprinkled vinegar, &c."

Carey reported further that "many were almost incessantly purifying, scouring, and whitewashing their rooms. Those who ventured abroad had handkerchiefs or sponges impregnated with vinegar or camphor at their noses, or else smelling salts with the thieves' vinegar. Others carried pieces of tarred rope in their hands or pockets, or camphor bags tied around their necks. . . . A person with a crape or any appearance of mourning, was shunned like a viper." Everyone looked out for himself and unconsciously people became selfish.[30] Rush wrote his wife that parents were deserting children who had become infected, and that "many people thrust their parents into the streets, as soon as they complained of a headache."[31]

On September 25 Rush noted that the disease was still spreading, and practically no one was perfectly well. "One complains of giddiness or headach—another of chills—others of pain in the back & stomach, and all have more or less quickness of pulse and redness or yellowness in the eyes. No words can describe the distress which pervades all ranks of people,—from the combined operations of fear, grief, poverty, despair and death.—More tears have been shed in my entry, and in my back parlour, within the last month, than have been shed perhaps for years before in our city. Never can I forget the awful sight of mothers wringing their hands,—fathers dumb for a while with fear & apprehension—and children weeping aloud before me, all calling me to hasten to the relief of their sick relations."[32] The picture is one of woe and gnawing grief. Physicians were almost powerless in the face of the calamity. One can only imagine how difficult it must have been, for example, to obtain necessary supplies with the avenues of distribution clogged or closed. The city was paralyzed to such an extent that three of the four local newspapers ceased to circulate.

One of the most interesting pictures of the city during the epidemic was penned by Charles Brockden Brown in his novel, *Arthur Mervyn; or Memoirs of the Year 1793*. Arthur Mervyn, a country boy, came to Philadelphia penniless while the fever was raging. "In proportion as I drew near the city, the tokens of its calamitous condition became more apparent," we read in the first volume. "Every farm-house was filled with supernumerary tenants; fugitives from home; and haunting the skirts of the road, eager to detain every passenger with inquiries after news. The passengers were numerous; for the tide of emigration was by no means exhausted. Some were on foot, bearing in their countenances the tokens of their recent terror, and filled with mournful reflections on the forlornness of their state. Few had secured to themselves an asylum; some were without the means of paying for victuals or lodging for the coming night; others, who were not thus destitute, yet knew not whither to apply for entertainment, every house being already overstocked with inhabitants, or barring its inhospitable doors at their approach.

"Families of weeping mothers, and dismayed children, attended with a few pieces of indispensable furniture, were carried in vehicles of every form. The parent or husband had perished; and the price of some moveable, or the pittance handed forth by public charity, had been expended to purchase the means of retiring from this theatre of disasters; though uncertain and hopeless of accomodation in the neighboring districts. . . .

"I pursued the track which I had formerly taken, and entered High-street after nightfall. Instead of equipages and a throng of passengers, the voice of levity and glee, which I had formerly observed, and which the mildness of the season would, at other times, have produced, I found nothing but a dreary solitude.

"The market-place, and each side of this magnificent avenue were illuminated as before, by lamps; but between the verge of the Schuylkill and the heart of the city, I met not more than a dozen figures; and these were ghost-like, wrapt in cloaks, from behind which they cast upon me glances of wonder and suspicion; and, as I approached, changed their course, to avoid touching me. Their clothes were sprinkled with vinegar; and their nostrils defended from contagion by some powerful perfume.

"I cast a look upon the houses, which I recollected to have formerly been, at this hour, brilliant with lights, resounding with lively voices, and thronged with busy faces. Now they were closed, above and below; dark, and without tokens of being inhabited. From the upper windows of some, a gleam sometimes fell upon the pavement I was traversing, and shewed that their tenants had not fled, but were secluded or disabled."

Further on Arthur Mervyn came to an infected house through which he wandered. "Effluvia of a pestilential nature assailed me from every corner. In the front room of the second story . . . the bed appeared as if some one had recently been dragged from it. The sheets were tinged with yellow, and with that substance which is said to be characteristic of this disease, the gangrenous or black vomit. The floor exhibited similar stains."

That was the Philadelphia in which Benjamin Rush fought with enduring courage to save his fellows from the onslaught of the pestilence. An air of hopelessness weighed down upon the city and death stalked through the highways and narrow alleys twenty-four hours of each day. No one was spared—rich men, poor men, scholars, laborers—all suffered. The wheels of the city government stopped and the fight with the fever occupied the whole attention of the city fathers. Members of the Legislature fled to their homes and the state government barely functioned.

There was no time to devote to rites for the dead in this confusion. Elizabeth Drinker observed in her diary, on September 10, 1793, that the victims were put into their coffins as soon as they had died, without changing their clothes or laying them out, and were buried in an hour or two after their death. On September 27 she heard that coffins were stacked in piles near the State House for the use of the poor. It was also reported that trenches were dug in the potter's field to receive the dead. Rush noticed that in many cases a deep yellow color appeared over the body a few minutes after death. In some the skin became purple and in others black.[33]

Rush was under constant strain. He could not sleep at night because of fatigue and frequent knocks at the door. He arose at six o'clock. His entire household was working on an emergency schedule. His mother and sister lived with him, and he employed a negro manservant and a mulatto boy. While the epidemic was at its height three of his five private students moved into the house. The entire household examined or prescribed for about 1,000 patients between September 8 and 15. Rush himself frequently interviewed patients and prescribed for them while at lunch or dinner. Indeed, his dining room became an auxiliary consultation office. On many days he examined more than 150 patients, making calls on horseback.

Finally, Rush as well as his household broke under the strain. During the month of September three of his pupils died of the fever. The other two were stricken but recovered. On October 1 his sister died. Shortly thereafter his faithful servant contracted the disease. His mother also was ill. The Doctor's wife and children, however, were safe in Princeton.

On the evening of September 14 Rush himself developed the unmistakable symptoms. He did what he could for himself and the next morning, notwithstanding the fact that he felt quite ill and had drawn ten ounces of blood from his own body at ten o'clock, he made calls and visited between forty and fifty patients by noon. When he returned to his home at two o'clock, he was exhausted and was seized with a chill, followed by high fever. He took one of the mercurial purges and went to bed; after sundown he took another dose and again bled himself to the extent of ten ounces. When the morning came he felt somewhat relieved after a cold bath, but remained in bed. On the 17th he received patients and went over the reports with his assistants. On September 18 he came downstairs and prescribed for not less than 100 patients in the parlor. Next day, although weak, he resumed his regular routine.

On September 22 Rush wrote Edward Pennington: "Ed Fisher and all my young men except one are ill. I was yesterday confined half the day to my bed & despair of being strong eno to go abroad today."[34] On the next day his assistant, Mr. Stall, died, and on September 24, another assistant, Mr. Alston.

Ten days later, on October 4, Rush suddenly collapsed on a bed in a sick room, was carried home and again put to bed. On October 9 he complained of chills, was bled plentifully, and given the mercurial powders. He became critically ill, however, and his attack lasted until October 21.

The epidemic reached its height in early October; indeed, the greatest weekly mortality list—720—appeared for the second week of October. "It is told today," reads Elizabeth Drinker's diary entry for October 5, "that the day before yesterday, 40 persons were sent to the Hospital, and a vast number buried—yesterday not so many laid in ye earth, but many sick." At the most critical period of the epidemic, exactly a week later, she recorded: "On fifth day last, 40 were sent to the hospital which with those there before amounted to 302 persons; 'tis now so full that another is said to be preparing. Seventeen graves 'tis said were dug in the Friends burying ground yesterday. 'Tis very affecting to walk through the streets of our once flourishing and happy city; the houses shut up from one corner to another, the inhabitants that remain keeping shut up—very few seen walking about. The disorder now, 'tis said, rages much in ye south part of ye city—that great numbers die in that part called Irish-Town. . . . The weather is much changed this evening; it blows hard from N.W. and is very cold."

In mid-October the city was living through its tensest moments. Nothing else mattered except deliverance from the dreadful scourge. Even the watches and clocks were almost always incorrect because along with others watchmakers were either ill or had fled the city, but time meant little either to the sick or well. One night the watchman cried ten o'clock, when it was only nine, and continued the mistake throughout the night. But no one cared.

Frightful pictures of conditions were brought to the attention of the city officials. On October 19 one of the carters in the service of the City Committee reported "that in the performance of his duty he heard the cry of a person in great distress, the neighbour informed him, that the family had been ill some days—and that being afraid of the disease no one had ventured to examine the house; he cheerfully undertook the benevolent task, went upstairs and to his surprise found the father dead, who had been lying on the floor for some days, two children near him also dead, the mother in labour; he tarried with her, she was delivered while he was there, and in a short time both she and her infant expired; he came to the City Hall, took coffins and buried them all."[35]

Finally, it was apparent that the epidemic was on the wane. After more than seven weeks of terror the fever seems to have been checked about the middle of October by the cold spell mentioned by Elizabeth Drinker. The number of cases declined steadily during the last two weeks in October. Through November and December there were only a few scattered cases. A special day of thanksgiving was proclaimed throughout the state on December 12.

The loss of life in actual numbers from the discovery of the first case of the fever in Water Street in early August until early November can only be approximated, because the vital statistics of the period are not reliable. The city proper had a population of less than 45,000. Between August 1 and November 9 there are records of 4,044 burials, but not all those who died were victims of the yellow fever. During the same period 191 children, whose parents died during the epidemic, were admitted to the emergency city orphanage. The deaths in September numbered 1,443.

On September 25 Rush reported to Elias Boudinot: "It is computed that 100 persons upon an average have been buried every day for the last eight or ten days. The sick suffer from the want, not only of physicians—bleeders—nurses & friends, but from the want of common necessaries of life. Five physicians—four students of medicine, and three bleeders have died of the disorder. But the mortality falls chiefly upon the poor, who by working in the sun, excite the contagion into action."[36]

From letters written by Rush to his wife one forms an idea of the number of patients treated by the Doctor. On September 5 he wrote that he was seeing nearly 100 patients daily, and that he was saving twenty-nine out of thirty of all who called him on the first day of the appearance of the illness. On September 8 he wrote: "I have this day been called to more new cases than I have time to count." Two days later he visited and prescribed for more than 100 patients. On September 11 he made seven calls before five o'clock in the morning. Within the next week he was unable to see at least from fifty to sixty patients daily. While recuperating from his first attack, on September 21, he made twenty-five visits, and on October 3, the day before he collapsed the second time, he made fifty calls.[37]

It was, of course, physically impossible for Rush to see all the patients who came to his door or who asked him to call. On one morning forty-seven were turned away before eleven o'clock. People stood in line outside the Doctor's door on Walnut Street. "Many of them left my door with tears," he recalled later, "but they did not feel more distress than I did, from refusing to follow them . . . and even yet, I recollect, with pain, that I tore myself at one time from five persons in Moravian-alley who attempted to stop me, by suddenly whipping my horse, and driving my chair as speedily as possible beyond the reach of their cries."[38]

Rush claimed that not less than 6,000 Philadelphians owed their lives to purging and bleeding although, throughout the epidemic, he was bitterly attacked by some physicians and laymen for prescribing the lancet. In determining the quantity of blood to be drawn, he was guided by the state of the pulse and temperature of the atmosphere. Many patients were bled twice and even three times daily. In early September he preferred tapping small quantities of blood frequently, but as the epidemic grew in intensity he did not hesitate to draw a pint to twenty ounces of blood at one time. From some persons he drew as much as seventy to eighty ounces in five days! He insisted that bloodletting was not prescribed indiscriminately and that the amount of blood drawn depended directly on the condition of the individual patient. Results proved to his satisfaction that bleeding and purging were the proper remedies. "At no period of the disease," he reflected later, "did I lose more than one in twenty of those whom I saw on the first day, and attended regularly through every stage of the fever; provided they had not been previously worn down by attending the sick."[39]

Not all the bleeding was done by professionally trained physicians and nurses. In a letter to an unknown correspondent, dated October 29, 1793, preserved in the J. Pierpont Morgan Library, one learns that unskilled hands at times performed the operation. Volunteer service went even beyond the sick room to the grave. "Richard Allen was extremely useful in performing the mournful duties which were connected with burying the dead," this letter goes on, in discussing the unselfish services rendered by the negroes of the city. "Many of the black nurses it is true were ignorant, & some of them were negligent, but many of them did their duty to the sick with a degree of patience & tenderness that did them great credit. During the indisposition & confinement of the greatest part of the physicians of the city, Richard Allen, and Absalom Jones provided copies of the printed directions for curing the fever—went among the poor who were sick,—gave them the mercurial purges,—bled them freely, and by these means, they this day informed me had recovered between two, and three hundred people." If Rush himself did not bleed indiscriminately, it is quite possible that the laymen who followed his printed directions without professional judgment most likely did.

Some patients there were who, influenced perhaps by the attacks made on Rush, the bleeder, refused to be bled. For Rush such patients were trying, for he was absolutely certain of the efficacy of the treatment. In Mitchell's *The Red City*, Schmidt, a victim of the fever, would not permit Dr. Rush to bleed him; instead he insisted on lying out on an open porch day and night. Eventually he recovered. Here is the dialogue:

"The doctor liked few things better than a chance to talk. He sat down again as desired, saying: 'Yes, I am tired; but though I had only three hours' sleep last night, I am still, through the divine Goodness, in perfect health. Yesterday was a triumph for mercury, jalap, and bleeding. They saved at least a hundred lives.'

" 'Are the doctors all to your way of thinking?'

" 'No, sir. I have to combat prejudice and falsehood. Sir, they are murderers.'

" 'Sad, very sad!' remarked Schmidt.

" 'I have one satisfaction. I grieve for the blindness of men, but I nourish a belief that my labor is acceptable to Heaven. Malice and slander are my portion on earth; but my opponents will have their reward hereafter.'

" 'Most comforting!' murmured Schmidt. 'But what a satisfaction to be sure you are right!'

" 'Yes, to know, sir, that I am right and these my enemies wrong, does console me; and too, to feel that I am humbly following in the footsteps of my Master. But I must go.' . . .

" 'Ah, my son,' he [Schmidt] said, 'only in the Old Testament will you find a man like that—malice and piety, with a belief in himself no man, no reason, can disturb.' "

That Rush was obstinate cannot be denied, but this trait was consistent with his marked individuality of character. The controversy between the opposing medical factions over methods of treatment hardly helped the fight against the fever. Philip Freneau, poet and journalist, cried out:

> Doctors raving and disputing,
> Death's pale army still recruiting.
>   What a pother,
>   One with 'tother,
> Some a-writing, some a-shooting.
>
> Nature's poisons here collected,
> Water, earth and air infected;
>   O! what pity
>   Such a city
> Was in such a place erected.

Those who survived set to work to clean and fumigate their homes and the city in general after the epidemic was over. By the middle of November those who had emigrated to the country had returned. Mrs. Rush and the children settled once more in the Walnut Street house on November 22. For fumigating purposes, some used nitre and aromatic spirits. In many households infected articles of furniture were buried under the ground; in others they were baked in ovens. Some housekeepers destroyed all the beds and clothing that had been infected; others threw them into the Delaware River. Many whitewashed their walls and painted the woodwork. Rush advised that the walls and floors be scrubbed, that the windows of the sick rooms be kept open for several days and nights, that beds and furniture be placed in the open air for a week or two.[40] On January 22, 1794, he made a further suggestion: "I have heard with great pleasure that the Corporation have taken measures to have all the beds, and cloathing which were infected by our late epidemic, exposed in such a manner as to destroy the contagion in them. To render this measure effectual, I beg leave to suggest that the beds &c of all those persons who have been persuaded to believe that they had not the yellow fever, but fevers of other kinds in their families, during its prevalence in our city, should not be exempted from the ordinance of the Corporation. By neglecting this precaution, the disease may be revived amongst us in warm weather."[41]

Was it possible for the disease to revive next summer or was it, as some claimed, a fever that had been brought in accidentally by foreign ships? This question of the origin of the fever was one that engaged physicians and laymen in bitter controversy for many months during and after the epidemic. The newspapers gave considerable space to the dispute, and in the end the public mind was only confused.

Before the end of August Rush had announced publicly that the disease was of domestic origin and traceable to the putrid exhalations from the damaged coffee on the dock on the Delaware. On August 25 a special meeting of the College of Physicians was held to consider the steps that should be taken in connection with the prevalence of the fever. Doctors Rush, Hutchinson, Say, and Wistar were appointed a committee to report on the subject.

As soon as it became known that Rush believed the origin to be domestic, a bitter controversy arose. Landowners and real estate speculators were aroused because, if it were true that the disease existed by reason of local conditions, families would move to other cities and business would be seriously injured. Dr. Adam Kuhn and Dr. Edward Stevens, a St. Croix physician, bitterly attacked Rush's view, and held that the disease was most certainly imported from the West Indies.

Rush, admitting that he was influenced by the theories of Dr. Thomas Sydenham, insisted that morbid exhalations create fevers at a distance of two or three miles in open country. Of course, he scoffed, loathsome and dangerous diseases have always been considered by all nations as of foreign extraction. In the year 1793, he pointed out, yellow fever prevailed in many parts of the United States, but outside of Philadelphia there was no suspicion or suggestion that it had been imported. He traced the first cases of the fever in Philadelphia to the sailors of the vessel who were first exposed to the effluvia of the coffee. Their sickness commenced the day on which the coffee began to emit its putrid odor. He pointed to the fact that in the West Indies yellow fever never attacks children, but in Philadelphia it did. The disease was undoubtedly local in character.

And why should not yellow fever appear in the Quaker City? "It is only a higher grade of a fever," he explained, "which prevails every year in our city, from vegetable putrefaction," and this epidemic was most certainly caused by "putrid vegetable exhalation."[42] Indeed heat, acting upon moist vegetable matter, may produce it in any part of the world. When the damaged coffee was exposed on the wharf on July 24, conditions favored its putrefaction and exhalation, with the resultant fever. The rapid progress of the disease from Water Street to other parts of the city was further evidence for Rush that his theory was correct. Further, he disclosed: "It is remarkable that it passed first through those alleys and streets, which were in the course of the winds that blew across the dock and wharf where the coffee lay." And had not many persons, who had worked or visited in the neighborhood of the wharf in early August, become ill? He also stressed the fact that the disease did not spread to rural sections, another support to his contention that it was most certainly domestic in origin.[43] For four or five years Rush believed that yellow fever was contagious; then he changed his mind.

Dr. William Currie did not believe that the disease was caused by the putrid coffee. If so, he asked, why was the disease confined to Water Street in the early stages of the epidemic; why did it not spread throughout the city at the same time? He held firmly that the disease was imported. He showed that yellow fever was prevalent in

San Domingo in 1793, and from this island, on account of the slave insurrections, many refugees had come to Philadelphia. On July 24 the sloop *Amelia*, from San Domingo, docked in the city. Then there was the French privateer, the *Sans Culottes*, which brought in her prize, the *Flora*, whose master fell a victim to yellow fever at Chester. There were aboard these vessels other sick persons "with evident symptoms of yellow fever." The crew of the privateer was made up of sailors who had visited infected ports. For Currie the evidence was conclusive that the fever was foreign in origin. Dr. Isaac Cathrall supported Currie, detailing that a Danish ship, the *Henry*, moved up to Kensington on August 16, and its captain and two sailors were in bed a few days later with marked symptoms of the yellow fever. Indeed, all three died, and the keeper of the tavern where they stayed contracted the disease and also died. Currie and Cathrall concluded that undoubtedly the disease was introduced by the foreign ships that arrived in Philadelphia in July and August.[44]

Some said the fever was brought into the city on August 7 by the brig *Mary* from Cape François, but Dr. Jean Deveze, a French army surgeon who was a passenger on the vessel, flatly denied this. There were only three sick persons on board, he said, and none manifested yellow fever symptoms. He claimed that the disease originated from "alterations of the atmospheric air" and was not contagious. He disagreed with Rush's method of treatment and, while volunteering at Bush Hill Hospital, he bled patients only in extreme cases and opposed the use of "ten and ten." He resorted to glysters, gargles, baths, lemonade, chicken broth, skimmed milk, emulsions, and sedatives.[45]

So tired and irritable from overwork was Rush that he viewed the opinions and theories of his opponents as personal affronts. Here was a man who had been working fifteen to eighteen hours daily for weeks; and, having seen a high percentage of his patients recover, he became convinced of the curative value of his treatment. Even if there was another side to the question he was too exhausted mentally to follow its argument. Adding this to his natural obstinacy, one easily understands the Doctor's state of mind. The attacks on his opinions of origin and treatment so embittered him that, on November 5, he resigned from the College of Physicians, the organization which he had helped to found. At the same time he presented to the College a copy of Sydenham's works!—this as a farewell slap. On November 26 the College, in reply to Governor Mifflin's appeal for information, stated that "No instance has ever occurred of the disease called yellow fever, having been originated in this city, or in any other parts of the United States . . . but there have been frequent instances of its having been imported."[46]

In a quiet moment Rush decided that the best thing to do would be to write about the epidemic dispassionately after the bitterness of the controversy had subsided. On November 8 he wrote James Pemberton: "I have kept a diary of everything that related to the disease, and to the operation of the remedies which I used to cure it, and shall when my health & leisure will permit, lay the result of all my observations before the public. It will be impossible to procure Dr. Bond's notes from his son. From the success which attended the use of mercury—jalap & the lancet in our late disorder, I am disposed to believe that it will never be so fatal hereafter as it has been. Its principal mortality was among those people who did not use those remedies, or if they did, in such a sparing manner as not to be effectual."[47] Rush's plan was carried to completion and, in 1794, there appeared his exhaustive volume: *An Account of the Bilious Remitting Yellow Fever, As It Appeared in the City of Philadelphia, in the year 1793.*

The epidemic passed into history; winter came and the city carried on, though its population was reduced by nearly ten per cent. Even if the future was to prove many of Rush's theories invalid and his conclusions incorrect, his courage and his almost superhuman efforts to minister to thousands of patients, from sunrise until long after sunset, day after day and week after week, will always attest to the nobility of his character. There was something heroic as well as deeply spiritual about his labors, and he can hardly be charged with ignorance or incompetence for adhering to practices which the limited knowledge of his day confirmed, but the discoveries of a later age were to discard.

IX

Further Epidemics

1794–1803

In the spring of 1794 Philadelphia was busy smartening and prink-
ing itself; more paint was used by housekeepers during the months
after the epidemic than for many years. Externally, at least, the city
looked cheerful and bright. Mothers and fathers, sisters and brothers,
though still bemoaning the loss of friends and family, were beginning to lose themselves in work, for there was much to be done to
make up for time and labor lost during the epidemic.

Washington and his cabinet and members of Congress were back
in the city again, with Jefferson and his Republicans in control of
the House. The Republicans, aroused because England was stopping
our ships, impressing alleged British seamen, and interfering with
our shipping in the French West Indies, demanded positive action.
A nonintercourse bill, to forbid trade with England, was actually
passed in the House but failed in the Senate only by the casting vote
of the Vice-President. Work was rushed on new frigates for the
navy, and coast defenses were maintained on a war basis. The capital was in an irritable mood, and Philadelphians realized that war
was, indeed, a possibility. President Washington, however, supported
by Alexander Hamilton and the Federalists, held out against measures of hostility and, in May 1794, John Jay, Chief Justice of the
Supreme Court, hastened to London to negotiate a treaty with England. At the moment, the dangerous sparks in the halls of Congress
failed to kindle the flame of war.

The violent upheaval through which France was passing stirred
the memories and emotions of all Americans. The Republicans in
and out of Congress were as sympathetic toward the French revolutionists as they were hostile to England. All royalty was viewed with
disfavor. Benjamin Rush wrote his old friend of Revolutionary
days, General Horatio Gates, that he admired and preferred a re-

publican form of government then as definitely as he did in 1777, and that he wished success to the French cause.[1]

He talked, wrote, thought, and read about the French Revolution as well as about the acute Republican-Federalist convulsions to which it gave rise in Congress. As the summer approached, however, his practice consumed so much time that the French Revolution and its complexities paled in importance.

During the spring, and particularly in early June, Rush, now living on Fourth Street near Locust, noticed a steady increase in the number of diseases of the "inflammatory complexion." He anticipated, therefore, that the fevers of the forthcoming summer and autumn would be of a violent and malignant nature, and was more disposed to entertain this opinion after observing the stagnating filth of the gutters throughout the city.

Direct evidence of a recurrence of the dreaded fever of 1793 appeared early in June. On June 6, Dr. Philip Syng Physick, a rising star in the medical profession, notified Rush that he had just treated a patient suffering from yellow fever. This bit of news did not surprise him, but it must have perturbed him, as he remembered the terrific days of 1793. A week later Rush himself called to see one Isaac Morris, diagnosed the case as yellow fever, and of course ordered the patient to be bled and purged. The patient recovered. During the last two weeks of June, Rush saw several cases that looked suspiciously like yellow fever. In July at least five patients manifested yellow fever symptoms, and in early August there were many more. On August 12 news reached Philadelphia that the disease had appeared in Baltimore. In fact, Rush believed that one of his own patients "brought the contagion of it in his body from that place."

By mid-August it was being bruited about that several persons in the city were down with yellow fever. In the inns and taverns and in the market places there was much whispering and deep concern about the state of the city's health. On August 25 two members of the State Committee of Health in Philadelphia called on Rush, who advised them that undoubtedly yellow fever had appeared in the city, but that his patients, at least, had so far yielded to treatment. Four days later Rush addressed the entire Committee, advising them that the filth in the gutters, and the stagnant water in the neighborhood of the city were the remote causes of the fever, and should be removed immediately if the spread of the disease was to be prevented. On September 1 Rush found that the disease had been carried through several families, and the number who fell ill rapidly multiplied. On the next day, therefore, he wrote the mayor, calling attention to the contagious nature of the fever and its existence in the city.

Rush's summary of the situation was bitterly attacked in some quarters. An anonymous correspondent, in the *Gazette of the United States*, declared that Rush's report would "not only render multitudes uneasy, and interrupt the usual course of business, but injure the interest and reputation of the city in several respects." The disease is not contagious, said the correspondent, and why, therefore, should any attention be given it by the newspapers or officials? After denouncing Rush's theory of the domestic origin of the epidemic of 1793, the correspondent concluded: "Be under no concern my fellow citizens, the yellow fever is not in our city, nor is it possible for it to be generated in it, in its present situation."

These attacks did not alter Rush's convictions and, on September 13, he wrote the Committee of Health that the disease was found to be contagious in many cases, and he urged that citizens indisposed be warned to apply for medical aid without delay. His suggestions were, however, received coldly, and a few persons went so far as to say that the Doctor was insane. According to Rush many yellow fever sufferers were dying daily, but some of their physicians, refusing to admit the existence of yellow fever in the city, attached other names to the illness. The conduct of the Committee of Health, he felt, was as unethical as that of the purblind physicians.

When the Committee called a meeting of all the physicians, on September 30, Rush refused to attend. He was wild with wrath next day, when the Committee announced publicly that the physicians' reports showed that not a single case of a contagious nature existed in the city. Yellow fever was not even mentioned. "Thus while nurses, bleeders, clergymen and occasional visitors of the sick, and in some instances, the sick themselves, united in deciding upon the character and name of our fever," wrote Rush later, "a majority of the physicians united in persuading the citizens that it existed only in the imaginations of two or three men."[2]

Meanwhile Rush was visiting and seeing in his office scores of patients daily. Call a spade a spade, he demanded; to conceal the identity of the disease was dangerous because it was most certainly contagious. "I saw one instance in which the disease was excited in twelve hours after the contagion was taken into the body," Rush reported. "A lady lately from Rhode Island who laid so near a sick gentleman in a public house as to be disturbed by his groans, humanely went into his room in the morning to offer him all the relief that lay in her power. She found him in the act of puking black matter, and was much shocked at the yellow color of his face. She did not suspect his disorder to be the yellow fever, for his physicians had denied or concealed it in the family. The speedy death of this gentleman induced her to change her lodgings. In the evening of the same day she went to the theatre, where she was seized with a chilly fit. The next day I was sent for to visit her. I found her ill with all the symptoms of the yellow fever. She was cured, but the danger and distress from which she escaped, furnished an affecting instance of the cruelty of concealing or denying the existence of contagious and malignant diseases."[3]

The first few cases of yellow fever did not frighten Rush, but by mid-September he concluded that the disease had reached the proportions of a mild epidemic. Where mercury, jalap, and the lancet had been used, the mortality rate was low. "The Kuneans" [Dr. Adam Kuhn and his disciples], Rush wrote John Redman Coxe, who was studying at Edinburgh, "call it an inflammatory remittent, & deny it to be the true yellow fever. Where a yellowness attends, they call it a jaundice. This conduct is necessary, otherwise they would be obliged to subscribe to the generation of the disease in our city, and to the use of depleting mediums. Dr. Kuhn lost Caleb Emlen's eldest son last week on the 5th day of a fever. He was yellow before as well as after his death. The Doctor called it a putrid fever. I did not hear what medicines he took but he was not bled." The clamor against Rush had become so intense, he told

Coxe, that a group of citizens proposed to drive him out of the city. He was denounced as a fanatic and as an enemy of the people. "I am not moved by insults, nor threats," was Rush's reaction, "but persist in asserting & defending all my opinions respecting the disease. The only revenge I seek of my fellow citizens is to save their lives, and the only notice I take of the slanders of my medical brethren, is to refuse to consult with them."

Rush felt that he achieved more success with his remedies in 1794 than in 1793 because the patients were given much better care. He bled more freely than in the previous year. In the letter to Coxe mention is made of a newly arrived Englishman from whom 140 ounces of blood in twelve bleedings were taken in six days, the lancet being used four times in one day! Within the course of the same six days this patient took nearly 150 grains of calomel with the usual proportions of jalap. He recovered.[4]

The epidemic was not extensive because, in Rush's opinion, occasional showers on several days checked the disease in September and October. Cases of yellow fever were reported occasionally by Rush throughout the whole of the moderate winter. He observed that "the head was affected in this fever, not only with coma and delirium, but with mania. This symptom was so common as to give rise to an opinion that madness was epidemic in our city." Sore eyes were also common during the prevalence of the fever. "The yellowness of the skin which sometimes attends this fever, was more universal, but fainter than in the year 1793."[5]

Just as the disease was less virulent and the yellow tinge fainter, so the number of cases was fewer by many than in 1793. Scarcely any citizens closed their houses and left the city, and at no time was there as much distress and anxiety as there was in the previous year. "Out of forty patients to whom I have been called since the 9th of June," Rush wrote on September 17, "and whom I saw on the first, or second day of the disease, I have lost only one, & she died only because her friends opposed bleeding at the time, & in the quantity I prescribed it." There were some, of course, who feared what the next day or week might bring, and so they fled to the country. They were a distracted group. On October 3, 1794, Henry Muhlenberg wrote Rush from Lancaster: "Your Philadelphians that marched through here, seemed to be very downcast and tired, and I fear some bad consequences. I really saw hardly one lively glad face."[6]

For the treatment of the fever Rush resorted to practically the same remedies which he had used in 1793. Bleeding, purging, cool air, cold drinks, and cold water were prescribed. A salivation was also employed to create "a diversion of congestion, inflammation and serous effusion, from the brain and viscera to the mouth," and then tonics were prescribed to restore strength to the system. It is almost unbelievable that from fifty to 150 ounces of blood were drawn from each patient! The tonics included fresh fruits, bread, milk, chicken broth, white meats, eggs, oysters, and malt liquors. Of more than 200 patients whom Rush saw in the first stage of the fever and treated in this manner, only four died.[7]

According to Rush, seventeen out of twenty-three of Dr. William Currie's patients were lost after he had stopped prescribing jalap, calomel, and bloodletting. Drs. Wistar and Kuhn, who were but little more successful, ascribed their "numerous deaths to bilious and intermitting fevers, gout-dropsies of the brain," and other diseases.

Rush always believed that his own success with this particular disease was unparalleled in the thirty-four years of his practice. "Out of upwards of 120 of 'strongly marked' cases," he wrote on November 4, "I lost but two where my prescriptions were followed on the first day of the disorder." This success pleased him almost as much as the harsh criticism of his enemies vexed him. It was openly charged that he was bleeding patients to death, that he was nothing but a horse doctor, and that he was insane.[8]

After the danger of a general epidemic had passed, Rush turned his thoughts to preventive measures for the future. The spread of a contagious disease could be prevented in cities, he thought, by quarantine. Whenever a contagious disease of domestic origin is discovered, "let all the families which are within fifty yards of the infected person or persons be ordered instantly to remove into houses or tents, to be provided for them at the public expense. . . . Let chains then be placed across the streets which lead to the sick, and let guards be appointed to prevent all access to the infected parts of the city, except by physicians, and nurses, and . . . other persons.

. . ."[9] Such a quarantine was too strict for practical observance, but he was advocating a practice that was to become universal in dealing with contagious diseases.

During the spring of 1795 Rush found time to see a few friends occasionally, but scant record of his social activities remains. He was still deeply interested in religion and enjoyed reading books on religious subjects. On May 7, 1795, Elizabeth Drinker recorded in her diary that she had just read the following works borrowed from Dr. Rush, viz.:

The Everlasting Gospel &c. concerning Eternal Redemption, by Paul Siegvolck, a German.

The three Woe Trumpets, of which the first and second are already past, and the third is now begun; by Elhanan Winchester, being the substance of two discourses &c.

The present state of Europe compared with antient prophesies. A sermon preached by Joseph Priestly.

The Lord Jesus Christ worthy of the love of all men, demonstrated in two discourses, by E. Winchester, and a sermon delivered by the same in London.

He read all the new books on medicine as they appeared, frequently receiving complimentary copies from the authors. That he read merely for entertainment and amusement is doubtful. He had been a sober youth and he grew even more serious as he approached middle age.

Death as well as new life entered the Rush home in the summer of 1795. On July 2, the Doctor's mother died and was buried in Christ Church burial ground in Philadelphia. A month later, on August 1, the twelfth child, Samuel, was born to Benjamin and Julia Rush.

During July and August of that year several cases of yellow fever appeared, Rush assuming the cause to be in putrid exhalations, and attributing the fact that the spread was checked to a heavy rainfall on August 30 and 31. The following June and July, 1796, sporadic cases of yellow fever were brought to his attention, but again the disease was effectively checked, according to Rush, by the rain in mid-July.[10]

Often Rush reflected on the epidemic of 1793. Besides the

ghastly and unhappy recollections, there rankled in his mind the memory of the vicious attacks made upon him. Although he had retired from political life after the government had been organized under the Constitution, he felt that not a little of the opposition to his medical opinions grew out of disagreement with his political views. This was either an unjust attitude on the part of his opponents or possibly a figment of Rush's imagination. The day after Christmas, in 1795, he gave vent to his feelings in a letter to General Gates. "Many of us have been forced to expiate our sacrifices in the cause of liberty," he said, "by suffering every species of slander & persecution. I ascribe the opposition to my remedies in the epidemic which desolated our city in 1793, chiefly to an unkind and resentful association of my political principles, with my medical character. My enemies triumphed over me for a while, only because they had contracted no guilt by voting for, or supporting the declaration of independence. I do not mention this fact by way of complaint. A kind and bountiful providence has showered a thousand blessings upon me which more than compensate for the losses and persecutions I have incurred by my Republicanism. I am easy in my circumstances—happy in my family, and since the year 1793 renovated in my constitution. Since the part I took in the establishment of the Government in 1787, I have retired wholly from political life. . . . I still love the common people with all their weaknesses and vices, both of which in our country I ascribe in part to the errors, and corruptions of our government."[11]

It is quite possible, of course, human nature being constituted as it is, although it is difficult to prove without documentary evidence, that some of Rush's political enemies did attack him through his medical practice. Philadelphia business men, too, were badgering him because he continued to assert that the yellow fever was domestic in origin. However, in the fall of 1796, from consultation with physicians in other cities, he was convinced that, in spite of the opposition in his own city, belief in the domestic origin of the fever had become universal in the United States.[12] When another epidemic of yellow fever struck the city in August 1797, Rush refused to budge on the question of domestic origin.

The winter of 1796–97 was, in general, a healthy one. On July

8 and again on the 25th, Rush treated two yellow fever patients, both of whom recovered.

He was not, it seems, too deeply preoccupied to indulge occasionally in mild diversion before he was to be plunged into another epidemic. "Went to see a learned pig," he wrote in his commonplace book on July 14. "He was a year old, was about one-half a foot high and had cost the owner one thousand dollars. He distinguished all the letters in the alphabet on cards and picked them up with his mouth. He spelled every word that was told him by bringing the letters of which those words were composed and laying them at his owner's feet. He did several small sums in addition, subtraction and multiplication. He distinguished colors, and lastly he told the name of the card taken out of a pack by taking up with his mouth the corresponding card from a pack on the floor."[13]

During the first week in August, ten persons who manifested yellow fever symptoms died, and when news of these deaths was gossiped about the city, considerable excitement ensued. Rush believed that this time the fever was derived from the foul air of a ship, just arrived from Marseilles, which had discharged her cargo at Pine Street wharf, and from the foul air of a ship from Hamburg, docked in Kensington, north of Philadelphia proper. It was also caused, he decided, by putrid exhalations from the gutters and marshes at a distance from the Delaware River. For several weeks the disease was confined to the southern part of the city and to Kensington. Casually, Rush made an observation, the supreme importance of which he was never to realize. Mosquitoes were very numerous! There were even more of them than during the summer of 1793. After the first week in September practically every patient he visited was ill with yellow fever.

The citizens were, of course, greatly alarmed. People do not completely forget a catastrophe within the span of four years, and then, too, there had been at intervals sporadic reminders of the devastating epidemic of '93. It was estimated in certain quarters that two-thirds of the residents had left the town, but this figure is certainly an exaggeration. The President, John Adams, went to his home in Braintree, Massachusetts, and the cabinet secretaries moved their offices to various towns in the vicinity of Philadelphia. Sixteen merchants moved their wares to Wilmington, Delaware. Tents were pitched on the east bank of the Schuylkill River for those who had been exposed to the fever. The Legislature went so far as to appropriate $10,000 for the relief of yellow fever sufferers.[14]

Fearing that the disease might spread beyond control, the City Health Office, at the request of the College of Physicians, appointed a special committee of five physicians to administer relief. A quarantine was also imposed. "When persons with infectious fevers have been situated in confined places," reported the *Gazette of the United States* on September 2, "every person belonging to the house, as well as those adjoining, except the necessary attendants, have been pressingly advised to remove—yellow flags have been placed at the door to prevent unnecessary intercourse—and in the neighbourhood of Penn Street, where the infection appeared most malignant, a fence has been erected to stop the communication with that part of the city. The city hospital with several out buildings has been kept in complete order for the reception of the sick, and a number of tents pitched for the accomodation of families, whose connexion with the sick made it necessary for them to remove."

According to Dr. Currie, in the *Gazette* of September 3, about 200 patients had been stricken with yellow fever, and of these between sixty and seventy had died, including twenty-seven sent to the City Hospital during the epidemic. Currie told a physician in Wilmington that he was bleeding and purging patients freely.

On September 6 the *Gazette* noted that the City Hospital Committee had appointed a number of persons to work at the city burial ground day and night to bury such bodies as were sent by order of the Health Officer or the City Hospital. Ten days later it was reported that the City Hospital, which had been opened for only four weeks, had admitted 169 patients, of whom sixty-nine had died. Rush seemed to think that "there were evident marks of the disease attacking more persons three days before, and three days after the full and change of the moon, and of more deaths occurring at those periods than at any other time."[15] This sounds like the backwash of astrology running into eighteenth-century medicine.

In reviewing the symptoms and incidence of the disease in 1797 Rush found little difference in the state of the pulse from what he observed in 1793 or 1794. As in previous years he found "the action of the arteries" very irregular. "I perceived a pulse, in several cases," he recorded, "which felt like a soft quill which had been shattered by being trodden upon." The excretions bore no distinctive marks, nor was the nervous system impaired. Indeed, few patients became delirious after having been bled, but "where blood-letting had not been used, patients frequently died of convulsions." In several cases the senses of sight and touch were impaired, but glandular swellings were uncommon. "The skin was cool, dry, smooth, and even shining in some cases. Yellowness was not universal. Those small red spots, which have been compared to moscheto bites, occurred in several of my patients." More than a century was to pass before the actual part played by the mosquito was discovered.

Rush observed, further, that the number of moderate cases was insignificant compared with those of a malignant or dangerous nature. "It was upon this account," he concluded, "that the mortality was greater in the same number of patients, who were treated with the same remedies, than it was in the years 1793 and 1794." The disease was, on the whole, of a more malignant character than in the epidemics of the other two years. During the months of August, September, and October, the number of deaths totalled 1,000 to 1,100. Nine physicians died. During the epidemic not more than twenty-four physicians were visiting patients, and of these eight were stricken with the fever.[16]

After the fever had played havoc once again in the city, Governor Mifflin was anxious to determine its origin definitely, with a view to prevention in the future. The College of Physicians reported to the Governor that the disease had positively been imported by two ships from the West Indies, and advised more rigid quarantine regulations for the port. The members of the medical faculty of the University of Pennsylvania stated, with an equal degree of positiveness, that the fever was caused by putrid exhalations from the gutters and streets of the city and from the ponds and marsh lands in the vicinity, as well as from foul air of the ships from Marseilles and Hamburg docked along the river front. The faculty recommended once more that the gutters and marshes be drained.[17]

In opposition to the College of Physicians and its pronouncements, and in agreement with the faculty of the University, Rush and a few friends organized the Academy of Medicine of Philadelphia, which, during its short existence, sought to prove that the origin of the fever was entirely domestic. The Academy addressed letters to Governor Mifflin, with Rush's signature topping those of thirteen other physicians, stating that the fever was derived from exhalations from the gutters, streets, ponds and marshes; and secondly from the noxious air emitted from the hold of the ship *Navigation,* Captain Linstroom, from Marseilles, in the southern part of Philadelphia; and in Kensington from the ship *Huldah,* Captain William Warner, from Hamburg. It was suggested that in the summer months ships with cargoes liable to putrefy be unloaded outside the city proper.[18]

During the last weeks of the epidemic as well as later, most of the attacks made on Rush were leveled against his method of treatment rather than against the theory of domestic origin of the disease.

Rush used practically the same treatment he introduced in 1793. He began by bleeding; some patients recovered completely after a single bleeding; others, he said, required the loss of upwards of 100 ounces of blood. In many cases a third remedy, salivation, was employed. "Besides the usual methods of introducing mercury into the system," Rush pointed out, "Dr. Stewart accelerated its action, by obliging his patients to wear socks filled with mercurial ointment; and Dr. Gillespie aimed at the same thing, by injecting the ointment, in a suitable vehicle, into the bowels, in the form of glysters." Because of the strong prejudice against bloodletting, he was anxious to combat the fever with mercury alone, although he was afraid to trust to it without the assistance of the lancet.[19]

On September 14, 1797, the *Gazette of the United States* gave space to a testimonial from Dr. Philip Syng Physick. "With a view of inspiring confidence in blood-letting, in the cure of yellow fever," he wrote while convalescing, "I take this method of informing my fellow citizens, that I lost during my late attack of that fever, 176 ounces of blood by twenty two bleedings in ten days. The efficacy of this valuable remedy was aided by frequent and copious evacuations from my bowels, and a moderate salivation." He felt deeply grateful to Dr. Rush for his recovery. Strangely enough, the very newspaper in which this testimonial appeared shortly began to attack Rush bitterly.

It was found that a vegetable diet was advantageous; indeed, Rush perceived that in some cases convalescents died from eating animal food too soon. Again he advised cold water applied to the body, cool, fresh air, and general cleanliness. "Blisters were applied as usual," Rush reported, "but, from the insensibility of the skin, they were less effectual than applications of mustard to the arms and legs. It is a circumstance of notice, that while the stomach, bowels, and even the large blood-vessels are sometimes in a highly excited state, and overcharged, as it were, with life, the whole surface of the body is in a state of the greatest torpor. To attempt to excite it by internal remedies is like adding fuel to a chimney already on fire."[20]

After analyzing thousands of cases during several epidemics, Rush concluded that fevers for the most part afflict the poor, and that to prevent or to cure them, remedies must be cheap, and easy to apply. "From the affinity established by the Creator between evil and its antidotes, in other parts of his works," the religious-minded Rush suggested, "I am disposed to believe no remedy will ever be effectual in any general disease, that is not cheap, and that cannot easily be made universal."[21]

It was because of his deeply religious and sensitive nature and his intense sincerity that the attacks made by his opponents hurt him all the more. His every action was the expression of the most honest and unselfish motives. However, in fairness to his opponents, it must be stated that his opinions, not his motives, were questioned, but the high-strung, overworked, and harassed man was unable to realize the difference. Even friends who disagreed quite justifiably with his medical views on the epidemic were too frequently set down as personal enemies. That he was so cocksure and stubborn was most unfortunate, for the antagonism he stirred up against himself cut him off from many of his contacts with people, and caused him great unhappiness.

By the end of October he felt utterly alone and deserted. His fellow men seemed to be surrounding him with drawn bayonets. On

October 31, writing John Dickinson that the epidemic was on the decline, he added: "Such seasons as we have just witnessed are called the 'Doctors harvests.' To me it has been an harvest but it has been of unprofitable labor, anxious days, sleepless nights, and a full and overflowing measure of the most merciless persecution. I have not merited the indifference with which the citizens of Philadelphia have butchered my character. When the fever first appeared in our excellent city, my dear and excellent wife spent many hours in urging me to leave it. My second daughter a girl of 13 years of age added tears to the entreaties of her mother to prevail upon me not to expose myself a second time to the dangers and distresses of the year 1793. To their entreaties & tears I made the following reply: 'If I thought by remaining in the city, I should certainly die; I should think it my duty to stay. I will not quit my post.' "[22] No one ever thought of asserting that Rush lacked courage. Indeed he was one of the sterling heroes of his day, but the heroic element in his character did not offset his obstinate and dogmatic manner. His contemporaries were too close to the scene of action to appreciate in proper perspective the fearlessness which characterized his labors in the many frightful months of the 1790's.

In late September, 1797, so incensed was Rush at the savage onslaught made upon him by his critics, that he entertained again the idea of leaving his native city. As he surveyed the situation, he felt that his future in Philadelphia was anything but bright. He complained to his friend, Dr. John R. B. Rodgers, of Columbia College, of the "persecutions of 1793" which had lately been revived against him. Again he mentioned the hostility of the old Tories toward him, because of his activities during the War for Independence, and the antagonism of the Federalists because of his support of Republican political principles. "Ever since the year 1793 I have lived in Philadelphia as in a foreign country," he wrote Rodgers in late September. "This situation is far from being agreeable to me, but it is much less so to my family. My business for several years past has been upon the decline in this city since the year 1793, and were I not employed by strangers I could not maintain my family by my Philadelphia patients." He suggested the possibility of his joining the medical faculty at Columbia. "Under the influence of these events," he went on, "I have contemplated leaving this city & settling in New York. One thing only is necessary to determine my conduct, & that is—a certainty of getting a professors Chair in yr University in which I can disseminate my medical principles. As I would practice only in consultations and prescribe only to such chronic patients as could visit me, I would prefer a residence out of town & near the University. The income of a professorship with that of my estate in Pennsylvania would be sufficient, with a garden, and pasture lot to maintain my family. If you think there is any chance of the above proposition succeeding, you are at liberty to announce it in confidence to some of the Regents of the University—if not—you will please to burn this letter." The letter was not even signed, so great was the excitement in which it was written.[23]

Rodgers, delighted at the prospect of Rush's coming to New York, assured his preceptor that he would welcome him with open arms. Rush's letter was handed to Dr. Mitchell, the Professor of Chemistry at Columbia, to Dr. Post, the Professor of Anatomy, and to Dr. Hamenly, all of whom seemed pleased with Rush's plan of removing to New York. Dr. Hamenly even volunteered to yield to Rush his chair in theory and practice if the faculty concluded that such an arrangement would be for the public good. Rodgers called a meeting of the medical faculty of the College on October 17 to see what could be done.[24]

On October 20 the medical faculty decided unanimously in favor of inviting Rush to join the staff at Columbia. "Dr. Hamenly who has the united Professorships of Theory & Practice offered to give up the Practice to you," Rodgers advised Rush. The professors formally resolved: "That the Faculty consider the appointment of Dr. Benj. Rush to the Practice chair as an event that will very much promote the interests of Columbia College & highly advance the reputation, credit and usefulness of the Medical School." Rodgers then inquired as to Rush's final decision.[25]

As far as the medical faculty was concerned the matter was settled; Rush was to come to Columbia. There was, however, in his path, a towering obstacle, which proved to be insurmountable. Alexander Hamilton, staunch Federalist and no friend of Rush's, was a member of Columbia's Board of Trustees. After the unanimous decision of the medical faculty it was expected that the appointment would be approved in the regular order of business without discussion. Hamilton, however, was definitely opposed to placing the Republican physician, regardless of his fame, on the staff of his institution, and he set himself on guard to block the recommendation.

Although, on November 2, when the trustees first met, Rush was nominated as joint professor of the theory and practice of physic, at the meeting on the following day, when the nomination was brought up for approval, Hamilton arose and proposed a resolution stating that no necessity existed for a new appointment to the medical faculty. Because Rush did not have enough interested friends on the Board to defeat the motion then and there, it was postponed for consideration until the next meeting. Rodgers, angered and provoked, wrote Rush: "The affair now rests there, & we shall try our strength at the next meeting of the Trustees whether the old haven of bigotry and political resentment shall triumph or not—I hope for the honor of Columbia College it will be foiled—but my dear Sir that will have no effect upon your reputation if you choose our city as your home, nor will it give you one pupil less at your class—whether the Trustees give you a standing in the College or not you will still have the interest of the Faculty & its good wishes & all its pupils." Rodgers suggested that no matter what happened at the University, Rush should offer a course of lectures in New York.[26]

When news of this sudden turn of events reached Rush, he decided immediately to strike New York from his mind. Moreover, he did not wish to have the question discussed again by the trustees. He was, nevertheless, disappointed and dismayed at the shock, as he had anticipated his election. Under stress of the first strong feelings of frustration, he went so far as to think seriously of giving up medicine entirely for agriculture. But it was one of those ideas which spring to mind in a disturbed moment and disappear before they come to fruition. He unburdened himself to Rodgers: "When I proposed removing from Philad^a to New York I contemplated a situation in which I could follow the wishes of my heart, to live in peace with every body, and where the principal source of hostility to me would cease from the universal prevalence of the same opinion which I have held of the domestic origin of the yellow fever. I expected to avoid the principal sources of hostility to me. In this wish & expectation I have been disappointed. I therefore request that you stop the business in its present stage, and aprise the Trustees of the University that I shall not accept the appointment shd it be offered to me after the obstacles that have been thrown in the way of it by Mr. Hamilton.

"It is peculiarly gratifying to me to know that the opposition to my appointment came from that gentleman.

"I beg my most grateful & affectionate acknowledgments may be made the medical faculty of the University for the liberal and disinterested friendship they have manifested to me upon this question.

"My determination to retire from my present scene of strife is unshaken, and I am happy in being able to inform you that the prospects of independence & usefulness have lately been opened to me in my native state far more respectable tho' much less agreeable than the one I wished for in your University. My wish is to retire to a farm where I shall have leisure. . . ." Unfortunately, however, Rush's income at this time was not large enough to permit of his retirement to the country, where he desired to devote the rest of his life to a complete statement of his system of medicine.[27]

The contemplated removal to New York now out of the question and the farmer's life only a dream, Rush remained in Philadelphia. To make matters worse, many of his former patients, having lost confidence in him by reason of the attacks on his medical opinions, were consulting other physicians. "From the year 1793 till 1797 my business was stationary in Philadelphia, after 1797 it sensibly declined," recorded Rush. "I had no new families except foreigners, added to the list of my patients and many of my old patients deserted me. Even the cures I performed added to the detraction that had taken place against my character, when they were effected by remedies that were new and contrary to the feelings of citizens. No ties of ancient school fellowship, no obligations of gratitude, no sympathy in religious or philosophical opinions, were able to resist the tide of public clamor that was excited against my practice. My name was mentioned with horror in some companies, and to some of the weakest and insignificant of my brethren false tales of me became a recommendation to popular favor."[28]

The expenses of his rapidly growing household were heavy and the diminution of income was a source of worry to Rush. At this time, 1797, there were five sons and two daughters ranging in age from two to twenty. Rush's responsibilities as a parent were weighty, and so he was thankful when a means of augmenting his income presented itself. Back in 1795 he had been asked to become director of the United States Mint at an annual salary of $750, but he had declined the invitation, believing that he would be criticized. People might feel that the position interfered with his practice. He declined the post also because, as he said: "My business was more profitable to me than three times the value of the office; thirdly, because it would prevent my introducing my son into business by withdrawing me from it, and fourthly, because I had devoted myself to the establishment of a new system of physic."[29]

When the office of treasurer of the Mint became vacant in the fall of 1797 Rush, pinched by economic considerations, cast aside his previous objections. Indeed, he was more than anxious to obtain the position and its salary. He made his wish known to President John Adams, through his wife's uncle, Elias Boudinot, then director of the Mint. Timothy Pickering who as secretary of state had been a neighbor of Rush's, also recommended him to the President. Adams, having fled the city when the epidemic had become critical, wrote Pickering from his home in Quincy, Massachusetts, on September 18. "Dr. Rush I have known, esteemed, and loved, these three and twenty years," he said. "His learning and ingenuity are respectable and his public and private virtues amiable. His services from the beginning of our great Revolution were conspicuous and meritorious. He had no small share in recommending our present Constitution, and might be eminently useful to the present administration." Adams disclosed that he had under consideration a large number of applicants and had been comparing their qualifications. "I hope my judgment is not too much influenced by my affections, if it leans in favor of Dr. Rush," he continued. "If your opinion is clearly with mine, you may make out his commission as soon as you please."[30]

Two weeks passed and again the President wrote his Secretary of State, on October 2: "The applications for the Treasury of the

Mint are so numerous and respectable, that whoever obtains it ought to think himself highly honored by his competitors, if not by his appointment. My prevailing opinion, which I have before intimated to you, is not altered."[31]

From the list of some forty applicants Rush was chosen and appointed treasurer of the Mint. The position was sought by many because it carried with it influence as well as an annual salary of $1,200. Rush was gratified by his appointment and he took up his duties in the first United States Mint building, erected in 1792 on the east side of Seventh Street near Arch. It was a plain brick building and was used for this purpose for forty years.

The demands of his new post, which he retained until his death, were not burdensome and hardly interfered with his medical practice and teaching. The duties of the Treasurer were specified by Director Boudinot in an official notice: "He is to receive all Bullion of the precious metals and copper, with the coin struck in the mint, and all monies advanced by the government on the Director's application, and issue the same on the warrants of the Director, and be accountable for the same—He must attend every day (unless excused by the Director) between the Hours of ten & twelve o'clock of the morning to receive deposits, issue bullion and pay the current accounts as occasion may require. The Treasurer being accountable for all Receipts & issues of every kind, his own interest as well as the ordering of the Department, will lead him to attend to the daily entries of everything relative to the business of the mint, agreably to the rules established for keeping the accounts, and will make it an indispensable duty to settle his accounts & balance them every quarter, that is on the last day of March, June, September, & December."[32]

After organizing the work in his customarily efficient manner, Rush found the duties much less arduous than they appeared. During the first few years of his incumbency he was able to devote more time to the job than was actually required because his practice had further dwindled as a result of the newspaper attacks that had been launched against him by John Fenno and William Cobbett in September and October, 1797.

Fenno, as editor of the *Gazette of the United States,* published his personal broadsides in the form of Letters to the Editor in which he struck at Rush's "lunatic system" of medicine. He tried to convince the public that Rush had gone far beyond any sane medium of treatment, that he was, indeed, a fanatic. "Humanity loudly calls on the obstinate adherents to the violent system, to advert now and then to the maxim,—Medium Iter Tutissimus Ibis" [You will travel most safely in the middle of the road].[33]

A series of attacks on Rush appeared in Fenno's newspaper. At the same time the editor occasionally published letters from readers in defense of the physician. On September 30 a correspondent, in praising Rush, stated that the attacks could not injure the reputation of "our American Hippocrates." He claimed that Rush's method of treatment was advocated by Philadelphia's most respectable physicians, and that the great man labored only to improve the science of medicine. "He finds an ample reward in the approbation of his own conscience"; the letter went on, "his endeavours have been crowned with success, and he has added largely to the stock of human happiness."

This and similar laudatory paragraphs failed to quench the fire produced by Fenno's tirades, and Rush finally brought suit against him for libel. Fenno was in a rage; he asserted that the liberty of the press was in danger, and on October 3 printed in his *Gazette* an article under the caption "Assault on the Liberty of the Press," in which Rush was once more bitterly denounced. Fenno claimed that he had attacked Rush's doctrines because he believed them to be dangerous to society. "The plain fact is," ran the editorial, "that the Dr. still retains that same principle of ambition and that same thirst for popularity, which has ever distinguished him through life. His great aim seems to have been to retire from the practice of medicine, with the fame of an Esculapius, and to carry to his grave the credit of some wonderful discovery, which shall rank him with Harvey, Chiselden, or Hunter, or Boylston. . . ." He was not succeeding in this aim and, when the French Revolution rendered blood the most popular topic of conversation, he hit upon the idea of bloodletting! Who loses seven patients out of eight? asked Fenno. Who says that almost every disease can be cured by bloodletting? Is it not true that the doctors who lose the fewest patients are those who bleed sparingly?

Harsh words these and not all true. Rush was, of course, ambitious, but so is every man with a spark of mental and physical energy. Whether or not he was thirsty for popularity to the point of prostituting his profession to fanciful theories is another question. He was undoubtedly sensitive to the opinions of his fellow men. On the other hand he derived satisfaction in pursuing, in the face of strong opposition, any course he deemed right. First and foremost he was an idealist and, had he merely craved popularity, he would not have been so bold in upholding ideas which he knew would alienate him from influential public groups. Often his fearless attitude resulted in decided unpopularity. That he was anxious to develop his own system of medicine and that he hoped to win credit for some discoveries in his field is true. Furthermore, Rush's record in the epidemic of 1793 does not indicate that he lost "seven patients out of eight." Far from it.

Before the suit against Fenno had progressed very far in the courts, Rush decided to drop it. Libel suits against Americans were rarely decided in favor of the plaintiff, and so it was surmised that Fenno would not be convicted by a jury of his fellow countrymen.[34] Furthermore, Rush really wanted to concentrate his legal attack on another opponent. An English journalist and pamphleteer, William Cobbett, who came to America in 1792 and opened a book shop on Second Street, opposite Christ Church, directed his vitriolic pen against Rush in *Porcupine's Gazette,* a newspaper which he began to publish in March 1797. Under the pen name of "Peter Porcupine" he devoted his talents to controversial paragraphs. He set out to influence the minds of his readers by taking daring shots at leading men and matters of public policy. In early September 1797, he opened fire upon the treatments prescribed by Rush. The Doctor was referred to in *Porcupine's Gazette* as a "poisonous trans-Atlantic quack" and the "Samson" of medicine who had actually slaughtered thousands of citizens. Bleeding was the bull's eye of the target, but the "injudicious" doses of mercury were also well within range of his fire. Soon scores of readers accepted Cobbett's view. Many times one heard ghastly tales of victims who bled to death, and macabre jests about "ten and ten" powders.

Again Rush's ire was aroused, this time to the point of fury. In October he announced that he would institute a suit for libel against the blustering slanderer, Cobbett. The newspapers were chock-full of letters and articles bringing Rush publicity which was hardly profitable. All his weaknesses were played up, his merits forgotten, as his name was bandied about by inveterate letter writers and the town gossips. Only a few friends sprang to his defense.

On September 19 there appeared in *Porcupine's Gazette* an article entitled "Medical Puffing," which Rush felt was outrageous as well as distinctly libelous. Cobbett started out with verse:

> The times are ominous indeed,
> When quack to quack cries purge and bleed.

He then called attention to the arts that Rush, the "remorseless Bleeder is making use of to puff his preposterous practice." He charged that Rush wrote letters to his friends whose replies in praise of his methods were published by prearrangement in the newspapers. After quoting from one of these letters, Cobbett commented: "Dr. Rush, in that emphatical stile which is peculiar to himself, calls mercury 'the Samson of Medicine.' In his hands and in those of his partizans it may indeed be justly compared to Samson; for I verily believe they have slain more Americans with it, than ever Samson slew of the Philistines. The Israelite slew his thousands, but the Rushites have slain their tens of thousands." Rush could hardly sit complacently and allow such scurrility to pass unnoticed, nor could he ignore the caption of a later article: "Can the Rush Grow Up Without Mire?"

Fuming with wrath Rush importuned Joseph Hopkinson, a young lawyer, to restrain Cobbett's pen through court action. Hopkinson had not yet celebrated his thirtieth birthday and this was his first important case. Later he was to achieve fame not only as an attorney but as the author of "Hail Columbia." Associated with him as counsel in the case were Moses Levy, Jared Ingersoll, and William Lewis. The suit for libel was inaugurated in the December, 1797, term of the Supreme Court of Pennsylvania, and Joseph Thomas, attorney for Cobbett, on December 30 filed a petition requesting that the case be removed to the United States Circuit Court, inasmuch as Cobbett was a British subject and the case involved a consideration of more than five hundred dollars. The petition was not acted upon until March 1798, when Chief Justice McKean denied the motion, holding that the amount of damages could not be determined without a formal trial.

After several postponements the case was finally brought to trial before the Supreme Court of Pennsylvania in December 1799. In the meantime McKean was elected Governor of the State and Edward Shippen became Chief Justice. On the 13th day of December Justices Shippen, Yeates, and Smith heard the arguments. Messrs. Rawle, Harper, and Tilghman represented Cobbett. For two days the lawyers presented arguments and evidence. Lawyer Hopkinson addressed the jury ably. "The attack made on Dr. Rush," he said, "is of the most deadly and violent kind that malice could invent, or abandoned depravity execute. He is accused of murder, or destroying the lives of his fellow citizens, in a time of dreadful calamity." He proceeded to defend the Doctor's professional conduct during the epidemics of 1793 and 1797, and attempted to show that Cobbett's attack was motivated by political and personal malice. He argued that Cobbett did not seek to present useful information to the public on an interesting question, or to correct any errors in Rush's system or method of treatment, but that the attack was a personal one against Rush and not against his system of medicine. Referring directly to Cobbett he exclaimed: "The eye of decency can seldom read his pages without offence, and virtue turns from them with indignation and disgust. Is there a species of editorial pollution that has not blackened them? If there be, it is because it has escaped the laborious industry, and acuteness of this strange man." And, turning finally to the jury, he rested the case with this appeal: "The injured father of an amiable family, the worthy citizen, the useful philosopher now sues before you—Professional science implores that countenance and protection without which she must wither and die —virtue, bleeding at every pore, calls for justice on her despoiler, and the anxious heart of every honest man pants with impatience to meet in you, the Defenders of Virtue, and the Scourgers of Vice."

Lawyer Ingersoll added that Cobbett had formed "a deliberate design of demolishing the reputation of Dr. Rush," and that by frequently referring to him as a quack, he showed that the man and not the medical system was the object of his attack.[35]

Satisfied with their plea, Hopkinson and his aides retired in an optimistic frame of mind. Lawyer Rawle came forward and presented the case for the defense. He insisted that in the pages of *Porcupine's Gazette* Cobbett had merely discussed a public question which was on the tongues and in the minds of all the citizens. Rawle read a letter written by Rush to Drs. Physick and Cooper, in August 1798, concerning the treatment of yellow fever. In this letter Rush had written that there was no precise method of treatment for all cases, and that bleeding and mercurial purges did not constitute the proper treatment in every stage and appearance of the fever. Therefore, argued Rawle, Rush admitted that more than one method of treatment was possible; and, consequently, everyone had the right to make his own observations. Rawle contended, further, that the plaintiff had not shown that he had sustained any injury and that no definite amount of damages was demanded; and that, therefore, it must be held that no direct injury was sustained from Cobbett's writings. If, he pleaded, Rush's system has been so useful and so infallible, "the feeble efforts of Mr. Cobbett could not destroy his celebrity."[36]

The outcome of the trial was uncertain, the atmosphere tense, when, toward the close of the second day, Justice Shippen turned to the jury to deliver his charge. In reviewing the case he explained that action had been brought against Cobbett for writing, printing, and publishing scandalous libels to defame and vilify Rush. Although Cobbett pleaded "not guilty," the attacks had actually been published and therefore the question to be decided was whether or not they constituted defamatory libels. "A libel," the Justice explained, "is defined by law, to be malicious defamation, expressed either in printing or writing, or by signs or pictures, tending to blacken either the memory of one who is dead, or the reputation of one who is alive, or to expose him to public hatred, contempt or ridicule."

"The charges against the defendant in the declaration," the Justice continued, "are various; but they may be reduced in substance to the following.—That he repeatedly calls the plaintiff a quack, an empyric; charges him with intemperate bleeding, injudiciously administering mercury in large doses in the yellow fever; puffing himself off; writing letters and answering them himself, stiling him the Sampson in Medicine; charging him with murdering his patients and slaying his thousands, and tens of thousands." He added that the Cobbett publications were "certainly libellous" and that "the liberty of the press . . . is a valuable right in every free country, and ought never to be unduly restrained; but when it is perverted to the purposes of private slander, it then becomes a most destructive engine in the hands of unprincipled men."[37]

The jury deliberated for two hours and, finally, returned its verdict. The decision was in favor of the plaintiff, who was awarded $5,000. Including the cost of the suit, Cobbett's rashness had cost him $8,000. He did not pay the full amount to Rush, however, for in the summer of 1801, Cobbett's attorney made a settlement for $4,000.[38] Rush donated the money to charity.

The verdict of the jury was a bitter pill for Cobbett to swallow. In fact it ruined him. His Philadelphia property fell under the sheriff's hammer and the sheets of part of a new edition of *Porcupine's Collected Works* were sold as waste paper.

Cobbett, however, was by no means ready to retire from the field. He decided to hammer at Rush regardless of the verdict against him. Just a month after the trial, on January 13, 1800, he launched another attack. "Rush and his five thousand dollars having made a great noise," Cobbett felt called upon to reopen the whole subject. He now stated that, in 1793, Rush had originated the practice of bleeding patients and had become head of the "Bleeders." He referred to Rush's defense of his remedies in letters to newspapers and to other physicians and asked: "And, if this be not puffing, if it does not resemble the conduct of Quacks, I beg the learned brethren of the lancet to tell me what it is." He questioned the honesty of the Court, writing: "I always had my doubts . . . that Rush, that sleek-headed saint-looking Rush, knew the judges and juries better than my friends did, and the result has, at last, proved that my doubts were but too well founded."

Cobbett craved revenge, and in the middle of February he published the first number of a small periodical, *The Rush Light,* in order, as he said, "to assist the publick view, in the inspecting of various tenebrious objects," and to expose everyone connected with Rush and the Court which tried the suit. "Rush is remarkable for insinuating manners," he commented sarcastically, "and for that smoothness and softness of tongue, which the mock-quality call politeness, but which the profane vulgar call blarny. To see and hear him, you would think he was all friendship and humanity." He scoffed at Rush for joining different churches on various occasions to try to please all the sects, and for accepting "that lucrative sine-cure the treasureship of the mint" from John Adams, to whom he was opposed politically.[39] He attacked Rush's lawyers and the statements made by them.

In the second issue of *The Rush Light,* February 28, Cobbett listed his reasons for opposing Rush's system of depletion, and defended the articles which he himself had written during the epidemic of 1797. He believed that "Rush had constantly endeavoured to place himself at the head of something or other . . . he had ever been upon the search for some discovery, some captivating novelty, to which he might prefix his name, and thus reach, at a single leap, the goal at which men seldom arrive but by slow cautious and painful approaches." He was questioning the motives behind Rush's exercise of his duty as a scientist, to be constantly on the lookout for fresh facts.

In the next issue of the periodical, March 15, Cobbett again defended the charges that he had previously made against Rush. He was a "vain-boaster," as evidenced by his own publications concerning his work during the epidemic of 1793; further, he was a quack because he continually boasted about his medical superiority in public places and in the newspapers. Conceit, perhaps it was, but hardly quackery! Further, he stated, it is true that Rush "slew his patients."

The fourth number of the periodical carried the self-explanatory sub-title: "A Peep Into a Pennsylvanian Court of Justice."

At length Cobbett's ammunition gave out without doing much damage, and he sailed for England on June 1, 1800. Rush, of course, rejoiced at the departure of this plaguing journalist who had been a thorn in his side for almost three years. Cobbett's newspaper attacks, the final judgment of the court notwithstanding, had led numbers of patients and friends to desert the physician. For many months Rush furnished an absorbing topic of conversation in the inns and taverns, and as long as he was before the public eye— usually undiscriminating in controversial matters—his practice continued to decline. Seldom was he called by a new patient in these heartbreaking years.

In the midst of the fight with Cobbett the yellow fever again appeared in the city, in 1798. On April 7 Rush visited a yellow fever patient who died on the next evening, but he was not alarmed because no other cases had been reported. Two months passed, and on June 6 Dr. Samuel Cooper lost a yellow fever patient; four weeks later another patient died from the same disease. Between July 2 and July 20 about a dozen yellow fever cases were reported in different parts of the city remote from the Delaware River. Then on July 21 the ship *Deborah* from the West Indies was moored at Kensington, "where the foul air which was emitted from her hold produced several cases of yellow fever, near the shores of that village." In the month of August the disease appeared in nearly every corner of the city and particularly in those sections where there were foul gutters and open sewers. The fever attacked persons of all ages, both white and black. "In the blacks," observed Rush, "it was attended with less violence and mortality than in white people. It affected many persons who had previously had it." The poor in the city hospital were cared for by Rush and Dr. Physick, and so generous were Rush's services at the Pennsylvania Hospital that he was presented with a handsome silver platter as a mark of appreciation.

During August and September the weather was warm and dry and mosquitoes were plentiful. The epidemic was checked for a time by a frost on September 29, but it spread again with the return of warm weather. Rush believed, as in previous years, that the fever owed its origin to the exhalations from gutters, docks, cellars, common sewers, ponds of stagnating water, and also from the foul air of the ship *Deborah*.[40] As president of the Academy of Medicine, Dr. Physick addressed a letter to the Board of Health on August 9 in which he supported Rush's theory.[41]

Rush observed the same symptoms and used the same treatment as in former epidemics. In answer to a request for suggestions from Physick and Cooper, Rush wrote, on August 13, that in 1797 he concluded that death occurred in some cases after the administration of the bleeding and purging remedies on account of the "stagnation of acrid bile in the gall bladder." In order to stimulate the gall bladder and to discharge its contents he advised the use of "tartar emetic, gamboge, jalap and calomel, combined, or given separately, and in small or large doses, according to circumstances." He reported that he had not lost a single patient to whom he had given this powerful remedy; in some cases two doses were given in a single day.[42] This is the letter referred to by Cobbett's attorney during the trial.

During the epidemic Rush lived outside the city proper, on Sydenham Street, and devoted most of his time to charity patients in the city. Toward the end of August he felt that the epidemic was under control. Furthermore, it seemed that he was regaining some of the public favor which he had lost. "The way is now open and smooth for my usefulness," he wrote his wife on August 29. "Public confidence is again placed in me, and my opinions and advice have at last some weight. Under these circumstances I cannot think of retiring altogether. My business is confined chiefly to my old patients, to strangers, & the poor. I refuse applications daily to wealthy & respectable people. I go to town about 9 o'clock in the morning and return to our hut always before sunset. I am seldom fatigued, and have as yet felt none of the aches and pains of 1797."[43]

According to Rush the number of persons affected by the fever was four times as great in 1793 as in 1798, because in 1798 a larger percentage of the population left the city. The total number of deaths, however, from August to November, totalled 3,446 in 1798 compared with more than 4,000 in 1793. The death rate in 1798 was strikingly greater than in 1793. The widespread public disapproval, in 1797, of a "liberal and general use of the lancet" excited in the people fear and prejudice against its use the following year. Therein, according to Rush, lay the explanation of the high mortality rate in 1798.[44]

The fever again appeared in June and July of 1799, once more causing a general exodus from the city, but it did not reach the proportions of previous visitations. Rush continued to use the depleting remedies, although he occasionally prescribed other remedies in 1799 to satisfy public opinion. "We have yielded to public prejudice and importunity," he confessed to Timothy Pickering, "by prescribing yeast, lime water and milk, and several other simples, but all to no other purpose, than now and then, easing a troublesome symptom. From the experience of six years, I am satisfied the disease can be cured when in its malignant form, only by depleting remedies. These may admit of some variety in different seasons and constitutions, but the operation of them all, whether they act immediately upon the stomach, bowels, pores, salivary glands, or blood vessels, is to evacuate, and thereby to weaken and reduce the system preternaturally excited, or convulsed by the stimulus of a poison acting upon it. The success of my private practice by the use of the above remedies has been such as to encrease my attachment to them—having lost out of about 50 patients but two, and these I did not see 'till the 3rd day of the disease. They both moreover refused to submit to several of my prescriptions. . . ."[45]

The fever of 1799 disappeared rather quickly, and by August few cases were seen. There were only sporadic cases in 1800 and in 1801. In the fall of the latter year Rush was apparently in a better frame of mind and was facing the world with new courage, if we are to judge from a letter to Dr. Currie: "Dr. Rush is happy in being able to inform his friend Dr. Currie, that liberty, peace, order and plenty continue to pervade every part of the United States. Out of nearly five millions of people in our country, not more probably than twenty persons with healthy appetites, have passed this day without two or [more] comfortable meals. Of what country upon the face of the earth can the same thing be said on any one day of the year?"[46]

In the summer of the next year a few cases of yellow fever appeared. On August 5 the Board of Health, in more or less of a panic, publicly declared the fever to be contagious, and advised that the city be deserted immediately. The outbreak was mild although the fever continued throughout August and September, and not until October 5 did the Board suggest that the citizens return to the city.

In July of 1803 two deaths from yellow fever were reported in the last week of July, followed by several cases in August and several in different parts of the city in September, but chiefly in the neighborhood of Water Street near Walnut. On September 12 the Board of Health, contradicting its statement of the previous year, published an announcement that the fever was not contagious. It had been imported by a boat from New York. Five per cent of the victims died. This small proportion showed, according to Rush, that "this fever was of a less malignant nature than it had been in most of the years in which it had been epidemic."[47]

During the summer of 1804 and again in 1805 there were a few scattered cases of the fever.

In the ten years from 1793 to 1803, Rush had treated thousands of yellow fever patients, and from his vast experience he was able to draw important conclusions. In his account of the epidemics of 1793, 1794, and 1797, Rush stated definitely that yellow fever is contagious. Later, he changed this opinion, to which he had held so firmly, and admitted that he had erred in the earlier years. In the fall of 1802 Dr. Edward Miller of New York City spoke of Rush's "excellent paper on the non-contagiousness of yellow fever."[48] In 1793 Rush, although he believed at that time in the contagious nature of the fever, did not consider it highly communicable. His new view was propounded with his usual vigor. In the fall of 1803 he wrote John Coakley Lettsom, celebrated London physician, that "Many hundred instances have occurred this year, which clearly demonstrate that it [yellow fever] is not propagated by contagion, but wholly by means of an atmosphere, rendered impure by putrid exhalations." Six months later he again wrote Lettsom that he was sorry to differ with him on yellow fever, insisting that the disease was caused by putrid exhalations from dead animal and vegetable matter. "It is not contagious, and never spreads beyond the atmosphere in which it is created."[49]

Finally, in his "Facts Intended to Prove the Yellow Fever Not to Be Contagious," Rush maintained once more that the fever is not contagious in its simple state and that it spreads exclusively by means of exhalations from putrid matter which is diffused in the air. This is evident, he wrote, because authorities agree that the fever does not spread by contagion in the West Indies; nor does it spread in the country districts when carried thither from the cities. It does not spread in yellow fever hospitals when they are situated beyond the influence of the impure air in which it is generated; nor does it spread in cities from any specific matter emitted from the bodies of sick people. "It generally requires the coöperation of an exciting cause, with miasmata, to produce it. This is never the case with diseases which are universally acknowledged to be contagious." There are circumstances, he said, which seem to indicate, though incorrectly, that the disease is contagious. When a person is attended in a small filthy room, for example, the accumulated excretions of the body ultimately acquire the same properties as the putrid animal matters known to cause malignant fevers. Similarly, when a person sleeps on a bed used by a yellow fever patient, the disease is communicated in the same way as from any other putrid matter.

To prove that the fever is propagated by means of an impure atmosphere Rush demonstrated that it appears only in those climates and seasons of the year in which heat, acting upon moist animal and vegetable matters, fills the air with their putrid exhalations; and that it is unknown where marshes, ponds, docks, gutters, sinks, unventilated ships, and other sources of noxious air, are not found. Continuous and heavy rains check the fever, especially when followed by cold weather. It is completely checked by frost, and likewise destroyed, Rush believed, by intense heat and high winds. "The influence of damp weather, in retaining and propagating miasmata, will be readily admitted, by recollecting how much more easily hounds track their prey, and how much more extensively odours of all kinds pervade the atmosphere, when it is charged with moisture, than in dry weather."

If the view were to be accepted that yellow fever is noncontagious, friends and families would no longer desert patients nor become hysterical in their presence. "It will lead us to a speedy removal of all excretions," Rush visioned, "and a constant ventilation of the rooms of patients in the yellow fever, and thereby prevent the accumulation, and further putrefaction of those exhalations which may reproduce it. . . . By deriving the fever from our own climate and atmosphere, we shall be able to foresee its approach in the increased violence of common diseases, in the morbid state of vegetation, in the course of the winds, in the diseases of certain brute animals, and in the increase of common, or the appearance of uncommon insects." Finally, the changed conception of the nature of the disease would lead to the proper drainage of marshes, gutters, sewers, and cellars.[50]

During the remainder of his medical career Rush continued to hold yellow fever to be noncontagious, but he just as strongly retained his original belief in its domestic origin.

Colonel Percy M. Ashburn, medical historian of the United States Army, points out that dengue, breakbone fever, or scarlatina rheumatica, was recognized in the army only a century ago and suggests that Rush "described it as 'bilious remittent fever,' and under that name it was commonly confused by him and others with yellow fever and malaria." Another physician has observed that: "Although he never could have realized it himself, he probably wrote more correctly about dengue fever than about yellow fever."[51]

A century was to pass before the true nature of yellow fever transmission was determined. Rush was correct in connecting its incidence with warm and marshy areas, bad drainage and filth. He did not dream of the part the mosquito plays although, strangely enough, he came miraculously near the truth when on several occasions during the epidemics he made mention of the extraordinary number of mosquitoes. His belief that negroes are less susceptible to the disease than whites still holds.

Not yet has the causative germ of the fever been discovered. The disease was first recognized in the West Indies in 1647; it appeared in New York City in 1668, in Boston in 1691, and in Charleston, South Carolina in 1699. Dr. Josiah Clark Nott was one of the first to hint that the mosquito plays a part in the transmission of the disease, and his idea was advanced by Dr. Carlos Finlay in 1881. At the close of the Spanish-American War Major Walter Reed was sent to Cuba to study yellow fever at the head of an Army Board consisting of James Carroll, Aristide Agramonte, and Jesse W. Lazear. For experimental purposes fourteen cases were produced by mosquitoes, six by injection of blood, and two by the injection of filtered blood serum.

The story of the heroism of these men is well known. Carroll submitted to inoculation and nearly died of an attack. Lazear, after an accidental mosquito bite, succumbed to the disease. The results of the experiment were momentous. It was proved that the cause of the disease is either an ultramicroscopic organism or a filterable virus transmitted to man only by a mosquito, the stegomyia fasciata or calopus. At that point the fight against yellow fever was won.

The symptoms recognized today are fever climbing as high as 105°, flushed face, red nostrils and lips, a tongue coated but bright red at the tip and sides, nausea and vomiting, albumen in the urine, lemon-yellow skin, headache, hemorrhages from the nose, mouth, or gums. A quantity of blood in the material rejected from the stomach is looked upon as a dangerous sign.

The mortality in epidemics runs as low as ten per cent; in Rio Janeiro in 1898 it reached 94.5 per cent. The disease can and has been stamped out by destroying the breeding places of the mosquito. Had Philadelphia cleaned its alleys, gutters, and ponds, as Rush suggested, the city would indeed have been spared the devastation wrought by the epidemics in the 1790's.

The future was to disprove his theories and invalidate his treatments. The epithet of "bleeder" was to cling to him and damage his reputation among his contemporaries and his fame before posterity, but for his unselfish service, his courage, and the firmness with which he held to his course, he emerges a man of heroic cast.

X

Theory and Practice

THE eighteenth century was marked by great political changes: the rise to power and influence of Prussia and Russia, the downfall of the old régime in France, the partition of Poland, the expansion of the British Empire, and the successful revolt of the American colonies. Scientific discovery and the spirit of reform moved forward hand in hand. Among the progressive steps in natural science, which antedate the French Revolution, there are the experiments of Newton, DuFay, Franklin, and Coulomb in physics; the work of Leibnitz and Newton in mathematics; the findings of Scheele, Priestley, Cavendish, and Lavoisier in chemistry; the invention of botanical nomenclature by Linnæus; the pioneer researches of Buffon and Lamarck in physiology and zoölogy; and the exposition of the processes of digestion by Réaumur and Spallanzani, and of respiration by Lavoisier.

In Europe hospitals were increasing in number, while here and there in America new ones were being organized. The medical center of gravity shifted from France to England and Scotland, and the majority of doctors in the American colonies received their formal training under such distinguished Englishmen as Hunter, Cullen, Pott, and Guy. The American physician watched with no little interest the development of histology under Bichat, of pathology under Morgagni, of physiology under Haller. Medical theories in general went through a period of mushroom growth, while American medicine was influenced to a great degree by the theories of Thomas Sydenham, Hermann Boerhaave, William Cullen, and John Brown.

Sydenham was one of the first physicians to stress the importance of clinical experience over theory. He is known as the founder of modern clinical medicine, and was Rush's inspiration. He died in 1689, more than a half century before Rush was born, and yet he influenced Rush's medical ideas more than any other one person. He attempted to describe accurately what he observed without permitting theoretical explanations to confuse the picture. He asserted that physicians should learn to recognize diseases by observing them. Two-thirds of all diseases, he said, are fevers. His descriptions of disease won for him a place of honor in the medical history of the seventeenth century. American physicians were for a long time influenced by Sydenham's theory that, in an effort to expel a harmful substance from the body, nature developed specific symptoms; and, to cure disease the morbific matter must be eliminated through perspiration, in the stools, and in cutaneous eruptions.

Dr. Lettsom believed that in some phases of medicine Rush surpassed Sydenham. "In the inestimable work of Sydenham we contemplate the minuteness of perception and depth of meditation, constituting a mental energy which enabled him to discriminate facts," said Lettsom, "and with a vivid penetration, to form a beautiful concatenation of experience that perhaps was never equalled in medical science. Rush approached if not exceeded him in grandeur and compass of thought, though less discriminating in that felicitous arrangement of medical phaenomena which distinguished Sydenham, whilst his theories were less consonant to nature. Rush possessed a lively imagination, which his extent of judgment could alone controul, and lead to important discoveries; and though he sought to rise above the trammels of established opinions, and delighted to grasp at novelties, he did not wish to be paradoxical. If he acquired less facility of method and arrangement than Sydenham, he rivalled him in vigour of investigation, and still more in boldness and decision of professional practice."[1]

Rush said that, when he started to practise in Philadelphia, in 1769, the theories of the Dutch physician, Boerhaave, chief of the humoral school, governed the practice of every medical man in Philadelphia. Boerhaave it was who instituted bedside clinical teaching and, flourishing immediately after Sydenham, he established clinical observation on a systematic basis. Three constitutional predispositions, also termed diatheses, were recognized by Boerhaave: salt, putrid, and oily temperaments. His therapy was the depleting and debilitating use of bloodletting and purges. It was taught that fever is nature's effort to prevent death, that inflammation is the mechanical obstruction of the capillaries, and that circulation and digestion can be explained on mechanical principles.

Rush was also influenced by William Cullen, under whom he studied at Edinburgh. Cullen proposed a theory known as solidism—a dynamic something called "nerve principle" which was thought to produce spasm and atony, abnormal relaxation. He also preached simplicity in therapeutics, and held forth against the use of bloodletting. After a number of years, Rush discarded Cullen's system of theoretical nosologies, long lists of names which, Rush believed, burdened the memory. For Rush clinical facts were more important than names, and the pulse became the "nosometer of the system."

Rush adopted some of Dr. John Brown's terms in the formulation of his own system. Brown, also from Edinburgh, based his theory on the supposition that all living tissue is excitable. If the excitability is increased, there results sthenic disease, in which activity or energy is exhibited; if decreased, asthenic disease is the result. The treatment was simple. Decrease or stimulate as the case required, using plenty of alcohol or opium until the patient returned to that intermediate grade of excitement which spells health.

Having been influenced, like all the contemporary American physicians, by the theories of these medical solons of the seventeenth and eighteenth centuries, Rush ultimately worked out his own theories. His system was developed fully soon after he succeeded Dr. John Morgan to the chair of the Theory and Practice of Medicine, in 1789, in what later became the University of Pennsylvania. From that year until his death in 1813 the history of American medicine is, by and large, the history of Rush's work as a teacher, practitioner, and theorist. One finds in his methods much that resembles Sydenham's rare powers of observation of the symptoms of disease. So exact an observer was he that many of his descriptions of disease are still classic and reliable. He broke away from Cullen's system at this time, 1789, although it was then the basis of medical practice in Philadelphia. Stimulants and depressants were the two kinds of remedies recognized by Rush, while in the treatment of yellow fever in 1793, he became the chief advocate of phlebotomy.

His break with the Cullen school was a personal sacrifice because it led directly to loss of consultation practice. Many of the physicians in Philadelphia, faithful to Cullen's theories, refused any longer to refer patients to Rush, and this antagonism continued for several years. Rush, however, would not be hindered by this opposition, and persisted in the further development of his own theories.

Most diseases were classified as fevers, and all the medical systems revolved around the conception of fever. At first Rush accepted Boerhaave's theory that fever was caused entirely by a thickening of the blood, but, after he had studied at Edinburgh, he adopted Cullen's theory "of a spasm upon the extremities of the capillary vessels in every part of the surface of the body." Then, about 1770, he deserted this theory and remained in doubt as to the cause of fever for twenty years. At length he decided that all fevers are due to disturbances in the blood vessels, chiefly in the arteries. He thought that these disturbances were preceded by a debility, which so depressed the bodily function that it could be unduly influenced by various stimuli. Fever was produced by the reaction to these stimuli, and the varying degrees of reaction caused the varying degrees of fever.

Among the causes producing the general debility Rush listed: cold; passions of fear, grief, despair; famine; excessive evacuations "whether by the bowels, blood-vessels, pores, or urinary passages; heat, intemperance in eating and drinking; fatigue; and certain causes which act by over-stretching a part or the whole of the body, such as lifting heavy weights, external violence acting mechanically in wounding, bruising, or compressing particular parts; extraneous substances acting by their bulk or gravity, burning, and the like."

Stimulus is the one exciting cause of fever, said Rush. It produces morbid excitement in the blood vessels, more especially in the arteries. "Heat, alternating with cold, intemperance, passions of the mind, bruises, burns, and the like," he explained, "all act by a stimulating power only, in producing fever. This proposition is of great application, inasmuch as it cuts the sinews of the division of diseases from their remote causes. Thus it establishes the sameness of a pleurisy, whether it be excited by heat succeeding cold, or by the contagions of the smallpox and measles, or by the miasmata of the yellow fever."

The effort to unify the existing conception of disease was further defended by his statement that, since all fevers have their origin in disturbances of the blood vessels, all the local manifestations of disease such as pleurisy, or inflammation of the liver, stomach, or bowels, could be symptoms only of an original underlying disease. Rush insisted that there could be but one fever, however different the predisposing or precipitating causes might be. "Fire is a unit, whether it be produced by friction, percussion, electricity, fermentation, or by a piece of wood or coal in a state of inflammation," he said, in attacking the complexity of medical terminology.

Although there is but one fever, it is possible, he claimed, to assign specific names to many more or less permanent and fixed states of fever. He listed forty such states in three classifications. The first division includes those fevers which attack the whole arterial system with little or no local "affection," such as the malignant gangrenous, common inflammatory, bilious, and typhoid fevers. The second class comprises fevers that affect the whole arterial system, and are accompanied with marked local affections, viz., intestinal, pulmonary, rheumatic, arthritic, maniacal, apoplectic, paralytic, vertiginous, nephritic, dropsical, and ophthalmic fevers. In the third class are listed the "misplaced" states of fever, those that "appear to pass by the arterial system, and to fix themselves upon other parts of the body," such as: hepatic, convulsive or spasmodic, hysterical or hypochondriacal, and cutaneous fevers.[2]

Although not accepted by the American medical profession as a whole, Rush's theory of the "proximate cause of fever" served as a guide for many of his students as well as other physicians. Exerting, as it did, definite influence in American medicine, it must be considered an important chapter in our medical history, even if it was to be refuted by later findings.[3]

A flood of complimentary letters from physicians in all parts of the country is evidence of the high regard in which Rush's theories were held. From Baltimore his former student, Dr. Ashton Alexander, almost shouted: "Heaven my dear Sir who has chosen you the instrument of so much good will preserve you for the interest of mankind. Whilst the ignorant and incredulous physicians follow their unfortunate patients to the shades of death, you will be preserved by the confidence which you profess in your remedies, a confidence the more valuable because so deadly fought." Dr. Robert H. Archer, of Harford County, Maryland, in confessing that he had been converted to Rush's system, said: "When any new medical opinion is published to the world it should be the business of every practitioner of medicine to discover how far it is founded in truth. The new system of medicine which you teach has produced much contention among the physicians of America & I believe it has influenced the practice of nearly all. I attended for the first time a course of your lectures in 1794–95. I was startled. I came home— read—practised.—and never became more reconciled.—I however still had my doubts. I attended another course.—My doubts vanished, and I became a strong advocate for the new system.—The conversion was not too rapid not to have been the effect of Reason.— When prejudice has not fettered the mind, truth finds an easy entrance.—it produces pleasure." And Dr. John McClelland was convinced, as he wrote: "I have lately looked over your fourth volume of Medical Inquiries and think you have presented to the world a more satisfactory theory of the proximate cause of fever than any heretofore published.—And your defense of bloodletting will I hope remove the prejudices which have prevailed amongst physicians against that invaluable remedy."[4] From such opinions it is easy to judge that Rush's theories played an important part in American medicine in the generation following 1790.

Rush impressed upon his students the view that, if medicine was to progress, the artificial arrangement of diseases must be discarded. Cullen's *Genera Morborum* listed 1,387 diseases, each one requiring a different treatment. This multiplication of names seemed to Rush to be absurd, and in his lectures he warned the students that the name of a disease is comparatively worthless; the nature of it is everything. He believed that the prevailing system had led physicians to prescribe exclusively for the symptoms of diseases, without due regard to the condition of the body, and that it had multiplied unnecessarily the materia medica, by employing nearly as many medicines as there are forms of disease. He was convinced that the number of medicines used was needlessly large, and that if physicians prescribed for the state of the disease rather than for the name, only a fourth of the medicines in use would be necessary. "By thus limiting their number," he thought, "we should acquire a more perfect knowledge of their virtues and doses, and thereby exhibit them with more success." In the new system, observation and judgment must take the place of reading and memory, and prescriptions must conform to clinical conditions. This will shorten the road to medical knowledge "so that a young man will be able to qualify himself to practice physic at as much less expense of time and labour than formerly, as a child would learn to read and write by the help of the Roman alphabet, instead of Chinese characters."

Since Rush's system rejected the nosological arrangement of diseases, and considered that every morbid state of the body required either depletion or stimulation, the art of healing, therefore, consisted in knowing from the pulse and other signs whether or not depletion or stimulation was indicated, and in deciding then on the proper remedy.[5]

By attempting to break down the accepted nosology Rush believed that a step forward was being made in medicine. "Science has much to deplore from the multiplication of diseases. It is as repugnant to truth in medicine, as polytheism is to truth in religion. The physician who considers every different affection of the different systems in the body, or every affection of different parts of the same system, as distinct diseases, when they arise from one cause, resembles the Indian or African savage, who considers water, dew, ice, frost, and snow, as distinct essences: while the physician who considers the morbid affections of every part of the body, (however diversified they may be in their form or degrees) as derived from one cause, resembles the philosopher, who considers dew, ice, frost, and snow, as different modifications of water, and as derived simply from the absence of heat."[6] The approach to the subject and the line of attack were, indeed, modern.

Rush was one of the first physicians to recognize the relationship between infected teeth and arthritis, and to suggest that the teeth be examined in the treatment of all chronic diseases and extracted if decayed. The following account of focal infection is considered a classic description:

"Some time in the month of October, 1801, I attended Miss

A. C. with rheumatism in her hip joint, which yielded for a while, to the several remedies for that disease. In the month of November it returned with great violence, accompanied with a severe toothache. Suspecting the rheumatic infection was excited by the pain in her tooth, which was decayed, I directed it to be extracted. The rheumatism immediately left her hip, and she recovered in a few days. She has continued ever since to be free from it.

"Soon after this I was consulted by Mrs. J. R. who had been affected for several weeks with dyspepsia and toothache. Her tooth, though no mark of decay appeared in it, was drawn by my advice. The next day she was relieved with her distressing stomach complaint, and has continued ever since to enjoy good health. From the soundness of the external part of the tooth, and the adjoining gum, there was no reason to suspect a discharge of matter from it had produced the disease in her stomach.

"Some time in the year 1801 I was consulted by the father of a young gentleman in Baltimore, who had been affected with epilepsy. I inquired into the state of his teeth, and was informed that several of them in his upper jaw were decayed. I directed them to be extracted, and advised him after to lose a few ounces of blood, at any time when he felt the premonitory symptoms of a recurrence of his fits. He followed my advice, in consequence of which I had lately the pleasure of hearing from his brother that he was perfectly cured. . . ."

Rush proceeded to set down a few general conclusions: "When we consider how often the teeth, when decayed, are exposed to irritation from hot and cold drinks and aliments from pressure by mastication, and from the cold air, and how intimate the connection of the mouth is with the whole system, I am disposed to believe they are often the unsuspected causes of general, and particularly nervous diseases. When we add to the last of those diseases the morbid effects of the acrid and putrid matters, which are sometimes discharged from the carious teeth, or from the ulcers in the gums created by them, also the influence which both have in preventing perfect mastication, and the connection of that animal function with good health, I can not help thinking that our success in the treatment of all chronic diseases would be very much promoted, by directing our inquiries into the state of the teeth in sick people, and by advising their extraction in every case in which they are decayed. It is not necessary that they should be attended with pain, in order to produce disease, for splinters, tumors and other irritants before mentioned, often bring on disease and death, when they give pain, and are unsuspected causes of them. This translation of sensation and motion into parts remote from the place where impressions are made, appears in many instances, and seems to depend upon an original law of the animal economy."[7]

These observations and conclusions on focal infection must certainly be listed with those of prime importance in the medical history of modern times.

During the War for Independence Rush became interested in inoculation as a means of preventing the incapacitation and death of soldiers from smallpox. As chairman of the Medical Committee of Congress, when he was a member of that body, he was instrumental in having thousands of recruits inoculated before they went into active military service. Consequently, the mortality rate from smallpox in the Continental Army was low. While he was in service in the medical department of the army, Rush kept notes on the various methods used in inoculating the soldiers and, in 1781, he published *The New Method of Inoculating for Smallpox*. His technique was strikingly modern.

As a result of these observations, he concluded that healthy subjects might be inoculated "in every stage of life, and in almost every condition of the human body," although in infancy the periods before and after dentition were preferable. He advised against inoculating in the summer season because of the frequency of "bilious" disorders. A slight puncture should be made in the left arm with a needle or lancet, the puncture being large enough to draw only one drop of blood. No plaster or bandage should be placed over the puncture.

The patient, Rush insisted, should be specially prepared for the inoculation. No wine or spirits should be taken for forty-eight hours before inoculation, and during that time a vegetable diet should be prescribed, together with moderate exercise in the fresh air. To regulate the eruptive fever after inoculation, Rush recommended that the patient lose twelve to fourteen ounces of blood.

Less than twenty years after Rush had perfected his system of inoculation, Edward Jenner, in 1798, began to use vaccine at the St. Thomas Hospital in London. Rush was deeply impressed with the importance of Jenner's discovery, and his prophecy that vaccination would wipe out smallpox was to be fulfilled. A few years after vaccination came into general use Rush wrote: "All you have heard, & read of the Kinepox is true. I consider its substitution to the small pox as the greatest discovery of the 18th Century. It bids fair to annihilate the small pox in a few years, and thereby to save many millions of lives. The advantages over the variolus inoculation are as follows:

1. It requires no previous preparation in diet or medicine.

2. It may be performed in all seasons of the year.

3. It seldom confines a patient to his house, or interrupts his business.

4. It risks no sense, and never impairs beauty.

5. It is not contagious.

6. It is never mortal. Its supposed mortality has arisen from its being accidentally combined with other diseases.

7. It frequently removes old, & constitutional indispositions."[8]

Just what "constitutional indispositions" Rush had in mind is not known, but on this point he was in error.

In the spring of 1803, Rush was one of fifty physicians in Philadelphia who recommended vaccination as a positive preventive against smallpox. "We the subscribers, Physicians of Philadelphia," the newspaper notice read, "having carefully considered the nature and effects of the newly discovered means of preventing, by vaccination, the fatal consequences of the small-pox, think it a duty thus publicly to declare our opinion, that inoculation for the Kine or Cow pock is a certain preventive of the Small Pox; that it is attended with no danger, may be practised at all ages and seasons of the year, and we do therefore recommend it to general use."[9]

Among the pages of Rush's lecture notes on the Practice of Physic, now preserved in the University of Pennsylvania Library, is a picturesque paragraph in which the Doctor points out that dress is a cause of disease. "Who would suppose," asked Rush, "that the covering of primeval innocence would have any effect in producing disease? Dress in producing diseases acts from 1st Quality 2d Quantity 3 Fashions. Two thirds of the diseases of the autumn in this city are caused by too thin clothing. Tis an old saying 'Pride is never too hot nor too cold.' Many change their clothes with the season of the year but 'tis absurd—they should be changed with the changes of the weather. In children, diseases are occasioned by clothes being too tight round the head or breast as swaddling cloths, tight breeches, tight shirt collars etc. are sources of disease. I have even known tight buckled shoes produce disease as vertigo a case of which I was witness to. 'Tis remarkable that the very complexion of the body is changed by clothing. . . . Flannel shirts worn next the skin will prevent many diseases. I have known the use of flannel shirts to preserve the health of a whole army. No vermin are bred in it when worn months without washing. Cotton is of the same nature—very different is linnen when worn long it favours the production of lice & pestilential diseases."

Hydrophobia, the disease produced by the bite of a rabid animal, "is a malignant fever, pre-eminent in power and mortality, over all other diseases," Rush believed. He listed its symptoms: "Chills, great heat, thirst, nausea, a burning sensation in the stomach, vomiting, costiveness; a small, quick, tense, irregular, intermitting, natural or slow pulse; a cool skin, great sensibility to cold air, partial cold and clammy sweats on the hands, or sweats accompanied with a warm skin diffused all over the body, difficulty of breathing, sighing, restlessness, hiccup, giddiness, headach, delirium, coma, false vision, dulness of sight, blindness, palpitation of the heart and convulsions."

To prevent the disease after infection has occurred, Rush advised that the virus be destroyed by cutting or burning out the wounded part, or by long and frequent sprinklings of water upon it in order to wash away the saliva. Once the disease had developed, the cure was to be found in bloodletting to the extent of one to two hundred ounces(!), the use of purges, and sweating.[10]

For tetanus, Rush suggested as remedies large and frequent doses of opium, quarts and even gallons of wine daily, ardent spirits, bark, cold and warm baths, oil of amber, salivation and blisters. He told about a New England quack who, upon being asked why he prescribed ardent spirits in such quantities as to produce intoxication, replied that he had always observed the jaw to fall in drunken men, and anything that would produce that effect, he supposed to be proper in the locked jaw.[11]

In February and March of 1789, there was an epidemic of measles in Philadelphia. Rush recorded such symptoms as severe headache, swelling of the eyelids so as to obstruct vision, toothache, and nasal hemorrhage. In the throat and lungs the measles produced a soreness and hoarseness, pains in the breast, and a distressful cough. Vomiting was frequent; and in the bowels griping, diarrhoea, and occasionally bloody stools. Rush prescribed bleeding in all cases attended by great pain, a cough, and a hard pulse. Opiates, too, were used, and barley water, bran, flaxseed tea, and a mixture of water and cider.[12]

Gout was a comparatively common complaint in the eighteenth century, and was conceived by Rush to be a disease of the entire system affecting the ligaments, blood vessels, stomach, intestines, brain, liver, nerves, muscles, cartilages, bones, and skin. It most frequently attacks persons of a "sanguineous temperament," he thought, but sometimes affects those of nervous and phlegmatic temperaments. The idle and wealthy are more subject to it than the working and temperate section of the population. In some cases it is an hereditary disease "depending upon the propagation of a similar temperament from father to son."

The remote causes of the gout, which induce a general predisposing state, were listed as indolence, great bodily labor, long protracted bodily exercise, intemperance in eating and in sexual indulgence, acid aliments and drinks, strong tea and coffee, worry, violent or continued exercise of the mind in study or business and, lastly, the use of alcoholic drinks. The exciting causes frequently consist in a sudden application or unusual intensity of the remote causes.

Rush believed that, in its onset, gout might be prevented by the loss of a few ounces of blood, or by a gentle physic followed by a warm foot-bath. Many remedies were resorted to by him in cases of "great morbid action in the blood-vessels and viscera." The first was bloodletting, which he believed not only lessened or removed the pain but also prevented further congestion tending toward apoplexy or pneumonia. Purging, vomiting, and nitre were also recommended. The affected limbs should be left uncovered in order to benefit from the cool air, the Doctor advised, and "diluting liquors, such as are prescribed in common inflammatory fevers, should be given in such quantities as to dispose to a gentle perspiration." Stimulating liquors should be avoided. Fear and terror, it was claimed, have in some instances cured a sudden outbreak of the disease.

In that state of the gout "in which a feeble morbid action takes place in the blood-vessels and viscera," the remedies used were to produce vigorous action. Rush prescribed opium, wine, porter, brandy, thirty drops of ether, aromatic substances such as ginger and cloves, oil of amber "where the gout produces spasmodic or convulsive motions," bark, warm baths, salivation by means of mercury, and massaging.

He also offered a few suggestions for prevention. In the first place a moderate and simple diet is essential: "In general, fish, eggs, the white meats and broths may be taken in small quantities once a day, with milk and vegetables at other times. A little salted meat, which affords less nourishment than fresh, may be taken occasionally. It imparts vigour to the stomach, and prevents dyspepsia from a diet consisting chiefly of vegetables. . . . From the disposition of the gout to return in the spring and autumn, greater degrees of abstinence in eating and drinking will be necessary at those seasons than at any other time." He advised against overwork, especially mental fatigue. The sexual appetite should be indulged with moderation, and costiveness should be prevented.[13]

Although Rush's treatment of the gout passed into the discard long ago, it was at the time considered a great improvement over previous methods.

Rush himself never suffered from gout. He was, however, forced to bed from time to time because of a tendency toward pulmonary tuberculosis. He said that he inherited from his paternal ancestors a predisposition to tuberculosis, and that between the ages of eighteen and forty-three he had occasional attacks of the disease, but because of the constant and faithful use of the remedies which he prescribed in his practice, he was able to enjoy at the age of sixty an uninterrupted exemption from pulmonary complaints. Because of his own predisposition he was, of course, especially interested in the nature and cure of tuberculosis and other pulmonary disorders.[14]

To prevent serious colds he recommended frequent cold baths to lessen the sensitivity of the body; loose fur or woolen garments; wrapping or rubbing with ice or snow the parts of the body which are frozen; and warm feet, because "the effects of cold are first felt in those parts [the feet] upon the account of their remoteness from the action of the heart and brain."

He pointed out that pulmonary tuberculosis was unknown among the North American Indians, and was scarcely seen among settlers on the frontier lands. It was less common in country places than in the city, but increased in both places "with intemperance and sedantary modes of life." Further, "ship and house carpenters, smiths, and all those artificers whose business requires great exertions of strength in the open air, in all seasons of the year, are less subject to the disease, than men who work under cover, and at occupations which do not require the constant action of their limbs. Women, who sit more than men, and whose work is connected with less exertion, are more subject to consumption." The greater prevalence of the disease among women was due, it was believed, to their light dresses and the exposure of the shoulders and upper parts of the arms. At first he declared the disease to be contagious, but this view he later discarded.

It is remarkable that he was able to diagnose tuberculosis in the so-called "pretubercular" state, although the stethoscope had not yet been invented. He was ignorant of the tubercle bacillus, and did not have the use of tuberculin. The symptoms which he recorded are concise and definite and are still useful today: "A rapid pulse especially towards evening, slight fever increased by the least exercise, burning and dryness in the palms of the hands, occasional flushing in one and sometimes both cheeks, a hoarseness, a slight pain in the breast, a deficiency of appetite, general indisposition to exercise or motion of every kind."

The way to cure the patient, Rush believed, "is to revive in the constitution by means of exercise or labour, that vigour which belongs to the Indians." Work in the country, horseback riding, open-air occupations in general, and cold baths, were all considered positive remedies.

Although horseback riding and vigorous exercise would hardly be prescribed by the physician of our own day, there is much in Rush's treatment of tuberculosis that is in accord with present-day ideas. He insisted that the whole system be strengthened by exercise and a generous vegetable diet, and that persons with an hereditary predisposition to the disease should choose occupations that call for work in the outdoors. He warned that the patient must "avoid fatigue." Although he resorted to bloodletting in some cases in the inflammatory stage, still his treatment differs little from that employed today. Above everything he recommended fresh air in a dry situation, distant from the sea.[15]

In his own day Rush was recognized as a specialist in pulmonary disorders and was consulted frequently, not only by local physicians but by medical men and patients throughout the country. "I have been desired to prescribe for a patient of yours a Mrs. Burns who it is said is afflicted with the pulmonary consumption," he wrote a fellow physician, "I have nothing to add upon that disorder to what I have published in the 2nd volume of my medical inquiries & observations, but that I continue to use small & frequent bleedings in it with great success. Blisters should be kept constantly running from her sides, breast, or limbs.——Exercise on horseback in good weather should be used after the reduction of the pulse, and the cessation of inflammatory symptoms. Even the cold bath has been used by me with advantage after the inflammatory stage of the disorder has passed away. It will be most proper and beneficial in warm weather. Begin with water of a moderate temperature." To his former student, Dr. John Redman Coxe, he wrote: "I have lately used the cold bath in the pulmonary consumption. It is an excellent substitute for riding on horseback in hot weather, and in very debilitated habits. I have preceded the use of it by bloodletting to prevent haemorrhage from the lungs."[16]

For his able and original work in diagnosis and treatment Rush deserves high credit for his contributions in the field of pulmonary tuberculosis.

His survey of the sources of diseases prevalent in this country in the summer and fall is interesting both to the antiquarian and to the scientist.[17] He called attention to exhalations from marshes impregnated with decayed and decaying vegetable and animal matter, and enumerated various substances which, when in a state of putrefaction, might cause disease. He noted cabbage; potatoes—"nearly a whole ship's crew perished at Tortola, by removing from her hold, a quantity of putrid potatoes"; pepper; Indian meal; onions; mint; coffee; cotton; hemp, flax, and straw; old canvas; "old books and old paper money, that had been wetted, and confined in close rooms and closets"; the timber of an old house; green wood confined in a closed cellar during the summer; the stagnating air of the hold of a ship; bilge water; water long confined in hogsheads; the stagnating air of cellars; stagnating rain water; "the matters which usually stagnate in the gutters, common sewers, docks and alleys of cities, and the sinks of kitchens; air emitted by agitating foul and stagnating water—Dr. [Benjamin] Franklin was once infected with an intermitting fever from this cause"; a duck pond; and "weeds cut down, and exposed to heat and moisture near a house." Rush was correct in believing that the source of certain diseases can be traced to putrefied matter, although the fact that the cause is to be found in the disease-producing germs thriving in such matter was not yet known. Again he was on the track of a revolutionary discovery to be made in the years to come.

He had an idea that miasmata from all these sources might produce such common diseases of the summer and fall as malignant or bilious yellow fever, inflammatory bilious fever, mild remittent fever, dysentery, colic, and cholera morbus.

What appealed to Rush was the possibility of preventing these diseases. As an early exponent of preventive medicine, his suggestions were marked by their sanity, simplicity, and practicality. If the source of a disease were found to be in the immediate vicinity of the city, he proposed that, whenever possible, Philadelphians should flee the neighborhood temporarily. For those who could not get away he advised a simple and small diet "accomodated to the greater or less exposure of the body to the action of the miasmata, and to the greater or less degrees of labour or exercise which are taken"; bloodletting; laxative medicines—"hundreds, perhaps thousands of the citizens of Philadelphia were indebted for their preservation from the yellow fever to the occasional use of a calomel pill, a few grains of rhubarb, or a tablespoonful of sweet, or castor oil, during the prevalence of our late pestilential fevers"; and "a plentiful perspiration, or moderate sweats, kept up by means of warm clothing and bed-clothes. The excretion which takes place by the skin, is a discharge of the first necessity."

In order to "obviate the internal action of miasmata, by exciting a general or partial determination to the external surface of the body," Rush prescribed warm baths to keep the skin clear and the pores open; cold baths; salt-water sponge baths morning and night; and oil rubs—"the natives of Africa, and some American Indians, use this preventive with success during their sickly seasons."

Avoid all exciting causes, he warned, such as heat and cold, the early morning and night air; fatigue from such amusements as fishing, gunning, and dancing, and from unusual labor or exercise; intemperance in eating and drinking; new foods and drinks—"during the prevalence of malignant fevers the stomach is always in an irritable state"; violent emotions or mental disturbances; and continuance of hard labor.

After disposing of the methods by which individuals might protect themselves against the common summer and fall diseases, Rush turned to the means of exterminating the diseases. Here he had in mind a sanitary garbage collection and disposal system, wider and cleaner streets, adequate sewerage, and a stricter ship quarantine. He called upon the towns to remove or to destroy all the putrid substances listed by him as fever-producing. "The advantages of burning offal matters, capable of producing fevers," he noted, "have been demonstrated by those housekeepers, who, instead of collecting the entrails of fish and poultry, and the parings and skins of vegetables, in barrels, instantly throw them into their kitchen fires. The families of such persons are generally healthy."

He appealed for more air space in the cities, the elimination of narrow streets and alleys, deep lots reserved for yards and gardens for all the residences, and sewers "to convey, when practicable, to running water, the contents of privies and the foul water of kitchens." He went so far as to propose, as William Penn had previously done, that every other block in cities be left unoccupied.

Long before we had any definite knowledge of the breeding habits of the mosquito, Rush demanded that all marshes be either drained or flooded completely, and that after timber land has been cleared, it should be cultivated without delay.

In order to prevent the inhalation of any of the unwholesome air from the holds of incoming ships Rush asked for a rigid quarantine. "In commercial cities," he pleaded, "no vessel that arrives with a cargo of putrescent articles should ever be suffered to approach a wharf, before the air that has been confined in her hold has been discharged. The same thing should be done after the arrival of a vessel from a distant or hot country, though her cargo be not capable of putrefaction, for air acquires a morbid quality by stagnating contiguous to wood." He was far ahead of his day in many of the suggestions he made.

Over a long period of years Rush gathered material for *An Account of the State of the Body and Mind in Old Age, With Observations On Its Diseases, and Their Remedies.*[18] From his clinical records he discovered the circumstances which favor longevity. First and foremost is heredity—descent from long-lived ancestors. "I have not found a single instance of a person," he wrote, "who has not lived to be 80 years old, in whom this was not the case. . . . The knowledge of this fact may serve, not only to assist in calculating what are called the chances of lives, but it may be made useful to a physician." Temperance in eating and drinking is the second factor, followed by "the moderate exercise of the understanding . . . business, politics, and religion, which are the objects of attention of men of all classes, impart a vigour to the understanding, which, by being conveyed to every part of the body, tends to produce health and long life." Another factor is equanimity of temper —"the violent and irregular action of the passions tends to wear away the springs of life." Marriage is almost essential, thought Rush. He had met with only one unmarried person beyond eighty years!

Persons who emigrate to new countries acquire fresh physical and mental vigor from the new environment. Rush did not find that sedentary occupations militate against long life unless accompanied by intemperance. Chronic diseases in themselves do not shorten human life, he held further; nor does the loss of teeth affect the life span to any marked degree. Prematurely bald or gray gentlemen may be cheered by Rush's hint that "I have not observed baldness, or grey hairs, occurring in early or middle life, to prevent old age."

As to the phenomena of the body and mind which occur in old age, the great sensitivity to cold seemed to Rush to be the most marked. He was acquainted with a woman, aged eighty-four, who slept under three blankets and a quilt in the heat of summer. Old persons, he found, are more responsive to aural than to visual images —"Dr. [Benjamin] Franklin informed me, that he recognized his friends, after a long absence from them, first by their voices."

Continuing his observations, Rush held that the appetites of old persons usually increase, the pulse is generally full, the breath peculiarly bitter, dreaming universal, while the eyes of very old persons change from a dark color or blue to a light color. The memory is the first faculty of the mind that fails in the declining years, but the fear of death, Rush decided, seems to prevail much less in old age, than in early or middle life.

That fewer people die of supposedly incurable than of curable diseases, was Rush's opinion, expressed in a lecture to his students "On the Causes of Death In Diseases That Are Not Incurable."[19]

There are many causes of death in curable cases due directly to the physicians themselves, he stated quite frankly. First of all there is the physician's ignorance "arising from original incapacity, or a want of proper instruction in medicine"; and his negligence in failing to answer calls promptly, and in a lack of attention to all symptoms of the disease. By charging excessively for their services some physicians cause patients to delay seeking medical advice until it is too late. Forgetfulness in visiting patients regularly or in sending medicine in time for use often leads to fatal consequences. Prescriptions of physicians written in a careless and illegible hand, causing errors in compounding medicines, and fraudulent medicines, occasionally cause death in curable diseases. However, "a sudden indisposition attacking a physician, so as to prevent his regular and habitual visits to his patient" might be set down as an act of fate.

Rush listed as many as fourteen causes of death which originate with the sick persons themselves. Ignorance of the public at large as to medical matters tops the list. This is followed by prejudice in the choice of a physician, that is, in selecting a doctor from the same sect or party regardless of his talents. To follow fashion in the choice of a physician is not wise: "In this country wealth gives the tone to medical reputation." Fatal results also occur by neglecting to apply in due time for medical aid; by failing to comply with the physician's directions; by neglecting to make use of the medicines at the time and in the manner prescribed; by indulging in food and drink improper in quality or quantity; by returning to work or study prematurely; and by habits of secret drinking. Fear has often rendered fatal diseases which would otherwise have yielded to medicine. "A peculiar irritability" of temper has likewise been known to prove fatal. "A dread of the expenses of medical services has sometimes, by preventing an application to a physician, occasioned death from diseases that might have been cured by a single dose of physic." "An excess of delicacy" which causes patients to conceal the nature of their diseases leads to inaccurate diagnosis and treatment.

More important in Rush's eyes than his discussion of the responsibility for unnecessary death, was his defense of bloodletting. His contemporaries believed that his fame as a great medical man would rest on his bold and effective use of the lancet.

In his theory of the proximate cause of fever, Rush explained that fever is caused directly by the morbid and excessive action of the blood vessels, and that it is also related to abnormal sensitivity in their muscular fibres. In defending bloodletting, Rush pointed out that the blood is the most powerful stimulus acting upon the vessels and fibre and, by withdrawing a part of it, the principal cause of the fever is diminished in its potency. "The effect of blood-letting is as immediate and natural in removing fever," he claimed, "as the abstraction of a particle of sand is to cure an inflammation of the eye, when it arises from that cause. . . . By artificial blood-letting, we can choose the time and place of drawing blood, and we may regulate its quantity by the degrees of action in the blood-vessels." When used at the proper time and in quantity proportional to the force of the disease, it frequently strangles a fever in its forming state.

LIBRARY AND SURGEON'S HALL

To prove his point Rush marshaled more than a score of benefits gained from bloodletting in the "inflammatory state of fever." It imparts strength to the body by removing the pressure of indirect debility; it reduces the abnormal frequency of the pulse; it speeds up the pulse when it is too slow; it checks the nausea and vomiting which attend the malignant state of fever; it so affects the bowels as to make them more easily moved by a physic; it renders the action of mercury more speedy and more certain in exciting a salivation; it disposes the body to sweat spontaneously; it acts as a corrective for a dry and a black tongue; and it removes or lessens pain in every part of the body, and more especially in the head. One might imagine that, after this recital, Rush had won and rested his case. However, he went on to show that venesection removes or mitigates the burning heat of the skin; removes chilliness unaffected by cordial drinks or warm bed clothes; checks profuse sweats and diarrhoea; relieves coma; induces sleep; and prevents the chronic diseases of cough, consumption, jaundice. It is especially valuable, too, from the standpoint of convalescence because: "It prepares the way for the successful use of the bark and other tonic remedies, by destroying, or so far weakening, a morbid action in the blood-vessels, that a medicine of a moderate stimulus afterwards exceeds it in force, and thereby restores equable and healthy action to the system." On the whole he felt the lancet to be safer and more helpful than the ordinary depleting remedies: vomits, purges, sweats, salivation, and blisters. The amount of blood to be drawn from a patient was determined largely by his pulse, and also by his condition, constitution, age, and weight.

Because the pulse was such a significant guide, Rush drew up directions for taking it. He suggested that the arm be so placed as to be free from the pressure of the body upon it, and that the muscles be completely relaxed. In all obscure or difficult cases he advised that the pulse be felt in both arms. "Apply all the fingers of one hand, when practicable, to the pulse," he admonished. "For this purpose it will be most convenient to feel the pulse of the right hand with your left, and of the left hand with your right. Do not decide upon blood-letting, in difficult cases, until you have felt the pulse for some time. The Chinese physicians never prescribe until they have counted 49 strokes. Feel the pulse at the intervals of four or five minutes, when you suspect that its force has been varied by any circumstance not connected with the disease, such as emotions of the mind, exercise, eating, drinking, and the like." When the pulse was depressed or imperceptible in the wrists, it was suggested that pulsations of the arteries in the temples and neck be felt.

The amount of blood to be drawn in an inflammatory fever could not be decided by referring to a table of figures. Rush believed that "much more blood may be taken when the blood-vessels are in a state of morbid excitement and excitability, than at any other time." He believed generally in copious bloodletting. "If the state of the pulse be our guide, the continuance of its inflammatory action, after the loss of even 100 ounces of blood, indicates the necessity of more bleeding, as much as it did the first time a vein was opened. In the use of this remedy it may be truly said, as in many of the enterprizes of life, that nothing is done, while anything remains to be done. Bleeding should be repeated while the symptoms which first indicated it continue, should it be until four-fifths of the blood contained in the body are drawn away." This proposal is almost too fearful to contemplate—the loss of four-fifths of one's blood.

In cases in which the pulse acts with force, Rush held that ten to twenty ounces could be withdrawn at one time. When the pulse is much depressed it is better to take only a few ounces at a time, repeating the process three or four times a day.[20]

On the face of it Rush's brief for bloodletting seems today to be little short of preposterous. Furthermore, he carried phlebotomy and the depleting system farther than anyone ever had before, and his disciples, in the last years of the eighteenth century and in the early years of the nineteenth, followed and popularized his methods in all parts of the country. How stoutly he was defended by contemporary physicians may be judged from this letter, only one of many: "Your Theory & Practice of Medicine gains ground rapidly," reported a physician in South Carolina. "The terrible dread of bleeding has entirely disappeared, & the administration of calomel & jalap is now exercised everywhere & by every old woman. . . . And to whom is the credit due, but to you my good Sir, the author of such

Principles & Practice as will stand the test of time & last so long as there shall be matter to act upon or man to exercise them."[21]

The state of medicine and public health was surveyed by Rush, in 1805, in *An Inquiry Into the Comparative State of Medicine, in Philadelphia, between the years 1760 and 1766, and the year 1805.*[22] He observed the dress of the people. By 1805 wigs had gone into disuse and round hats with high crowns had come into fashion. Umbrellas, which until that time had been used by women only, were now being carried by men in wet weather. Tight dresses were uncommon and stays were not used, facts which Rush lamented! "The benefits to health which might have been derived from the disuse of that part of female dress, have been prevented by the fashion of wearing such light coverings over the breasts and limbs."

Relishes, common in previous years, and bitters and punch as appetizers were seldom served. Late suppers were a thing of the past. More vegetables were consumed than formerly, and meat was served only once a day, at dinner. Malt liquors were taken regularly with meals, but the taverns and beer houses were not as busy as in years gone by, nor was drunkenness as common.

For several reasons the health of the people in Philadelphia was generally better. Improvements in the construction of houses caused them to be warmer in winter and cooler in summer. The universal use of stoves in churches prevented many colds. The drinking-water supply had been greatly improved and the public baths were more frequently patronized.

On the other hand, however, habits and conditions prevailed which affected the robustness of the people unfavorably. Ice cream eaten in excess or upon an empty stomach seemed to Rush to be quite deleterious to good health. The use of tobacco was becoming more general. The city suffered from an inadequate sewage disposal system, filthy gutters, pools of stagnant water here and there, and putrefied matter on the docks. Rush also pointed to the contamination of the drinking water since, as he said, "the pump water is impregnated with many saline and aerial matters of an offensive nature."

In 1805 Rush found that a mild bilious fever was still a universal complaint throughout the city. "Inflammations and obstructions of the liver have been more frequent than in former years, and even the pneumonies, catarrhs, intercurrent, and other fevers of the winter and spring months, have all partaken more or less of the inflammatory and malignant nature of the yellow fever." Pulmonary tuberculosis, scarlatina anginosa, cholera infantum, and gout continued to be common diseases. Mental diseases were on the increase. Smallpox, however, was "nearly extirpated." Apoplexy and palsy were less prevalent, Rush supposed, because of the decreased consumption of meat and liquors. "Perhaps," he continued, "the round hat, and the general use of umbrellas, may have continued to lessen those diseases of the brain."

During the last quarter of the eighteenth century several new remedies came into favor. In the field of preventive medicine, vaccination had, by 1805, supplanted inoculation. Digitalis, lead, and arsenic were new remedies; and cold air, cold water, and ice were also prescribed freely. The use of mercury was revived, and leeches were used in diseases removed beyond the influence of the lancet. "Opium and bark, which were formerly given in disguise, or with a trembling hand, are now, not only prescribed by physicians, but often purchased, and taken without their advice" by many persons. Exercise, fresh air, and the seashore came to be recommended in chronic cases.

Rush believed that the new medical theories and the new remedies buoyed up the general health of the people and definitely caused the death-rate to decline. By 1805, smallpox had almost ceased to be a mortal disease; most fevers yielded to medical treatment; pulmonary tuberculosis was warded off in many cases; and gout was yielding to the lancet. "Madness, which formerly doomed its miserable subjects to cells or chains for life, has yielded to bleeding, low diet, mercury, the warm and cold baths, fresh air, gentle exercise, and mild treatment, since its seat has been discovered to be in the blood vessels of the brain," Rush reported optimistically. "Since the care and extraction of teeth have become a distinct branch of the profession of medicine," he continued, "several diseases which have arisen from them, when decayed, have been detected and cured." Although not all of Rush's findings still hold in the light of present medical discoveries, it is true that real progress was made between 1769, the year he started to practice, and 1805.

In many quarters Rush's system had been accepted, a system which "rejects the nosological arrangement of diseases, and places all their numerous forms in morbid excitement, induced by irritants acting upon previous diseases. It rejects, likewise, all prescriptions for the names of diseases, and, by directing their applications wholly to the forming and fluctuating states of diseases, and the system, derives from a few active medicines all the advantages which have been in vain expected from the numerous articles which compose European treatises upon the materia medica."

If medical science is to go forward, "Let us strip our profession of everything that looks like mystery and imposture," Rush persuaded his students, "and clothe medical knowledge in a dress so simple and intelligible, that it may become a part of academical education in all our seminaries of learning. . . . Let us study the premonitory signs of diseases, and apply our remedies to them, before they are formed." The morbid and natural history of the pulse must also be completed because "it is the string which vibrates most readily with discordant motions in every part of the body."[23]

Rush himself contributed more than any American physician of his time to the progress of medicine. He pleaded vigorously for simplification of medical nomenclature, and the elimination of all but a few key medicines. The task of prescribing was made easy inasmuch as he considered every morbid state of the system to be such as required either depletion or stimulation. The recognition of the connection between decayed teeth and disease was one of Rush's outstanding contributions to medical science. He fought strenuously against smallpox and was an ardent proponent of inoculation and, later, of vaccination. He was, indeed, one of the first advocates of preventive medicine. He wrote illuminatingly and in detail on the cause and treatment of many diseases such as hydrophobia, tetanus, fevers, measles, yellow fever, gout, cancer, tuberculosis, smallpox, and dropsy. He described cholera infantum in 1773.

He was the chief exponent of bloodletting. For Rush bloodletting constituted a therapeutic measure to which he resorted in most diseases. It was a practice which aroused bitter antagonism as well as unquestioning faith. His supporters thought that upon this one principle, if upon no other foundation, his immortality would rest. Posterity was to judge him otherwise. They condemn this error in his judgment; and the fame, which he is awarded and richly deserves, stands upon other ground.

His writings, his lectures, and his practice profoundly influenced American medicine for many years. He was a great practical physician, extraordinarily successful in the treatment of disease and exceptionally accurate in observing symptoms and analyzing causes. He was a pioneer in many fields, and dedicated his life sincerely and unselfishly to a profession which did not always use him kindly, but one which brought to him the deep and abiding satisfaction of service rendered to his fellow man.

XI

First American Psychiatrist

A CENTURY and a half ago there was no book, either written or published in America, on psychiatry and the treatment of the insane. Information on the subject was practically nonexistent. Insanity was still often linked with the devil, and insane patients shockingly abused. In the hospitals, with few exceptions, there were no quarters for them at all. The physician as well as the layman was ignorant of the nature of the disease. It was the custom to incarcerate the insane with ordinary criminals, to confine them in almshouses with paupers, or to let them wander about at large.

When the Pennsylvania Hospital was formally opened in 1752, a section was specially designated for the care of the insane. The Public Hospital for Persons of Insane and Disordered Minds, organized at Williamsburg, Virginia, in 1763, was the first state hospital in America exclusively for the insane, its first patients being admitted in 1773. It was not, however, until after about 1830 that the movement for the erection of state hospitals for the insane was well on its way.

In this branch of medicine Benjamin Rush found a virgin field. When he joined the medical staff of the Pennsylvania Hospital, in 1783, the roll of patients included twenty-four "lunatics." Twenty years later, in 1804, forty-nine lunatics were registered. For the thirty years, from 1783 until 1813, that Rush was on the staff of the Hospital, he manifested particular interest in the insane patients. During this period he made valuable observations and kept careful records which were later incorporated in his epoch-making study of insanity. The humane and judicious treatment of the insane, as a method of caring for the mentally ill, received the first real impetus through his personal efforts and constant pleading. Almost immediately after joining the staff of the Pennsylvania Hospital, he protested against what he considered cruel and improper treatment of the insane. He hammered at the door of the directors' meetings until he was heard, until adequate accommodations were provided for, and humane treatment was given the insane patients.

As the most distinguished physician in Philadelphia in 1789, he could not be merely turned away without consideration. The Board of Managers of the Hospital were moved to action when, on November 11, 1789, they gave a hearing to Rush's complaint: "Under the conviction that the patients afflicted by madness, should be the first objects of the care of a physician of the Pennsylvania Hospital, I have attempted to relieve them, but I am sorry to add that my attempts which at first promised some improvement were soon afterwards rendered abortive by the cells of the hospital. These apartments are damp in winter & too warm in summer. They are moreover so constituted, as not to admit readily of a change of air; hence the smell of them is both offensive and unwholesome." He added that "few patients have even been confined in these cells who have not been affected by a cold in two or three weeks after their confinement, and several have died of consumption in consequence of this cold. These facts being clearly established, I conceive that the appropriating of the cells any longer for the reception of mad people will be dishonourable both to the science and humanity of the city of Philadelphia."[1]

Rush then carried his fight to the people. He published articles on the subject in the local newspapers and got in touch with the members of the State Legislature. At length, on the last day of February 1792, he was able to chalk up a real victory when the lower house of the Assembly passed a bill appropriating $15,000 for the construction of an insane ward, referred to by Rush as the "mad-house."[2]

The west wing of the Pennsylvania Hospital was at length completed in late November 1796, and a month later the insane patients were removed from the old quarters into the new section. Following Rush's appeal for bathing facilities, two rooms were set aside, one with a cold and one with a hot bath, supplied with water from a tank beneath the ceiling. These baths were put into use in late October 1799.

When Rush requested this installation of baths, in April 1798, he also suggested another great reform in the treatment of the insane. Occupational therapy was a most important step forward. He proposed that wherever possible the patients be assigned definite tasks or occupations: "Certain employments should be devised for such of the deranged people as are capable of working; spinning, sewing, churning, &c. might be contrived for the women; Turning a wheel, particularly grinding Indian corn in a hand mill, for food for the horse or cows of the hospital, cutting straw, weaving, digging in the garden, sawing or plaining boards &c. &c. would be useful for the men." The proceeds from this labor might "afford a small addition to the funds of the hospital." A few years later, in 1803, he made another recommendation: "That a well qualified person be employed as a friend and companion to the lunatics, whose business it shall be to attend them and when the physicians direct their enlargement, to see them safe to their apartments."[3] After centuries of ignorance and misunderstanding, the insane patient was at last coming to be treated as a human being, suffering from an unfortunate ailment.

Rush was not yet satisfied, however, and in 1810 he made further recommendations to the Board. The directors received most of his suggestions favorably, although action was not taken immediately, in every case, because of lack of funds.

He requested: "That small and solitary buildings be erected at a convenient distance from the west wing of the hospital for the reception of patients in the high and distracted state of madness, in order to prevent the injuries done by the noises to persons in the recent, or convalescent state of that disease, and to patients in other diseases, by depriving them of sleep, or by inducing distress from sympathy with their sufferings.

"That separate floors be appropriated for each of the sexes. . . .

"That an intelligent man and woman be employed to attend the different sexes, whose business shall be to direct and share in their amusements and to divert their minds by conversation, reading, and obliging them to read and write upon subjects suggested from time to time by the attending physicians.

"That no visitor be permitted to converse with or even to see the mad people."

Rush pointed out that "degraded as they are by their disease, a sense of corporeal pleasure, of joy, of gratitude, of neglect, and of injustice is seldom totally obliterated from their minds."[4]

The insane as well as the other patients frequently complained of the cold during the winter. The fires in the hospital were covered at twilight. Rush conceived the idea that more deaths occurred during the night than during the day, probably because the patients were exposed, in a debilitated state, to a reduced temperature. In December 1812, he demanded that the hospital rooms be kept as warm during the night as during the day, and asked for the appointment of a person to feed the fires.[5]

It is apparent from the reforms instituted by Rush in the Pennsylvania Hospital that his positive views on the subject of insanity were both enlightened and advanced. He looked upon insanity not as a single disease but as a combination of many diseases, claiming that it is not merely a mental disease, but a disease of the whole body. Furthermore, he held that insanity is not always the result of a diseased brain and nerve centers; but, on the contrary, is caused by arterial excitement. He believed that diseases of the mind could be brought "under the dominion of medicine by just theories of their seats and proximate causes."[6]

From his correspondence it is evident that he began to put his theories of insanity into concrete form about the year 1795. In October of that year he wrote one of his former students: "I have lately adopted a new theory of mania. I suppose it in nearly all cases to be accompanied by inflammation in the brain. This, the water, blood, pus, & hardness found in the brain after death all demonstrate —for they follow inflammation in other parts of the body. The hardness is a real scirrus analagous to schirrus in the liver. In consequence of the adoption of this theory, I have lately cured three deplorable cases of madness by copious bleeding (100 ounces in one case). It was aided afterwards by the cold bath." A few months later he wrote again: "My remedies for the recent cases were bleeding to 100 ounces down to 30 ounces—strong purges—low diet—kind treatment, and the cold bath." Shortly thereafter he reported enthusiastically: "My late success in the treatment of mania has brought me an encrease of patients in that disorder. My remedies are frequent but moderate bleedings, purges, low diet, salivation, and afterwards the cold bath."[7]

After many years of treating insane patients both privately and in the Pennsylvania Hospital, he had gathered countless facts which finally emerged in his greatest as well as his last volume on medicine. *Medical Inquiries and Observations, Upon the Diseases of the Mind* appeared in 1812, a year before his death and, although now much out of date, it remains one of the most significant books ever written by an American on the subject. Indeed, for a half century it was used as a standard reference work by physicians and medical students, continuing in use for so long a period because it was a pioneer work as well as a distinguished one. Isaac Ray's *Medical Jurisprudence of Insanity* was published in 1838, but not until 1883 did another systematic work on insanity, a successor to Rush's volume, appear. Furthermore, there was up to Rush's day no work of importance in this field of medicine published in Europe.

Rush considers the nature and pathology of insanity and its causes, physical, mental, moral, naming and defining them in an original and striking manner, even if he is at times needlessly prolix. He was one of the first physicians to recognize distinctly the corporeal nature of insanity and to insist that it be subjected to medical as well as moral treatment.

Throughout the book the term "derangement" is used to signify the diseases of all the faculties of the mind—"every departure of the mind in its perceptions, judgments, and reasonings, from its natural and habitual order, accompanied with corresponding actions." It is claimed that "the cause of madness is seated primarily in the blood-vessels of the brain, and that it depends upon the same kind of morbid and irregular actions that constitute other arterial diseases. There is nothing specific in these actions. They are a part of the unity of disease, particularly of fever; of which madness is a chronic form, affecting that part of the brain which is the seat of the mind."[8]

There are many reasons for believing that the cause of insanity, "madness," is seated in the blood vessels of the brain. First of all, many of "its remote and exciting causes" are the same as those of fever, and such brain diseases as apoplexy, palsy, and epilepsy, which it was believed had their seats in the blood vessels. Secondly, the ages and constitutions of persons most subject to insanity correspond to the age-grouping of victims of arterial diseases. Thirdly, all the symptoms of an ordinary fever, except a hot skin, are seen in insanity. Fourthly, insanity alternates with several diseases which are seated in the blood vessels: rheumatism, intermitting fever, and dropsy. Fifthly, "from its blending its symptoms with several of the forms of fever. It is sometimes attended with regular intermissions, and remissions," and, as he explained, "I have once seen it appear with profuse sweats, such as occur in certain fevers, in a madman in the Pennsylvania Hospital. These sweats, when discharged from his skin, formed a vapour resembling a thick fog, that filled the cell in which he was confined to such a degree as to render his body scarcely visible." Sixthly, the blood drawn from insane patients is the same type as that drawn from patients in certain fevers. In the seventh place, the appearance of the brain after death is similar to that of one after death from apoplexy and other diseases said to be affections of the blood vessels of the brain. Lastly, the remedies which cure insanity are the same as those that cure fever or disease in the blood vessels from other causes, and in other parts of the body.

Although the primary seat of insanity is in the blood vessels, it also extends, according to Rush, to the nerves and to that unknown part of the brain which is the seat of the mind.[9]

There are more than a score of remote and exciting causes of insanity classified in several groups. The first division includes those causes that act directly upon the brain such as injuries; certain local disorders induced by tumors and abscesses; such diseases of the brain as apoplexy, palsy, epilepsy, vertigo; exposure to the sun's rays; and certain odors. Rush noted a place in Scotland where insanity was sometimes induced by lead fumes; patients, who were afflicted, bit their hands, and tore the flesh on other parts of the body.

The second group includes causes which induce insanity by acting upon the brain in common with the whole body, such as gout, dropsy, tuberculosis, pregnancy, and fevers. Inanition from lack of nourishment, excessive use of alcoholic drinks, inordinate sexual desires and gratifications, great pain, extraordinary labor or exercise, extremely hot or cold weather, are all included in this group.

Corporeal causes, which act sympathetically upon the brain, comprise the third division. These are: narcotic substances such as opium and hemlock; the suppression of any usual evacuation such as the menses, milk, semen, or blood from the hemorrhoidal vessels; worms in the alimentary canal; and irritation from foreign matters retained in the irritable parts of the body. "I once knew some small shot," Rush related, "which were lodged in the foot of a small boy, induce madness several years after he became a man."[10]

Then there are direct and indirect causes of derangement which act upon the body through the medium of the mind. Of the causes that act directly on the mind, intense study is listed first, "whether of the sciences or of the mechanical arts, and whether of real or imaginary objects of knowledge. The latter more frequently produce madness than the former. They are, chiefly, the means of discovering perpetual motion; of converting the base metals into gold; of prolonging life to the antediluvian age; of producing perfect order and happiness in morals and government, by the operations of human reason; and, lastly, researches into the meaning of certain prophecies in the Old and New Testaments."

Second in this category is the frequent and rapid transition of the mind from one subject to another. In Rush's time it was said that booksellers were sometimes deranged from this cause, turning as they do from one book to the next in quick succession. The weakening effects of such sudden transitions of the mind were also thought to be evident after a person had read a volume of separate articles or magazines. "The brain in these cases," commented Rush, "is deprived of the benefit of habit, which prevents fatigue to a certain extent, from all the exercises of the body and mind, when they are confined to single objects."

Among the causes of an indirect nature the constant exercise of the imagination plays a part. Then there are the impressions that act primarily on the heart: joy, terror, love, fear, grief, distress, defamation, ridicule, loss of liberty, property, beauty, and inordinate love of praise. Rush believed that excess joy produced insanity among many of the successful adventurers in the South Sea speculation in England in 1720; Charles VI of France was deranged from a paroxysm of anger. Terror, likewise, has often induced insanity in persons who have escaped from fires, earthquakes, and shipwrecks. In 1803 an actor committed suicide in Philadelphia soon after being hissed off the stage. Loss of one's savings and wealth has led to insanity, the interesting observation being made that insanity "occurs oftener among the rich who lose only a part of their property, than among persons in moderate circumstances, who lose their all." An American Indian, Rush recorded, became deranged and destroyed himself when he saw his face in a mirror after having recovered from a violent attack of smallpox. The loss of an eye in a fight in a country tavern caused one of Rush's patients to go insane, while "a clergyman in Maryland became insane in consequence of having permitted some typographical errors to escape in a sermon which he published upon the death of General Washington."

The understanding also becomes deranged occasionally through the medium of the moral faculties. A guilty conscience, real or imaginary, is a frequent cause. "An instance of insanity occurred in a married woman . . . of the most exemplary character, from a belief that she had been unfaithful to the marriage bed. . . . An accident discovered that the supposed criminal connection was with a man whose very person was unknown to her."[11]

After long study Rush finally concluded that insanity occurs more commonly from mental than from corporeal causes. Its origin is usually psychic rather than physical.

The circumstances and conditions which predispose the body to be acted upon by these causes are many and varied. Heredity plays an important part. "A peculiar and hereditary sameness of organization of the nerves, brain, and blood-vessels sometimes pervades whole families, and renders them liable to this disease from a transient or feeble operation of its causes." A predisposition to insanity was said to be connected with dark-colored hair. There is a greater predisposition to insanity between the ages of twenty and fifty, than in any other age group. "The reason why children and persons under puberty are so rarely affected with madness must be ascribed to mental impressions, which are its most frequent cause, being too transient in their effects, from the instability of their minds, to excite their brains into permanently diseased actions." Rush met with few old people who suffered from mental diseases. Women are more predisposed to insanity than men, he thought, by reason of menstruation, pregnancy, parturition, and "by living so much alone in their families." At the same time, however, "the distressing impressions made upon the minds of women frequently vent themselves in tears, or in hysterical commotions in the nervous system and bowels, while the same impressions upon the minds of men pass by their more compact nervous and muscular fibres, and descend into the brain, and thus more frequently bring on hypochondriac insanity."

It seemed to Rush that single persons are more predisposed to insanity than married persons. "The absence of real and present care," he pointed out, "which gives the mind leisure to look back upon the past, and to anticipate future and imaginary evils, and the inverted operation of all the affections of the heart upon itself, together with the want of relief in conjugal sympathy from the inevitable distress and vexations of life, and for which friendship is a cold and feeble substitute, are probably the reasons why madness occurs more frequently in single than in married people."

The rich are more predisposed to madness than the poor, being more sensitive to all its remote and exciting causes.

Climate has a definite influence on the mind. Insanity is uncommon in uniformly warm climates, more common in climates alternately warm and cold, but most common in such as are usually moist, cold, and cloudy.

Particular forms of society, and particular opinions and pursuits, predispose the body to derangement. It is a rare disease among savages, but in commercial countries where fortunes are suddenly made and lost, it is common. It is most prevalent at those times when speculation is substituted for regular business.[12]

All these causes, remote and exciting, direct and indirect, cover in one way or another the etiology of insanity as we know it today, even if current medical terms assigned to the various phases of mental diseases have been changed. Although future findings have completely outmoded Rush's classification of causes, the general conception was remarkable.

He divided diseases of the mind into two large sections: general intellectual derangement, and partial intellectual derangement including tristimania (sadness)—an original term with him—and anemomania (monomania or paranoia), a type of hypochondriasis.

Partial intellectual derangement, and particularly hypochondriasis, he defined as consisting in "error in opinion, and conduct, upon some one subject only, with soundness of mind upon all, or nearly all other subjects. . . . It [the error] is directly contrary to truth, or it is disproportioned in its effects, or expected consequences, to the causes which induce them. . . . When it relates to the persons, affairs, or condition of the patient only, and is attended with distress, it has been called hypochondriasis. When it extends to objects external to the patient, and is attended with pleasure, or the absence of distress, it has been called melancholia. . . . Perhaps the term tristimania might be used to express this form of madness when erroneous opinions respecting a man's person, affairs, or condition, are the subjects of his distress."[13]

For partial intellectual derangement Rush recommended more than a score of remedies, divided into two groups. The first group, supposed to act directly upon the body, is headed by bloodletting. To understand the reason for this treatment one must bear in mind Rush's claim that the primary seat of insanity is in the blood vessels of the brain, and that it depends upon the same kind of morbid and irregular action that accompanies other arterial diseases. He insisted that early and copious bleedings, twenty to forty ounces at a time, could calm insane patients and occasionally cure them in a few hours. His records tell of one patient who lost 470 ounces of blood in forty-seven bleedings! It is recorded, too, that a preacher, suffering from tristimania, called on Dr. Thomas Bond for advice. He said he was possessed of a devil, and that he felt him constantly in aches and pains in every part of his body. The Doctor felt his pulse which he found to be full and tense, and advised him to sit down in the parlor, persuading him to permit a vein in his arm to be opened. While the blood was flowing the patient cried out: "I am relieved, I felt the devil fly out of the orifice in my vein as soon as it was opened." He then recovered rapidly from his derangement.

Bloodletting went into disuse as a treatment for insanity shortly after Rush's death.

This first group of remedies also includes purgatives and emetics, which, by exciting the stomach and the bowels, often remove morbid excitement from the brain, and thus restore the mind to its healthy state. Not only is a reduced diet recommended but also stimulating food, drinks, and medicines: "The diet should consist of solid animal food, with such vegetables as are least disposed to acidity, and both should be rendered palatable by condiments. The drinks should consist of old Madeira or sherry wine, and porter diluted with water, or taken alone, provided the stomach be not affected with a morbid acid."

The warm bath was considered most beneficial when it induced sweats. It was also proposed, however, that the body be immersed in cold water for several hours. Counter-irritants were suggested: mustard applied to the feet, sufficiently strong to cause pain, itself a remedy. Salivation is also helpful, Rush advised, because mercury acts by abstracting the morbid excitement from the brain to the mouth, and by changing the cause of the patient's complaints, and fixing them wholly upon his sore mouth.[14]

The second group of remedies includes those that act upon the body through the medium of the mind. The physician was advised to listen sympathetically and seriously to the patient, thus to give him every opportunity to relieve his subconscious mind. Rush frequently asked patients to write down an account of their symptoms. They felt better for the writing and often he learned much that was enlightening about them. Was it possible that Rush, in using this procedure, called by Freud mental catharsis, anticipated the theory and practice of the psychoanalyst?

Destruction of all old associations and ideas is another treatment suggested in this group of remedies. As soon as possible, a patient's dress, room, his company and general environment should be changed, but above all, whenever possible, the body and mind of the patient should be kept busy. Occupation is definitely helpful, but care must be used in providing harmless instruments and tools. "Happiness," said Rush, "consisting in folded arms, and in pensive contemplation, beneath rural shades, and by the side of purling brooks, never had any existence, except in the brains of mad poets, and love-sick girls and boys." He recalled the case of a patient, whom he was unable to help, who recovered after he had returned to work on his Maryland farm. Rush attributed the cure to profuse perspiration!

Amusements, such as shooting, hunting, quoits, chess, and checkers, which interest the mind or exercise the body, were considered helpful. Music and "committing entertaining passages of prose and verse to memory, and copying manuscripts, have been found useful in relieving hypochondriasm. They divert and translate attention and action from the understanding to a sound part of the mind." It was also suggested that mention be made of a parent, relative, or a friend from whom the patient has received acts of kindness, protection, or relief in early life. Single persons sometimes find relief from mental disorders in matrimony—"the constant pursuits and wholesome cares of a family generally prevent and cure such as are transient and imaginary." Long trips relieve the mind from the monotony of objects and persons. The strong emotion of terror is also helpful "by the concussion it gives to both body and mind." Rush had the record of a woman opium addict in New York City. On one of his visits the physician took from his pocket a large snuffbox, and the patient immediately asked for some snuff. When she opened it, however, an artificial snake jumped to her shoulder and she became convulsed with terror, and rapidly recovered, living forty years thereafter. In another case a fall down a steep hill cured an insanity of twenty years' standing.[15]

Turning to mania or tonic madness, one of the three forms of general intellectual derangement, Rush listed its premonitory signs as watchfulness, high or low spirits, great rapidity of thought, eccentricity in conversation and conduct, terrifying or distressing dreams, great irritability of temper, jealousy, instability, and extraordinary acts of extravagance such as the purchase of things not needed. "The face is pale or flushed, the eyes are dull or wild, the appetite is increased, the bowels are costive, and the patient complains sometimes of throbbing in the temples, vertigo and headache." Rolling eyes, a ferocious countenance, whistling, imitating the noises of animals, walking with a quick step are some of the symptoms.

In visiting a patient suffering from mania Rush suggested that, on entering the cell or chamber, the physician should catch the patient's eye "and look him out of countenance." An animal's dread of the steady glare of the human eye had long been recognized. The tiger, the mad bull, and the enraged dog fly from it. A man deprived of his reason assumes so much of the nature of those animals that he is for the most part easily terrified or composed by the eye of a man who possesses his reason. A desired effect is produced by "looking the patient out of countenance" with a steady eye, and varying its aspect from the highest degree of sternness down to the mildest degree of benignity, for "there are keys in the human eye . . . which should be suited to the state of the patient's mind, with the same exactness that musical tones should be suited to the depression of spirits in hypochondriasis." Rush himself used this method.

The deranged patient can be made amenable through the voice: "In governing mad people it should be harsh, gentle, or plaintive, according to circumstances." The physician's countenance should supplement his eye and voice in ruling the patients. Always keep promises made to the patients, Rush warned, and treat them with all the respect "due to their former rank and habits."

If all treatments fail, several means of coercion were suggested. Privation of customary pleasant food, a fifteen- to twenty-minute shower bath, and cold water poured under the coat sleeve so that it might descend into the arm pits and down the trunk of the body, are included. More successful, however, was confinement in a strait-jacket, or in a chair of Rush's own design called a tranquillizer.[16] The violent patient was strapped in the tranquillizer, his head being fixed rigidly by lowering a hinged block fastened to the back. By lessening muscular action or reducing motor activity the tranquillizer was supposed to control the rush of the blood toward the brain. It was claimed also that it reduced the force and frequency of the pulse. Because of the large number of bruises and fractures resulting from its use, however, this device was soon dispensed with.

Rush also designed a machine called a gyrator for use in "torpid madness." This machine was based on the principle that insanity depends on the amount and force of blood flowing to the brain. It was a kind of turn-table on which the patient was so placed that centrifugal force increased the flow of blood to the brain. The head was placed at the greatest distance from the center of motion, and on revolving the gyrator, the blood was forced to the head and accelerated the heart action from seventy to 120 beats a minute.

Of the remedies for mania that are applied to the mind through the medium of the body, bloodletting was considered by Rush the most important. He advised that on the first attack twenty to forty ounces of blood be drawn, and that the process be repeated "not only while any of those states of morbid action in the pulse remain which require bleeding in other diseases, but in the absence of them all, provided great wakefulness, redness in the eyes, a ferocious countenance, and noisy and refractory behavior continue, all of which indicate a highly morbid state of the brain." Other remedies are darkness, which invites silence, erect position of the body, vegetable diet, purging, emetics, nitre, cold air, water, ice, salivations, peruvian bark, and solitude.[17]

Manalgia, in which "a universal torpor takes place in the body and mind," is another form of general intellectual derangement. Its symptoms are taciturnity, downcast looks, total neglect of dress and person, indifference to all surrounding objects, and insensibility to heat and cold. One patient slept in the cupola of the Pennsylvania Hospital for nine years and on the coldest days never came near a fire. "A fixed position of the body sometimes attends this form of madness. Of this there have been two remarkable instances in our hospital. In one of them, the patient sat with his body bent forward for three years, without moving, except when compelled by force, or the calls of nature. In the other, the patient occupied a spot in a ward, or entry, or in the hospital yard, where he appeared more like a statue than a man." In manalgia the skin is dry, cold, pale, and yellow; the eyes, if originally dark, become light in color; the appetite is weak; and there is a strong attachment to tobacco among the patients who have been in the habit of taking it.

According to Rush, "Nebuchadnezzar seems to have been affected with this low grade of madness. He was said to resemble a beast, probably from the uncommon growth of his hair, beard, and nails." This type of insanity might last from ten to fifty years.

Among the remedies for manalgia which act upon the mind through the medium of the body, Rush recommended the warm bath; the cold shower bath—"the impulse imparted to the head by the descent of the water upon it adds very much to its efficacy"—and the cold shower bath following a one- or two-hour warm bath in order to give the system the necessary shock. Malt liquors, wine, and cider are listed as remedies. Artificial diarrhoea, in manalgia, was said to excite "a revulsive action or disease, in a less delicate part

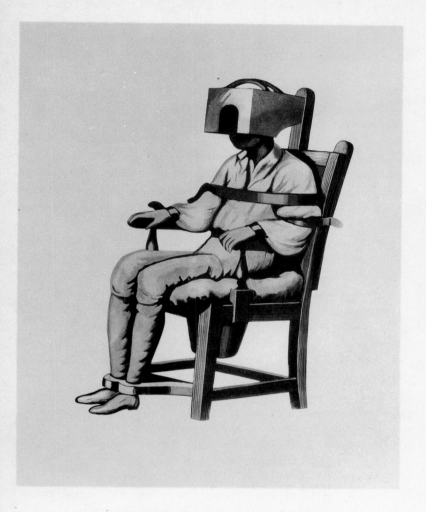

TRANQUILLIZER OR STRAIT-JACKET

of the body than the brain." Music, work, and exercise are also suggested.

Rush quoted Dr. Samuel Johnson as saying that Dean Swift had a temporary return of his reason during the continuance of an abscess in his eye.

Great pain, particular odors, loud and uncommon sounds are other remedies for manalgia found in Rush's list. As auxiliary aids opium, iron, strong tea and green coffee, garlic, valerian, and electricity were also used. The application of electricity in 1812 is especially interesting; many decades were to pass, however, before it was generally utilized by physicians.

Rush finally recommended that the passions and emotions be excited, and he gave as an example the effect of a fit of anger in the case of a patient in the Pennsylvania Hospital who, for several months, had refused to speak. He amused himself by drawing. One day Dr. Bond looked over his shoulder and saw a picture of a flower. "A pretty cabbage," remarked the Doctor. "You are a fool and a liar," shouted the patient, "it is a flower." From that time he spoke as usual.[18]

Surveying insanity in general, Rush made some comments on the possibility of recovery from mental diseases. A young person is easier to cure than an old person. Intermissions of violent mental excitement, abscesses in any part of the body, a running nose after it has long been dry, warm and moist hands after they have long been cold and dry, the continuance or revival of hysterical symptoms after being long absent, a moderate diarrhoea, are all favorable signs. Insanity caused by brain lesions is seldom cured, and that which follows epilepsy, never. "Madness is difficult to cure, when it arises from the revival of an old and dormant passion, excited by association, especially when that passion is love or grief. It is remarkable, that the love which causes madness does not revive with its cure." Return of the ability to spell correctly after it has been suspended is a favorable sign. The return of an habitual disease or appetite is likewise favorable. In one case a patient's habit of stammering returned as soon as he began to recover from insanity. The revival of an appetite for gingerbread in another patient was soon followed by his recovery; and in another case a girl, who had been in the habit of copying poetry while well, asked one day for her pen, ink, and books, and recovered shortly thereafter.[19]

In discussing the derangement of the passions Rush discourses upon love. It becomes a disease only when it is disappointed in its object. As a disease, it is recognized by such symptoms as sighing, wakefulness, perpetual talking, or silence concerning the beloved one, and fondness for solitude. It may be discovered in a man by blushing and increased frequency of the pulse when the name of the beloved is mentioned. It may be determined in a woman "by her retiring to decorate herself upon the appearance of the man in company whom she loves. It always renders a woman awkward, but it polishes the manners of men. The effects of unsuccessful love are dyspepsia, hysteria, hypochondriasis, fever, and madness. The last has sometimes induced suicide, while all others have now and then ended in death."

When the disorder is accompanied with fever or with intense nervous excitement, Rush proposed the following remedies: bloodletting; a new love; avoidance of the person beloved and a vacation in distant parts; exciting in the mind a more powerful passion such as ambition; constant employment—"the disease is half cured when the distressed lover ceases to think of the object of his affections." According to Ovid the lovelorn should determine and "dwell upon all the bad qualities, and defects in the person and accomplishments of his mistress."[20] With the exception of bloodletting, Rush's remedies are still recommended to distressed lovers, with probably the same uncertain results.

Although many of his cures for the various forms of mental disease gradually fell into disuse and today are merely of antiquarian interest, yet in a number of instances Rush's approach was correct. In advocating the use of mental catharsis he was a century ahead of his time. Although one might smile at innumerable passages in *Medical Inquiries and Observations, Upon the Diseases of the Mind*, nevertheless it must be said that Rush gave to the medical profession an able exposition of the forms of mental disorder. Indeed, this book is considered by some authorities one of the most notable books on the subject in English. Rush wrote it after thirty years of practice in the Pennsylvania Hospital. Here, in one of the few institutions in

America in the eighteenth century, the insane were segregated. The care they received was accorded to them as human beings and not as beasts.

This study of mental diseases was so unique and so complete that it remained the only comprehensive American treatise on the subject until the year 1883. One of its distinguished features is that it treats the subject from the pathological point of view, holding that insanity is definitely a disease of the brain. The assumption that the seat of the disease is in the blood vessels of the brain is not far removed from present-day theories concerning some of the mental disorders. Rush made the further original suggestion that insanity skips one or more generations. To his efforts can be attributed more advancement in the hospitalization and treatment of the insane than to any other physician of his time. The introduction of occupational therapy was particularly significant. Although his resort to bloodletting was discredited decades ago, and although the tranquillizer and gyrator, which he invented, went into the discard shortly after his death, Rush remains, nevertheless, a pioneer in the study of psychiatry and once more stands as a benefactor of his distressed fellow men.

XII

Reformer and Philosopher

THE intellectual pursuits of Benjamin Rush were not followed merely along the paths of medical practice and research. Far from it. An avid curiosity and a deep sense of civic duty led him to inquire into public problems. A stubborn belief that the results of his observations and findings were of value to his fellow man, and that his opinions embodied the essence of truth, led him to frequent publication of his reflections. On public questions he often played the propagandist, and running through his missionary writings is a cocksureness which is sometimes annoying and frequently obscures their worth.

Rush discussed the evils of strong drink and tobacco; he took up penal reform and held forth against the death penalty; he raised his voice against slavery; he inquired into the manners and customs of the neighboring Indians and Pennsylvania Dutch; he crusaded for the abolition of oaths; he made illuminating observations on our natural resources and the use thereof; he drew up a plan for a state school system; he wrote several excellent biographical sketches and eulogies, and occasionally expounded weighty philosophical questions such as the influence of physical causes on the moral faculty.

He made his first venture into authorship at the age of nineteen, and continued to wield his pen until he died. One wonders how it was possible for such a busy man to have found time to fill so many pages on such diverse subjects. He himself once remarked that ideas, whether acquired from books or reflection, produced a plethora in the mind which can be relieved only by depletion through the pen or tongue.

Rush was one of the first out-and-out advocates of abolition in America. Three years before American independence from England was declared, he wrote his first attack against the institution of slavery. The *Address to the Inhabitants of the British Settlements Upon Slave-Keeping* is a summary of arguments against the practice. The vices charged against the negro—idleness, treachery, theft—

are the offspring of slavery itself. The slave is driven to crime by his master's methods. Rush believed that the sugar, rice, and indigo industries could be carried on successfully without slave labor. The importation of slaves was justified by some persons on the ground that the slaves become acquainted with and adopt the religion of their new country. "This is like justifying a highway robbery," reasoned Rush, "because part of the money acquired in this manner was appropriated to some religious use. . . . A Christian slave is a contradiction in terms." He also disagreed with those who held that, by treating slaves well, we render their situation happier in America than in their own country: "Slavery and vice are connected together, and the latter is always a source of misery. Besides, by the greatest humanity, we can show them, we only lessen, but do not remove the crime, for the injustice of it continues the same."

What was the practical way to put an end to slavery? First of all, suggested Rush, let slave trade be abolished immediately by organizing a general boycott against those citizens who continue to import slaves and against the ships that carry them. Limit the period of servitude of the slaves already in the country, and then: "Let young negroes be educated in the principles of virtue and religion—let them be taught to read and write—and afterwards instructed in some business, whereby they may be able to maintain themselves." They should be thus prepared for freedom. When emancipation finally came, ninety years later, the slaves had not been prepared for it and a tragic era followed.

Rush went on, in this pamphlet, to condemn the dissolution of family ties occasioned by the theft of individual slaves in Africa, and the separation of individuals in negro families in America. He called on the advocates of liberty in America to "bear testimony against a vice which degrades human nature, and dissolves that universal tie of benevolence which should connect all the children of men together in one great family." He appealed to the ministers of the gospel, claiming that "Slavery is an hydra sin, and includes in it every violation of the precepts of the law and the gospel. In vain will you command your flocks to offer up the incence of faith and charity, while they continue to mingle the sweat and blood of negro slaves with their sacrifices."

This *Address* accompanied a petition to the Legislature of Pennsylvania asking for an increase in the import duty on negro slaves. It was written anonymously, and when Rush was discovered to be the author, he hastily penned a *Vindication of the Address to the Inhabitants of the British Settlements* in reply to a pamphlet which tried to show that slavery was not forbidden by Scripture.

In the *Vindication* Rush maintained that abolition was in no sense a Utopian scheme, that slavery had been abolished in parts of Europe and was, indeed, slowly losing its hold in America. He declared that reason and humanity were moving many West Indian planters to favor free labor.

He stressed the cruelty and injustice suffered by the negroes, quoting from accounts of frightful punishments in the West Indies. If a slave struck a white man in these islands, the death penalty was imposed. It was not considered a punishable offense in Jamaica for a white person to kill a slave found stealing or running away at night. A runaway slave, when captured, might lose a foot as punishment. Such cruel treatment, and the system of slavery itself moved Rush deeply, and made of him one of the early leaders in a movement which was not to end until arms settled the issue nearly a century later.

Again in the temperance movement Rush was a pioneer. As early as 1772 he published *Sermons to Gentlemen Upon Temperance and Exercise*. He divided people into two classes, those who should and those who should not use wines and strong drink. Wine may be taken by the sick, said the preacher-physician, in nervous fevers, and in chronic diseases in which the stomach is upset. It is sometimes indispensable for the inhabitants of low marshy countries where perspiration does not flow freely. In moderate quantities it maintains a proper balance between solids and fluids, thus preventing disease; and for old people or such as are in the decline of life it "prolongs the strength and powers of nature."

Wine should not be used by anyone under thirty-five years of age, unless he is suffering from a disease requiring a stimulant. Rush also believed that "studious people or those who have occasion to exercise their thinking faculties much, should abstain from wine.

Thinking is a stimulus to the constitution, and wears out the springs of life beyond the most laborious exercise of body."

Thoughts on the subject lay dormant in Rush's mind for more than a decade before he published his famous blast: *Enquiry into the Effects of Spirituous Liquors Upon the Human Body.* This pamphlet, reprinted over and over again in many forms for a half century, was a general survey of the effects of liquor on the body and mind, and on society in general. It was an ardent appeal for temperance.

Rush also carried his doctrine into the classroom, advising the students to avoid as far as possible medicines that contain distilled spirits. "Perhaps there are few cases in which it is safe to exhibit medicines prepared in spirits, in any other form than in drops. Many persons have been innocently seduced into a love of strong drink from taking large or frequent doses of bitters infused in spirits. Let not our profession be reproached, in a single instance, with adding to the calamaties that have been entailed upon mankind, by this dreadful species of intemperance."[1] He wrote Dr. Lettsom in London: "I believe they [liquors] are safe in those medicines only which are given in drops. Where it is necessary to give tinctures by spoonfuls, or in larger quantities, I direct them to be made with water instead of spirit."[2]

The *Enquiry* defines spirits as "all those liquors which are obtained by distillation from fermented juices or substances of any kind," and shows that they quicken the circulation and produce heat in the blood. After a time, however, "they become what is called sedative; that is, they diminish the action of the vital powers, and thereby produce languor and weakness." Ultimately spirituous liquors lead to "a sickness in the stomach," to dropsy, obstruction of the liver, insanity, palsy, apoplexy, and epilepsy. All forms of inflammatory fevers are rendered more frequent and more obstinate by their use. The toll of lives from intemperance, according to Rush, was tremendous: "Spirituous liquors destroy more lives than the sword. War has its intervals of destruction—but spirits operate at all times, and seasons upon human life." In cities they are responsible for debts, disgrace, and bankruptcy, and in rural districts for idleness with all its attendant evils.

The effects of liquor on the moral fibre are terrifying, causing one to be peevish and quarrelsome, and to "violate promises and engagements without shame or remorse."

Rush admitted that liquors are beneficial to one who is faint or exhausted, or to one who has been exposed to wet weather. In no other cases, however, are spirits absolutely essential for well-being. One might substitute cider, which is "perfectly inoffensive and wholesome," or beer, which is both wholesome and nourishing. Furthermore, brewers should be exempt from taxation. A pleasant and cooling drink, the best that can be contrived in warm weather, is a mixture of vinegar and water sweetened with sugar and molasses.

The heavy liquors are, then, practically superfluous to physical well-being, and their consumption might be materially decreased if the price were to be increased through heavy taxation.

Because of Rush's personal interest in the subject, the College of Physicians, September 4, 1787, went on record in favor of temperance, and appointed him chairman of a committee to prepare a memorial to the State Legislature "setting forth the pernicious effects of spirituous liquors upon the human body, and praying that such a law may be passed as shall tend to diminish their consumption." On November 6, 1787, the College adopted the Memorial which stated:

"That among the numerous diseases which are produced by the use of distilled spirituous liquors, they would only mention, the dropsy, epilepsy, palsy, apoplexy, melancholy and madness, which too seldom yield to the powers of medicine. That where distilled spirituous liquors do not produce those terrible and obstinate diseases they generally impair the strength of the body so as to lessen its ability to undergo that labour, either in degree or duration, which it is capable of without them. That the prevailing ideas of the necessity and advantages of using distilled spirituous liquors to obviate the injurious effects of extreme heat or cold upon the human body are altogether without foundation, and that they increase the evils they are taken to remove."[3]

The temperance movement in America was thus given its start and, in 1885, a delegation of the W.C.T.U. gathered at the grave of Benjamin Rush who, without realizing the far-reaching effects of his crusade, gave impetus to a movement which has lived down to the present. Over Rush's grave one finds this tablet:

"On the 3rd of November, 1885, the officers and delegates of the National Women's Christian Temperance Union from forty states and numbering 300 by their representatives planted this oak tree in token of their reverence for the memory of Dr. Benjamin Rush, instaurator of the American temperance reform, one hundred years ago."

The *Enquiry* yielded some positive results. In a letter to Rev. Jeremy Belknap, distinguished Boston divine, in 1788, Rush explained jubilantly: "My . . . object shall be the extirpation of the *abuse* of spirituous liquors. For this purpose I have every year for several years past republished the enclosed tract [the *Enquiry*] two or three weeks before harvest. The effects of this perseverance begin already to shew themselves in our State. A family or a township is hit with the publication one year, that neglected or perhaps ridiculed it the year before. Associations are forming in many places to give no spirits at the ensuing harvest. The Quakers and Methodists take the lead in these associations, as they have often done in all enterprises that have morality or the happiness of society for the objects. Many storekeepers among the Quakers now refuse to buy or sell spirituous liquors. In a short time I expect there will be an act of the Quaker society to forbid the sale, or even use, of them altogether, except as a medicine."[4] In 1788 Rush made a stirring appeal for temperance before the Philadelphia annual conference of the Methodist Episcopal Church, and won many converts. Twenty-three years later, in 1811, he visited the sessions of the General Assembly of the Presbyterian Church, in Philadelphia, and presented a thousand copies of his *Enquiry* to the ministers and elders.

The effects produced by the tract were encouraging, but there was more to be done to safeguard the future. Rush looked to the press. "Let us try the force of the press upon spirituous liquors in every part of the United States," he requested Belknap. "I call upon you, my worthy tho' unknown friend, to act the part of a pioneer in this business in Massachusetts. Your success will be certain, & your reward great, both here & hereafter. . . . The good effects of our labors will appear in the next generation. Habitual drunkards are beyond the influence of reason, but young men will feel its force upon this subject & act accordingly. In the year 1915 a drunkard I hope will be as infamous in society as a lyar or a thief, and the use of spirits as uncommon in families as a drink made of a solution of arsenic or a decoction of hemlock."[5]

The usefulness of newspapers for propaganda purposes was thus recognized when the American daily press was in its infancy. Rush set the year 1915 as the time when a drunkard would be "infamous"; he missed American prohibition by five years.

He watched the results of his propaganda carefully. On July 4, 1788, during a special celebration in Philadelphia on the first Independence Day after the adoption of the Federal Constitution, Rush was pleased to observe that of the 17,000 persons who participated "there was scarcely one person intoxicated, nor was there a single quarrel or even dispute, heard of during the day." This extraordinary circumstance Rush assigned to the fact that no liquors, except beer and cider, were consumed on the festival grounds. Here was tangible evidence that his labors were bearing fruit.[6]

His next battle was to be fought against the use of tobacco. He gathered data for a tobacco tract during the summer of 1790, and in late August advised Belknap: "The next time I appear before the public as an author will probably be in an 'Inquiry into the Influence of Tobacco upon the Health, Life, Morals, Manners, and Property of Mankind.' I have lately discovered that the use of that vile weed, especially in chewing & smoaking, predisposes very much to the intemperate use of strong drinks. The use of tobacco in any way is uncleanly. Now uncleanliness has been proved to be unfriendly to morals. Many diseases are produced by it, some of which become fatal. The price of it is moreover considerable, amounting in a lifetime to many pounds, and the time spent in *procuring & using it,* if employed in profitable labor, would yield a handsome beginning for a son or daughter, or endow a charity school, or nearly build a church."[7] Against smoking and chewing were, in one short letter, charged diseases of the mind as well as of the body, uncleanness, and extravagant expenditures. By November the last line of the essay, mentioned in the letter, was written and ready for press. Rush knew that its publication would increase the number of his enemies but, he wrote Belknap on November 19, "I am scandal proof."[8]

The tract on tobacco was published as *Observations Upon the Influence of the Habitual use of Tobacco Upon Health, Morals, and Property*, and sought to prove that tobacco impairs the digestion and leads to pulmonary tuberculosis and nervous diseases. Furthermore, it creates an artificial thirst, a desire for strong drink, leading to drunkenness, and idleness, a corruption of the moral sense. When used in the form of snuff, tobacco "seldom fails of impairing the voice by obstructing the nose. It moreover imparts to the complexion a disagreeable dusky color."

It is a matter of common observation that smoking frequently annoys persons who do not use tobacco and, according to Rush, "a habit of offending the senses of friends or strangers by the use of tobacco, cannot therefore be indulged with innocence." And what of the possible damage to clothing and furniture caused by tobacco burns and stains! He also made some calculations on the time lost in using snuff. A man who takes a pinch of snuff every twenty minutes, consuming half a minute every time he uses the box, wastes five whole days a year!

The campaign against tobacco was not supported by any influential groups and, with no positive victory in prospect, Rush turned to other fields.

He was always in sympathy with the under dog. The sufferings of the negro slave had early attracted his attention, and now he turned to the sorry plight of prisoners, suffering under a medieval penal system. Punishments, at this period, had not been adjusted to fit the varying degrees of crime, while the psychology of the criminals themselves was never considered. Public punishments, the whipping post and stocks, were resorted to universally, and provided spectacles for curious citizens who happened to be passing by. Rush saw no excuse for subjecting a criminal to punishment in public, and he insisted that a definite attempt at reformation be made. The criminal was punished and society took its revenge, but no steps were ever taken to help him return to society a decent citizen.

At the home of Benjamin Franklin, where the Society for Promoting Political Enquiries met on March 9, 1787, Rush read a paper on penal reform called *An Enquiry Into the Effects of Public Punishments Upon Criminals, And Upon Society,* which was immediately printed in pamphlet form, winning many adherents to its views.[9]

This *Enquiry* holds that reformation of the criminal cannot be effected by public punishments, inasmuch as these penalties are always associated with infamy, and they destroy in the criminal the sense of shame, "one of the strongest out-posts of virtue." Further, they are usually too short in duration to change obstinate habits of vice; and they have, on the other hand, tended to increase crime, since "a man who has lost his character at a whipping-post, has nothing valuable left to lose in society."

The *Enquiry* also sets forth that, by exciting a sense of terror in the minds of the spectators, public punishments lead to further crime. The admiration which fortitude under suffering arouses in some instances excites a spirit of envy. If, indeed, criminals are insensible to these punishments, the effect must be still more fatal to society; it removes terror instead of exciting it. Distress of all kinds, when actually seen, leads to sympathy and a disposition to relieve the distress. "While we pity," wrote Rush, "we secretly condemn the law which inflicts the punishment: hence, arises a want of respect for laws in general." When, however, criminals are viewed without sympathy, indignation, or contempt, the spectator regards the punishment as a mere arbitrary act of cruelty: "Hence will arise a disposition to exercise the same arbitrary cruelty over the feelings and lives of their fellow creatures." Furthermore, public chastisements acquaint the spectators with crimes hitherto unknown to them.

The use of convict labor in road building, as it has persisted in many states in our own day, Rush believed absolutely wrong, because such practice renders labor of every kind "disreputable."

How, then, should the criminal be punished? It is a familiar fact, Rush pointed out, that the individual loves liberty, and that he loathes separation from the society of his family and friends. Is it not, therefore, a severe punishment to take liberty and the freedom of social intercourse from the malefactor? Prisoners should be confined in a large jail located in an accessible part of the state. This jail should include a house of worship, a garden, and a shop where prisoners can work at trades. The place should not be called a prison or any other name "that is associated with what is infamous in the opinion of mankind." Punishments should be of varying degrees, related directly to the temper of the criminals or the progress of their reformation. Rush was, indeed, one of the first Americans to insist, as he did in this *Enquiry*, that the only purpose of punishment is the reformation of the criminal. He remarked that we spend public money willingly to build almshouses and hospitals for the relief of men and women with physical disorders; why, then, should we not maintain institutions for the treatment of diseases of the mind as manifested in criminality?

Punishments, including bodily pain, labor, solitude, and silence, should be planned so as not to mar the future life of the culprit, because "the infamy of criminals is derived, not so much from the remembrance of their crimes, as from the recollection of the ignominy of their punishments," and "public punishments have scars which disfigure the whole character." Rush believed that ultimately the gallows, pillory, stocks, whipping post, and wheelbarrow would be abolished. He was looking far into the future; the whipping post was still being used in some parts of the United States in the twentieth century.

Rush was one of the first American advocates of penal reform to demand the abolition of capital punishment. "I am not more satisfied of the truth of any proposition in Euclid than I am of the truth of this declaration. *Murder is propagated by hanging for murder*," he wrote Belknap. "How disgraceful to our republics, that the monarchs of Europe should take the lead of us in extending the empire of reason & humanity in this interesting part of the government."[10] He declared, in the *Enquiry*, that "Laws . . . which inflict death for murder are . . . as unchristian as those which justify or tolerate revenge. . . . The power over human life is the sole prerogative of him who gave it. Human laws, therefore, rise in rebellion against this prerogative, when they transfer it to human hands." Why not confine the murderer, he asked, and attempt to reform him? Exile as a form of punishment is unwarrantable because it deprives society of the advantages which reformation might bring.

Ten years after this first blast against penal methods, Rush followed up his attack in *An Enquiry Into the Consistency of the Punishment of Murder by Death, With Reason and Revelation.* It is stated in this dissertation that capital punishment lessens the horror attached to killing and thus tends to increase the number of murders; and that people who are tired of life commit murder in order to be hanged—believing this course preferable to suicide! Persons serving on juries who find capital punishment revolting refuse to convict murderers. Further, "it has been said, that a man who has committed a murder, has discovered a malignity of heart, that renders him ever afterwards unfit to live in human society. This is by no means true in many, and perhaps in most of the cases of murder. It is most frequently the effect of a sudden gust of passion, and has sometimes been the only stain of a well-spent or inoffensive life."

Before this paper was written, in 1797, important changes had been effected in Pennsylvania's penal system. In 1793 the Attorney-General of Pennsylvania, William Bradford, with a view to establishing the principles laid down by Rush in 1788, published a paper denouncing the death penalty in the State. Rush's original plea, backed by Bradford, now brought action. In 1794 Pennsylvania's criminal code was completely revised, and capital punishment was reserved for deliberate homicide only. In the ten-year period, 1779–89, twenty-six persons had been put to death in Pennsylvania for burglary, twenty-three for robbery, and four for rape. Pennsylvania's reforms were influential in bringing about changes in criminal codes throughout the country, and Rush, as one of the pioneers in the movement for penal reform, deserves a large share of the credit.

His interest in prison welfare was expressed not only by the written word but also by actual help rendered the prisoners themselves. Not infrequently he took or sent gifts to the Philadelphia jail. In the late summer of 1796 we find him buying watermelons, and on Christmas day of that year providing turkey dinners for the inmates "as a proof that they are still remembered in their present suffering condition by some of their fellow creatures."[11]

The prisoners, not ungrateful for the watermelons and other delicacies, sent Rush cards of thanks from time to time. "The prisoners now confined in the new jail," reads one of these cards writ-

ten in September 1800, "return you their most grateful and un-
feigned thanks for those most elegant water-melons this day received
from yourself. And as this is not the first instance wherein a number
of us have been the objects of your remembrance and benevolence,
you may be assured sir, that our hearts are enlarged with thankful-
ness and gratitude for the most genuine advice and counsel we have
received from you Sir, along with the said present. And our earnest
desire is, that we may each one of us be prepared for greater mercies,
and in due time have them bestowed upon us. And may you sir, be
blessed with many and happy days, and when you shall be called to
make your exit from this vain life and world; may the remembrance
of your virtues and numberless acts of benevolence to the poor and
distressed flourish here on earth, till time shall be no more!"[12]

Rush was just as sincere in his efforts to insure a high standard
of honesty in all relationships of everyday life. The administration
of oaths in public and legal matters was a source of constant annoyance to him. Did not the system of oaths fix a special standard of
honesty for set occasions? Why should men not be honest at all
times?

In his *An Enquiry Into the Consistency of Oaths With Reason
and Christianity*, published in 1789, Rush called on Congress to
frame laws that would command respect and obedience without the
necessity of oath-taking.[13] "Oaths produce an idea in the minds of
men," he objected, "that there are two kinds or degrees of truth; the
one intended for common, and the other for solemn occasions."
Reverence for the casual kind of truth is easily lost; but truth, indeed, has no scale or subdivisions which oaths create. Because oaths
are contrary to reason, and because they have a pernicious influence
on morals, and are contrary to the spirit of the gospel, legislators and
clergymen should consider "how far they are responsible for all the
falsehood, profane swearing and perjury that exist in society."

Shortly after its publication Rush sent to Jeremy Belknap a copy
of this attack on oaths and requested that it be republished in the
Boston newspapers, writing: "It will probably for a while be disregarded, but the time will come when it will produce its effect. I am
not more satisfied, that what is called legal swearing is contrary to
the gospel, than I am that two and two make four. For this reason,

I now 'swear not all.' The universal practice of swearing required by all our laws, led me first to examine the lawfulness of oaths. The inquiry ended in a conviction of their folly & iniquity. In this, as in many other instances we see, that good grows out of evil, as truth does from error, & pleasure from pain. . . ."[14]

His outcry reached deaf ears, and oath-taking still remains a basic if sometimes perfunctory procedure in our legal system.

*   *   *   *   *   *   *

In the field of morals Rush's convictions were probably best summed up in *An Address to the Ministers of the Gospel of Every Denomination in the United States, Upon Subjects Interesting to Morals*, in 1788.[15] Herein he listed the practices which exert a pernicious influence upon morality. He turned back to spirituous liquors, insisting that they beget quarrels, and are responsible for much profane and indecent language. Since meetings of citizens for military drills are usually attended with intemperate drinking, fighting, and profanity, the militia is also an evil influence. Fairs, too, furnish an occasion for drunkenness and gambling.

Lawsuits should be prevented whenever possible, because "they are highly disreputable between persons who profess christianity." The "licentiousness of the press," horse racing, and cockfighting are all inimical to the good life. Clubs which exist only for dining purposes are also undesirable. "Amusements of every kind, on Sundays, beget habits of idleness and a love of pleasure, which extend their influence to every day of the week." This stand on Sunday amusements was almost universal in colonial days and in the early years of the Republic. The Pennsylvania law of 1794, prohibiting sports and public amusements on Sundays, was not in any way liberalized until 1933.

More constructive than the *Address to the Ministers*, but still chimerical and impractical, was Rush's *A Plan for A Peace-office of the United States*.[16] The Secretary of Peace, under this plan, would have power to establish and maintain free schools in every city, township, and village in the United States, and to furnish every family in the United States with a copy of an American edition of the Bible. Around the office of the Secretary of Peace beautiful pictures of pleasing subjects were to be hung, but in the office of the Secretary of War, on the other hand, were to hang horrible scenes of ghastly battles picturing broken bones, unburied bodies, hospitals, villages on fire, and rivers dyed with blood. And "to subdue that passion for war, which education, added to human depravity, have made universal, a familiarity with the instruments of death, as well as all military shows, should be carefully avoided." Military uniforms, titles, and parades should be abandoned. "Reviews tend to lessen the horrors of a battle by connecting them with the charms of order . . . military dresses fascinate the minds of young men . . . were there no uniforms, there would probably be no armies."

These noble ideas bore little fruit, however, and a century and a quarter after their publication, the United States entered the most destructive and far-reaching war in the history of the world. Strength of numbers is not necessarily evidence of the justness of a cause; the martyr for truth and liberty must fight a lone battle. As a pacifist Rush stood alone with the Quakers.

Turning from morality, and from governmental and political problems, he gave some thought to the daily press. To the editor of the *Federal Gazette* he addressed "Directions for conducting a newspaper in such a manner as to make it innocent, useful and entertaining."[17] Living 3,000 miles from Europe, he said, we have little interest in European quarrels and events, and the less published in America about them, therefore, the better. Avoid filling the newspaper, he advised the editor, with anecdotes of British vices and follies, for "what have the citizens of the United States to do with duels, the elopements, the kept mistresses, the murders, the suicides, the thefts, the forgeries, the boxing matches, the wagers for eating, drinking and walking, &c. &c. of the people of Great Britain?" Such news destroys whatever delicacy exists in the minds of young people. Further, if any of these vices are committed in the United States, the less said about them the better.

The editor was warned against using the newspaper as a vehicle for private scandals or personal disputes, or for attacking a man who is unable to fight back, or for publishing an article that he would not wish his wife or daughter to read. Newspapers were urged to publish a short account of all laws passed in all the States, the congressional debates, weather reports, and monthly lists of local deaths. The advancement of agriculture, industry, and commerce was held to be the principal object of a newspaper.

When this word of advice was written, in 1789, the first daily newspaper in America was celebrating its fifth anniversary; it was a four-page paper with little local news and many advertisements. The great metropolitan newspapers of the twentieth century and the scandal-mongering tabloids were far beyond the imagination of the provincial critic of 1789.

Rush himself might have made a fighting editor of the Horace Greeley type. His essays are forceful and concise and the propaganda pieces are written with a gusto. Some of the articles provide delightful reading, forbidding as the titles sometimes sound. Among them is his summary of experiments and observations on the mineral waters of Philadelphia, Abington, and Bristol. Rush studied the chemistry of these waters, listed the diseases in which they are remedial, and offered directions for their use. The Philadelphia mineral water was found in a well twenty-six feet deep, near the corner of Sixth and Chestnut Streets opposite Independence Hall. "The water, when it first comes from the pump, has a slight foetid smell, is somewhat turbid, and after standing a few hours exposed to the air, deposits a yellow sediment." This water and the waters in Abington and Bristol, north and northeast of Philadelphia, were said to be emetic and purgative, and "they likewise quicken the pulse, and promote perspiration." They were recommended for treatment in hysteria, palsy, epilepsy, gout, "in an old obstinate diarrhoea," in obstructions of the liver and spleen, chronic rheumatism, and diseases of the kidney and bladder; but they were considered deleterious, however, in cases of acute rheumatism and acute gout. "They afford the most certain relief in all cases of a want of appetite, when it originates from a defect in the stomach." The best time for drinking them, is either early in the morning, at noon, or in the evening, on an empty stomach. The mineral water in Philadelphia was used for many years, but whether or not it possessed any real medicinal properties it is impossible to say.

Maple sugar was another of our natural resources that Rush was anxious to protect and to develop. In *An Account of the Sugar-Maple Tree of the United States*, he presented an imposing array of facts and figures on the methods of obtaining maple sugar, and on the advantages of the sugar.[18] This essay, carefully and concisely written, contains most interesting data. Here one finds facts on the nature of maple wood, the rate of growth of the trees and their geographical distribution, the amount of sap obtainable, and a dozen and one related subjects. It is stated that a tree of ordinary size yields in a good season from twenty to thirty gallons of sap, from which are made from five to six pounds of sugar. Directions are given for reducing sap to sugar by freezing, by spontaneous evaporation, and by boiling.

Rush advocated the development of the maple-sugar industry, not only for commercial reasons, but also because he believed it would help solve the slave problem, inasmuch as most of the cane sugar used in the country was produced by slaves in the West Indies. The rapid extension of the maple-sugar business would result in "the happy means of rendering the commerce and slavery of our African brethren, in the sugar Islands as unnecessary, as it has always been inhuman and unjust."

In 1795 Rush signed a proposal for the sale of lands and property of the "Society for promoting the manufacture of sugar from the sugar maple tree, and furthering the interest of Agriculture in the State of Pennsylvania."[19] His vision of a widespread maple-sugar industry did not materialize.

Rush was a trained observer, besides being keenly interested in his neighbors. This is the explanation of the excellence of his studies of the Indians, and the Pennsylvania Germans. His paper on the *Natural History of Medicine Among the Indians in North America*, read before the American Philosophical Society in February 1774, is one of his most distinguished and scholarly studies, and it still remains one of the most important contributions on the subject. Though a medical paper, it is nontechnical in character and has a definite appeal for the layman.

This study is concerned with the North American Indians of the eighteenth century who inhabited the territory between 30° and 60° latitude. These people, we are told, lived largely like savages by fishing and hunting. Maize, or Indian corn, was an original grain among them.

There are several customs of the Indians which had direct bearing on particular diseases from which they suffered. The treatment they accorded their children deserves attention in this connection. To harden them against the action of heat and cold, the natural enemies to health among the Indians, the babies were plunged into cold water daily; the strong survived. To facilitate their being moved from place to place, they were tied to boards where they lay on their backs for as long as a year and a half. Babies were breast fed for a long period of time after birth. The children who lived were healthy and free from disease in infancy.

The diet of the Indians bore a direct relation to the incidence of disease among them. It was partly animal, partly vegetable. In the summer much more fish than animal meat was eaten; roots and fruits were eaten throughout the year. Salt was not used until Europeans introduced it. Meat was preserved from putrefaction by cutting it into small pieces and exposing it in the summer to the sun, and in the winter to the frost. Meat juices were preserved in the form of soups, a fact which explains why "the use of the spoon preceded that of the knife and fork." There was no set time for meals among the Indians who obeyed "the gentle appetites of nature, as often as they call them." After spending a whole day on the chase they frequently ate for three or four hours at one sitting, a custom which naturally placed a great strain on the digestive system.

Women engaged in arduous domestic labor and married at about the age of twenty when their constitutions were strong enough for childbearing. In childless marriages it was possible to obtain a divorce easily and quickly. Men were employed in hunting and in warfare, which "call forth every fibre into exercise, and ensure them the possession of the utmost possible health." Seldom did men marry before the age of thirty, and late marriages, said Rush, were responsible for healthy children. Among the men it was considered a mark of heroism to bear the most excruciating pain without flinching, and "upon this account they early inure themselves to burning part of their bodies with fire, or cutting them with sharp instruments. No young man can be admitted to the honors of manhood or war, who

has not acquitted himself well in these trials of patience and fortitude."

Both men and women oiled and painted their bodies. Bear grease
mixed with clay, resembling the color of the skin, was used universally. "This pigment," according to Rush, "serves to lessen the sensibility of the extremities of the nerves." Men and women enjoyed
the cold bath which "fortifies the body, and renders it less subject
to those diseases which arise from the extremes and vicissitudes of
heat and cold." Further, it should be remarked, there were no deformed Indians, because the severity of their customs destroyed the
weak and deformed.

The constitution of Indian society was such that most of the passions which affect the body adversely were not experienced. Equality
of power and property barred envy and ambition.

The very type of life which developed the strong and fearless
Indian of song and story also subjected the weaker brothers to disease. "We need only recollect the custom among the Indians, of
sleeping in the open air in a variable climate—the alternate action of
heat and cold upon their bodies, to which the warmth of their cab-
bins exposes them—their long marches—their excessive exercise—
their intemperance in eating, to which their long fasting, and their
public feasts naturally prompt them: And, lastly, the vicinity of their
habitations to the banks of rivers, in order to discover the empire of
diseases among them in every stage of their lives. They have in vain
attempted to elude the general laws of mortality, while their mode
of life subjects them to these remote, but certain causes of disease."
The fevers produced by cold were "of the inflammatory kind, such
as pleurises, peripneumonies, and rheumatisms." The dysentery was
also a common disease among the Indians. They were also subject
to "animal and vegetable poisons," which frequently resulted in
death. Smallpox and venereal diseases were communicated to them
by the Europeans. "I have heard," said Rush, "of two or three cases
of the gout among the Indians, but it was only among those who
had learned the use of rum, from the white people."

The Indians used a few simple but potent remedies. Immediate
purging, sweating, and cold baths were resorted to universally. "The
patient is confined in a closed tent or wigwam, over a hole in the

earth, in which a red hot stone is placed; a quantity of water is thrown upon this stone, which instantly involves the patient in a cloud of vapour and sweat; in this situation he rushes out and plunges himself into a river; from which he retires to his bed." This remedy was the prescription for fevers and nervousness caused by fatigue. In many complaints no stimulating food was given to the patient, cold water only being taken internally. Bleeding was used as a remedy in some disorders, sharp stones and thorns being employed frequently to discharge blood. One of the methods used to restore life to drowned persons was hopelessly useless. It consisted in suspending the patient by the heels, in order that the water might flow from his mouth. The practice was based on the belief that a person drowns from swallowing an excessive quantity of water. In the treatment of smallpox the Indians likewise demonstrated their lack of scientific knowledge. It is not to be wondered at that small-pox was usually fatal inasmuch as they plunged themselves into cold water in the earliest stages of the disease. Most of the Indian anti-dotes to poisons likewise had no positive value.

Because of their inability to cope with new diseases brought by the whites, Rush predicted that in a few centuries the Indians would be entirely exterminated. He ascribed to "the extensive mischief of spirituous liquors" the mortality "peculiar to those Indian tribes who have mingled with the white people." Many of the diseases found in civilized communities, he added, result from abandoning "the simple diet, and manners, of our ancestors." Finally, he suggested that "agriculture is the true basis of national health, riches and popu-lousness."

Another paper, *An Account of the Vices Peculiar to the Indians of North America*,[20] seems to be a wholesale denunciation of the character of the aborigines. It is stated that they were "strangers to the obligations both of morality and decency, as far as they relate to the marriage bed," and that their "nastiness'" was exemplified in their dress and in their total disregard of decency "in the manner of their natural evacuations." Drunkenness, gluttony, and cruelty seemed to Rush to be more general among the Indians than among the whites. Idleness was a universal vice among the tribes. "They are not only too lazy to work, but even to think." Theft and gambling were also common. "But the infamy of the Indian character is completed by the low rank to which they degrade their women," is the final charge in Rush's catalog of Indian vices.

From the Indians Rush turned to his white neighbors in Pennsylvania, and took notes on their manners and customs as he traveled about. The evolution of the conservative citizen through the stages of frontier life is discussed in *An Account of the Progress of Population, Agriculture, Manners, and Government in Pennsylvania, in a Letter to A Friend in England.*[21] Pennsylvania was peopled largely by Quakers, Germans, and Scotch-Irish, almost all of whom made their livings in agricultural pursuits. Rush describes a settler's cabin: "The floor of this cabbin is of earth, the roof is of split logs—the light is received through the door, and, in some instances, through a small window made of greased paper. A coarser building adjoining this cabbin affords a shelter to a cow and a pair of poor horses. The labor of erecting these buildings is succeeded by killing the trees on a few acres of ground near his cabbin; this is done by cutting a circle round the trees, two or three feet from the ground. The ground around these trees is then ploughed and Indian-corn planted in it."

The settler "eats drinks and sleeps in dirt and rags in his little cabbin"; he believes in natural rights and is hostile to governmental regulation. This first type of settler improves the land and ultimately sells it to a second type, who has a little money and therefore improves the property, but still remains hostile to any government. He does not give enough attention to his land; he contracts debts and, after a period of years, sells to a third settler, usually a man of property and good character. This man of property improves the place, grows a greater variety of farm products, and boasts a small garden. He builds a real dwelling, a large one, usually of stone. As his wealth increases he values the protection of the laws, pays his taxes, supports the schools, and becomes a conservative and law-abiding citizen. Rush estimated that two-thirds of the Pennsylvania farmers belonged to this class after the War for Independence. It is possible that in the territory east of the Susquehanna River the percentage of conservative farmers was even higher.

The German settlers particularly engaged Rush's attention, and in his *An Account of the Manners of the German Inhabitants of*

Pennsylvania[22] he asserted that the State was greatly indebted to them for its prosperity. They arrived in Pennsylvania with but little property, "a few pieces of gold or silver coin, a chest filled with clothes, a bible, and a prayer or an hymn book constituted the whole stock of most of them."

Although most of the German settlers were farmers, many of them were skilled artisans. As farmers they were most economical. "They keep their horses and cattle as warm as possible in winter, by which means, they save a great deal of their hay and grain; for those animals when cold, eat much more than when they are in a more comfortable situation."

Rush also noted that the Pennsylvania German farmers were influenced by the phases and appearance of the moon in their planting, pruning, sowing, and reaping. Their farms could be distinguished from those of other settlers "by the superior size of their barns; the plain, but compact form of their houses; the height of the enclosures; the extent of their orchards; the fertility of their fields; the luxuriance of their meadows, and a general appearance of plenty and neatness in everything that belongs to them."

They are, said Rush, a religious, hospitable, and peaceful people, little addicted to convivial pleasures, but fond of vocal and instrumental music. The descendants of the original German settlers in rural Pennsylvania still remain a quiet, thrifty, peace-loving, religious people, living the simple life. This study of the Pennsylvania Germans and the survey of diseases and medical practice among the Indians are notable essays.

In the realm of philosophy Rush's *An Enquiry into the Influence of Physical Causes Upon the Moral Faculty* is equally significant. This careful, erudite paper was delivered before the American Philosophical Society on February 27, 1786. Containing many of his ideas on morality, it attracted considerable attention when published in pamphlet form. It is easily one of his most distinguished nonmedical compositions.

In this paper the Doctor demonstrated the influence of physical causes, particularly those springing from disease, upon memory, imagination, and individual judgment, pointing out the analogy between their influence upon the intellectual powers of the mind, and upon the moral faculty. Here is a suggestion of the modern approach to criminology.

By "moral faculty" Rush meant "a power in the human mind of distinguishing good and evil; or in other words, virtue and vice"; it "performs the office of a law-giver, while the business of conscience is to perform the duty of a judge. The moral faculty is to conscience, what taste is to judgment, and sensation to perception."

The memory, imagination, and judgment are affected directly by diseases, particularly by fevers and insanity. One's temperament might be changed entirely by a spell of sickness, and how often, observed Rush, by way of example, "do we hear persons of the most delicate virtue, utter speeches in the delirium of a fever, that are offensive to decency or good manners!" Patients in the delirium of a fever often indulge in extraordinary flights of the imagination, and the insane often astonish attendants with a remarkable display of memory. The same patients manifest similar extraordinary changes of the moral faculty. "I have more than once," noted Rush, "heard the most sublime discourses on morality in the cell of an hospital, and who has not seen instances of patients in acute diseases, discovering degrees of benevolence and integrity, that were not natural to them in the ordinary course of their lives?"

What of dreams? Do they affect the memory, the imagination, and the judgment? "Dreams are nothing but incoherent ideas, occasioned by partial or imperfect sleep." Rush believed that judgment and memory are deranged in dreams, and that changes in the state of the brain in sleep frequently affect the moral faculty likewise— "hence we sometimes dream of doing and saying things when asleep, which we shudder at, as soon as we awake."

Rush believed "in the freedom of moral agency in man" because he conceived it to be essential to man's nature as a responsible being in society. "In those cases where the moral faculty is deprived of its freedom, by involuntary diseases, I conceive that man ceases as much to be a subject of moral government, as he does to be a subject of civil government, when he is deprived by involuntary diseases, of the use of his reason."

What are the particular causes which act mechanically upon the moral faculty depriving the individual of his freedom? Long before the influence of climate on civilization became such an important factor in discussions of the subject, Rush set forth, in his distinguished paper, that the moral and intellectual characters of nations as well as individuals are influenced by climate. "Revenge—levity—timidity—and indolence, tempered with occasional emotions of benevolence, are the moral qualities of the inhabitants of warm climates, while selfishness tempered with sincerity and integrity, form the moral character of the inhabitants of cold countries. The state of the weather, and the seasons of the year also, have a visible effect upon moral sensibility." Rush conceived the idea that the most vicious murders are probably those caused by constant recurrence of fogs and rains in November in Great Britain. Heat, however, as we now know, seems to be more directly associated with crimes of violence and religious fanaticism involving physical torture and sacrifice, than fog or rain.

Rush believed that diet and the passions are directly related, that fermented drinks, for example, when used excessively, rouse "every latent spark of vice into action." "Habitual drunkenness never fails to eradicate veracity and integrity from the human mind." On the other hand, however, "water is the universal sedative of turbulent passions—it not only promotes a general equanimity of temper, but it composes anger." Moral sensibility is affected adversely by extreme hunger, causing one to be irritable and sulky; hunger frequently drove the Indians to war.

The parent of every vice is idleness; and rural life, therefore, is a happy one chiefly "because its laborious employments are favorable to virtue, and unfriendly to vice." This was written at a time when less than three per cent of the population of the thirteen original States lived in towns and cities. This thesis is still used by many vice crusaders who find in the cities a flood of temptations.

"The effects of excessive sleep," wrote Rush, "are intimately connected with the effects of idleness, upon the moral faculty,—hence we find that moderate, and even scanty portions of sleep, in every part of the world, have been found to be friendly, not only to health and long life, but in many instances to morality."

He believed, further, that bodily pain has a tendency to cure vice.

There are still those who feel that painful illness is the penalty imposed by Providence for wrongdoing.

The helpful effects of solitude on the moral faculty Rush confined to "persons who are irreclaimable by rational or moral remedies," and "where the benefit of reflection, and instruction from books, can be added to solitude and confinement, their good effects are still more certain." The positive effects of music upon the moral faculty make it possible "to discover the virtues and vices of different nations, by their tunes, as certainly as by their laws. The effects of music, when simply mechanical, upon the passions, are powerful and extensive."

Even odors act directly upon the moral faculty. Foul odors irritate the spirit as well as the body, but "agreeable odors seldom fail to inspire serenity, and to compose the angry spirits—Hence the pleasure, and one of the advantages of a flower garden."

While it is not possible for us to accept all the principles set down by Rush in this notable examination of the influence of physical causes upon the moral faculty, it must be borne in mind that many of these observations were, in 1786, exceedingly provocative and often remarkably advanced. They should not be overlooked even today by the careful student of ethics, penology and criminology, and psychology.

In his biographical sketches and eulogies Rush consciously aimed to emphasize some of the principles enunciated in his philosophical papers and tracts on the good life. In his delightful vignette of Christopher Ludwick, Baker-General of the War for Independence, one sees clearly why Rush wrote it. "The history of the life and character of Christopher Ludwick, is calculated to show the influence of a religious education upon moral conduct; of habits of industry and economy, upon success in all enterprises; and to inspire hope and exertion in young men of humble employment, and scanty capital, to aspire to wealth and independence, by the only means in which they are capable of commanding respect and affording happiness."[23] Here, then, was an opportunity for Rush to unfold "the influence of a religious education upon moral conduct."

This and other biographical excursions were, it seems, honestly inspired by the exemplary lives which the subjects led. The eulogy on Dr. William Cullen, his teacher, delivered before the College of Physicians in Philadelphia, on July 9, 1790, was a highly commendable piece of work. The inspiring eulogy on David Rittenhouse, distinguished astronomer, was delivered before the American Philosophical Society on December 17, 1796 in the presence of President Washington, members of Congress, and a host of distinguished guests.

The whole world of men, things, and ideas was Rush's province. The subjects into which he delved are almost encyclopedic in scope. He was one of the first Americans to plead' for the abolition of slavery and for temperance. He recommended the conservation and advantageous utilization of our natural resources. He was one of the early advocates of a thorough-going reform in our penal system and was instrumental in having the death penalty abolished, except in cases of first-degree murder, in Pennsylvania. He offered countless suggestions for making the world a better place in which to live, and he bent every effort to spread his gospel through eloquent speeches and voluminous writings in newspapers, magazines, pamphlets, and books. His style is forceful, enthusiastic, polished, and often dramatic. Indeed, many of his philosophical and biographical essays can still be read with a measure of satisfaction in their high literary quality and enjoyment in their diverse contents.

XIII

The Man of Affairs

A MAN of no mean intellectual attainments, even outside the realm of his profession, Rush gave expression to his talents through his activities in numerous societies. He was associated with the best of contemporary minds in groups scientific, philosophical, philanthropic, religious, and cultural. Nearly every Philadelphia society of standing found the name of Benjamin Rush on its rolls, in many cases among the charter members or officers. He did not join these organizations merely for the material gain he might have received in his practice through such affiliations. He was whole-heartedly in sympathy with all liberal and philanthropic movements, and lent to them his financial support as well as valuable time and services. He attended meetings and contributed lengthy and careful papers to the scientific and philosophical societies. It is amazing that the physician, up to his ears in his own work, found the spare moments to tend all the irons he had in the fire.

In 1769 he was elected a member of the American Philosophical Society and, between 1770 and 1801, he filled successively the offices of curator, secretary, councillor, and vice-president (1797–1801). Over a period of forty years he delivered important addresses before that distinguished body. The first of these, delivered in 1774 when he was twenty-nine years of age, "An Inquiry into the Natural History of Medicine among the Indians of North America, with a Comparative View of their Diseases and Remedies With Those of Civilized Nations," was marked by a wealth of observation and by mature thought. It remains one of the most important contributions on the American Indian.

Rush's connection with the American Philosophical Society gave him an opportunity not only to discuss the scientific problems in which he was interested, but also to form contacts with such leaders of thought as Benjamin Franklin, Thomas Jefferson, and David Rittenhouse.

On his return to America in 1769, Rush was struck by the evils of negro slavery and, during the first few years of practice, he was further moved by the pathetic cases of individual slaves who came under his professional care. In 1773 his address to the colonists on the slavery question appeared, and this pamphlet, together with additional observations published a year later, did much to consolidate the anti-slavery forces, and to bring into being an organized body. In 1774 Rush, James Pemberton, and other Philadelphians founded the first anti-slavery society in America, The Pennsylvania Society for Promoting the Abolition of Slavery and the Relief of Free Negroes Unlawfully Held in Bondage. The active work of the Society was curtailed, however, by the War for Independence. Later, in April 1787, it was enlarged and reorganized with Benjamin Franklin as President, and Benjamin Rush and Tench Coxe as secretaries. After serving as secretary for several years, Rush became President of the Society, in 1803, and retained this post until his death in 1813.

Rush demanded immediate relief and assistance for the slaves in Philadelphia. He addressed negro meetings and was a welcome visitor in every negro assemblage in the city. Racial antagonism, Rush believed, would not have been so bitter if the whites could have been persuaded to take a healthy interest in the welfare of the negroes, and to try to understand their peculiar difficulties. Why should not a white citizen attend the funeral of a respected negro? On June 18, 1792, Rush himself attended the funeral of a negress, Mrs. William Gray. About fifty white persons were present, Rush noted, and "the sight was a new one in Philadelphia, for hitherto, a few cases excepted, the negroes alone attended each other's funerals. By this event it is to be hoped the partition wall which divided the blacks from the whites will be still further broken down and a way prepared for their union as brethren and members of one great family."[1]

Feeling that it was essential for the negroes to have dignified houses of worship, Rush started in 1791 a movement for a negro church in Philadelphia. He recorded the event casually, on July 25, in one of his pocket notebooks: "Met about a dozen free blacks at Wm. Wileber's in New Street, & read to them sundry articles of faith & a plan of church government which I had composed for them. They appeared well satisfied with it, and agreed to deliberate upon it previously to its being adopted and laid before the public."[2]

He carried the appeal across the Atlantic, asking the British anti-slavery leader, Granville Sharp, to collect funds for the Philadelphia church which was to serve a negro population numbering about three thousand. Sharp responded by sending £14 14s., representing contributions from six London patrons.[3]

The African Church was erected on South Second Street, and on August 22, 1793, Rush was a guest at a dinner given to celebrate the completion of the church roof. About a hundred white persons were present, and Rush was gratified by the wholesome spirit of the occasion: "Never did I see people more happy, some of them shed tears of joy."[4]

Always a friend of the oppressed or unfortunate, he was a frequent visitor at the local prison. When the Philadelphia Society for Alleviating the Miseries of Public Prisons was organized, in May 1787, Rush joined immediately, and was elected one of its physicians. "The business of the Physicians," reads the by-laws, "shall be to visit the prisons when called upon by, or to give advice to the acting committee respecting such matters as are connected with the preservation of the health of persons confined therein, or subject to the government of the officers of the prison."[5] The Society attempted to improve the unwholesome conditions in the Walnut Street jail which, it was charged, was managed by the warden for his own profit. Individual members as well as committees visited the jails weekly, investigated the conditions, and suggested reforms in discipline and general penal methods.

His accomplishments outside medicine were recognized even by foreigners while Rush was still a young man. In 1772 he was elected a corresponding member of the London Society for the Encouragement of Arts and Manufactures. In 1786 he was elected a member of the Milan Society of Arts and Science; in 1791, a member of the German society, Naturae Curiosorum; and, in 1811, an honorary member of the Royal Humane Society of London.

When the Society for Promoting Political Enquiries was organized in Benjamin Franklin's home, in February 1787, Rush was assigned to the Committee on Papers. This Society was organized for "mutual improvement in the knowledge of government, and for the advancement of political science." One of the first papers presented before this body was Rush's "An Inquiry into the Effects of Public Punishments on Criminals and Upon Society," being a plea for punishment in private and an attack on a Pennsylvania law providing for public punishments. Rush's point of view was, for the most part, attacked in the press, but the objectionable law was nevertheless repealed three years after its passage. His eulogist, David Ramsay, says that the address was designed to arouse public opinion against the law of 1786 which substituted hard labor for some offenses which had previously carried the death penalty. "The labour which the convicts, under this new law, were to perform was, however, to be public; and they were accordingly chained to the wheelbarrows, and were employed to clean the streets and repair the roads: as a mark of infamy their heads were shaved and they wore a particular habit."[6] It was this system which Rush fought, not the mitigation of the penalty.

He was one of the physicians and one of the managers of the Philadelphia Humane Society, organized in 1780 to aid in the resuscitation of drowned persons. The bustling life along the waterfront gave urgency to the formation of such an association. In the spring of 1793 he was notified that he had been elected an honorary member of the Humane Society of Massachusetts "in testimony of the high esteem they entertain of your public & private character & your great exertions in the cause of humanity." In 1812 he was elected an honorary member of the Columbian Chemical Society in Philadelphia. He also belonged to the Pennsylvania Society for the Encouragement of Manufactures and Useful Arts, the American Society for Promoting Useful Knowledge, the American Academy of Arts and Sciences, and the Library Company of Philadelphia.

His participation in the activities of many civic bodies and learned societies, interested largely in public problems, was a concrete expression of a conviction set forth in his *Address to the People of the United States* that "Every man is public property. His time and talents—his youth—his manhood—his old age—nay more, his life, his all, belong to his country."

Everyone with a few spare dollars jangling in his pocket hoped to turn a profit after the close of the War for Independence, in speculation in land. Philadelphia was an active center for speculators, especially those trading in the lands of central and western Pennsylvania. Rush, although hard at work with his practice and civic endeavors, was drawn into the speculative wave. He became interested in lands largely in Lycoming, Northumberland, and Mifflin counties in central Pennsylvania. He bought and sold land from time to time, sometimes at a profit, sometimes at a loss. In 1784, in association with Colonel Isaac Franks, wealthy Philadelphia merchant and trader, he purchased nineteen tracts of land in what is now Indiana County, Pennsylvania.[7]

Rush then purchased several tracts along the Loyalsock Creek, above Sunbury, in Lycoming County. For his agent, Benjamin Young, he drew up a list of "Directions," dated September 18, 1787, indicating the type of information he considered essential. Young was instructed to proceed to Sunbury, and then north to the Loyalsock where tracts were to be examined at and above the forks. He was requested to give particular attention to the following points:

"1. The nature of the soil—is it sandy—clayey or stoney.

2. The quality of the timber & quantity of underwood & cleared land.

3. The number of creeks & springs—& mill seats—specifying on what tracts each are seated.

4. The effects and marks of the late frosts on the lands.

5. The quality of the grass on each tract.

6. The situation for houses.

7. The quality of the soil & timber on the adjoining hills or mountains.

8. The quality of land on this side Wm. Plunkett's tract—for 2 or 3 miles.

9. Examine where & what is the line of the islands in the creeks.

10. Examine the fish in the creek, & report such animals—fruits —seeds—flowers—stones etc. as you may see, that are new, or curious.

11. Examine the distance from the creek of a boiling spring on or near Chase's tract.

12. Keep an exact journal of every days transactions, from the

day you leave home 'till you return record everything that strikes you immediately after you see or hear it.

13. Be very careful to whom you shew the draughts, & by no means tell any one what quantity of land belongs to me on the Loyalsock except the person who goes with you. You may confess 900 acres.

14. Examine the thickness & height of the most striking trees."[8]

From this document it appears that the land agent must of necessity have been a man versed in a knowledge of all outdoors—of timber, game, vegetation, soil, and water.

It is not possible to reconstruct a clear-cut, comprehensive picture of Rush's speculation in the lands of his state, because few of the letters and documents are available.

In September 1789 Rush authorized an agent, William Cooper, to sell certain of his holdings in the Loyalsock Creek section, on the west branch of the Susquehanna River, about thirty-five miles above Sunbury and about twelve miles east of Williamsport. "The creek on which these lands lie is navigable from the forks of the Susque-hannah at certain seasons of the year. It abounds with trout above most of the creeks in the state. Its waters flow with great rapidity. . . . The lands on the creek a few miles below the forks consist wholly of rich bottoms, and abound with white walnut—sugar-maple—beach—hemlock—the different kinds of oak—hickory—sycamore—& large white pine." This long letter from Rush to Cooper bore the earmarks of high-pressure land-development advertisements of a later day, and several deeds on record indicate that it brought results.[9]

The astute speculator kept watch for wind of any public improvement which might increase the value of his lands. A movement in favor of road building was now in swing, and Rush pulled whatever strings he could in favor of Lycoming County roads. Late in 1792 he wrote a Colonel Johnson: "The Society for promoting roads & state improvements, are about to report in favor of a road from Wyalusing to the Forks of Loyalsock—also in favor of improving the navigation of the Loyalsock creek to the forks. As a landholder on those waters I call upon you to concur with your influence to have those improvements adopted. They will open a communication to an immensely rich country. The road will connect the East and West branches of the Susquehannah together—and afford an easy access for Eastern settlers into the heart of our State, and lastly the road & the clearing the creek will render both practicable & carry a plan for establishing a sugar plantation at the forks similar to the one lately establish[ed] on the Delaware—but on a smaller scale, and with the addition of a [?] and grist mill. . . ."[10]

In 1794–95 many land deals were executed. The Loyalsock district lured Joseph Priestley, scientist, who forwarded Rush a brief letter from New York, February 5, 1794: "I will buy the lands upon the terms agreed upon between us, & will pay the first sum within six weeks which I hope will be no material inconvenience to you, as I think you said it might be so long before you could get the deeds out of the office."[11]

Two weeks later, February 18, Rush sent one William Brown £577 to cover the purchase of 20,000 acres of land in Bedford County. In August he sold to Robert Morris 1,035 acres along the Susquehanna River at 10s. an acre. At this time his holdings included 20,000 acres in Bedford County, 3,100 in the Loyalsock district, 3,009 around Towanda, 1,734 in the neighborhood of Brush Creek, 12,700 in Mifflin County, and 1,014 in the Sugar and Log Creek section. These holdings totaled more than 41,000 acres.

In January 1795 the Doctor bought 10,000 acres at 3s. 9d. an acre from William Brown and James Harris, but the location does not appear in the records. A month later he disposed of 3,200 acres along Clearfield Creek at 3s. an acre, and 5,400 acres in the Lycoming Creek district. In April of the same year he sold his brother six tracts of land at 3s. 9d. an acre, and in September he bought a farm in the Brush Valley at 4s. 2d. an acre from a Dr. Alberti.

In April 1796 he exchanged with Dr. Alberti 500 acres of land on the Crooked Creek in Lycoming County for 500 in Brush Valley, and gave him 5s. an acre for 4,171 acres adjoining the above tract. In July he advised a prospective buyer that he wished to dispose of 5,500 acres of land on Pine Creek, a branch of the Tioga River in northern Pennsylvania, and added that he would accept 10s. an acre "in notes endorsed by R Morris payable one year hence." The market was rising. In August he sold 514 acres on Sugar Creek at 15s. an acre, and the Pine Creek land at the price originally specified.[12]

In 1797, a year which found him fighting another epidemic in Philadelphia, he sold 200 acres of land in Brush Valley at 4s. an acre, and bought 860 acres in Mifflin County for $400. In August he was perturbed when word was received from one of his agents that the Land Commissioners had advertised taxes, amounting to £5 1s. 4d. for the year 1794, due from Rush on 10,000 acres in Loyalsock Township and 2,950 acres in Muncy Township. If not paid by September the lands would be sold by the sheriff. Agent Tulloh explained that he would be pleased to take care of the matter so as to avoid any difficulty.[13]

Tulloh was empowered by Rush, in 1800, to sell a large portion of the original Loyalsock purchase, and the following printed announcement was distributed:

"To Farmers

"Large tracts of Land in Loyalsock township, Lycoming County, are now parcelled off in Lots for settlement.—Those lands are well watered and timbered, and have at a great expence been laid open by roads leading to the County town of Williamsport, from which they are distant about 12 miles; these roads also intersect the great road leading to upper Canada, and the Genesee, so that the farmer may calculate upon a ready sale for his produce almost at his door.

"Those persons willing to become settlers, will meet with generous encouragement by applying to Mr. Andrew Tulloh, Williamsport, Lycoming County."[14]

In April 1802 Tulloh, as attorney for Rush, made an agreement to lease to Elisha Kingsbury 200 acres of what was known as the Cascade tract along the waters of Wallis' Run in Loyalsock Township. Kingsbury agreed to build "a good and sufficient grist mill" and, to expedite its construction, Tulloh agreed to supply 200 pounds of iron as a loan. The mill was to be for the convenience of all settlers in the vicinity. Rush, however, disapproved of the arrangements and he so advised Tulloh: "I have always resolved to keep the Cascade tract of my lands on Wallis's Run in order to allure one of my sons to settle in that country, or that it might serve to sell the other adjoining tracts. Under the influence of this resolution I once refused a Guinea an acre for it in cash. You will excuse me therefore for not confirming your contract with a settler upon it." Tulloh was upset, for carpenters had already started work on the mill. However, a few weeks later, on June 29, Rush notified Tulloh to go ahead with the original plans.[15]

Building operations made little progress and finally Kingsbury, the lessee, vacated, as a letter to Rush from Robert M. McClure, another agent, indicates: "According to your directions I have purchased out, and taken a release from Kingsbury of all his claim to your Cascade tract, for which I gave him twenty dollars. he at first asked one hundred & fifty dollars and did not till a few days ago comply with the offer I made him of twenty. he has cut down & burned part of the timber on about three acres and built a cabbin up to the square on the land. he has not made any preparations for building a mill which I think will be of use. I have been speaking with several millwrights to know on what terms they would undertake to build a mill, but they refuse entering upon any terms untill they see the situation. I shall if you think proper employ one to go with me and view the Cascade and let you know what will be the lowest terms on which it can be done. Your taxes I will attend to & take care that the proper credits are entered in the commissioners books."[16]

The real estate business demanded careful consideration and constant attention. Prospective purchasers were dealt with largely through agents to whom instructions had to be sent frequently. Rush found it advisable to keep in close touch with his agents about general conditions in the neighborhood of his holdings so as to know when the land was ripe for development or sale. Complaints of tenants and purchasers were sometimes carried over the agents' heads direct to Rush, and these he tried to settle by correspondence.

"I am one of the settlers upon your land," wrote one William Roberts in 1801, "I live on a part of M. Theophilis Rees land. I am in the settlement between 3 and 4 years a shoemaker by trade and the only one that works the trade in the settlement and when the advertisements that 50 acres of every tract was given for settling I apply'd to the agent here Simon James for James Knox's tract. I began my improvement upon it but afterwards Mr. Samuel Philipps informed me that he received a letter from you in which you say that this tract with 2 more has been disposed of. Now sir if it is in your power to let me have 50 acres it will be more handy to me for my trade than any other not taken up."[17]

It was not uncommon for several persons to claim title to the same tract of land, and Rush frequently had on his hands controversies over titles to lands bought or sold by him. "Several persons in the county of Clearfield," wrote one protestant in 1809, "have set up claims to the lands I purchased of you in that county and I have been compelled to institute ejectments against the claimants which ejectments are now pending in the Circuit Court of this State. . . . I understand that the persons claiming the lands allege that no lines were run on the ground for the several tracts which I bought of you. Should this unfortunately be the truth the lands will be lost. . . . Should I lose these lands for want of a survey or by reason of any other defect in the title you gave me I shall have to call upon you to refund the consideration money and interest."[18]

As time went on, after 1797, and the income from his practice declined, Rush welcomed any profit from the sale of his land holdings. In March 1810 he was asked to name a price on 800 acres of land which he held at the headwaters of the Crooked Creek. Whether or not any transaction took place is unknown.[19] In 1812 he sold 1,528 acres on the west side of the Susquehanna River below the mouth of Sugar Creek in Luzerne County.[20]

From her father, Richard Stockton, Mrs. Rush inherited 227 acres of land at Mount Lucas, near Princeton, and this tract was sold in March 1793 for 112 pounds, 5 shillings New Jersey currency. In April of the next year Dr. and Mrs. Rush sold twenty-one acres of land, adjoining the Princeton University campus, for £500.[21]

The activities of this indefatigable man of affairs were by no means confined to his professional work as teacher and physician. An idealist and altruist, he labored constantly and strenuously for the alleviation of human misery and the betterment of mankind. At the same time a realist and man of action, he was prudent, clear headed, and generally shrewd in providing for himself the means whereby he could enrich his life.

XIV

Educator

THE institutions of learning which gradually grew up in the colonies during the seventeenth and eighteenth centuries were modeled after the schools and colleges of the Old World. Directly related to the European background of the settlers, there were three distinct types of school organization. In the South the aristocratic idea of education prevailed, whereby the upper classes received classical and secondary training, often under tutors, while the masses were left, except for industrial apprenticeship, without even elementary instruction. It was customary for the sons of the wealthy throughout the colonies to pursue their education abroad. In the North—Massachusetts and Connecticut—there were definite governmental support of educational institutions and the first approximation of a public school system. The Middle Colonies, however, developed an organization of parochial schools. Each church was responsible for its school. These colonies, dominated largely by Calvinism and Lutheranism, looked upon the school as a necessary adjunct to the church. It was through universal instruction that the faith could be preserved.

In Pennsylvania, although William Penn had provided for universal education, the schools were parochial, growing up about the large variety of sects which settled in the colony. There were Germans, Swedes, Dutch, English, Welsh, Scotch and Irish Presbyterians, and Roman Catholics. In Philadelphia, as early as 1689, a Friends' Public School was established. Thus the tradition of education in Pennsylvania, even through the eighteenth century, was one of close alliance with religion even where government aid was sought. Benjamin Rush, therefore, though far-seeing and liberal in his insistence upon the desirability of universal instruction and upon the duty of the state in helping to provide for it, could not see beyond this concept of sectarianism in education.

Rush's general theories of education, as well as the specific proposals for instruction advanced in his letters and essays are, however, often far ahead of his time. Many of his principles are practised in schools today. He visualized the future needs of the nation's school system with uncanny astuteness. The fight for the establishment of a common school system in Pennsylvania was an uphill one. Although provision for free education had been made in the state constitution, it was not until the early nineteenth century that acts were passed to make the constitutional mandate effective. Free tuition was provided at public expense at existing private schools for the children of the poor, but many were too proud to admit their poverty, and the funds set aside by the state merely helped to support the private, church, and neighborhood schools.

Rush's ideas on the foundation of a general educational system are to be found in such an essay as "A Plan for Establishing Public Schools in Pennsylvania . . ."; his theories on method and technique are expressed in such a paper as "Thoughts upon the Amusements and Punishments Which are Proper for Schools"; and "A Defence of the Use of the Bible As A School Book" is a good example of his educational propaganda. In the fields of organization, administration, and curriculum, he covered nearly every aspect of education. He urged the phonetic method of teaching English; he advocated along with Franklin that less time be devoted to the classical languages; he suggested that athletics and amusements relieve the student at times from the discipline of study.

In the spring of 1784 Rush wrote that he had finished an essay on the mode of instruction appropriate to a republic.[1] It was not published, however, until 1786, as *A Plan for Establishing Public Schools in Pennsylvania, and for Conducting Education Agreeably to a Republican Form of Government*. This essay, addressed to the citizens and legislature of Pennsylvania, outlined a system of education for the new American republic.

Learning boasts many advantages, writes Rush. It is friendly to religion and promotes adequate notions of the Deity; it is favorable to liberty, for "without learning, men are incapable of knowing their rights, and where learning is confined to a few people, liberty can be neither equal nor universal." Furthermore, learning cultivates proper regard for laws and government; it is "friendly to manners," contributing to the pleasures of society and conversation; it promotes agriculture, the basis of national wealth; and "manufactures of all kinds owe their perfection chiefly" to it.

Convinced of the importance of placing these indisputable advantages within reach of the masses, Rush proposed a plan to make schooling available in all parts of the state. The base of the structure would be built around free schools in every township or in districts comprising 100 families. In these schools the curriculum would include reading, writing, English, German, and arithmetic. Four colleges, scattered throughout the state and concentrating on mathematics and science, would feed a university in the state capital where instruction would be offered in law, physics, theology, international law, and economics. All citizens would be taxed for the support of these schools whether or not they had children in attendance. Ultimately, theorized Rush, the schools would decrease taxes by instructing the citizens in sound methods of government and finance, and by increasing the profits of agriculture and manufacturing. Education for democracy, indeed!

A general system of education was definitely needed in Pennsylvania, the essay further demonstrated, because of the existing diversity in racial groups. The population of the state as a whole would become more homogeneous through the public schools, and consequently more amenable to peaceable government.

The keystone of any system of instruction, in Rush's mind, was religion. It is the only foundation of a useful education. There can be no virtue without religion, and without virtue liberty cannot flourish; and liberty, indeed, is the very essence of republican government. The religion of the New Testament is one of the essentials of education. "A Christian . . . cannot fail of being a republican, for every precept of the Gospel inculcates those degrees of humility, self-denial, and brotherly kindness, which are directly opposed to the pride of monarchy and the pageantry of a court. A Christian cannot fail of being useful to the republic, for his religion teacheth him, that no man 'liveth to himself.' "

Next to his obligations to his Creator, the student should be taught love of country as a vital principle of his daily life. Duty to country comes even before duty to family. However commendable the peaceful domestic life may be, the citizen must be prepared to accept

public responsibility at the call of his fellow citizens. The spirit of
nationality should frankly dominate the scholastic atmosphere. Although the student must be imbued with a love of mankind and be
taught to regard all his fellow men with understanding, he must
cherish with a more intense and peculiar affection the citizens of his
own state and of the United States. This spirit of narrow national-
ism has never been removed from our educational system. Every
young man must be taught to amass wealth, but it must be only to
increase his power of contributing to the demands of the state.

Occasional amusement is necessary, but study and business are the
principal pursuits in life.

Practical work in manual occupations in the intervals of study,
and in the busy seasons of the year, was one of Rush's suggestions
made a century and a quarter before it was adopted at Antioch College and similar institutions.

Rush would hardly have approved of our present college dormitories and campus life. He believed that students should live with
adults, that their manners would be improved by subjecting them to
those restraints which the difference of age and sex naturally produce in families. The influence of Rush's own student days at Nottingham was still powerful.

The curriculum should include music because of "its mechanical
effects in civilizing the mind." During the first twelve years of formal schooling, instruction should be offered in reading, writing,
arithmetic, and in the modern languages which are necessary for one
to speak, particularly French and German. "The state of the memory in early life," accurately observed Rush, "is favorable to the
acquisition of languages, especially when they are conveyed to the
mind, through the ear." To read and write English facilely and
fluently is a goal which every student should strive to reach. Public
speaking should be stressed in the schools of a republic, and history
taught in order to ensure a deep knowledge of the science of government. Chemistry, in unfolding the effects of heat and the combinations of elements, not only enlarges "our acquaintance with the
wonders of nature and the mysteries of art," but is useful in agriculture and industry.

Shortly after the publication of this plan for the diffusion of knowledge Rush suggested to his London friend, Richard Price, that, to be long-lived, republics must resort to popular education. "Republics are slow in discovering their interest," he wrote, "but when once they find it out they pursue it with vigor and perseverance. Nothing can be done by our public bodies till they can carry the people along with them, and as the means of propagating intelligence and knowledge in our country are as yet but scanty, all their movements are marked with appearances of delay and procrastination. To remedy these inconveniences, colleges, newspapers, and posts are establishing in all our States."[2]

On March 28, 1787, he made a public appeal for free schools in Philadelphia through the columns of the *Independent Gazetteer*. Only by means of free schools can the blessings of knowledge be extended to the poor of the community, and nothing should prevent the establishment of such schools in the populated districts of Pennsylvania and in Philadelphia. How can a republican nation be free and happy when the common people are ignorant? Rush called upon the citizens of Philadelphia to apply to the Legislature for permission to tax property for school purposes. The temperance advocate had a suggestion right at hand. "The price of a bottle of wine," he calculated, "will pay the tax of an ordinary freeholder for a whole year to those schools," and by decreasing the extent of crime the expenditures for jails would be substantially diminished. In this article he also proposed that girls receive instruction in needlework, spinning, and knitting. Carrying further the prevailing idea of the inseparability of church and school, he added that children of parents of the same denomination be educated together, in order that religion and education be more intimately associated.

One of the very first suggestions for the establishment of a national or federal university came from Rush in January 1787, in an *Address to the People of the United States*.[3] In keeping with the principles of a republican form of government, it is necessary that knowledge of every kind be broadcast throughout the nation and, for this purpose, demanded Rush, let Congress, instead of appropriating a half-million dollars to build a capital city, vote a fourth of this sum for a federal university where every subject connected with government could be adequately taught. The plan called for

traveling correspondents to be sent to Europe to gather data on industrial and agricultural discoveries and improvements. This university was, indeed, to be a post-graduate school for students from the
several state colleges, and ultimately government offices would be
open only to graduates of the federal university. It was to be more
or less of a civil service training school.

This unique idea was not merely pigeonholed in Rush's mind, for
in the fall of 1788 a definite plan of a federal university was
evolved.[4] Convinced that the new government would fail unless the
citizens were properly trained to play their parts in the scheme of
things, he called upon Congress to create, in the district allotted for
the capital, such a federal university, a post-graduate school designed
to prepare young men for public life. He suggested that courses be
offered in literature, law, history, political science, agriculture, commerce and industry, mathematics, natural philosophy, chemistry,
natural history, philology, German, French, and "all those athletic
and manly exercises . . . which are calculated to impart health,
strength, and elegance to the human body." A botanical garden and
museum were essential divisions of the institution. He proposed again
that young men be sent abroad "to collect and transmit knowledge
for the benefit of our country"—the traveling fellowship idea of a
later age.

Instruction in philology, he stated, would "become the more
necessary in America, as our intercourse must soon cease with the
bar, the stage and the pulpits of Great Britain from whence we received our knowledge of the pronunciation of the English language.
. . . The cultivation and perfection of our language becomes a
matter of consequence, when viewed in another light. It will probably be spoken by more people, in the course of two or three centuries, than ever spoke any one language, at one time, since the
creation of the world." Perhaps it was, at the time, a rash one, but
none the less a keen prophecy.

Under Rush's plan the professors were to receive salaries of £150
to £200 annually in addition to fees of two to three guineas paid by
the students for each lecture course. Thirty years after the founding of the university only holders of its degrees would be permitted
to hold government offices. Perhaps the plan of admitting only uni-

versity graduates into the civil service might be criticized as undemocratic, but Rush explained: "We require certain qualifications in lawyers, physicians and clergymen, before we commit our property, our lives or our souls to their care. . . . Why then should we commit our country, which includes liberty, property, life, wives and children, to men who cannot produce vouchers of their qualifications for the important trust? We are restrained from injuring ourselves, by employing quacks in law; why should we not be restrained in like manner, by law, from employing quacks in government?" The failure of our government, particularly municipal government, to function honestly and efficiently can be traced to the "quacks" and self-seekers in official positions. The reasonableness and wisdom of Rush's conception is only too evident when the personnel of the public service is surveyed.

Although he was an avowed opponent of war and military expansion, Rush nevertheless asked that special attention be given to military science, inasmuch as it was probable that for some time to come wars would continue "to be the unchristian mode of deciding disputes between Christian nations."

The nation could not carry on successfully and gloriously without a university such as Rush projected. "We shall never restore public credit, regulate our militia, build a navy, or revive our commerce, until we remove the ignorance and prejudices, and change the habits of our citizens; and this can never be done, till we inspire them with federal principles, which can only be effected by our young men meeting and spending two or three years together in a national university, and afterwards disseminating their knowledge and principles through every county, township and village of the United States." To save itself, then, the nation should educate men specifically for its government service.

At about the same time, 1787, Rush became aware of the need of facilities for the education of women, and was one of a group which established the Young Ladies' Academy, in Philadelphia. Although it did not offer all the advance subjects taught by private tutors, it went far beyond the elementary education of the day. At the close of the quarterly examination period, on July 28, 1787, Rush accepted an invitation to deliver the commencement address at the Academy. He spoke on "Thoughts Upon Female Education, Accomodated to the Present State of Society, Manners, and Government, in the United States of America."[5] Drawing his ideas largely from Fenelon's essay on the education of women, written in 1688, Rush made a plea for more practical training in the preparation of girls for the domestic, social, and religious life. The Doctor's address was published and extensively quoted; subsequently it influenced opinion throughout the country.

Because early marriages shorten the period of formal schooling, the education of girls must be confined to the more useful branches of literature and to those subjects helpful to mothers, said Rush. Inasmuch as every citizen has an equal share in the government, it is necessary "that our ladies should be qualified to a certain degree by a peculiar and suitable education, to concur in instructing their sons in the principles of liberty and government." A fair knowledge of the English language is most essential; every girl should know how to read, speak, and spell correctly; she should also be taught to write a fair and legible hand. "I know of few things more rude or illiberal," said the commencement orator, "than to obtrude a letter upon a person of rank or business, which cannot be easily read." Some knowledge of bookkeeping and arithmetic is necessary, and "an acquaintance with geography and some instruction in chronology will enable a young lady to read history, biography, and travels, with advantage; and thereby qualify her not only for a general intercourse with the world, but as an agreeable companion for a sensible man." Under no circumstances should vocal music be neglected: "The distress and vexation of a husband—the noise of a nursery, and even the sorrows that will sometimes intrude into her own bosom, may all be relieved by a song, where sound and sentiment unite to act upon the mind." Dancing is quite proper as a course of study; it is not only healthful but also develops grace and poise in the feminine figure. All these studies should be linked up in some way with regular instruction in the Christian religion and daily Bible reading.

Not only did Rush advocate the study of music in all the curricula he prepared, but he was also in sympathy with any movement which might bring it closer to the people. In 1787, the year in which the society was organized, Rush was elected to the board of managers of the Uranian Academy. The purpose of the society was to improve church music in Philadelphia. An audience of some 600 attended the first concert of this Academy, held at the Reformed German Church in Race Street, in April 1787.[6]

On the subject of method and technique of teaching Rush offered some suggestions in *Thoughts Upon the Amusements and Punishments Which Are Proper for Schools*, published in 1790.[7] He recommended that the recreation of students should consist of such exercises as are directly related to occupations in adult life: agriculture, mechanical pursuits, and the learned professions. In the agricultural course, give premiums to those who produce the largest crops or keep their plots in most proper order; in the mechanics course, let the students construct models for diversion. The young men in the professional courses are enjoined to derive their amusement from cultivating the land. Gunning as a sport for schoolboys was highly objectionable. "Why," he asked, "should we inspire our youth, by such exercises, with hostile ideas towards their fellow creatures? Let us rather instill into their minds sentiments of universal benevolence to men of all nations and colours. Wars originate in error and vice. Let us eradicate these, by proper modes of education, and wars will cease to be necessary in our country." For Rush, the idealist, education was to be the salvation of mankind and only through wise universal instruction was the highest good of the state to be achieved.

In the eighteenth century and for a long time thereafter the rod still served as the most effective instrument of discipline, and the schoolmaster as the only despot in a free country. Rush could look back upon his own school life with pleasure. His early instruction had been strongly tinged with religion and spirituality, and in his own recommendations he was reflecting the influence of his old schoolmaster, Dr. Finley. Very rarely did Dr. Finley resort to corporal punishment, and Rush in his turn felt that method of discipline never to be necessary and always to be harmful. Among other consequences, "the effects of thumping the head, boxing the ears, and pulling the hair, in impairing the intellects, by means of injuries done to the brain, are too obvious to be mentioned. The fear of corporal punishments, by debilitating the body, produces a corresponding debility in the mind, which contracts its capacity of acquiring knowledge." In a free country corporal punishment is contrary to the spirit of liberty. Instead, Rush suggested private admonition, detention at the close of the daily school session, and "holding a small sign of disgrace, of any kind, in the middle of the floor, in the presence of a whole school." Let schoolmasters cease to be tyrants if they would enjoy the respect ordinarily associated with their profession!

Several of Rush's essays on education are definite and undisguised attempts at propaganda. Such a one is his "Observations Upon the Study of the Latin and Greek Languages, As a Branch of Liberal Education, With Hints of A Plan of Liberal Instruction, Without them, Accomodated to the Present State of Society, Manners and Government in the United States."[8] He speaks out against the teaching of dead languages, inasmuch as teacher and student alike encounter difficulty in the process. "Many sprightly boys of excellent capacities for useful knowledge, have been so disgusted with the dead languages, as to retreat from the drudgery of schools to low company. . . . The Latin and Greek languages are the first tests of genius in schools. Where boys discover a want of capacity for them, they are generally taken from school, or remain there the butts of their companions. . . . The study of some of the Latin and Greek classics is unfavorable to morals and religion. Indelicate amours, and shocking vices both of gods and men, fill many parts of them. Hence an early and dangerous acquaintance with vice; and hence, from an association of ideas, a diminished respect for the unity and perfections of the true God." Again he reiterates his faith in religion as the keystone of the educational arch. A republican form of government cannot endure unless knowledge is disseminated universally; therefore, the teaching of the classics does not deserve a place in its educational structure, because only a few students would be reached by Greek and Latin. Strange and fallacious is his assertion that the study of Latin and Greek is an obstacle to the cultivation and perfection of the English language, and that it renders our language unintelligible to the greatest part of the people who hear or read it because of the substitution of Greek and Latin words for familiar English words.

To a "passion" for ancient writers Rush ascribed the lack of originality in authors of his own day. His explanation is amusing: "A judicious critic has observed, that the descriptions of Spring, which are published every year in England, apply chiefly to the climates of Greece and the neighborhood of Rome. This is the natural effect of a servile attachment to the ancient poets. It insensibly checks invention and leads to imitation."

Rush saw no reason why a knowledge of Latin and Greek should be required of a lawyer, physician, or clergyman "except it be to facilitate the remembrance of a few technicalities which might be retained without it," the essential technical contributions being available in English. Professional linguists only, therefore, should study Latin and Greek.

The suggested course of study without the classics called for the teaching of elocution, spelling, reading, and writing during the first eight years. It was specified that grammar be taught only by the ear because "ideas acquired through that organ are much more durable, than those acquired by the eyes. We remember much longer what we hear, than what we see; hence, old men recollect voices, long after they forget faces." After providing the student with these tools of learning, it is the duty of the school to furnish him with ideas. This goal in education is too often disregarded, perhaps because it is so very difficult to achieve.

Then there were to be courses in natural history and geography. Quite sound is his advice that the student should pursue the study of French and German, but again only by ear. Rather strange, however, is his next observation. "Great care should be taken not to permit him to learn these languages before he is twelve years old, otherwise he will contract so much of the French and German accent as will impair the pronunciation of his native tongue." Between the ages of twelve and fourteen the student is ready for arithmetic and simple mathematics and then, during the next four years, instruction should be offered in grammar, oratory, criticism, higher mathematics, philosophy, chemistry, metaphysics, physics, history, government, the principles of agriculture and commerce.

Naturally, the classicists were outraged at these revolutionary educational theories advanced, not by a schoolmaster, but by a physician;

and his friends took him severely to task about his extraordinary stand. John Adams wrote him: "I cannot give up my dear Latin and Greek although Fortune has never permitted me to enjoy so much of them as I wished. I dont love you the less however for your indifference or even opposition to them. Pray do you carry your Theory so far as to wish to exclude French, Italian, Spanish and Tudesque?"[9]

Again and again Rush insists upon using the Bible as an instrument of instruction. In the course of a lengthy letter on the wisdom of the Bible he commented: "I consider the Bible as I do the works of Nature. . . . As in the works of nature discoveries have often been made by accident, & by men of plain understandings without education, so truths have often been brought to light from the Bible by accident; or by persons of little or no education. As a familiarity with the works of nature leads to discoveries in philosophy, so a constant & attentive perusal of the Scriptures leads to a discovery of the truths of the Gospel. As discoveries encrease in a geometrical proportion in philosophy by means of discoveries, so the more we know of the extent of the objects of revelation, the more easily we comprehend the minutest parts of it. . . . I never read a chapter of the Bible without seeing something in it I never saw before."[10]

In the fall of 1789, he informed Jeremy Belknap that pressure of work had delayed his prospective discourse on the use of the Bible in schools. During the winter the pamphlet was written, and in November of the next year the author again wrote Belknap: "I only watch for time to copy my defence of the Use of the Bible as a School book to prepare it for the press."[11] This piece of propaganda finally appeared in March 1791 as *A Defence of the Use of the Bible As A School Book*, and was addressed to Belknap.

Many arguments in support of the Bible as a school text are set forth in this pamphlet. It is important to impress the minds of children with the great truths of Christianity before they are preoccupied with less vital subjects. There is, too, "a peculiar aptitude in the minds of children for religious knowledge." Because it contains more truths than any other book in the world it satisfies the native love of truth in the human mind. "The interesting events and characters, recorded and described in the Old and New Testaments, are

accomodated above all others to seize upon all the faculties of the
minds of children. The understanding, the memory, the imagination, the passions, and the moral powers, are all occasionally addressed by the various incidents" in the Bible. And is it not the only
book capable of giving support to old age? Furthermore, "this divine
book, above all others, favours that equality among mankind, that
respect for just laws, and all those sober and frugal virtues, which
constitute the soul of republicanism."

An opportunity presented itself in 1790 for Rush to apply his
theories of religious training. The Methodist Conference decided to
open schools for the children of the poor in Philadelphia. At the
subsequent convention of the Universalists, it was resolved that each
church establish a school where children could receive instruction in
reading, writing, and in singing psalms on Sunday. When Rush got
wind of the recommendation, he backed the resolution energetically.
Presenting the proposal that the schools be dependent on no single
denomination, he won the support of the Rev. Dr. William White,
of the Episcopal Church, Mathew Carey, a leading publisher, and
also of influential Roman Catholics. At a citizens' mass meeting
called in January 1791, "The First Day or Sunday School Society"
of Philadelphia was organized, supported by life members paying
ten dollars and annual members paying a dollar. The first meeting
of the subscribers was held at Joseph Sharpless' Academy on Second
Street on January 5, 1791, and, three months later, the first non-
sectarian Sunday school in this country opened its doors. It was so
well attended that a second school was established in the following
May.[12] White was elected President and Rush one of the visitors.
The scholars were chiefly children of "poor persons and of apprentices who would otherwise be debarred from the plainest education."[13]

In 1808 Rush assisted in the organization of the Philadelphia
Bible Society.[14] A year before he had dreamed of inaugurating a
drive for a seminary where young men could be trained for the
ministry. Such an institution was needed for four reasons:

"1. It will encrease the number of ministers by lessening the
expenses of their education (which at present amount, when conducted at Colleges, in some instances to a thousand pounds) and thus

destroy the distressing disproportion between the number of Congregations & of ministers in the Presbyterian Church of the United States.

"2. It will prevent Candidates for the ministry being infected with the follies and vices of young men educated for secular professions, or ridiculed by them for their piety.

"3. It will render education more appropriate to the subsequent duties and labors of the ministers of the Gospel by confining their preparatory studies to subjects connected with theology, and shortening the time now employed in acquiring a knowledge of things not related to that divine science. No more Latin should be learned in these schools than is necessary to translate that language into English, and no more Greek than is necessary to read the Greek testament.

"4. The plan we have contemplated will favour the growth of practical and habitual godliness in young men intended for the ministry."[15]

This scheme, however, was not carried through.

The theories and principles of education advanced by Rush are significant for their comprehensiveness, their attention to detail, and their progressiveness. They are highly colored by his profound belief in education as a safeguard of liberty and of the republic, and by his firm conviction in religious instruction as an integral part of any educational system.

He worked out definite plans and curricula for elementary schools and colleges. He presented concrete suggestions for the education of women, maintenance of discipline, teaching of science, limitation of the study of the classics, training for government service, and instruction in religion, morals, and the Bible. With such men as Jefferson and Franklin, Rush deserves a place among our constructive educators.

Many of his theories were to find practical expression and many of his dreams were to become realities in the establishment of a college which stands today as a worthy monument to a man whose progressive ideas and tireless efforts contributed materially to the advancement of American education.

XV

Dickinson College

HAVING conceived the idea of actually establishing a college, Rush finally was able to go ahead with his plans. The task entailed soliciting funds, obtaining a charter, supervising the establishment of the institution and organizing its curriculum. As early as 1781 or 1782, before the British troops had returned to England and before the peace preliminaries with King George's representatives had been drawn up in Paris, Rush began to discuss with his friends the plan for a college at Carlisle, Pennsylvania.

His motives in advocating the new college were threefold. In the first place, since he considered higher education "absolutely necessary to preserve liberty in the state," this college might indeed be "the best bulwark of the blessings obtained by the Revolution." In the second place the college in Philadelphia was too far from the frontier counties, and furthermore the expense attached to educating a young man in the city was unduly great. Finally, increased opportunity for higher education should be offered the citizens of Pennsylvania.[1]

He chose Carlisle, in the beautiful Cumberland Valley, for the site of the college because it would attract students from the growing western counties and states and could offer them instruction for less money "than at any other equally improved village in the State." Besides, it was considered one of the most healthful spots in Pennsylvania.

It is possible that baser motives, too, might have prompted Rush. He had been in conflict over educational and religious questions with the Rev. Dr. John Ewing, Provost of the University of the State of Pennsylvania and pastor of the First Presbyterian Church from which Rush had resigned. For slights, real or imagined, suffered at the hands of enemies within the Presbyterian Church, as well as some of his influential fellow citizens in political control, Rush had discovered a way to retaliate.[2] He would found his own college on the frontier which would draw the Presbyterians to "one common center of union."

In September 1782 he drafted some "Hints for Establishing a College at Carlisle in Cumberland County, Pennsylvania," asserting that "Every religious society should endeavor to preserve a representation of itself in government." In colonial Pennsylvania the Presbyterians had suffered from inadequate representation; in 1782, however, they so dominated the politics of the state that other denominations felt it necessary to combine against them. To combat this opposition Rush held that the Presbyterians should strengthen their position by opening schools, "the true nurseries of power and influence." While they were still in political control, he suggested that they should obtain a charter from the Legislature for a college at Carlisle.

Rush proposed that the Board of Trustees be comprised of twenty-four members, and that all officers and teachers be members of the Presbyterian Church in order to maintain a direct relationship between religion and education. A campaign was launched for funds to provide for a church, a chapel, a library, a laboratory, and a classroom building. Houses were to be purchased for the use of the principal and teachers of the college. There were to be no student dormitories: "The custom of crowding boys together under one roof is the remains of monkish ignorance. It exposes them to many vices and unfits them for future commerce and connections in the world. Men are made to live in families. They cannot therefore be too early and too constantly preserved in a close connection with them."[3]

After his plans were reduced to definite terms in the "Hints," Rush corresponded with influential Pennsylvanians, mostly Presbyterian ministers, asking for support. In the fall of 1782 he distributed a circular letter, beseeching aid in petitioning the Legislature for a charter. This letter pointed to the distance of the College of New Jersey (Princeton) from the homes of many of its Pennsylvania students, and to the high cost of transportation for the students. Again he indicated a major disadvantage of the college in Philadelphia in that it was located in a city, expensive and not conducive to a high moral tone of the student body. However, the members of the Presbytery and others at Carlisle, although favoring the plan in general, drew up a list of objections.[4]

Especially hostile to Rush's project was his old enemy, Dr. Ewing, and the politically powerful Philadelphian, Joseph Reed. Ewing tried to convince the ministers of Cumberland County that a new college would divide the Presbyterians; that it could not possibly succeed because of lack of funds; and that it was merely a scheme by which Rush hoped to take revenge for the loss of his professorship in the College of Philadelphia.[5] Rush branded the story too absurd to be contradicted, insisting that he was not at all actuated by resentment against the new University for turning him out of his professorship, but that he was serving the best interests of religion and of the Presbyterian Church.[6]

When the scheme was laid before the meeting at Carlisle, the Presbytery demurred, fearing that any attempt at organizing a college would alarm other denominations; that the support and endowment of such an educational institution would be evidence of partiality in the distribution of public property; that the Pennsylvania Legislature was too busy with urgent business to stop to consider a petition for a charter. These objections notwithstanding, Rush's general scheme was approved and he was requested to draw up the petition to be presented to the Legislature.[7]

Meanwhile, during the spring of 1783, he attempted to win over the influential citizens who were not friendly to his cause. One of the leading opponents in Carlisle was General John Armstrong, a strong factor in Pennsylvania political life, who objected to any institution that might compete with the college at Princeton. The General was associated with the group in control of Philadelphia politics and was not coöperative.[8]

On March 19, 1783, Rush detailed for General Armstrong the advantages to be derived by the state, and by the Presbyterians in particular, "from a nursery of religion and learning on the west side of the river Susquehanna." The letter explained that "The manner in which the Presbyterians seized their present share of power in the University of Philadelphia [when the Legislature withdrew the College of Philadelphia's charter in 1779] has given such general offense, that there is little doubt of an attempt being made in the course of a few years to restore it to its original owners. The old trustees say that the present charter is contrary to the Constitution of the state and to every principle of justice. . . . But supposing the present trustees held the university by the most equitable and constitutional tenure, it cannot be viewed as a nursery of the Presbyterian Church. . . . Religion is best supported under the patronage of particular societies. . . . Religion is necessary to correct the effects of learning. Without religion, I believe, learning does real mischief to the morals and principles of mankind. . . . Colleges are the best schools for divinity" and the Presbyterian Church needs them to train its ministers. Religion was, therefore, the chief factor in the movement for a new college.

Rush also indicated that the project was being backed by all classes of people and was certain, therefore, to succeed. The Quaker John Dickinson, President of the State, and the wealthy Philadelphia Episcopalian William Bingham were supporting it, and Rush hinted that General Armstrong, therefore, would certainly jump on the band wagon and enjoy some of the glory which would come to the founders. Finally, inasmuch as the scheme offered an opportunity for profit in real-estate speculation, Rush expected that it would win the favor of General Armstrong, a wealthy landowner. He told Armstrong that just as the land values increased around Princeton after the founding of the college, property likewise would jump in value in Carlisle and its vicinity.[9]

This letter aroused General Armstrong's curiosity and interest, although he was not yet willing to lend his support. At this juncture a happy thought ran through the mind of Rush's friend Colonel John Montgomery. He advised Rush to flatter the General by appointing him a trustee of the new college. The invitation was extended; General Armstrong was delighted, agreed to become a trustee, and from that day was a loyal supporter of the institution.[10]

By April 1783 the wind began to blow in a favorable direction. The Carlisle Presbytery formally approved the plan for a college, a board of twenty-four trustees was chosen, and arrangements completed to petition the Legislature for a charter at the fall session.[11] Subsequently, however, when the Synod met in Philadelphia, so powerful was the opposition that several of the recently elected trustees succumbed to its arguments and resigned. Rush then suggested that the Board be increased to thirty, and that several Germans be chosen so that the German inhabitants of the state could be solicited for funds. The reconstructed Board numbered forty members, including the Germans and ministers of thirteen denominations.[12]

The petition to the Legislature, bearing sixty-four signatures, stressed the importance of education, the provisions for it incorporated in the state constitution of 1776, and the special advantages of the location at Carlisle, near the new and growing settlements in the north and western parts of the State.[13]

"The ice is at last broken and leave has been obtained to bring in a bill to found a college at Carlisle," Rush informed Colonel Montgomery on September 1. "Joseph Mont[gomer]y opposed the plan [?] violently and plead [?] hard for the sickly banks of the Susquehanna where the youth would enjoy fogs, and the society of boatmen, waggoners and such like companions for half a century to come. He lost his motion by only four votes. . . . He now says he shall urge with all his might for a college but it shall be anywhere in the County of Cumberland but not in Carlisle until the people in the other towns have been consulted. All this is to gain time and finally to divide and destroy the scheme. Ewing and Reed could not oppose us with more specious and insidious maneuvers. Do come to town immediately—we suffer daily from the want of your advice and passionate honesty. . . . Everything hangs upon the next two weeks. If we fail this session—you will see petitions (composed in Philadelphia) next year from Harrisburg—Chambersburg—Shippen's Town and even Pittsburgh—against the town of Carlisle. . . . Do set off the next day after you get this letter. We have not a moment to lose. I am so wholly taken up with my business that I can do nothing. . . . Haste—haste, my friend, or we are undone."[14] There was, it seems, a great deal of political log-rolling in the legislative halls.

Rush's fear was unfounded, and on September 9, 1783, six days after the Anglo-American peace treaty had become operative, the Legislature passed "An Act for the Establishment of A College at the Borough of Carlisle, in the County of Cumberland, in the State of Pennsylvania."[15] It was enacted "That there be erected and hereby is erected and established in the borough of Carlisle, in the county of Cumberland, in this state, a college for the education of youth in the learned and foreign languages, the useful arts, sciences and literature. . . ."

In honor of President Dickinson the institution was designated Dickinson College. The management of the College was put in the hands of a Board of Trustees not to exceed forty in number, Rush, of course, being among them. More than one-third of the original trustees were clergymen. It was stipulated that "persons of every religious denomination among Christians shall be capable of being elected trustees."

The charter granted, no time was lost in organizing. The Board held three meetings in less than three weeks, the first convening in President Dickinson's residence in Philadelphia on September 15, 1783, when Dickinson was immediately elected President of the Board and the Rev. William Linn, Secretary. Later some of the business was conducted at Rush's house on Second Street below Chestnut.[16]

The pressing problems relating to the raising of funds, and to the academic organization and appointments probably occupied more of Rush's time than his practice of medicine throughout the remaining months of 1783. The War for Independence had created a small class of new rich to whom an appeal for contributions might be made. At the same time, however, the God of Chance and Continental paper currency had ruined an untold number of individuals and firms who were in no position to assist in founding a college. The new nation, with prices fantastically high and money fantastically worthless, could hardly be expected to support anything but self-liquidating projects. The task Rush and his fellow trustees took up was, on the face of it, a hopeless one.

The subscription books were formally opened and the drive was set in motion on September 19, 1783, when President Dickinson advised the solicitors to report pledges obtained at a Board meeting six months hence, on April 6, at Carlisle.[17]

There seems to have been no high-powered executive director for this campaign, but Rush was easily its life and spirit. He buttonholed his wealthy friends in Philadelphia, wrote to prospects throughout the state, and lost no opportunity to land a chance pledge.

LAST RESIDENCE OF BENJAMIN RUSH

Drawn from memory by C. A. Poulson.

In order to attract dollars from the Presbyterians, it was proposed that each congregation be visited by two clergymen.[18] To Rush's annoyance, Colonel Montgomery and General Armstrong had not come to Philadelphia to assist in soliciting funds, and he was left with the full burden. Nevertheless, he reported, optimistically, that the subscriptions would probably soon total £10,000.[19] Although £3,000 had been collected in Philadelphia, Rush was convinced that an additional £2,000 might be squeezed out of the Quaker purses.[20] In the rural districts the solicitors were frequently turned down with the cry of heavy taxes, depreciated currency, and the general post-war depression. Unfortunately, many of the contributions were in land office certificates, the payment of which was by no means certain, and in parcels of land, often untenanted and unproductive. By September 1784 only £6,000 had actually been collected.[21]

Failing to get sufficient cash, Rush begged equipment. Reporting to Dr. John Coakley Lettsom, April 8, 1785, a year after the close of the first drive, that the College was handicapped without a library, Rush asked him to beg a few books among his friends: "The sweepings of their studies will be very acceptable in our illiterate wooden country."

The Commonwealth of Pennsylvania, with a depressed treasury, could not be counted on for any considerable appropriation, and certainly for none at all in 1784 or 1785. Rush pleaded constantly with the members of the Legislature for financial aid, and at last, on April 7, 1786, there was passed "An Act for the Present Relief and Future Endowment of Dickinson College . . .," appropriating £500 and 10,000 acres of land.[22]

More than two years then passed without any further legislative action. On October 3, 1788, there was donated to the College a lot, measuring 240 by sixty feet, located on the north side of Pomfret Street between Hanover and Bedford Streets. This lot had originally been granted to the Province in 1773 by the proprietors of Pennsylvania, Thomas and Richard Penn, for use as a grammar school which was erected thereon. As soon as the title to the lot and building were legally vested in the Board of the College, repairs and improvements were immediately made.[23]

Six months later, March 27, 1789, the Legislature reported favorably "An Act for Raising by Way of Lottery the Sum of Eight Thousand Dollars for Defraying the Expense of Erecting A Common Hall in the City of Philadelphia and Two Thousand Dollars for the Use of Dickinson College." Four-fifths of the net profit from the lottery were to be used to erect the Philadelphia City Hall at Fifth and Chestnut Streets, and one-fifth to assist the College inasmuch as the institution's funds were "found inadequate for the purposes by them intended."[24] The lottery was subsequently advertised and conducted.

Current expenses to the extent of $1,500 were defrayed by the Legislature in 1791. Four years later, a charitable spirit again pervading the legislative halls, $5,000 was voted the College. This time, however, a provision was included in the Act calling on the College to give free instruction in reading, writing, and arithmetic to ten poor boys.[25] In 1806 the state again dug into its pocket to the extent of $4,000, of which sum a large part was used for the purchase of laboratory apparatus.[26]

For the next fifteen years the College struggled without aid from the Commonwealth, and then between 1821–29, when the Theological Seminary of the German Reformed Church was maintained as part of the College, an annual appropriation of $10,000 was granted, provided only that a regular annual report on the affairs of the institution be submitted to the state authorities. This was a liberal appropriation, indeed, and is evidence of a close relationship between the College and the state.

The financial problem was almost insurmountable. With subscriptions totaling only £6,000 in their hands, the trustees opened the College, after applications had been received from ten students in the fall of 1784.

While the campaign for funds was in progress, in 1783–84, Rush turned his attention to the work of organization. Not only was his mind occupied with the question of faculty appointments but also with the problems of curriculum. He wrote "A mode of education proper in a republic" to lay before the first regular annual meeting of the Board of Trustees on April 6, 1784.

During his student days in Edinburgh, Rush had become acquainted with a Presbyterian minister of Montrose, Scotland, the

Rev. D. Charles Nisbet, whose name was before the Board of the College of New Jersey when Dr. Witherspoon was chosen President of that institution. After 1776 his sympathy with the American colonies won friends on this side of the Atlantic. In the late fall of 1783 Rush corresponded with Nisbet, discussing the plans for the new college, and suggesting that he might be interested in accepting the presidency. At the same time he enlarged upon Nisbet's qualifications in letters to several trustees, and urged his election as head of the institution. One of the trustees, Rev. Dr. John King, hesitated: "His being a Foreigner would admit of no objection but is a Circumstance for some reasons more desirable— but we should be satisfied that we are capable of holding up such encouragement as would invite a man from thence where if he is really such [as pictured] he will have the greater inducement to stay."[27] There was much truth in King's contention, the embryo college having little to offer a man of recognized ability and reputation. Nevertheless, six weeks before the meeting of the Board, Rush had won over the influential members in favor of Nisbet and on April 6, 1784, he was elected Principal by a unanimous vote of the trustees, his annual salary being fixed at £250. Provision was made for a house to accommodate his family, and fifty pounds sterling was voted to defray moving expenses.[28]

Nisbet did not, however, jump at the invitation; he was not certain that he would be happy in central Pennsylvania. Dr. Ewing of the University, and Dr. Witherspoon of Princeton, according to Rush, advised Nisbet to stay in Scotland, suggesting that the college funds were inadequate, that the courses at Dickinson would be of a low standard and the position, therefore, would be unattractive to a man of Nisbet's talent and professional training.[29]

More of the adventurous than the rational spirit was required if a man were to accept this invitation to come to America. Without a taste for romance, an academician would have been miserable in a frontier community in the 1780's. It must have been in a particularly adventurous moment, when the fates advised him to gamble with the unknown future, that he decided to come to Dickinson. This was in August 1784.

Before his affairs in Montrose were settled, his trunks packed, and neighbors bidden farewell, Nisbet learned of the political unrest in Pennsylvania and the possible consequences to the finances of Dickinson College. John Dickinson, President of the Council, was the leader of the conservative party in power at the moment, but he was afraid that the opposition might gain control of the Legislature in the next election and overthrow the incumbent party in the entire state government. Back in 1779 the Legislature, for purely political reasons, had stupidly closed the College of Philadelphia; and Dickinson now feared that, if the opposition came into power in 1785, the charter of the new college might be annulled. As President of the Board of the new institution he advised Nisbet of the danger ahead; he did not believe it wise, at least for the present, for the Scotchman to give up a permanent position in his native land for a dubious commission in the new republic. Dickinson painted a gloomy picture indeed.[30]

When news of this letter reached Rush's ears, he was furious, and wrote on November 13: "Whether he [Dickinson] wished to annihilate our college and thereby to prevent any future draughts being made upon him for its support, or whether he is under Quaker influence as to the future power of the Presbyterians, I know not, but certain it is he is become the most formidable enemy to our college that ever we have yet known." Rush went directly to Dickinson and laid before him in no uncertain terms the consequences of his letter. "I have set forth the disgrace we must incur in Scotland and the operation of his letter upon the reputation of the trustees. But all this has had no effect upon him. He positively refuses to contradict his letter. We parted with his saying that 'it became us to act with prudence.' I replied in a warm tone that 'Prudence, where honor was concerned, was a rascally virtue.' "[31]

Finally Dickinson was prevailed upon to place the situation before Nisbet in a better light. The Philadelphians on the Board of Trustees officially discountenanced Dickinson's admonitions that Nisbet remain in Scotland, and instead assured him that the College was unquestionably a permanent institution. Rush also suggested that the trustees in Carlisle write Nisbet and set his fears at rest.

In the middle of November, Dickinson wrote Nisbet that the clouds had cleared, that the Assembly evidenced a more liberal and harmonious spirit than was exhibited before the session opened. "Many of the friends of the College at Carlisle are fully convinced," he assured Nisbet, "that no attempts will be made against that establishment; or that, if they should be, that they will be unsuccessful. I must confess that my hopes are much stronger than they were in favor of the institution."[32]

This correspondence must certainly have made matters difficult for the family in Montrose. The outlook was confused and uncertain. During the long winter months Nisbet turned the proposition over in his mind hundreds of times and, at length, decided to accept. He headed for Philadelphia, arriving on a warm day in June 1785. He was cordially received by Rush, then residing in a three-story house of stately proportions at the northwest corner of Lodge Alley (Gothic Street) and Second Street. The house, which boasted a beautiful garden, had been built by William Logan, son of William Penn's secretary, James Logan, about 1750.

Being well acquainted with all the leaders in the community, Rush was able to introduce Nisbet to the men whose power and influence might mean much to him and to Dickinson College. There was the ingenious Benjamin Franklin, back from France, and just elected President of the State Council to succeed Dickinson; James Wilson, one of the leaders of the bar, whose home at the southwest corner of Third and Walnut Streets was the scene of many gatherings of the intelligentsia; and the wealthy William Bingham. Wilson and Bingham were trustees of the college at Carlisle.

Rush was especially anxious to have Nisbet meet not only the influential leaders but also representative business men; it was important, too, to acquaint the citizens at large with the new institution. With this in mind he wrote John Montgomery on June 8, 1785, to arrange for a committee of citizens and trustees to meet Nisbet on the road outside of Carlisle, for a parade to escort the college president into the town with the courthouse bell ringing, and for a special address of welcome. This program was designed to attract prospective students who might read about the affair in the Philadelphia newspapers.[33]

In 1785, the ninth anniversary of the Declaration of Independence fell on a Monday. On that morning Nisbet and his party left

York and took the road to Carlisle. They were met by the local company of light horse and escorted into the town where the citizens were celebrating Independence Day. The address of welcome, as arranged by Rush, was delivered, but Nisbet was so excited by the enthusiasm that he was able to respond with only a few words.[84]

Nisbet's own enthusiasm was not destined to last long. The College had been opened in the fall of 1784, and immediately after he took over the reins, he found serious fault with the organization. The teachers were overburdened with classroom work, the students being ungraded. Classes were run on the plan of the Little Red School House. Unfortunately the defects of organization could not be corrected because of lack of funds.

One cannot blame the sensitive scholar for losing faith in Rush, who had made lavish promises that never materialized. Where were the funds and where was the congenial house for the principal? A house was provided, but it did not measure up to expectations. Nisbet and members of his family became ill, not long after their arrival, with the fever prevalent in that part of the country during the summer. The Nisbets were not accustomed to extremely warm weather and furthermore they found adjustment to the new environment difficult. Thin-skinned, Dr. Nisbet was ever ready to take offense. Faced with difficulties in getting cash and in running the College as a going concern, Rush was not always sympathetic when Nisbet complained about conditions at Carlisle. He did advise the trustees, however, that the principal's residence was inadequate. A better one could not be found.

In August, a month after Nisbet's arrival, Rush visited Colonel Montgomery in Carlisle for several days but failed to call on the head of the College. Nisbet was deeply hurt, and on August 10, 1785, he titled a piece of note paper: "Tomb of Dickinson's College," and wrote Rush in a bitter tone: "And is this thy kindness to thy friend? To have been two whole [days] in the place, without favouring [me?] with a single moment's tete-a-tete? . . . Please let me know by the bearer, if or when I am to be favoured with a few minutes conference before you leave the place." The disappointed man signed the message: "Your much injured."

After a warm Pennsylvania summer, Nisbet concluded—only two months after his arrival—that Scotland was heavenly country. He thought about the prospect of returning and he let it be known in Montrose that he was ready and anxious to come back to his former post. He simply could not live in health in America, he wrote Rush the first week in September, and added that he had decided to return to Scotland because he could be of no service to the College while in poor health. His purse was almost empty, and when told by the trustees that they could not pay for his return transportation, he was insulted. He was, indeed, a poor man, and he called upon Rush to have the money voted as a point of honor.[35]

October rolled around with its invigorating, brisk days, and the brown-yellow-red woodlands. The harvest season came with fruits and grains galore. Nisbet felt the exhilaration, but his pride would not permit him to reverse his decision. In accepting his formal resignation as head of Dickinson, dated October 18, 1785, the trustees finally agreed to reimburse him for expenses incurred in returning to Scotland.

After all the pother Nisbet did not sail eastward. The fates intervened. The vessel, on which he was scheduled to sail, did not arrive in port on this side on time. While waiting, Nisbet surveyed the situation once more and weighed the details anew. The crisp, cool November weather stirred his spirit. At the same time rumors were current that the college treasury was about to be bolstered up. Perhaps, too, another minister had already been appointed by the Montrose church? What with one thing and another, late November saw a change of heart and Nisbet decided to throw in his destiny with Dickinson College and the new republic.

The problem that then confronted the trustees was not altogether an easy one to solve. The resignation of the administrative head had been accepted, and now he was appealing to the trustees to be reinstated. Rush was satisfied that Nisbet would be reëlected. "We cannot do otherwise," he wrote Colonel Montgomery on November 28, 1785, "without incurring the folly of instability and thereby of resembling himself." Rush was in favor of a new contract carrying a lower salary for Nisbet until the College and his reputation could recover from the blow they both received by his conduct. He went on to complain: "When I urge the measure of re-electing him, you cannot suppose I can feel much regard for him or his family. He has treated me cruelly and his son still worse—but I freely forgive them both—and if they mend their manners and if the Doctor will do his duty and give over whining and complaining I shall love and serve him as well as if nothing had happened." The last statement was overgenerous for Rush, because his prejudices were always deep and the personal affronts he received were never forgotten and rarely forgiven.

Nisbet was officially reappointed, but he continued to be dissatisfied and unhappy. A conservative clergyman, aloof from the commercial and political activities of city and state, he found it difficult to make close contacts with men of affairs, with the trustees, and with the legislators who controlled the public purse. He was not the much publicized college president of a later age, who can count among his talents the ability to conduct successful endowment campaigns for his institution. Rush, a liberal, and thoroughly acquainted with American customs and frontier life, had little sympathy with the narrow views espoused by the hidebound Scotch scholar who could not meet the challenge of his new surroundings. The misunderstandings that arose between the two men grew so bitter that at one time Rush threatened to resign from the Board.

The relationship between Nisbet and the Board of Trustees as a whole was not cordial. The Principal carried out plans without consulting the Board. This failure on his part to coöperate explains, to some extent, the lack of system under which the College labored. The students, who were permitted to enroll at any time during the year, were not graded. New students attended classes with those who were far advanced in the same subject. There was no definite course of study, and the graduation requirements were vague. Books were scarce and could not be bought in Carlisle. The small college library was a happy hunting ground for the unscrupulous young bibliophile, who could steal books month after month, inasmuch as there was no attendant. The classrooms were inadequate in size and number.

Nisbet and the trustees could have learned much about administration from the colleges already flourishing. Harvard was just celebrating its one hundred and fiftieth anniversary; William and Mary was over ninety years old, and Yale eighty-five.

An all too rosy picture of the College and its facilities in 1786 might be glimpsed from the following advertisement, drawn up by the Board of Trustees on December 19, 1786, and inserted in the *Pennsylvania Packet* on February 7, 1787:

"The house in which the classes are taught at present is situated in a pleasant part of the town, and is sixty feet long and twenty-three broad. Three large rooms are finished for the purpose of teaching; there is also a library room and an appartment for the philosophical apparatus.

"The library already consists of two thousand, seven hundred and six volumes, in the Hebrew, Greek, Latin, English, French, German, Low Dutch and Italian languages, the donations of gentlemen in England, Scotland and Philadelphia.

"The philosophical apparatus contains a complete electrical machine, a camera obscura of a new construction, a prism, a telescope, a solar microscope, a barometer and thermometer, upon one scale, and a large and elegant set of globes.

"The Rev. Dr. Nisbet gives lectures daily on logic, metaphysic, and moral philosophy. The Rev. Dr. Davidson teaches geography, history, chronology, rhetoric, and belles lettres; and as there is no professor of natural philosophy yet chosen, the above gentlemen have undertaken for the present season, to give lectures and instruction in that science. The senior class, consisting of twenty students, are studying natural and moral philosophy, having already studied the classics and mathematics, and other branches usually taught in other colleges. Mr. Robert Johnson teaches the several branches of the mathematics. Mr. James Ross with proper assistants teaches the Greek and Latin languages. The tuition money is only five pounds per annum to be paid half-yearly, and twenty-five shillings entrance; boarding can be had at twenty six pounds per annum, in genteel houses, including washing, mending, fire and candles; twelve boarding houses are now open, equal to any at other seminaries, and the greatest attention will be paid to the morals of the students by Dr. Nisbet and Dr. Davidson, who officiate in the Presbyterian church on Sundays."

Two months later Rush wrote John Dickinson jubilantly: "I have great pleasure in informing you that your College is in a very flourishing condition. Pupils are coming & expected in great numbers from Maryland, Virginia & even North Carolina. Twenty young men will graduate there in May. The philosophical apparatus has been received in good order, & has given great satisfaction to the masters & scholars. The citizens of Carlisle have lately bought & given to the College for the use of the Principal a neat commodious stone house. Thus after all our difficulties & disappointments, heaven has at last crowned our labors & wishes with success."[36]

The College, in fact, presented a different picture. The discipline problem was a serious one because the charter had given the Board and the principal joint power to deal with this matter. In the summer of 1785 the Board drew up a "Plan of Education" enumerating penalties for infractions of specified rules, and setting up a faculty discipline committee. Rush seems to have been responsible for this impracticable plan, and Nisbet justly complained that the trustees should not interfere in the administration of discipline. And yet, notwithstanding the conflicts in the administrative circle, sixty-seven students were on the rolls in 1791 and "it is expected," the report stated, "that 20 will be prepared this fall to receive their first degree in the arts."[37]

A year later, however, Nisbet was complaining again about mediocre lectures and unsatisfactory arrangement of classes. From 1796 to 1798 an unsuccessful attempt was made to divide the student body into freshman, junior, and senior classes, and to offer a three-year course. In November 1798 the students went on strike, demanding a short, one-year course. When they failed to appear in their classrooms it was decided, at a hasty conference of the President of the Board of Trustees and the faculty, to meet their demands and to graduate students after one year's study.[38] Not until 1814, ten years after Nisbet's death, was the present four-year course inaugurated.

The trustees and students alike frequently objected not only to methods of instruction but also to the course content. Practically no time for student discussion was allowed in the classroom. In his own course Nisbet used the lecture method entirely. The intellectually curious student was given no opportunity to ask questions. Notwithstanding protests on the part of the trustees, the lecture method was not abandoned. The pedagogical mind is set and slow to change.

Nisbet threw himself open to criticism because he permitted his personal political prejudices to enter into his treatment of technical subjects in the classroom. He was avowedly a Federalist, and his criticism of Jefferson and his disciples antagonized many students and citizens. He frequently compared European institutions with American, always at the expense of the latter. He failed to realize that, regardless of the justice of his criticism, the spirit of nationality in America was developing so rapidly that there was no tolerance of criticism from a foreigner. It was reported that he openly censured several trustees, especially Rush.

Rush spent many anxious hours over the affairs of the College in the 1790's. The increasing number of complaints caused him no end of worry. Cool and frank discussion between Rush and Nisbet was out of the question. The Board of Trustees as a body had little influence over the Principal. Although the situation was an unhappy one, Rush believed that the institution was strong enough to survive all attacks from within and without. "I deplore with you the conduct of the Principal of our College," he wrote Colonel Montgomery. "He discovers in everything which you have mentioned, a want of the virtues of a Christian, and the manners of a gentleman. Alas! poor human nature! But let us not despair. God was the father, and Providence has been the nurse of our college. No weapon formed, or thrown against it, either from within, or without will ultimately prosper."[39]

Definite progress, however, was made before the turn of the century. In 1799 work was started on a twelve-room building in the center of an eight-acre plot. In January 1803 part of this building was occupied and then, only a month later, the entire edifice was reduced to ashes. This catastrophe was a severe blow to Rush, and he was obviously beginning to give up hope as he wrote: "It has added a fresh instance to the number of the unsuccessful issues of my life." His work in the army medical department during the War for Independence had been marred by his controversy with General Washington and Dr. Shippen, and his unselfish service during the yellow fever epidemics of the 1790's had been blighted by the bitter controversies with the medical profession and laymen. And now one of his pet projects, just beginning to show tangible signs of permanence, faced extinction.

There was still hope, however, for the friends of the College came to the rescue magnificently. Before the end of the summer sufficient funds had been collected for a new building; architect Benjamin Henry Latrobe drew the plans, and the foundations were laid. This West College, still occupied, was opened in 1806.

Nisbet did not live to preside in the new building. After his death in January 1804, Rev. Dr. Robert Davidson, one of the teachers and pastor of one of the Presbyterian churches in Carlisle, acted as President pro tempore for several years. When news of Nisbet's death was received in Philadelphia, Rush, for all his disaffection for the man, referred to him as a walking library, knowing a great deal about many and a little about all subjects. He told the story of Nisbet's acquaintance with odd books that few people had read: "He lived next door to a pastry cook at Montrose in Scotland, who used to import old books from London by the barrel to put their leaves under his pies. Before he tore them up he permitted Dr. Nisbet to look over them and to take such as he wanted at a trifling price for his own use. These books the Doctor read and from them extracted a great deal of rare and uncommon knowledge." Rush admitted that Nisbet was an excellent companion and an entertaining conversationalist, but on the other hand he was possessed of a "querulous disposition and more disposed to find fault than to praise." Society did not profit proportionately from his uncommon abilities and knowledge. "He rather resembled a fountain," was Rush's figure, "which poured forth streams in a royal garden for the amusement of spectators than a rich and copious stream that fertilized in its course an extensive country."[40] The fact that Rush and Nisbet were much alike in character and personality explains in part their failure to work in accord with each other.

When the time came to elect a permanent president, Rush set about the task with his accustomed vigor and enthusiasm. His renewed interest in the College manifested itself in fresh activity in behalf of the institution. In the summer of 1808 he shipped out several boxes of "philosophical apparatus purchased for the College."[41]

In July he took the first steps in his effort to place his friend, Rev. Dr. Samuel Miller of New York City, at the head of Dickinson. Rush wrote Miller that Judge Hamilton, one of the trustees, had advised him that there was general agreement in favor of Miller's appointment.[42] To several trustees and friends of the College, Rush had previously mentioned Miller's name as a possible successor to Nisbet. Rush painted for Miller a bright future for the institution. "From the late donations of the legislature (though small) it bids fair to revive from the situation to which it was depressed before Dr. Nesbitt's death. 2,000 dollars are immediately to be laid out in purchasing a philosophical & clinical apparatus & 2,000 more in purchasing books. The building for the accomodation and instruction of the students is finished, but as yet not occupied for the former purpose. The erection of this house & the payment of a debt contracted to Dr. N, will nearly absorb all the funds of the College, so that the principal resource for the support of the three professors now belonging to the College is derived from the tuition money of about 50 students." Several trustees proposed that the principal manage the new building as a private boarding house for students and retain the profits in lieu of salary. Thus if the new principal were an outstanding figure, he would attract more students and thus increase his income. Rush asked Miller to consider the appointment, not only because he was the man best qualified to set in motion a revolution in education, which the country needed, but also because the climate at Carlisle would be a boon to his health since he was suffering from tuberculosis.[43]

Although Miller declined Rush's invitation to become a candidate for the position, the trustees, nevertheless, proceeded to elect him by unanimous vote in October. The letter to Rush in which Miller positively refused to consider the offer, had been handed to the Board during the summer, and Rush was, therefore, surprised, but none the less pleased, at the action of the trustees. "A wide field of usefulness will now be opened to you," he hastened to predict in a congratulatory message to Miller. "You will become the patriarch of the western counties of the United States. You will have the honor of introducing a system of education into our country accomodated to the forms of our government, and to our state of society and manners. You will be able to abolish customs, and studies in the College of monkish origin, and which have nothing but antiquity to recommend them." Over and above his salary, Rush pointed out that Miller could make two to three hundred dollars as pastor of the church in Carlisle; and again he called attention to the sanative climate: "Think among other things of the air of New York so unfriendly to weak lungs."[44]

Miller could not be persuaded, however, and on the last day of October wrote Rush, definitely declining the principalship of Dickinson.[45]

The search for a principal was renewed. Rush sent inquiries to colleges from one end of the country to the other. One could hardly expect a distinguished educator to head a small, little-known college. After considerable difficulty, a possibility finally presented itself in the person of the Rev. Jeremiah Atwater, a graduate of Yale, and President of Middlebury College, Vermont. President Timothy Dwight of Yale had, at an earlier date, called Rush's attention to Atwater's accomplishments. After some preliminary correspondence, the position at Dickinson was offered to Atwater, who notified Rush in the late summer of 1809 that he would accept. He arrived at Carlisle in September. He was thirty-five years of age, and in Rush's judgment, "learned, well-read, pious, and heartily disposed to enter upon his duties as Principal of the College with zeal and disinterestedness."[46]

Here was a man with experience in the management of a small college and an understanding of its problems. The trustees as well as the students were pleased with the new Principal, who on his side was so well satisfied that he wrote Rush he felt perfectly at home at Carlisle.[47]

Without delay Atwater took hold and resuscitated the dying institution, reorganizing it root and branch. Soon the student enrollment began to climb. In 1809 there were sixty-one students; in 1810, seventy-seven; and in 1811, 110. The following year Rush bought some new laboratory apparatus and also two hundred dollars' worth of books for the library. In 1811 Joseph Priestley's son-in-law, Dr. Thomas Cooper, was appointed to Dickinson's first chair of chemistry. Things were humming, and at the close of this year, 1811, Rush was able to describe the College to John Adams as "a flourishing institution—the President, a Dr. Atwater, has given it great celebrity."[48]

Sanguine expectations of a smoothly running organization were not to be realized. Like his predecessor, Atwater soon recognized that joint control of discipline problems by the faculty and trustees was an impossible arrangement. Discord led to bitter feeling and in 1815, two years after Rush's death, Atwater and two professors resigned. In the year 1816 the College was forced to close and did not again open its doors to students until 1821, when a substantial appropriation from the Legislature made reorganization possible. Then for about ten years the College prospered until the old trouble over the administration of discipline arose again.

Today Dickinson College, with an enrollment of more than 550 students, offers courses in the liberal arts and sciences, leading to the degrees of Bachelor of Arts, Bachelor of Philosophy, and Bachelor of Science.

The institution owes its existence to Benjamin Rush. He it was who conceived it, founded it, and solicited funds to sustain it during the early years. In spite of the disagreeable squabbles with Nisbet, he gave much of his time to its affairs, purchasing equipment and supplies, looking for principals and teachers, and drawing up plans of organization. His ideas were not always practicable, but they were offered after careful study and thought. Mindful of his unselfish devotion the trustees, in 1790, placed on its minutes a resolution stating that "the Board are deeply sensible of the very great services of the Doctor, and not only most cordially approve of his conduct, but hereby declare their warmest acknowledgements, for his extraordinary zeal and diligence in promoting the good of the Institution—and that this expression of our gratitude be transmitted to him by the President."[49]

XVI

Last Years

RUSH was fifty-six years old when the last of the serious yellow fever epidemics struck Philadelphia in 1802. He was in the full vigor of his middle years, his dynamic spirit having overpowered an ever-present physical handicap of weak lungs. The decade he was still to live he spent in bustling activity, dividing his time and energy between his professional duties and his many and varied outside concerns, personal and philanthropic. He was constantly at work on lectures, pamphlets, and books, scientific and philosophic, and on the preparation of manuscripts for the press. During April 1810 he edited nine lectures on general subjects, and two others on the pleasures of the senses and of the mind, compiling besides a new syllabus for his lectures. Throughout the summer of 1812 he was transcribing lectures and preparing his notable volume on diseases of the mind.[1]

The troubles arising at Dickinson College were his troubles. He had to look out for his interests in the speculation he was carrying on in western lands. The propaganda bee never left his bonnet, and up to the end he crusaded against slavery, intemperance, and existing penal codes. He kept up correspondence and personal contacts with former students, personal friends, and colleagues, and the outstanding minds among his contemporaries.

In the earlier years he had felt very close to Franklin. Indeed, he felt so greatly indebted to the sage that he once planned a book which was to be a collection of the fragments of wisdom he had treasured in his memory as they fell in conversation from the lips of the genius of eighteenth-century America. Rush helped to patch up the differences that held John Adams and Jefferson aloof from each other between 1801 and 1811. The reconciliation he effected between these two men, which was to renew a friendship lasting till their deaths in 1826, was deeply satisfying to Rush, occurring as it did but two years before his own death. Jefferson recalled with pleasure evenings of delightful conversation spent with Rush.[2]

These men respected Rush as a scientist and philosopher. He was a gifted and convincing conversationalist, blessed with an agreeable voice, charming and courteous in manner. A remarkably retentive memory was an additional asset.

Dictatorial by nature, this father of a large family followed the activities of his children closely. His marriage to Julia Stockton had been a fortunate and happy one to which Mrs. Rush must have contributed largely in patience and understanding. To the mother the children. could turn for sympathy and affection; from the father came admonitions and advice. When his son James went abroad to study medicine in the summer of 1809, Dr. Rush drew up for him a guide to conduct, worthy of Polonius:

"1. Commit yourself and all that you are interested in daily to the protection of your Maker, Preserver and bountiful Benefactor. Keep a journal from the day you leave Philadelphia in which insert all the physical facts you hear in conversation, the companies you go into and interesting matters you hear in them, with the names of each of them when small and select. The days on which you begin a new book or enter upon any new study or business. The subjects of sermons, speeches, &c. Avoid lodging in houses where there are handsome young ladies. Avoid particular attentions &c. where you visit.

"2. Attend public worship. Avoid driving out in large companies on Sunday. Attend the Courts, General Assembly and Debating Societies.

"3. Converse on medicine with physicians as much as possible; find out what new medicines or new forms of old medicines they are in the habit of giving.

"4. Keep in a separate book an account of your expenditures, contracts, &c. Preserve all your receipts. Also finally recollect the saying of Sir John Baynard to his son when he set out on his travels: 'Remember while you are in the world the world sees you.' Also the saying of Israel Putnam to your father in 1766: 'Keep older and wiser company than thyself.' Also of George Dilwyn to B. Chew Jr.: 'Remember thou hast a character to lose.' "[3]

What recreation the twenty-three-year-old medical student was to have the father failed to say. The doctor himself rarely indulged in diversion or entertainment. He found it difficult to relax, and thus further mental stimulation and increased activity were his medicine for a tired mind and body. Work was his chief recreation, and his energy and capacity for it astoundingly great. It was this high-geared living which drove Rush to bed from time to time, but his extraordinary recuperative powers soon had him back on his feet again working harder than ever.[4]

Rush was always an inveterate diarist and recorder, observing keenly everything he saw or heard or read, and digesting his impressions in pithy and polished style. Even casual conversations and chance meetings in the stagecoach or on the road found their way into his notebooks. So completely had he disciplined his mind that he could read or write with perfect concentration in the midst of household noises or the buzz of conversation. Study and contemplation were for Rush two of the vital satisfactions of his life. "While children dispute, and fight about gingerbread, and nuts, and Party men about posts of honor," he wrote a friend and former student, "the pleasure of one evening's successful investigation of a moral & physical truth—or an hour spent in literary or philosophical society, will more than outweigh all that ambition ever conferred upon her votaries."[5]

Rush was easily the ranking teacher of medicine in America. During a career of forty years he taught more than 3,000 students who had nothing but praise for their conscientious and able master. To some he gave financial aid to help them over the difficult years of apprenticeship and medical school through which he himself had passed under Dr. John Redman and in Edinburgh. Through his classes in the College and University he spread the theories of Cullen, under whom he had studied, in conflict with the medical system of Boerhaave then prevailing among physicians in Philadelphia. After 1790 he was to teach his own system evolved during twenty years of practice.

Rush could look back upon a life of service to his country and his fellow men. During the War he was absolutely unselfish in his devotion to the cause of independence. As a member of the Continental Congress he was the only Doctor of Medicine to sign the Declaration. Later he served as Physician-General of the Middle Department of the Army. The hornets' nest he brought about his ears in this latter post let loose against him humiliating charges, unquestionably unfounded, of complicity in a conspiracy against General Washington. To this day over Rush's memory hangs the cloud of this unjust reproach.

It is upon his fame as a physician that Rush's immortality will rest. Excellently trained for his day, conscientious and skillful, he built up a large and profitable practice and earned the respect of physicians and laymen in all parts of the country. His contributions both in the theory and practice of medicine were invaluable, and even today his descriptions of focal infection, cholera infantum, and dengue are considered classics. His excursions into the almost virgin field of psychiatry were remarkable for their originality and insight.

In courage, devotion, and physical sacrifice no one gave more generously than Rush during the frightful days of Philadelphia's yellow fever epidemics. Thus his lot seemed doubly bitter when he was met with the enmity and wrath of fellow physicians for his wide and general use of the lancet upon which he pinned his faith for his success in combating the scourge. So spectacular was the battle that was fought, that the epithet of "bleeder" will never detach itself from his name.

By his very bearing he inspired perfect confidence in his ability. Above medium height, he held his slender body erect and carried himself with dignity. A well-shaped hand and long, slim fingers attest to the skill of his surgical technique. His face was long and thin with a high rounded forehead, high cheek bones and firm jaw. The stubborn determination and will with which he faced all difficulties were evident in his strong, well-defined features—bright piercing eyes under heavy brows, thin aquiline nose, long upper lip and resolute mouth. In youth he wore a neat powdered wig, but in middle age his rather long, thin, gray hair somewhat softened his sharp features. He was always meticulous about his appearance and wore his clothes with an air of elegance.

His portrait painted by Thomas Sully was executed in 1813, after Rush's death, from a family picture. It now hangs in the Pennsylvania Hospital. Here, too, is a bust by William Rush, a cousin, presented to the Hospital in October 1813, six months after the Doctor's death.

Although he had been forced to bed from time to time, only six weeks before death came he was able to write that he enjoyed "uncommon health." "Now and then I am reminded of my age," he said, "by light attacks of the *tussis senilis* [a cough], but they do not impair my strength nor lessen my facility in doing business."[6] During the last year or two of his life a cough increased in intensity and frequency. The rainy, damp days of the spring in March 1813 seemed to affect him adversely, and the cough became serious.

After visiting his patients, as usual, on Wednesday, April 14, complained of a chill and general indisposition at dinner in the evening, and at nine o'clock he went to bed. Becoming very cold he drank some brandy and soaked his feet in hot water. During the night fever developed and severe pains in his side made for a restless night. Breathing became difficult as dawn came. Early in the morning a bleeder was summoned and ten ounces were drawn from his arm. After losing the blood, he felt relieved, and slept. At ten in the morning Dr. Dorsey found the pulse calm, but the pain continued. Next morning he was weak and in a state of exhaustion; wine-whey was prescribed and proved for a time to brace him. His pulse, however, gradually became weaker and Dr. Dorsey gave a diagnosis of typhus. Stimulants were administered, and external irritation kept up, but without effect. On Saturday morning he awoke with severe pains and asked that a bleeder be called again. He believed that his pulmonary tuberculosis was reaching an acute stage and this was probably more nearly correct than Dorsey's diagnosis. After consulting with Dr. Physick, Dr. Dorsey ordered three ounces of blood to be drawn. On Sunday morning Rush seemed to be in better spirits, and he conversed freely, but at four o'clock in the afternoon his temperature began to rise and by nine o'clock his condition had become critical. When morning came, he realized that the end was near, and at about five o'clock in the afternoon of Monday, the 19th of April, he expired, rational and composed, his mind functioning normally. "Be indulgent to the poor," were his last words, uttered to his son.[7]

The first of our great physicians had passed away in his sixty-eighth year. In all parts of the country men and women mourned the death of a great physician and a man of the people, respected by the rich and cultured, and loved by the poor and oppressed.

The local newspaper, in announcing the death of "the great and good Doctor Benjamin Rush" indulged in superlatives. "The columns of a newspaper are not the place," ran the notice on April 20, "nor our feeble pen the instrument, for commemorating the transcendent virtues, talents and usefulness of such a man. Biography and history will no doubt hereafter do them the justice they deserve. In the meanwhile it is the painful duty of every press to contribute its transient notice of an event, which has deprived the country of a patriot, society of a most superior and fascinating member, and science of an illustrious ornament. It is true that threescore years and ten being accomplished, ought to teach us that much longer life could not be expected. But the loss is only the more irreparable, when age has matured and mellowed genius, without diminishing or blunting any of its inestimable faculties. Few men, if any, in this or any other county, have so eminently combined public with professional services as Dr. Rush. From the time of his signing the Declaration of Independence to the last moment of his career, he has always displayed the first requisites for a great statesman: while his multiform works in medical science have been the almost annual productions of his knowledge in this department. Just as he had completed a great, original performance on the Diseases of the Mind, this great, original man has been suddenly withdrawn from this world. Such is mortality! As a father, a husband, a brother, a friend, a companion, a citizen, in every sphere of existence, his attributes were of the highest character, his loss leaves a chasm which time alone can fill."[8]

Two days later, April 22, the *American Daily Advertiser* carried the simple notice: "The friends of the late Dr. Rush are respectfully invited to attend his funeral this afternoon, at four o'clock." He died in his home at 98 South Fourth Street where he had been living since 1807, when he moved from the southeast corner of Fourth and Walnut Streets. His last residence was an attractive three-story red and black brick house, with a frontage of eighty-nine feet, and with a spacious garden in the rear. It was built and originally occupied by Justice Edward Shippen of the Supreme Court of Pennsylvania.

The funeral was attended by a large gathering including deputations of the American Philosophical Society, Pennsylvania Society for the Abolition of Slavery, and the Pennsylvania Hospital. Young and old, rich and poor, all bowed in honor of one of the nation's most distinguished citizens.

The great man was buried in the Christ Church Burial Ground at Fifth and Arch Streets, Philadelphia, fifty yards east of the grave of Benjamin Franklin. The inscription on the gravestone reads:

In memory of
Benjamin Rush M.D.
Who died on the 19th of April
in the year of our Lord 1813
Aged 68 years

Well done good and faithful servant
enter thou into the joy of the Lord

Matt. 25c 23v

News of the death brought grief to men far off. Dr. David Hosack, of New York, wrote James Rush that his father was "not only an honor to his profession and his country but an ornament to human nature the benefactor of the human race." To Mrs. Rush he also wrote: "In this city as in his own every mark of respect is paid to his memory and his death regretted not only by his profession and his numerous friends but by all classes of our citizens."[9] "As a man of science, letters, taste, sense, philosophy, patriotism, religion, morality, merit, usefulness, taken all together," said John Adams, "Rush has not left his equal in America; nor that I know in the world. In him is taken away, and in a manner most sudden and unexpected, a main prop of my life."[10] The depth of Adams' feeling is further expressed in a letter to Richard Rush: "In what terms can I address you? There are none that can express my sympathy with you and your family, or my own personal feelings on the loss of your excellent father. There is not another person, out of my own family, who can die, in whom my personal happiness can be so deeply affected. The world would pronounce me extravagant and no man would apologize for me if I should say that in the estimation of unprejudiced philosophy, he has done more good in this world than Franklin or Washington."[11]

Mrs. Adams was equally moved and she wrote her daughter of the death of "our ancient friend, our physician, the constant correspondent and endearing companion; the benevolent, learned, and ever to be regretted Rush. It is indeed a heavy stroke to your father. . . . A friend of so many years ripening, whom no changes had warped, who had passed together with him through many political conflicts, in the most perilous times, is a loss not to be repaired."[12] Thomas Jefferson wrote John Adams: "Another of our friends of seventy-six is gone, my dear Sir, another of the co-signers of the Independence of our country. And a better man than Rush could not have left us, more benevolent, more learned, of finer genius, or more honest."[13]

"Since the death of Washington and Hamilton, whose virtue and greatness had been the boast of their fellow citizens and whose lives shed a lustre on the age which gave them birth, no instance of mortality has occurred in the United States to awaken so extensively the public sensibility as the death of Dr. Rush," was the editorial comment of Joseph Dennie in his magazine, *The Portfolio*. "Having long been at the head of the first school of medicine in our country, distinguished both at home and abroad as one of the ablest medical writers of the age, and conspicuous for the services he had rendered as a practitioner, no less than for his public spirit and benevolence as a man, he had an equal hold on the pride, the affections and the hopes of his fellow citizens."[14] Equally laudatory was editor Delaplaine's comment: "Considered in relation to the entire compass of his character—as a practitioner, a teacher, a philosopher, and a writer, Dr. Rush must be acknowledged to have been the most distinguished physician that America has produced. In no quarter of the globe has it fallen to the lot of many individuals to occupy so extensive a sphere, and to comply with duties so numerous and diversified, in the public and private, the literary and practical departments of medicine." Discussing Rush's personal qualities the article went on: "He was temperate in his diet, neat in his dress, sociable in his habits, and a well bred gentleman in his intercourse with the world. In colloquial powers he had few equals, and no one, perhaps, could be held his superior. His conversation was an Attic repast, which, far from cloying, invigorated the appetites of those who partook of it. Yet none could enjoy it without being conscious of intellectual refreshment—so ample were his resources, and so felicitous his talent for the communication of knowledge."[15]

A lengthy elegiac poem on the death of Rush appeared in 1813 and was a glowing tribute to the great physician. A poet, who was too modest to sign his name to his verse, exclaimed:

> Lamented Rush! when free from anxious fears,
> I marked thy merit in the prime of years;
> Thy energetic mind, thy fond desire
> Science to court, whose Promethean fire
> Broods o'er the gloom of ignorance and night,
> And warms to new existence and delight!
>
> .   .   .   .   .
>
> He scorned opposing crowds, and meekly wise
> Pursued research with microscopic eyes;
> Determined truth by every mean to try,
> Where others dared not gaze 'twas his to fly;
> He rescued truth from mad opinion's maze,
> And caught from science her inspiring rays;
> Beamed o'er the healing art a radiant light,
> Like orient phosphor o'er the mists of night!

Of Rush's work in the War for Independence, the poet sang:

> Boldly he sprung to aid his country's cause,
> To guard her sacred rights and equal laws;
> His deep conceptions and his nervous pen
> Were both employed to assert the rights of men.

And on the epidemic of 1793, he wrote:

> Bold to repel his fury Rush was seen,
> With mind determined and undaunted mien:
> That mild philanthrophy which marked his way,
> Beamed with new splendour on that fatal day![16]

Rush was undoubtedly the most conspicuous character in the medical profession in eighteenth-century America, raising his profession to a higher level than it had ever attained before. He was a pioneer in his field and often a bold experimenter. In 1887 S. Weir Mitchell, eminent physician and litterateur, called Rush "the greatest physician this country has produced," and "a sanitarian far in advance of his day."

Rush was to the University of Pennsylvania what Cullen was to Edinburgh and Boerhaave to Leyden. His account of the yellow fever epidemic of 1793 won for him international fame. He was the most striking and impressive figure in the medical life of the country in his time, and yet his very strength of character caused him to make many enemies. His was a restless soul; he was impatient and impulsive, and his quick and unequivocal decisions frequently led him to unfair judgments of men and things. He was often intolerant of the views of others, holding fast to his own opinions, dogmatic, pugnacious, and impatient of contradiction, sometimes wrong-headed as well as strong-headed. His shortcomings must, however, be pardoned on the grounds of individualism, for Rush's mind was highly original and, because he was an individualist of the first order, he many times appeared stubborn and conceited. In his controversies with other physicians over the medical theories which he proclaimed, he was not infrequently cocksure and censorious. He could on occasion be hypercritical and caustic.

Although he was domineering as a teacher, nevertheless he was one of the most pleasing and intelligent medical lecturers in the country. He was magnetic in the lecture hall and profoundly influenced the students who studied under him, his lectures and his writings standing as guideposts of medical theory and practice in America for many years. "To him, more than any other man in America," in the uncomplimentary opinion of Colonel P. M. Ashburn of the Army Medical Department, "was due the great vogue of vomits, purging, and especially of bleeding, salivation, and blistering, which blackened the record of medicine and afflicted the sick almost to the time of the Civil War."[17] His work must be judged, of course, in consideration of the status of medicine in 1770 rather than of the findings of medical experimentation in the twentieth century.

Even if he could lay no claim to fame in the history of medicine, he would be hailed for his philanthropic work and social service, as an advocate of slavery abolition, penal reform, and popular education. At times he probably wrote with an eye to publicity, but always he was motivated by the desire to do good for mankind.

Rush also stands out as one of the very few medical writers whose works have attracted the general reader. His style is clear and concise, sometimes moving and exciting, and abounding in classical allusions, apt figures, and poetical references. So interested was the King of Prussia in Rush's account of the yellow fever epidemic that, in 1805, he presented the Doctor with a coronation medal; two years later the Queen of Etruria sent him a gold medal; and in 1811 he received a diamond ring from the Czar of Russia.

Benjamin Rush was a leader in many fields: he was a great physician, a talented teacher, a competent scientist, an able organizer, a felicitous writer, a vigorous social reformer, an earnest philanthropist, a creative scholar, and a devoted patriot.

APPENDIX

Rush Visits His Birthplace

THE following letter to John Adams, written on July 13, 1812, is an account of the Doctor's visit to his birthplace at Byberry nine months before his death:

"My Dear Friend.—Can you bear to read a letter that has nothing in it about politics or war? I will, without waiting for an answer to this question, trespass upon your patience, by writing to you upon another subject.

"I was called on Saturday last to visit a patient about nine miles from Philadelphia. Being a holiday I took my youngest son with me, instead of my black servant. After visiting my patient, I recollected I was within three or four miles of the farm on which I was born, and where my ancestors for several generations had lived and died. The day being cool and pleasant, I directed my son to continue our course to it. In approaching, I was agitated in a manner I did not expect. The access was altered, but everything around was nearly the same as in the days of my boyhood, at which time I left it. I introduced myself to the family that lived there, by telling them at once who I was, and my motives for intruding upon them. They received me kindly, and discovered a disposition to satisfy my curiosity and gratify my feelings. I asked permission to conduct my son up stairs, to see the room in which I drew my first breath, and made my first *unwelcome* noise in the world, and where first began the affection and cares of my beloved and excellent mother. This request was readily complied with, and my little boy seemed to enjoy the spot. I next asked for a large cedar tree that stood before the door, which had been planted by my father's hand. Our kind host told me it had been cut down seventeen years ago; and then pointed to a piazza in front of the house, the pillars of which, he said, were made of it. I next inquired for an orchard planted by my father. He conducted me to an eminence behind the house, and shewed me a number of large apple trees, at a little distance, that still bore fruit, to each of which I felt something like the affection of a brother. The building, which is of stone, bears marks of age and decay. On one of the stones near the front door, I discovered with some difficulty the letters J. R. Before the house, flows a small, but deep creek, abounding in pan-fish. The farm consists of ninety acres, all in a highly cultivated state. I knew the owner to be in such easy circumstances, that I did not ask him his price for it; but begged, if he should ever incline to sell it, to make me or one of my surviving sons the first offer, which he promised to do.

"While I sat in his common room, I looked at its walls, and thought how often they had been made vocal by my ancestors, to conversations about wolves and bears, and snakes, in the first settlement of the farm; afterwards about cows and calves and colts and lambs; and the comparative exploits of reapers and thrashers; and at all times with prayers and praises, and chapters read audibly from the bible; for all who inhabited it of my family were pious people, and chiefly of the sect of quakers and baptists. On my way home I stopped to view a family grave-yard, in which were buried three and part of four successive generations, all of whom were the descendants of Captain John Rush, who, with six sons and three daughters, followed William Penn to Pennsylvania, in the year 1683. He commanded a troop of horse under Oliver Cromwell; and family tradition says he was personally known to him, and much esteemed by him as an active and an enterprising officer. When I first settled in Philadelphia, I was sometimes visited by one of his grandsons, a man of eighty-five years of age, who had lived with him when a boy, and who often detailed anecdotes from him of the battles in which he had fought under Cromwell, and once mentioned an encomium on his character by Cromwell, when he supposed him to be killed. The late General Darke of Virginia and General James Irvine, are a part of his numerous posterity; as the successor to the eldest sons of the family, I have been permitted to possess his sword, his watch, and the leaf of his family bible that contains the record of his marriage, and of the birth and names of his children, by his own hand. In walking over the grave-yard, I met with a headstone, with the following inscription:

" 'In memory of James Rush, who departed this life March 16th, 1727, aged forty-eight years.

> " 'I've tried the strength of death, at length,
>   And here lie under ground,
>   But I shall rise, above the skies,
>   When the last trump shall sound.'

This James Rush was my grandfather. My son, the physician, was named after him. I have often heard him spoken of as a strong-minded man, and uncommonly ingenious in his business, which was that of gunsmith. The farm still bears marks of his boring machine. My father inherited both his trade and his farm. While standing near his grave, and recollecting how much of my kindred dust surrounded it, my thoughts became confused, and it was some time before I could arrange them. Had any or all of my ancestors appeared before me, in their homespun or working dresses, (for they were all farmers or mechanics), they would probably have looked at one another, and said, 'What means that gentleman by thus intruding upon us?'

"Dear and venerable friends! be not offended at me. I inherit your blood, and I bear the name of most of you. I come here to claim affinity with you, and to do homage to your Christian and moral virtues. It is true, my dress indicates that I move in a different sphere from that in which you have passed through life; but I have acquired and received nothing from the world which I prize so highly as the religious principles which I inherited from you, and I possess nothing that I value so much as the innocence and purity of your characters.

"Upon my return to my family in the evening, I gave them a history of the events of the day, to which they listened with great pleasure; and partook, at the same time, of some cherries, from the limb of a large tree, (supposed to have been planted by my father), which my little son brought home with him.

"Mr. Pope says there are seldom more than two or three persons in the world who are sincerely afflicted at our death beyond the limits of our own family. It is, I believe, equally true, that there are seldom more than two or three persons in the world who are interested in anything a man says of himself beyond the circle of his own table or fireside. I have flattered myself that you are one of those two or three persons to whom the simple narrative and reflections contained in this letter will not be unacceptable from, my dear and excellent friend, your affectionately,

BENJAMIN RUSH"

"To John Adams, Esq."

NOTES

Notes

CHAPTER I

1. *Pennsylvania Gazette*, December 24, 1745.
2. *Ibid.*
3. W. D. Staughton, *An Eulogium in Memory of the late Dr. Benjamin Rush*, 6.
4. For complete genealogy see L. A. Biddle, ed., *A Memorial . . . of Dr. Benjamin Rush.*
5. The Julian calendar, established in the time of Julius Caesar, was superseded in 1582 by the Gregorian calendar, promulgated by Pope Gregory XIII. Unlike the other Western European nations, England refused to adopt the Pope's reform, and by the eighteenth century, there was an error of eleven days. It was not until 1752 that Parliament caused the change to be made.
6. Joseph C. Martindale, *A History of the Townships of Byberry and Moreland*, 228.
7. Rush, Correspondence, XXXIV, 81.
8. L. A. Biddle, *op. cit.*, 10–11.
9. Rush, Correspondence, XXXIX, 8, June 27, 1765.
10. L. A. Biddle, *op. cit.*, 17.
11. *Ibid.*, 19. It was in 1778, after he had resigned in disgust from the Army medical department that Rush again thought about turning to law.
12. *Memoir of the Life and Character of Redman.*
13. MS., Stan V. Henkels catalog, No. 1452, Rush to Enoch Green, 1761.
14. Rush, Correspondence, XXXIX, 7, May 21, 1765.
15. G. W. Norris, *History of Medicine in Philadelphia*, 37–38.
16. Rush, Correspondence, XXXIX, 7, Rush to Ebenezer Hazard, Philadelphia, May 21, 1765.
17. *Ibid.*, 12, Philadelphia, November 8, 1765.
18. L. A. Biddle, *op. cit.*, 125–27.

CHAPTER II

1. T. P. James, *Memorial of Thomas Potts*, 172–74.
2. MS., Historical Society of Penna., Gratz Collection.
3. Rush, *Essays, Literary, Moral*, 330–31.
4. L. A. Biddle, ed., *Memorial*, 30–31.
5. Francis R. Packard, *Medicine in Philadelphia in the Eighteenth Century.* Transactions of the College of Physicians of Philadelphia, 1931, 172–73.
6. L. A. Biddle, *op. cit.*, 30.
7. Rush, Correspondence, XXII, 10, 11.
8. J. C. Lettsom, *Recollections of Dr. Rush*, 4.
9. David Ramsay, *Eulogium upon Benjamin Rush*, 16.
10. L. A. Biddle, *op. cit.*, 24–26.

11. *Ibid.*, 31–33, 38.
12. Rush, Correspondence, XXXIX, 24, Rush to Ebenezer Hazard, London, October 24, 1768.
13. L. A. Biddle, *op. cit.*, 35.
14. *Ibid.*, 49.
15. MS., J. Pierpont Morgan Library, Rush, Account of a Journey to Paris.
16. L. A. Biddle, *op. cit.*, 44.
17. MS., Rush, Account of a Journey to Paris.
18. Rush visited John Wilkes in the Newgate prison, London.
19. L. A. Biddle, *op. cit.*, 45.
20. *Ibid.*, 52.

CHAPTER III

1. *Pennsylvania Gazette*, January 19, 1769.
2. *Ibid.*
3. *Ibid.*, February 16, 1769.
4. *Pennsylvania Packet*, March 16, 1772.
5. *Ibid.*, April 26, 1773.
6. *Ibid.*, January 2, 1775.
7. *Ibid.*, April 22, 1776.
8. George B. Wood, *History of the University of Pennsylvania*, 27.
9. F. R. Packard, *History of Medicine in the United States*, 206–07.
10. Rush, Correspondence, XXIV, 54, Cullen to John Morgan, September 18, 1768.
11. F. R. Packard, *op. cit.*, 207.
12. Rush, Correspondence, XXII, 11.
13. Scharf and Westcott, *History of Philadelphia*, II, 1589.
14. Joseph Carson, *History of the Medical Department of the University of Pennsylvania*, 74.
15. F. R. Packard, *op. cit.*, 208.
16. Joseph Toner, *Annals of Medical Progress*, 99.
17. L. A. Biddle, ed., *Memorial*, 53–54.
18. *Ibid.*, 58.
19. *Ibid.*, 55.
20. Rush, *Medical Inquiries and Observations* (ed. 1805), IV, 366–80.
21. *Ibid.*
22. L. A. Biddle, *op. cit.*, 56–57.
23. *Ibid.*, 56.
24. *Pennsylvania Packet*, July 20, 1772.
25. *Ibid.*, August 2, 1773.
26. *Ibid.*, December 12, 1774.
27. Anne H. Wharton, *Salons, Colonial and Republican*, 15–24.
28. Extracts from the Journal of Sarah Eve.
29. L. A. Biddle, *op. cit.*, 85–86.
30. *Pennsylvania Packet*, January 15, 1776.
31. MS., Rush, Notebook, Letters and Thoughts, 13.
32. L. A. Biddle, *op. cit.*, 128.

CHAPTER IV

1. Charles Francis Adams, ed., *The Works of John Adams*, II, 357.
2. L. A. Biddle, ed., *Memorial*, 81–82.
3. MS., Speech at Carpenter's Hall, March 16, 1775. MS. in possession of
A. P. Wetherill, University of Pennsylvania.
4. L. A. Biddle, *op. cit.*, 83.
5. MS., Historical Soc. of Penna., Conarroe Papers, I, 27.
6. L. A. Biddle, *op. cit.*, 84–85.
7. Moncure D. Conway, *Life of Thomas Paine*, I, 67.
8. Moses C. Tyler, *Literary History of the American Revolution*, I, 458.
9. *Lee Papers*, I, 325, Lee to Rush, New York, February 25, 1776.
10. John G. Johnson, *Criticism of Mr. Wm. B. Reed's aspersions on the
character of Dr. Benjamin Rush*, 55.
11. Rush, Manuscript notes of debates in the Continental Congress, II, 10,
April 8, 1777.
12. MS., Library of Congress, Morgan Collection of the Signers. Rush to
Dr. Walter Jones, Philadelphia, July 30, 1776.
13. *Journals of Congress*, V, 634, 636, 812, 854; VI, 886.
14. C. F. Adams, *op. cit.*, II, 499–500. A. E. Lipscomb, ed., *Writings of
Thomas Jefferson*, I, 50. *Journals of Congress*, VI, 1081.
15. S. Weir Mitchell, *Historical Notes of Dr. Benjamin Rush*, 4.
16. *Ibid.*, 6–7.
17. *Ibid.*, 10.
18. *Ibid.*, 12.
19. Rupert Hughes, *George Washington*, III, 11.
20. MS., Hist. Soc. of Penna., Wayne MSS., III, 84, 104.
21. L. A. Biddle, *op. cit.*, 93–99.
22. S. Weir Mitchell, *op. cit.*, 21–22.
23. MS., New York Historical Society, Gates Papers, Box 11, No. 57,
Philadelphia, March 1, 1779.
24. MS., Rush, Letters, Facts and Observations upon a variety of subjects,
33–37. Rush to Dr. David Ramsay, Philadelphia, November 6, 1778.
25. *Lee Papers*, 236–37, Lee to Rush, September 1778.
26. *Pennsylvania Packet*, February 26; March 2, 1785.
27. *Ibid.*, November 18, 1780; November 15, 1781.
28. MS., Rush, Letters and Thoughts, 10, Rush to Lady Jane Belschers.
April 21, 1784.
29. C. F. Adams, *op. cit.*, VII, 214–15.
30. *Pennsylvania Packet*, June 27, 1780.
31. MS., New York Historical Society, Gates Papers, Box 16, Nos. 41 and
67, Rush to Gates, June 12, 1781; September 5, 1781.
32. MS., J. Pierpont Morgan Library, Rush to ——, Philadelphia, October
30, 1781.
33. *Pennsylvania Packet*, September 5, 1782.
34. Rush, *Considerations upon the present Test-Law of Pennsylvania*, 4–17.
35. *Price Letters*, Mass. Hist. Soc. Proceedings (1903), Second series, XVII,
341, Rush to Richard Price, April 22, 1786.

36. *Ibid.*, 352–54, Rush to Richard Price, October 27, 1786.

37. Charles Warren, *Making of the Constitution*, 270–71.

38. *Price Letters*, Mass. Hist. Soc. Proceedings (1903), Second series, XVII, 367–69, Rush to Richard Price, June 2, 1787.

39. MS., Mass. Hist. Soc., Pickering Papers, Rush to Timothy Pickering, August 30, 1787.

40. J. B. McMaster and F. D. Stone, *Pennsylvania and the Federal Constitution*, 149–50.

41. *Ibid.*, 214–15.

42. *Ibid.*, 294–95.

43. *Ibid.*, 299–300.

44. *Belknap Papers*, Mass. Hist. Soc. Collections, Series 6, IV, 397–98, Rush to Jeremy Belknap, Phila., February 28, 1788.

45. MS., Rush, Letters and Thoughts, 81.

CHAPTER V

1. Louis C. Duncan, *Medical Men in the American Revolution*, 7–8.

2. MS., Library of Congress.

3. Louis C. Duncan, *op. cit.*, 16–17.

4. Rush, *Medical Inquiries and Observations* (ed. 1805), I.

5. *Ibid.*, I, 269–78.

6. James Tilton, *Economical Observations on Military Hospitals*, 13.

7. "Surgeon Waldo's Diary," *American Historical Magazine*, V, 131.

8. Paul L. Ford, "Dr. Rush and General Washington," *Atlantic Monthly*, May 1895.

9. *Ibid.*

10. *Ibid.*

11. MS., Rush, Letters, Facts, and Observations, 1, 4.

12. MS., Library of Congress, Rush to William Duer, Princeton, December 8, 1777.

13. *Ibid.*, Rush to William Duer, December 13, 1777.

14. Rush, *Directions for Preserving the Health of Soldiers; Recommended to the Consideration of the Officers of the Army of the United States.*

15. MS., Library of Congress, Washington to Rush, Valley Forge, January 12, 1778.

16. Rush, Correspondence, XXIX, 120c, Rush to Mrs. Rush, Yorktown, January 15, 1778.

17. Edmund C. Burnett, ed. *Letters of the Members of the Continental Congress*, III, 59, John Witherspoon to William C. Houston, York Town, January 27, 1778.

18. MS., Hist. Soc. of Penna., Conarroe Papers, I, 27, Rush to James Searle, Esq., January 29, 1778.

19. A. Biddle, ed., *Old Family Letters*, 11–12, John Adams to Rush, February 8, 1778.

20. MS., Library of Congress, Papers of the Continental Congress.

21. Rush, Correspondence, XLIII, 46, John Witherspoon to Rush, Yorktown, February 2, 1778.

22. MS., Stan V. Henkels catalog No. 1183, Richard Peters to Robert Morris, February 3, 1778.

23. Rush, Correspondence, XXIX, 119, Rush to Dr. John Morgan, n.d.

24. MS., New York Historical Society, Gates Papers, Box 9, No. 31.

25. MS., Library of Congress, Papers of the Continental Congress, Rush to George Washington, Princetown, February 25, 1778.

26. W. C. Ford, ed., *Writings of George Washington*, VI, 438, Washington to the President of Congress, Valley Forge, March 21, 1778.

27. Rush, Correspondence, XLIII, 47, Congressional Committee to Rush, Yorktown, April 7, 1778.

28. MS., Library of Congress, Papers of the Continental Congress, Rush to the Congressional Committee, April 20, 1778.

29. L. A. Biddle, ed., *Memorial*, 100–01.

30. Louis C. Duncan, *op. cit.*, 294.

31. *Ibid.*, 298.

32. *Pennsylvania Packet*, December 23, 1780.

CHAPTER VI

1. MS., Rush, Manuscript notes of debates in the Continental Congress, II, 14.

2. MS., Library of Congress, Rush to Washington, Philadelphia, August 30, 1777.

3. S. Weir Mitchell, *Historical Notes of Dr. Benjamin Rush*, 18.

3a. *Atlantic Monthly*, May, 1895.

4. *Ibid.*

5. *Ibid.*

6. W. C. Ford, ed., *Writings of George Washington*, VI, 453.

7. MS., Rush, Letters, Facts, and Observations, 29–32; 37.

8. *Lee Papers*, Coll. New York Historical Soc., 1873, 370–75, Lee to Rush, September 26, 1779.

9. A. Biddle, ed., *Old Family Letters*, 73–74; 87, John Adams to Rush, August 23, 1805; December 4, 1805.

10. MS., Rush, Letters and Thoughts, 14–15.

11. George Washington, *Diaries*, III, 229.

12. MS., Library of Congress, Washington Papers.

13. MS., Hist. Soc. of Penna., Gratz Collection, Rush to Gen. Washington, Philadelphia, April 26, 1788.

14. Rush, Correspondence, XXIX, 129, 131, 132, 133.

15. Charles Thomson was secretary of the Continental Congress from its beginning to its end.

16. Rush, Correspondence, XXIX, 136.

CHAPTER VII

1. L. A. Biddle, ed., *Memorial*, 62 *seq.*

2. Joseph Carson, *History of the Medical Department of the University of Pennsylvania*, 97–98. Rush, *Six Introductory Lectures*, 8–9.

3. Harriet W. Warner, ed., *Autobiography of Charles Caldwell*, 116, 119.

4. David Ramsay, *Eulogium*, 128.

5. Thomas G. Morton, *History of the Pennsylvania Hospital*, 451.

6. Rush, Correspondence, XXV, 42, Thomas E. Bond to Rush, Philadelphia, March 12, 1804.

7. David Ramsay, *op. cit.*, 19.

8. MS., Hist. Soc. of Penna., Logan Papers, XIII, 111.

9. Rush, Correspondence, XI, 122, A. M. Lane to Rush, October 4, 1791.

10. MS., Rush, Letters, Facts, and Observations, 205–08.

11. Wyndham B. Blanton, *Medicine in Virginia in the Eighteenth Century*, 83.

12. David Ramsay, *op. cit.*, 9.

13. Rush, *Sixteen Introductory Lectures*, 171–72.

14. *Ibid.*, 114.

15. *Ibid.*, 9–18.

16. *Ibid.*, 295–317.

17. Robert Hare (1781–1858) was a distinguished scientist, member of the faculty of the University of Pennsylvania, and co-inventor of the oxyhydrogen blowpipe.

18. MS., Edgar Fahs Smith Collection, University of Pennsylvania.

19. Rush, *Sixteen Introductory Lectures*, 232–55.

20. MS., Rush, Practice of Physic, I, 1–2, University of Pennsylvania.

21. Rush, *Sixteen Introductory Lectures*, 318–39.

22. David Ramsay, *op. cit.*, 119–21.

23. Wm. Parker and J. P. Cutler, *Life, Journals and Correspondence of Rev. Manasseh Cutler*, 279–80.

24. Rush, Correspondence, XVII, 3, November 30, 1803.

25. J. H. Musser, *Memoranda of the Life and Works of Benjamin Rush*, 4–6.

26. MS., College of Physicians, Rush to Elisha Hall, July 6, 1789.

27. L. A. Biddle, *op. cit.*, 64–73.

28. Henry E. Biddle, ed., *Extracts from the Journal of Elizabeth Drinker*, 263.

29. Rush, Correspondence, VIII, 9.

30. *Ibid.*, I, 7, T. B. Adams to Rush, May 29, 1802.

31. Rush, "Account of Martin's cancer powder," *American Museum*, I, 37–40.

32. MS., College of Physicians, Rush to Dr. Elisha Hall, July 6, 1789.

33. Anderson Galleries catalog, May 18, 1926, Rush to Dr. Josephus B. Stuart, May 24, 1810.

34. Rush, Correspondence, XI, 95, Rev. John M. Crery to Rush, March 4, 1793.

35. MS., Hist. Soc. of Penna., Dreer Collection, Rush to Elisha Boudinot, Philadelphia, February 27, 1798.

36. Rush, Correspondence, I, 8, 9, William Adamson to Rush, June 7, 1804; July 23, 1804.

37. MS., Hist. Soc. of Penna., Society Collection, Rush to Elizabeth Micklin, July 24, 1812; January 2, 1813.

38. Rush, Correspondence, III, 8, John W. Campbell to Rush, Petersburg, Virginia, January 8, 1808.

39. Charles F. Heartman catalog, June 29, 1926, Rush to David Howell, Phila., April 27, 1804.

40. MS., Massachusetts Hist. Soc., Timothy Pickering Papers, XLIII, 208, Rush to Timothy Pickering, November 19, 1808.

41. Rush, Correspondence, I, 11.

42. *Ibid.*, I, 32, 33, 37, 39; VI, 11, 13, 20.

43. *Ibid.*, I, 132.

44. MS., Massachusetts Hist. Soc., Shattuck Papers, March 1, 1809.

45. Collection of Captain F. L. Pleadwell, Rush to Rev. Dr. Green, April 26, 1803.

46. Rush, *Sixteen Introductory Lectures*, 182–209.

47. *Pennsylvania Packet*, February 8, 1786.

48. MS., Massachusetts Hist. Soc., Belknap Papers, I, 364, Rush to Rev. Jeremy Belknap, Philadelphia, July 15, 1788.

49. Thomas J. Pettigrew, *Memoirs of the Life and Writings of the Late John C. Lettsom*, I, 186–87.

50. L. A. Biddle, *op. cit.*, 70.

51. Rush, *Sixteen Introductory Lectures*, 210–31.

52. *Alumni Register*, Univ. of Penna., 1902–3, 65, Rush to Dr. Petrikin, Philadelphia, April 21, 1812.

CHAPTER VIII

1. *Pennsylvania Packet*, January 1, 1790.

2. Elizabeth Drinker, *Journal*, 183.

3. MS., Massachusetts Hist. Soc., Belknap Papers, II, 60, Rush to Jeremy Belknap, March 2, 1791.

4. *Belknap Papers*, Mass. Hist. Soc. Col., Series 6, IV, 487–89, April 5, 1791.

5. L. A. Biddle, ed., *Memorial*, 133–35.

6. *Ibid.*, 141.

7. Rush, *An Account of the Bilious Yellow Fever*, 13–14.

8. Rush, *Medical Inquiries and Observations* (ed. 1805), I, 115–33.

9. Rush, "Enquiry into the causes of the increase of bilious and remitting fevers in Pennsylvania," *American Museum*, 1787, I, 130–33.

10. Noah Webster, *Pestilential Diseases*, I, 300–01.

11. Rush, *Account of Bilious Yellow Fever*, 8–11.

12. A. Biddle, ed., *Old Family Letters relating to the Yellow Fever*, 3–8.

13. *American Daily Advertiser*, August 24, 1793.

14. Rush, Correspondence, XXXV, 2.

15. Rush, *Account of Bilious Yellow Fever*, 36–70.

16. Mathew Carey, *A Short Account of the Malignant Fever*, 22–24.

17. *American Daily Advertiser*, August 27, 1793.

18. A. Biddle, ed., *Old Family Letters relating to the Yellow Fever*, 7, Rush to Julia Rush, August 26, 1793.

19. Rush, *Account of Bilious Yellow Fever*, 84. Mathew Carey, *Short Account*, 30–31.

20. Rush, *Account of Bilious Yellow Fever*, 193–203.

21. Rush, Correspondence, XXXVIII, 21, September 1, 1793.

22. A. Biddle, ed., *Old Family Letters relating to the Yellow Fever*, 9.

23. Rush, *Account of Bilious Yellow Fever*, 123–25.

24. Rush, Correspondence, XXXVIII, 12, 28, 50, 55, 77, 100.

25. MS., College of Physicians, Samuel Coates to Joseph Paschall, September 25, 1793.

26. Rush, *Account of Bilious Yellow Fever*, 93–98.

27. *Ibid.*, 99–110.

28. *Ibid.*, 123.

29. MS., Hist. Soc. of Penna., Society Collection.

30. Mathew Carey, *Short Account*, 32–33.

31. A. Biddle, ed., *Old Family Letters relating to the Yellow Fever*, 31, September 18, 1793.

32. MS., Hist. Soc. of Penna., Society Collection, Rush to Elias Boudinot, September 25, 1793.

33. Rush, *Account of Bilious Yellow Fever*, 113–22.

34. MS., Hist. Soc. of Penna., Society Collection.

35. *Minutes of the Proceedings of the Committee of Citizens*, 79–80.

36. MS., Hist. Soc. of Penna., Society Collection.

37. A. Biddle, ed., *Old Family Letters relating to the Yellow Fever*, 15–57.

38. Rush, *Account of Bilious Yellow Fever*, 346.

39. *Ibid.*, 315.

40. *Ibid.*, 141.

41. MS., Hist. Soc. of Penna., Gratz Collection, Case 7, Box 33.

42. Rush, *Account of Bilious Yellow Fever*, 147–58.

43. Rush, *An Enquiry Into the Origin of the Late Epidemic Fever*. Rush, Correspondence, XXXVIII, 43, Answers to queries relating to the yellow fever.

44. William Currie, *An Impartial Review*. Mathew Carey, *Short Account*, 14–20.

45. Jean Deveze, *An Enquiry*, 12–50.

46. Rush, *Account of Bilious Yellow Fever*, 145–46.

47. MS., Hist. Soc. of Penna., Etting Papers of the Signers, 86.

CHAPTER IX

1. MS., New York Hist. Soc., Gates Papers, Box 17, No. 239, Philadelphia, March 23, 1794.

2. Rush, *Medical Inquiries and Observations*, IV, 1–24.

3. *Ibid.*, 55–56.

4. MS., Hist. Soc. of Penna., Dreer Collection, Rush to John Redman Coxe, September 19, 1794. MS., Yale University Library, Daggett Papers, Rush to David Daggett, September 17, 1794.

5. Rush, *Medical Inquiries and Observations*, IV, 24–41.

6. Rush, Correspondence, XXIII, 69. MS., Yale University Library, Daggett Papers, Rush to Daggett, September 17, 1794.

7. Rush, *Medical Inquiries and Observations*, IV, 83–84.

8. MS., Hist. Soc. of Penna., Dreer Collection, Rush to John Redman Coxe.

9. Rush, *Medical Inquiries and Observations*, IV, 59.

10. *Ibid.*, III, 437–43.

11. MS., New York Hist. Soc., Gates Papers, Rush to Gen. Gates, Philadelphia, December 26, 1795.

12. MS., Princeton University Library, Rush to Samuel Bayard, September 22, 1796.

13. L. A. Biddle, ed., *Memorial*, 154–55.

14. Rush, *Medical Inquiries and Observations*, IV, 1–14.

15. *Ibid.*, IV, 28.

16. *Ibid.*, 14–32.

17. *Ibid.*, 33.

18. *Proofs of the Origin of Yellow Fever in Philadelphia and Kensington*, 1–10.

19. *Ibid.*, 33–43.

20. *Ibid.*, 47–49.

21. *Ibid.*, 42.

22. MS., Hist. Soc. of Penna., Logan Papers, X, 10.

23. Rush, Correspondence, XXV, 24. This letter to Dr. Rodgers is undated, but was probably written in late September, 1797.

24. *Ibid.*, XXV, 25, John R. B. Rodgers to Rush, New York, October 17, 1797.

25. *Ibid.*, XXV, 27, New York, October 20, 1797.

26. *Ibid.*, XXV, 23, New York, November 4, 1797.

27. *Ibid.*, XXV, 22, Rush to Rodgers, November 6, 1797.

28. L. A. Biddle, *op. cit.*, 73.

29. *Ibid.*, 149.

30. O. Pickering and C. W. Upham, *Life of Timothy Pickering*, III, 457.

31. *Ibid.*, III, 458.

32. Rush, Correspondence, XXIX, 48.

33. *Gazette of the United States*, September 18, 1797.

34. Scharf and Westcott, *History of Philadelphia*, I, 498–99.

35. T. Carpenter, *A Report of An Action for a Libel*.

36. *Ibid.*

37. *Ibid.*

38. Rush, Correspondence, XXIX, 88, Brockholst Livingston to Rush, New York, July 15, 1801.

39. Peter Porcupine (William Cobbett): *The Rush Light*, February 15, 1800.

40. Rush, *Medical Inquiries and Observations*, IV, 65–77.

41. Wm. Currie, *Memoirs of the Yellow Fever*, 11–13.

42. *Ibid.*, 20–23.

43. MS., Princeton University Library.

44. Rush, *Medical Inquiries and Observations*, IV, 88.

45. MS., Mass. Hist. Soc., Papers of Timothy Pickering, XXV, 189, Rush to Pickering, September 24, 1799.

46. MS., Library of Congress, Philadelphia, Novemb[r] 20, 1801.

47. Rush, *Medical Inquiries and Observations*, IV, 123–142.

48. Rush, Correspondence, XXVII, 101, Edward Miller to Rush, New York, November 30, 1802.

49. T. J. Pettigrew, ed. *Selections from the Medical Papers and Correspondence of the late John Coakley Lettsom*, 195–99, Rush to Lettsom, October 13, 1803, and May 13, 1804.

50. Rush, *Medical Inquiries and Observations*, IV, 226–67.

51. Percy M. Ashburn, *History of the Medical Department of the U.S. Army*, 278. Joseph McFarland, "The Epidemic of Yellow Fever in Philadelphia," *Medical Life*, XXXVI, 449–96.

CHAPTER X

1. J. C. Lettsom, *Recollections of Dr. Rush*, 16.

2. Rush, *Medical Inquiries and Observations* (ed. 1796), IV, 122–78; (ed. 1805), III, 16–37.

3. For contemporary criticism of Rush's theory of fever see: J. T. Rees, *Remarks on the Medical Theories of Brown, Cullen, Darwin, & Rush*, 67 seq., John Mace, *The Proximate Cause of Disease*, 57–62.

4. Rush, Correspondence, I, 26; I, 114; XI, 76. Ashton Alexander to Rush, August 29, 1797; Robert H. Archer to Rush, 1797; John McClelland to Rush, July 30, 1798.

5. Rush, *Six Introductory Lectures*, 149, 153–55. Rush, *Medical Inquiries and Observations* (ed. 1796), I, 151. David Ramsay, *Eulogium*, 20–21.

6. Rush, *Account of Bilious Yellow Fever*, 93.

7. Rush, *Medical Inquiries and Observations* (3rd ed.), 351. Ralph H. Major, *Classic Descriptions of Disease*. In 1912 Frank Billings called attention, for the first time, to the importance of focal infection as a cause of arthritis and nephritis, and attempted to prove experimentally that bacteria, isolated from these foci of infection, would, when injected into animals, reproduce the lesions. Billings, therefore, verified by more complete clinical observations the suggestions made by Rush. See Frank Billings, "Chronic infections and their etiologic relations to arthritis and nephritis," *Archives of Internal Medicine*, IX (1912), 484.

8. Alwin J. Scheuer, catalog No. 6, 1931, No. 2646, Rush to ——, February 15, 1802.

9. *American Daily Advertiser*, April 19, 1803.

10. Rush, *Medical Inquiries and Observations* (ed. 1805), IV, 163–68.

11. *Ibid.*, I, 247–66.

12. *Ibid.*, II, 337–49.

13. *Ibid.*, II, 227–93.

14. *Ibid.*, II, 149.

15. *Ibid.*, I, 199–214. Henry F. Stoll, "Benjamin Rush as a Phthisiotherapist," *The Medical Record*, February 8, 1908.

16. MS., College of Physicians, Rush to Dr. John McCleland, Franklin County, Pa., April 2, 1797. Rush, Letters to Dr. John Redman Coxe, August 12, 1795.

17. Rush, *Medical Inquiries and Observations* (ed. 1805), III, 163–218. An

inquiry into the various sources of the usual forms of summer & autumnal disease in the United States, and the means of preventing them.

18. *Ibid.*, 426–46.

19. Rush, *Six Introductory Lectures*, 65–80.

20. Rush, *Medical Inquiries and Observations* (ed. 1796), IV, 183–234.

21. Rush, Correspondence, I, 69, William Allston to Rush, Georgetown, S.C., July 25, 1806.

22. Rush, *Medical Inquiries and Observations* (ed. 1805), IV, 380–98.

23. Rush, *Six Introductory Lectures*, 156–68.

CHAPTER XI

1. Thomas G. Morton, *History of the Pennsylvania Hospital*, 143–44.

2. L. A. Biddle, ed., *Memorial*, 133.

3. Thomas G. Morton, *op. cit.*, 144.

4. *Ibid.*, 149–50.

5. Rush, Correspondence, XXXI, 52, Rush to the managers of the Pennsylvania Hospital, December 26, 1812.

6. Frank Woodbury, "Benjamin Rush, Patriot, Physician and Psychiator," *Transactions of the American Medico-Psychological Association*, XX, 427–30.

7. MS., Hist. Soc. of Penna., Dreer Collection, Rush to John Redman Coxe, October 5, 1795; January 16, 1796; April 28, 1796.

8. Rush, *Medical Inquiries and Observations Upon the Diseases of the Mind*, 17–18.

9. *Ibid.*, 18–28.

10. *Ibid.*, 30–36.

11. *Ibid.*, 36–47.

12. *Ibid.*, 47–71.

13. *Ibid.*, 74–75.

14. *Ibid.*, 98–105.

15. *Ibid.*, 106–27.

16. *Ibid.*, 142–46; 175–84.

17. *Ibid.*, 184–212.

18. *Ibid.*, 216–32.

19. *Ibid.*, 248–57.

20. *Ibid.*, 314–17.

CHAPTER XII

1. David Ramsay, *Eulogium*, 126.

2. T. J. Pettigrew, *Memoirs of Lettsom*, II, 435–37, Rush to J. C. Lettsom, August 16, 1788.

3. W. S. W. Ruschenberger, *An Account of the Institution and Progress of the College of Philadelphia*, 23, 183–84.

4. *Belknap Papers*, Mass. Hist. Soc. Collections, Series 6, IV, 403–04, Rush to Jeremy Belknap, Philadelphia, May 6, 1788.

5. *Ibid.*, 416–18, Rush to Jeremy Belknap, August 19, 1788.

6. Rush, "Observations on the Federal Procession," *American Museum*, IV, 77.

7. *Belknap Papers*, Mass. Hist. Soc. Collections, Series 6, IV, 468–69, Rush to Jeremy Belknap, Philadelphia, August 25, 1790.

8. *Ibid.*, 473.

9. MS., Hist. Soc. of Penna., Logan Papers, XIII, 102, Rush to John Dickinson, April 5, 1787.

10. MS., Mass. Hist. Soc., Belknap Papers, II, 26, Rush to Jeremy Belknap, October 13, 1789.

11. L. A. Biddle, ed., *Memorial*, 152.

12. Rush, Correspondence, XXI, 7, September 16, 1800.

13. Rush, *Essays, Literary and Moral*, 125–35.

14. MS., Mass. Hist. Soc., Belknap Papers, II, 10, Rush to Jeremy Belknap, May 16, 1789.

15. Rush, *Essays, Literary and Moral*, 114–24.

16. *Ibid.*, 183–88.

17. *American Museum*, V, 488–89, October 1789.

18. Rush, *Essays, Literary and Moral*, 275–94.

19. MS., Hist. Soc. of Penna., Phila. Misc. Papers, Box 76.

20. Rush, *Essays, Literary, Moral*, 257–62.

21. *Ibid.*, 213–25.

22. *Ibid.*, 226–48.

23. Rush, *Life of Christopher Ludwick*, 6.

CHAPTER XIII

1. L. A. Biddle, ed., *Memorial*, 138.

2. Rush, Letters and Observations, 33.

3. Rush, Correspondence, XXVIII, 106. Granville Sharp to Rush, London, n.d.

4. L. A. Biddle, *op. cit.*, 146.

5. *Pennsylvania Mercury*, May 25, 1787.

6. David Ramsay, *Eulogium*, 114.

7. Morris Jastrow, "Documents Relating to the Career of Col. Isaac Franks." *Publications of the American Jewish Historical Society*, V, 7–34.

8. Rush, Correspondence, XXXII, 80. Directions for Benjamin Young.

9. *Ibid.*, 90. Rush to Wm. Cooper, Philadelphia, Sept. 12, 1789.

10. Library of Congress. Photostats: American Letters and Documents, 1652–1845.

11. Rush, Correspondence, XXX, 56.

12. Rush, Manuscript Notes of Debates in the Continental Congress, III. Rush, Correspondence, XXXII, 110; VII, 115.

13. Rush, Correspondence, XVII, 63. Andrew Tulloh to Benj. Rush, August 3, 1797.

14. *Ibid.*, 69.

15. *Ibid.*, 68, 70, 72.

16. *Ibid.*, XI, 83. Robert McClure to Benj. Rush, Williamsport, May 16, 1803.

17. *Ibid.*, XIV, 97. Wm. Roberts to Benj. Rush, Cambria, September 10, 1801.

18. *Ibid.*, V, 48. James G. Fisher to Benj. Rush, February 15, 1809.

19. *Ibid.*, X, 42; XXVI, 73.

20. MS., Collection of Benjamin Rush, Kirkland, Pa.

21. MS., Princeton University Library.

CHAPTER XIV

1. Rush, Correspondence, XLI, 60. Rush to John Montgomery, March 9, 1784.

2. *Proceedings of the Massachusetts Historical Society, 1903*, 341–42. April 22, 1786.

3. *American Museum*, I, No. 1, 9–13.

4. *Ibid.*, IV, November 1788, 442–44.

5. Rush, *Essays, Literary, Moral*, 75–92.

6. *Pennsylvania Packet*, March 19, 21; April 9, 1787.

7. Rush, *Essays, Literary, Moral*, 57–73.

8. *Ibid.*, 21–56.

9. A. Biddle, ed., *Old Family Letters*, 54. John Adams to Rush, New York, February 2, 1790.

10. MS., Collection of Benjamin Rush, Rush to Julia Stockton, September 7, 1788.

11. MS., Massachusetts Historical Soc., Belknap Papers, II, 26, 56. October 13, 1789, November 12, 1790.

12. J. B. McMaster, *History of the People of the United States*, II, 83.

13. *American Daily Advertiser*, March 25, 1791.

14. L. A. Biddle, ed., *Memorial*, 193.

15. MS., Collection of Benjamin Rush, Rush to ———, May 22, 1807.

CHAPTER XV

1. *Pennsylvania Packet*, February 17, 1785.

2. Rush, Correspondence, XLI, various letters.

3. *Ibid.*, 1. Hints for establishing a college.

4. *Ibid.*, 2, 6. November 13, 1782.

5. *Ibid.*, 93. The same charge was made by George Bryan, another political leader.

6. *Ibid.*, 20. Rush to General Armstrong, March 19, 1783.

7. *Ibid.*, 6.

8. *Ibid.*, 13, 26, 28.

9. *Ibid.*, 20.

10. *Ibid.*, 21. Rush to Montgomery, May 3, 1783.

11. *Ibid.*, XLI, 27. Montgomery to Rush, April 16, 1783.

12. *Ibid.*, 29. Rush to Montgomery, May 3, 1783.

13. *Ibid.*, 4.

14. *Ibid.*, 38.

15. Mitchell and Flanders, comp., *Statutes-at-Large of Pennsylvania*, XI, 114.

16. Charles F. Himes, *A Sketch of Dickinson College*, 9, 34.

17. Rush, Correspondence, XLI, 40.

18. *Ibid.*, 54. John King to Rush, January 12, 1784.

19. *Ibid.*, 57. Rush to Montgomery, February 17, 1789.

20. *Ibid.*, 60. Rush to Montgomery, March 4, 1784.

21. *Ibid.*, XXVI, 88. William Linn to Rush, September 13, 1784.

22. Mitchell and Flanders, comp., *Statutes-at-Large*, XII, 221–25.

23. *Ibid.*, XIII, 132.

24. *Ibid.*, XIII, 276–82.

25. *Ibid.*, XIV, 123, 282.

26. Charles F. Himes, *op. cit.*, 50.

27. Rush, Correspondence, XLI, 54.

28. *Ibid.*, 65.

29. *Ibid.*, 88.

30. *Ibid.*, 94. Dickinson to Nisbet, October 25, 1784.

31. *Ibid.*, 95.

32. *Ibid.*, 98. Dickinson to Nisbet, November 15, 1784 (copy).

33. *Ibid.*, 126.

34. *Ibid.*, 136. Nisbet to Rush, July 18, 1785.

35. *Ibid.*, 145. Nisbet to Rush, September 4, 1785.

36. MS., Historical Society of Penna., Logan Papers, XIII, 102, April 5, 1787.

37. *American Daily Advertiser*, August 10, 1791.

38. Rush, Correspondence, XLII, 95. Nisbet to Rush, November 12, 1803.

39. *Ibid.*, 72. October 16, 1797.

40. L. A. Biddle, ed., *Memorial*, 179–80.

41. MS., Hist. Soc. of Penna., Conarroe Papers, I, 42, Rush to Rev. Dr. Robert Davidson, Philadelphia, August 20, 1808.

42. MS., Princeton University Collection, Rush to Rev. Dr. Samuel Miller, Philadelphia, July 21, 1808.

43. *Ibid.*, Rush to Miller, Philadelphia, July 5, 1808.

44. *Ibid.*, Rush to Miller, Philadelphia, October 8, 1808.

45. Rush, Correspondence, XXVII, 130.

46. L. A. Biddle, *op. cit.*, 200.

47. *Ibid.*, 200.

48. Rush, Correspondence, XXIX, 138. December 26, 1811.

49. *Ibid.*, XLII, 64.

CHAPTER XVI

1. L. A. Biddle, ed., *Memorial*, 202, 212.

2. A. E. Lipscomb, ed., *Writings of Thomas Jefferson*, X, 379–85. Thomas Jefferson to Benj. Rush, Washington, April 21, 1803.

3. L. A. Biddle, *op. cit.*, 216.

4. *Ibid.*, 133–215.

5. B. C. Steiner, *Life and Correspondence of James McHenry*, 464. Rush to James McHenry, August 12, 1800.

6. See David Ramsay, *Eulogium*, 101. Rush to Dr. Finley, March 4, 1813.

7. William Staughton, *Eulogium*, 12. L. A. Biddle, *op. cit.*, 130a. William Pepper, "Benjamin Rush," *Journal of the American Medical Association* (1890), 13–14. James Rush, Correspondence, I, 1.

8. See L. A. Biddle, *op. cit.*, 130b.

9. MS., New York Academy of Medicine. David Hosack to James Rush, April 26, 1813; David Hosack to Mrs. Rush, May 10, 1813.

10. MS., Collection of Benjamin Rush, E. Gerry to Richard Rush, April 8, 1814.

11. MS., Historical Soc. of Penna., Gratz Collection, Case 1, Box 3, John Adams to Richard Rush, Quincy, May 5, 1813.

12. See K. M. Roof, *Colonel William Smith and Lady*, 314.

13. A. E. Lipscomb, *op. cit.*, XIII, 246. Jefferson to Adams, May 27, 1813.

14. *Portfolio*, October 1813.

15. Delaplaine, *Repository*, I, 27, 43.

16. Historical Society of Pennsylvania.

17. P. M. Ashburn, *History of the Medical Department of the United States Army*, 19.

BIBLIOGRAPHY

Bibliography

I. MANUSCRIPT SOURCES

Ridgway Library. This branch of the Library Company of Philadelphia, founded by Dr. James Rush, son of Benjamin Rush, boasts the largest and most important collection of Rushiana. Most of Benjamin Rush's published works are on the shelves; and his correspondence, more than 5,700 documents, is preserved here in forty-three stout volumes. Although this correspondence, dealing largely with medical matters, covers Rush's entire life, there are few papers dating before 1770. One finds scores of letters from physicians and patients asking for medical advice. Volumes VII, XIV, XVII, XX, and XXXII contain miscellaneous letters and papers dealing with land speculation. Letters relating to Rush's intention of moving to New York in 1797 are to be found in volume XXV. Volume XXIX contains many of the papers pertaining to the charges against Dr. Shippen and the suit against Cobbett. Family letters are found in volumes XXXIII and XXXIV. Letters, statistics, and documents on the yellow fever epidemics, totaling 360 pieces, have been collected in volumes XXXV, XXXVI, XXXVII, and XXXVIII. The papers in volumes XLI and XLII concern Dickinson College. The papers in this entire collection are referred to as "Rush, Correspondence."

The following Rush notebooks are also in the stacks of the Ridgway Library:

Manuscript Notes of Debates in the Continental Congress. 224 pp.

These three small notebooks contain Rush's diary in late 1777 and early 1778, and miscellaneous memoranda on medicine, land deals, and financial matters.

Quack Recipe Book. 126 pp.

A collection of remedies picked up by Rush from friends and quacks.

Letters, Facts and Observations Upon a Variety of Subjects. 214 pp.

An important notebook containing essays, several important letters of the Revolutionary period, conversations with Benjamin Franklin, and a list of Rush's medical apprentices from 1770 to 1812. A hundred pages of this book, covering the men and events of the War for Independence, were destroyed by Rush in a rash moment. It is possible that these pages contained a wealth of material on Rush's controversy with Dr. Shippen and General Washington.

Letters and Thoughts. 184 pp.

A few short essays, letters, and comments on passing events.

Notebook. 170 pp.

Notes on medical subjects, lecture outlines, and anecdotes.

College of Physicians of Philadelphia. The medical library of this institution is second only to the Surgeon-General's in Washington in size. It owns many Rush letters and papers, some of which are not catalogued. The College of Physicians has been fortunate in obtaining possession of the original manuscripts of Rush's Lectures Upon the Mind, covering 954 pages; the lectures on the Practice of Medicine; on Pathology; and A Course of Lectures on the Theory and Practice of Chemistry.

Historical Society of Pennsylvania. The library of this Society owns approximately 100 Rush letters and miscellaneous papers in the Dreer, Society, Gratz, and Sprague collections; the Logan, Wayne, Conarroe, Cadwalader, Irvine, Wallace and Etting Papers; and the Wilson and Norris MSS. The Dreer Collection includes Rush's original MS report to the Governor on the yellow fever epidemic of 1797.

Library of Congress. In the Washington Papers and the Papers of the Continental Congress are several Rush letters concerning the condition of the military hospitals during the War for Independence. The correspondence of Edward and Joseph Shippen, and Dr. Jonathan Potts also contains scattered references on this subject. This library owns the manuscript of the essay "On the Influence of Physical Causes on the Moral Faculty."

Massachusetts Historical Society. Many interesting letters to and from Rush are to be found in the Papers of Timothy Pickering, one of the Doctor's close friends. Letters concerning his fight against strong liquors and tobacco are in the Jeremy Belknap Papers. This library also owns the Papers of George Cheyne Shattuck, who studied under Rush in 1807.

J. Pierpont Morgan Library. In addition to several Rush letters on a variety of subjects, this library owns the manuscript of Rush's Account of A Journey to Paris, February 16 to March 27, 1769, thirty-two pages. Only recently was it discovered that this manuscript, originally credited to James Beekman, was from Rush's pen.

New York Academy of Medicine. The notebook of Rush's friend, Dr. David Hosack, contains several letters written by him to Rush.

New York Historical Society. Several letters written by General Horatio Gates to Rush are preserved in the Gates Papers.

New York Public Library. A volume of transcripts, comprising letters to Rush from John Dickinson, Charles Lee, Anthony Wayne, 1775–1813, contains some important material on the Revolutionary period. This library owns the best collection of the various editions of Rush's pamphlets on temperance.

Pennsylvania Hospital. A few letters written by Rush and dealing with hospital matters are preserved in the museum.

Princeton University Library. Several deeds, and the letters requesting Dr.

Samuel Miller to become President of Dickinson College, are to be found in this collection.

Benjamin Rush Collection, Kirkland, Pa. The Rush family own several miscellaneous letters and papers of their distinguished ancestor, and the manuscript notebook of Rush's lectures on physiology.

Surgeon-General's Library. In addition to a few Rush papers, this library owns the manuscript of Thomas Drysdale's Account of the Yellow Fever of 1794 As It Appeared at Baltimore, in A Series of Letters to Benjamin Rush.

University of Pennsylvania Library. Here one finds two important manuscript notebooks: Rush's lectures on the Practice of Physic, in two volumes, and his lectures on Chemistry and the Theory and Practice of Medicine.

Notes on Rush's Lectures, Taken by His Students. Manuscript Notebooks

Alison, Robert: Notes. 197 pp. 1771 (College of Physicians)
Anonymous: Chemistry. 404 pp. 1783–84 (Univ. of Penna.)
Archer, Benj.: Notes. 2 vols. 170 pp. 1804 (College of Physicians)
Bartram, Moses: Chemistry and the Theory and Practice of Medicine. 2 vols. (Univ. of Penna.)
Clark, M. Jr.: Physiology. 1809–11 (College of Physicians)
Dallam, William: Practice of Physic. 184 pp. 1798 (Wm. Pepper's Collection)
Darlington, Wm.: Institutes and Practice of Medicine, 2 vols. 1802–04 (College of Physicians)
Gordon, J. H.: Notes. 232 pp. (Princeton Univ.)
Griffiths, Elijah: Notes. 1797–98 (College of Physicians)
James, Thomas C.: Practice of Physic. 178 pp. 1786 (College of Physicians)
Kuhl, Marcus: Notes. 205 pp. (Surgeon-General's Library)
Lee, George: Pathology, Therapeutics, and the Practice of Physic. 226 pp. (Surgeon-General's Library)
Lowber, Edward: Notes. 1803–04 (Library of Congress)
Martin, William: Notes. 1793 (Hist. Soc. of Penna.)
Maxwell, Robert: Notes. 1807–08 (Edgar Fahs Smith Collection)
Mitchell, Thos. D.: Notes. 2 vols. 652 pp. 1809–11 (College of Physicians)
Shippen, J. G.: Practice of Physic. 412 pp. 1809 (College of Physicians)
Shippen, Jos. G.: Practice of Medicine. 820 pp. 1810 (College of Physicians)
Simonton, William: Notes. 4 vols. 1791 (Univ. of Penna.)
Smith, Elisha H.: Theory and Practice of Medicine. 1790–91 (Surgeon-General's Library)
Spangler, Jno.: Notes. 2 vols. 555 pp. 1790–91 (Univ. of Penna.)
Suffield, Appolos King de: Medical Lectures. 2 vols. 593 pp. (N. Y. Historical Society)

II. CONTEMPORARY NEWSPAPERS

Philadelphia newspapers:

American Daily Advertiser (Dunlap's): 1791–95.

American Daily Advertiser (Claypoole's): 1796–1800.

American Daily Advertiser (Poulson's): 1800–13.

Gazette of the United States, and Philadelphia Daily Advertiser (Fenno's).

In September and October, 1797, the Gazette devoted considerable space to attacks on Rush's treatment of yellow fever patients.

Independent Gazetteer, or, the Chronicle of Freedom.

The Pennsylvania Gazette: 1745–69.

The Pennsylvania Packet, or The General Advertiser: 1771–90.

This newspaper was issued three times weekly, but in 1784 it became the first daily newspaper in America.

Porcupine's Gazette: 1797–1800.

William Cobbett's newspaper, in which Rush's medical theories and practice were bitterly attacked.

III. RUSH'S PUBLISHED WRITINGS

Account of a Curious Sermon.

A letter to the *Columbian Magazine* about a sermon Rush heard in the South.

An account of Dr. Hugh Martin's cancer powder, with brief observations on cancers. *American Museum*, I, No. 1, January 1787, 37–40.

An analysis of an arsenic powder, read before the American Philosophical Society, February 3, 1786.

An account of the bilious remitting yellow fever, as it appeared in the city of Philadelphia, in the year 1793. Phila. 1794. 363 pp.

The best narrative of the epidemic of 1793. Rush discusses the symptoms of the disease, weather conditions, his remedies and controversies over them. There are some excellent descriptive paragraphs.

An account of the climate of Pennsylvania. Phila. 1789.

An account of the causes and indications of longevity, and of the state of the body and mind in old age; with observations on its diseases, and their remedies. New York. 1872. 12 pp.

This essay was first printed in Philadelphia in 1793.

An account of the diseases peculiar to the negroes in the West-Indies, and which are produced by their slavery. *American Museum*, IV, 81–82, July 1788.

An account of the late Dr. John Morgan, delivered before the trustees and students of medicine in the College of Philadelphia, on the 2nd of November, 1789. *Columbian Magazine*, November, 1789, 353–54.

An account of the life and character of Christopher Ludwick, late citizen of Philadelphia, and Baker-General of the Army of the United States during the Revolutionary war. Phila. 1801. 31 pp.

Account of the manners of the German inhabitants of Pennsylvania. Phila. 1875. 72 pp. This paper was written in 1789. This particular edition was edited by I. Daniel Rupp. A revised edition appeared in Lancaster in 1910.

An account of the state of the body and mind in old age; with observations on its diseases, and their remedies. In Sir John Sinclair's The code of health and longevity, Edinburgh, 1807. IV, 514–31

Account of the sugar maple-tree of the United States. Phila. 1792. 16 pp.
A survey of the methods of obtaining sugar from the trees, and of the advantages of maple sugar.

An address delivered at the commencement held in the College of Philadelphia, on the 15th of December, 1790, previously to the examination of the theses, and the conferring of the degrees of doctor of medicine. *American Museum*, VII, 256–58, December 1790.
A brief discussion of the system of medical education in Philadelphia and of the value of medical theses.

An address to the inhabitants of the British settlements in America, upon slave-keeping. Phila. 1773. 30 pp.
A summary of the arguments against slavery, written to accompany a petition to the Legislature of Pennsylvania asking for an increase in the duty on negro slaves. A forceful piece of propaganda.

Address to the people of the United States. *American Museum*, I, No. 1, 9–13, January 1787.
A vigorous essay, presenting one of the earliest proposals for a federal or national university.

The benefits of charity, a dream. *Columbian Magazine*, August 1787, 578–81.
An appeal for free schools in Philadelphia.

Beschreibung des gelben fiebers welches in Jahre 1793, in Philadelphia herschte. Tubingen. 1796. 472 pp.
An early German translation of Rush's account of the epidemic of 1793. Translated by P. Fr. Hopfengartner and J. F. H. Autenrieth.

Bible in schools. n.p. n.d. 8 pp.
Tract No. 231 of the American Tract Society.

A charge, delivered in the University of Pennsylvania, to the graduates in medicine, April 19, 1810. 7 pp.
Advises the young physicians to be punctual and to develop the notebook habit.

Considerations on the injustice and impolicy of punishing murder by death. Phila. 1792. 19 pp.
Another edition was printed in London in 1793.

Considerations upon the present Test-Law of Pennsylvania: addressed to the Legislature and Freeman of the State. Phila. 1784. 23 pp.
An able propaganda essay, seeking repeal of an objectionable law.

Description of the entertainment given by the Minister, on the account of the birth of the Dauphin of France. Phila. 1782. 4 pp.
A detailed account of the elaborate affair held in Philadelphia, July 15, 1782.

Directions for conducting a newspaper in such a manner as to make it innocent, useful, and entertaining. *American Museum*, IV, 488–89, May 1789. Signed "A Friend to the Union."

Directions for preserving the health of soldiers: recommended to the consideration of the officers of the army of the United States. Published by order of the Board of War. Phila. 1778. 14 pp.
An important series of recommendations, first published in No. 284 of the Pennsylvania Packet.
This pamphlet was reprinted by the Massachusetts Temperance Alliance in Boston, in 1865, for distribution to the Union soldiers.

Directions for the use of the mineral water and cold bath at Harrogate, near Philadelphia. Phila. 1786. 12 pp.
A short, specific set of directions.

Dissertatio physica inauguralis, de coctione ciborum in ventriculo. Edinburgh, 1768. 30 pp.
This is Rush's dissertation for the M.D. degree at Edinburgh.

The drunkards emblem, or an enquiry into the effects of ardent spirits upon the human body and mind with an account of the means of preventing, and of the remedies for curing them. Phila. 1804. 44 pp.

An enquiry into the causes of the increase of bilious and remitting fevers in Pennsylvania, with hints for preventing them. *American Museum*, I, 130–33, 1787.
Read before the American Philosophical Society, December 16, 1785.

An enquiry into the effects of public punishments upon criminals and upon society. Phila. 1787. 18 pp.
Read at Benjamin Franklin's home before the Society for Promoting Political Enquiries, March 9, 1781.
A modern view of the subject.

An enquiry into the effects of spirituous liquors upon the human body, and their influence upon the happiness of society. Phila. n.d. 2nd ed. 16 pp.
Reasons against spirituous liquors, and suggested substitutes.

An enquiry into the methods of preventing the painful and fatal effects of cold upon the human body. *Columbian Magazine*, 1787, 427–31.
Some of the suggestions are applicable today.

An enquiry into the natural history of medicine among the Indians. Phila. [1774] 118 pp.

An enquiry into the origin of the late epidemic fever in Philadelphia: in a letter to Dr. John Redman, President of the College of Physicians. Phila. 1793. 15 pp.
A defense of the domestic origin of the fever.

An enquiry into the relation of tastes and aliments to each other; and into the influence of this relation upon health and pleasure. *American Museum*, V, 559–62, 1789.

An enquiry into the utility of a knowledge of the Latin and Greek languages as a branch of liberal education with hints of a plan of liberal instruction without them, accomodated to the present state of social manners, and government in the United States. *American Museum*, V, 525–35, June 1789. Signed "By a citizen of Philadelphia."

Essays, literary, moral & philosophical. Phila. 1798. 378 pp.
A collection of twenty-five non-medical essays on a variety of subjects. Many of these chapters had already appeared in magazines.
A second edition of this volume appeared in 1806 with an additional essay, on premature deaths.

An eulogium in honor of the late Dr. William Cullen, Professor of the Practice of Physic in the University of Edinburgh. Phila. 1790. 30 pp.
Delivered before the College of Physicians, July 9, 1790.

An eulogium intended to perpetuate the memory of David Rittenhouse, late President of the American Philosophical Society. Phila. 1796. 46 pp.
Delivered before the Philosophical Society, December 17, 1796.

An eulogium upon the Reverend Gilbert Tennent. Phila. 1764.

Excerpts from the papers of Dr. Benjamin Rush. *Penna. Magazine of History and Biography*, XXIX, 15–30, January 1905.
Taken from the notebooks in the Ridgway Library.

Experiments and observations on the mineral waters of Philadelphia, Abington, and Bristol. Phila. 1773. 30 pp.
Read before the American Philosophical Society, June 18, 1773.
Analyzes the waters and outlines their use in the treatment of disease.

Extract of a letter from Dr. Benjamin Rush of Philadelphia, to Granville Sharp. London. 1792. 8 pp.
Asks for funds for a negro church about to be erected in Philadelphia.

Free thoughts upon the cause and cure of the pulmonary consumption. *American Museum*, V, 247–49; 368–70; 1789.

An inquiry into the effects of ardent spirits upon the human body and mind.
4th ed. Phila. 50 pp.
Other editions were issued in Boston (1790), Edinburgh (1810), New York (1811), Boston (1812), Philadelphia (1818), and Boston (1823).

An inquiry into the functions of the spleen, liver, pancreas, and thyroid gland.
Phila. 1806. 29 pp.
Rush's own copy with marginal notes is in the Ridgway Library.

An inquiry into the influence of physical causes upon the moral faculty. Phila.
1839. 28 pp.

An inquiry into the various sources of summer & autumnal disease in the United States, and the means of preventing them. To which are added facts, intended to prove the yellow fever not to be contagious. Phila.
1805. 113 pp.

Medical inquiries and observations.
This important work was first published in two volumes in 1789 and 1793. It was later enlarged by the addition of two volumes. The Account of the Yellow Fever epidemic of 1793, is the third volume (1794). The fourth volume appeared in 1796. In the preface to the 1796 edition Rush hinted that he was planning to write on the diseases of the mind. The second revised edition was published in four volumes in 1805, a third edition in 1809, a fourth in 1815 and a fifth in 1819. Phila. 1789–1819.

Medical inquiries and observations upon the diseases of the mind. Phila. 1812.
367 pp.
The first book on mental diseases published in this country. It was used in the medical schools for a half century. A second edition was published in 1818, a third in 1827, a fourth in 1830, and a fifth in 1835.

Medizinische untersuchungen und beobachtungen uber die seelen-krankheiten.
Leipzig. 1825. 298 pp.
A German translation of Rush's great work on diseases of the mind, translated by Georg Konig.

Memoir of the life and character of John Redman, M.D. 7 pp. Printed in the Medical and Philosophical Register.

The new method of inoculating for the smallpox. Phila. 1781. 28 pp.
A University of Pennsylvania lecture. Gives full directions. Philadelphians were inoculated for smallpox for the first time in 1730. A second edition of this lecture was published in 1789 and a third in 1792.

Observations on the duties of a physician, and the methods of improving medicine. Accomodated to the present state of society and manners in the United States. Phila. 1789. 11 pp.
Charitable in tone. A University of Pennsylvania lecture.

Observations on the Federal procession on the Fourth of July, 1788, in the city of Philadelphia; in a letter from a gentleman in this city to his friend in a neighbouring State. *American Museum*, IV, 75–78, 1788. The democratic nature of the celebration appealed to Rush.

Observations upon the origin of the malignant bilious, or yellow fever in Philadelphia, and upon the means of preventing it: addressed to the citizens of Philadelphia. Phila. 1799. 28 pp.

Observations upon the present government of Pennsylvania in four letters to the people of Pennsylvania. Phila. 1777. 24 pp.
A careful paper based on the authorities in political science.

On the different species of mania. Phila. 6 pp.

On the different species of phobia. Phila. 4 pp.
Shows Rush's keen sense of observation.

On the effects of ardent spirits. Phila. n.d. 8 pp.
Tract No. 7 of the Tract Association of Friends.

On the objects of their institution. Transactions of the College of Physicians, I, pt. I, 1793.
This address, on the means of promoting the science of medicine, was the first paper read before the College of Physicians when it opened in 1787.

An oration delivered February 4, 1774, before the American Philosophical Society, held at Philadelphia. Containing an enquiry into the natural history of medicine among the Indians in North America, and a comparative view of their diseases and remedies, with those of civilized nations. Phila. 1774. 118 pp.
Contains much information on the diseases of the colonists as well as the Indians, and interesting comments on medical and related subjects.

An oration delivered before the American Philosophical Society, held in Philadelphia on the 27th of February, 1786; containing an enquiry into the influence of physical causes upon the moral faculty. Phila. 1786. 40 pp.
A workmanlike, erudite essay and an important contribution. This essay attracted considerable attention.

A plan for the establishment of public schools and the diffusion of knowledge in Pennsylvania; to which are added, thoughts upon the mode of education proper in a republic. Addressed to the Legislature and Citizens of the State. Phila. 1786. 36 pp.

Plan of a federal university. *Federal Gazette*, October 29, 1788.
Suggests a post-graduate training school for government employees.

Recherches sur les functions de la rate, etc. Geneve, 1807. 143 pp.

Relacion de la calentura biliosa, remitente amarilla, que se manifesto en Filadelfia en el ano de 1793. 2 vols. Madrid. 1804. 416 pp.
A Spanish translation of Rush's account of the epidemic of 1793.

Remarks upon the hydrophobia. *Eclectic Repertory*, III, No. 3, 1813.

A second address to the citizens of Philadelphia containing additional proofs
of the domestic origin of the malignant bilious, or yellow fever. To
which are added, observations, intended to shew that a belief in that
opinion is calculated to lessen the mortality of the disease, and to prevent its recurrence. Phila. 1799. 40 pp.
This is really an abridgment of previous publications on the subject "as
to be intelligible to persons who have not studied medicine."

Sermons to gentlemen upon temperance and exercise. Phila. 1772. 44 pp.
A paper of especial interest in our own times when diet and athletics are
receiving considerable attention. Some of the paragraphs are delightfully
written.

Six introductory lectures to courses of lectures upon the institutes and practice
of medicine, delivered in the University of Pennsylvania. Phila. 1801.
168 pp.
Thoughtful, frank, stimulating talks.

Sixteen introductory lectures, to courses of lectures upon the institutes and
practice of medicine, with a syllabus of the latter. To which are added
two lectures upon the pleasures of the senses and of the mind with an
inquiry into their proximate cause. Phila. 1811. 455 pp.
A fascinating series of lectures, interesting to laymen as well as to physicians.

A speech delivered by Dr. Benjamin Rush, March 16, 1775, in Carpenters'
Hall, before the subscribers towards a fund for establishing manufac-
tories of woolen, cotton, and linen, in the city of Philadelphia. *American
Museum*, V, 581–84, 1789.
Rush strongly urged the development of American industries.

A syllabus of a course of lectures on chemistry. Phila. 1770. Reissued in 1773.
39 pp.
The first chemistry text-book written by an American and for many years
the only such text-book available in this country.

A syllabus of a course of lectures on the institutes and practice of medicine.
Phila. 1798. 19 pp.
Outline of the topics of Rush's lectures on physiology, pathology, and
therapeutics.

Syllabus of lectures, containing the application of the principles of natural
philosophy, and chemistry, to domestic and culinary purposes. Composed
for the use of the Young Ladies Academy in Philadelphia. Phila. 1787.
6 pp.

Thoughts on paper money. Phila. n.d.
An argument for specie instead of paper money, signed "Nestor."

Thoughts upon female education accomodated to the present state of society, manners, and government in the United States of America. Addressed to the visitors of the Young Ladies Academy in Philadelphia, July 28, 1787. Phila. 1787. 32 pp.
A liberal viewpoint.

Thoughts upon the amusements and punishments which are proper for schools. Addressed to George Clymer, Esq. Phila. 1790. 8 pp.

Three letters addressed to the public. Phila. 1783. 28 pp.
Rush is said to have written these letters on the nature of the federal union, the civil and military powers, and the public debt. Signed "Tullius."

Three lectures upon animal life, delivered in the University of Pennsylvania. Phila. 1799. 84 pp.
An important volume setting forth Rush's theory of life.

To the citizens of Philadelphia and of the districts of Southwark and the Northern Liberties. *Independent Gazetteer*, March 28, 1787. An appeal for free schools. Unsigned.

Two lectures upon the pleasures and senses of the mind. Phila. 1811.

A vindication of the address, to the inhabitants of the British settlements, on the slavery of the negroes in America, in answer to a pamphlet, entitled, Slavery not forbidden by Scripture, or a defence of the West-India planters from the aspersions thrown out against them by the author of the Address. By a Pennsylvanian. Phila. 1773. 54 pp.
Rush stresses injustice suffered by the negro slaves.

Books edited by Rush:

First lines of the practice of physic, for the use of students in the University of Edinburgh. By William Cullen. Edited by Benj. Rush. Phila. 1781. 2 vols. 384 pp., 184 pp.

Loose remarks on certain positions to be found in Mr. Hobbes' philosophical rudiments of government and society with a short sketch of a democratical form of government in a letter to Signior Paoli by Catherine Macaulay. With two letters one from an American gentleman to the author which contains some comments on her sketch of the democratical form of government and the author's answer. London. 1769.
Rush's letter is really an introduction to the volume.

Observations on the changes of the air and the concomitant epidemical diseases in the Islands of Barbadoes. To which is added, a treatise on the putrid bilious fever, commonly called the yellow fever; and such other diseases as are indigenous or endemial, in the West India Islands, or in the torrid zone. By William Hillary. With notes by Benj. Rush. Phila. 1811. 260 pp.
Rush's notes are helpful and suggestive.

Observations on the Diseases of the army. By Sir John Pringle. With notes by Benj. Rush. Phila. 1810. 411 pp.
Pringle was one of George III's physicians.
Observations on the epidemical diseases of Minorca from the year 1744 to 1749. By George Cleghorn. With notes by Benj. Rush. 2nd. American ed. Phila. 1812. 184 pp.
Rush says in his preface that this work "contains a greater mass of practical knowledge in a small compass, than any book perhaps of the same kind in medicine."
A treatise on the hidden nature, and the treatment of intermitting and remitting fevers; illustrated by various experiments and observations. By Jean Senac. Translated from the Latin by Charles Caldwell. Recommendatory preface by Benj. Rush. Phila. 1805. 299 pp.
The works of Thomas Sydenham, M.D. on acute and chronic diseases, with their histories and modes of cure. With notes, intended to accomodate them to the present state of medicine, and to the climate and diseases of the United States, by Benj. Rush. Phila. 1815. 513 pp.
Rush edited this work "to revise and enforce" Sydenham's "invaluable truths."

IV. CONTEMPORARY SOURCES

Adams, Charles Francis, ed. The works of John Adams, 10 vols. Boston. 1856.

Albers, I. A. Americanische annalen der arzneykunde, naturgeschichte, chemie und physic. Bremen. 1803. 210 pp.
Contains a review of Rush's *Six Introductory Lectures.*

Allen, James, Esq. Diary.
Penna. Magazine of History and Biography, IX, 278.

Alumni Register, Univ. of Penna., 1902–03, VII, 65.
Letter written by Rush to Dr. Petrikin in 1812 on competition in the medical profession.

American letters and documents, 1652–1845. Library of Congress. Photostats of MSS. in Independence Hall, Philadelphia.
Two Rush letters.

Anderson Galleries Catalog. May 18, 1926.
Letter of Rush to Dr. J. B. Stuart on a cancer cure.

Anonymous. Elegiac poem on the death of Benjamin Rush, who fell a victim to the prevailing typhus fevers, on the 19th of April, 1813. Phila. 1813. 32 pp.
A glowing tribute.

Atwater, Jeremiah. An inaugural address delivered at the public commencement of Dickinson College, September 27, 1808. Carlisle. 1809. 23 pp.
A statement of the trustees on the condition of the College is attached.

Ballagh, James C. The letters of Richard Henry Lee. 2 vols. New York. 1912.

Belknap Papers, Part III. Massachusetts Historical Collections. Sixth Series. Vol. IV. Boston. 1891.
Contains many letters written by Rush to Rev. Jeremy Belknap of Boston, between 1788 and 1792.

Biddle, Alexander, ed. Old family letters, copied from the originals. Philadelphia. 1892. 479 pp.
Largely intimate letters from John Adams to Dr. Rush.

Biddle, Alexander, ed. Old family letters relating to the yellow fever. Phila. 1892. 108 pp.
Letters written by Rush to his wife, August 21 to November 12, 1793.

Biddle, Henry E., ed. Extracts from the Journal of Elizabeth Drinker, from 1759 to 1807. Phila. 1889. 423 pp.
The wife of Henry Drinker of the shipping and importing firm of James & Drinker. Excellent descriptive entries during the epidemic of 1793. The Drinkers knew Rush socially and professionally.

Biddle, Louis Alexander, ed. A memorial containing travels through life or sundry incidents in the life of Dr. Benjamin Rush. Written by himself. Also extracts from his commonplace book as well as a short history of the Rush family in Pennsylvania. Lanoraie. 1905. 262 pp.
This important memorial was written in 1800. A most important source.

Bolton, Henry C., ed. Scientific correspondence of Joseph Priestley. New York. 1892. 240 pp.
Priestley was one of Rush's correspondents.

Brown, Samuel. A treatise on the nature, origin and progress of the yellow fever, with observations on its treatment; comprising an account of the disease in several capitals of the United States; but more particularly as it prevailed in Boston. Boston. 1800. 112 pp.
Quotes Rush.

Burnett, Edmund C., ed. Letters of the members of the Continental Congress. 3 vols. Washington. 1921.

Carey, Mathew. A short account of the malignant fever lately prevalent in Philadelphia; with a statement of the proceedings that took place on the subject in different parts of the United States. 3rd edition. Phila. November 30, 1793. 112 pp.
This small book went into several editions in a few months. Carey, a well-known publisher, served for a time as a member of the committee of citizens. He "aimed at telling plain facts in plain language." An engaging account.

Carpenter, T. A report of an action for a libel, brought by Dr. Benjamin Rush, against William Cobbett, in the Supreme Court of Pennsylvania, December term, 1799, for certain defamatory publications in a newspaper

entitled Porcupine's Gazette, of which the said William Cobbett was Editor. Taken in shorthand by T. Carpenter. Phila. 1800.
Contains the Judge's charge to the jury, and the arguments of counsel.

Chalwill, William G. A dissertation on the sources of malignant bilious, or yellow fever, and the means of preventing it. Phila. 1799. 31 pp.
A Univ. of Penna. doctoral dissertation.
Believes "that the effluvia or miasmata, arising from putrefying animal and vegetable substances, are the cause of this disease."

Porcupine, Peter (William Cobbett). The Rush-Light.
A serial pamphlet first issued on February 15, 1800. Four issues in February and March, 1800. New York. 46 pp. 66 pp. 48 pp. 48 pp.
A scathing attack on Rush.

Porcupine, Peter (William Cobbett). The American Rush-Light. London. 1800. 192 pp.
An English edition of the Rush-Light.

College of Physicians. Facts and observations relative to the nature and origin of the pestilential fever, which prevailed in this city, in 1793, 1797, and 1798. Phila. 1798. 52 pp.
The reports of the College to Governor Mifflin. Yellow fever is said to be contagious and imported.

Cresson, Joshua. Meditations written during the prevalence of the yellow fever, in the city of Philadelphia, in the year 1793. London. 1803. 23 pp.
Cresson kept a record during the epidemic until he himself was carried off by the fever.

Currie, William. An impartial review of that part of Dr. Rush's late publication, entitled "An Account of the Bilious Remitting Yellow Fever, as It appeared in the city of Philadelphia, in the year 1793, which treats of the Origin of the Disease." In which his opinion is shown to be erroneous; the importation of the disease established; and the wholesomeness of the city vindicated. Phila. 1794. 15 pp.
Cites arrival of vessels from the West Indies with sick persons on board.

Currie, William. Memoirs of the yellow fever which prevailed in Philadelphia, and other parts of the United States of America, in the summer and autumn of the present year, 1798. Phila. 1798. 145 pp.
Includes tables of weather conditions, daily returns of the sick, dead, etc. and "A collection of facts respecting the origin of the fever."

Currie, William. A sketch of the rise and progress of the yellow fever, and of the proceedings of the Board of Health, in Philadelphia, in the year 1799; to which is added, a collection of facts and observations respecting the origin of the yellow fever in this country; and a review of the different modes of treating it. Phila. 1800. 112 pp.
Says the fever was imported and did not originate from domestic sources.

Deveze, Jean. An enquiry into, and observations upon the cause, and effects of the epidemic disease, which raged in Philadelphia from the month of August till toward the middle of December, 1793. Phila. 1794. 145 pp. English and French texts.
Deveze and Benjamin Duffield were medical directors of the public hospital at Bush-Hill. A vivid account. Disagrees with Rush as to origin and treatment of the fever. A lively account.

Duane, William, ed. Extracts from the diary of Christopher Marshall kept in Philadelphia and Lancaster during the American Revolution, 1774–81. Albany. 1877. 330 pp.

Eve, Sarah. Extracts from the Journal of Sarah Eve, written while living near the city of Philadelphia in 1772–73. Phila. 1881. 31 pp.

Fitzpatrick, John C., ed. The Diaries of George Washington. 4 vols. Boston. 1925.

Ford, Paul Leicester. Dr. Rush and General Washington. *Atlantic Monthly*, May 1895, 633–40.
Ford uses a series of letters from Rush to John Adams to trace the spirit in back of the movement against Washington during the Revolution.

Ford, Worthington C., ed. Journals of the Continental Congress, 1774–89. 18 vols. Washington. 1904–10.

Ford, Worthington C., ed. The writings of George Washington. 14 vols. New York. 1890.

Hosack, David. An introductory discourse to a course of lectures on the theory and practice of physic: containing . . . a tribute to the memory of the late Benjamin Rush. Delivered at the College of Physicians and Surgeons, November 3, 1813. New York. 1813. 35 pp.
Hosack was professor of Theory and Practice in the University of the State of New York.

Jastrow, Morris. Documents relating to the career of Col. Isaac Franks. Publications of the American Jewish Historical Society, No. 5, 1896, 7–34. Rush purchased several tracts of land jointly with Isaac Franks.

Jones, Absalom, and Allen, Richard. A narrative of the proceedings of the black people, during the late awful calamity in Philadelphia, in the year 1793; and a refutation of some censures, thrown upon them in some late publications. Phila. 1794. 28 pp.
A defense of the part played by negroes during the epidemic.

Lee Papers. Collections of the New York Historical Society. New York. 1871–74. Four parts.
Charles Lee was a Major-General and second in command of the Continental Army. These volumes contain letters to and from Rush.

Lipscomb, Andrew E., ed. The writings of Thomas Jefferson. 20 vols. Washington. 1903.

Mace, John. The proximate cause of disease: by induction from the laws of animated nature. With an examination of the theories of Townsend, Reich, Darwin, Rush and Wilson. Phila. 1802. 79 pp.
Mace had a high regard for Rush's "superior talents and dignity" although he disagreed with his theory of the proximate cause of disease.

Maclay, William, The journal of. Introduction by Charles A. Beard. New York. 1927. 429 pp.
A few references to Rush.

Magaw, Samuel. A discourse delivered July 17, 1794 in the African Church of the city of Philadelphia, on the occasion of opening the said church, and holding public worship in it the first time. Phila. 1794. 24 pp.
Magaw was rector of St. Paul's. Rush was deeply interested in the African Church.

Mease, James. Observations on the arguments of Professor Rush, in favour of the inflammatory nature of the disease produced by the bite of a mad dog. Phila. 1801. 62 pp.
Mease rejects Rush's use of bloodletting as a remedy for this disease.

Mease, James. The picture of Philadelphia, giving an account of its origin, increase and improvements in arts, sciences, manufactures, commerce and revenue. Phila. 1811. 358 pp.

Miller, Samuel. A brief retrospect of the eighteenth century. Containing a sketch of the revolutions and improvements in science, arts, and literature during that period. New York. 1803. 2 vols.
A curious, old-fashioned book containing a lengthy section on medicine. Comments on the "intrepidity and benevolence displayed by Dr. Rush," during the epidemic of 1793.

Minutes of the proceedings of the committee appointed on the 14th of September, 1793, by the citizens of Philadelphia, the Northern Liberties, and the District of Southwark, to attend to and alleviate the sufferings of the afflicted with the malignant fever prevalent in the city and its vicinity. Phila. 1848. 243 pp.
The committee met daily and the minutes offer an excellent picture of conditions in the city during the epidemic.

Mitchell, James T. and Flanders, Henry F., compilers. The Statutes-at-Large of Pennsylvania from 1682 to 1801. Harrisburg. 1906.
See vols. XI, XII, XIII, for acts relating to Dickinson College.

Mitchell, Silas Weir. Historical notes of Dr. Benjamin Rush. *Penna. Magazine of History and Biography*, April, 1903.
Taken from notebooks in the Ridgway Library.

Morgan, John. A discourse upon the institution of medical schools in America . . . with a preface containing, amongst other things, the author's apology for attempting to introduce the regular mode of practising physic in Philadelphia. Phila. 1765. 63 pp.

Morgan, John. A vindication of his public character in the station of Direc-

tor-General of the military hospitals, and Physician-in-Chief to the American Army, 1776. Boston. 1777. 158 pp.
Dr. Morgan defends his work, and appends official correspondence in support of his claims.

The New England Journal of Medicine and Surgery, I, No. 1, 81–86. Boston. 1812.
A review of Rush's *Sixteen Introductory Lectures*, concludes: "We believe that few popular works connected with medicine can produce greater interest, or promote more liberal and enlightened views of the profession, than this volume of introductory lectures."

Niles, H. Principles and acts of the Revolution in America: or, an attempt to collect and preserve some of the speeches, orations, & proceedings. . . . Baltimore. 1822. 495 pp.
Contains Rush's "Address to the People of the United States."

Nisbet, Charles. An Address to the Students of Dickinson College, on his re-election to the office of Principal of the said college. Carlisle. 1786. 16 pp.
A sermon on morals, manners, and the duties of a student.

Nisbet, Charles. The usefulness and importance of human learning. A sermon preached before the Trustees of Dickinson College. Met at Carlisle, May 11, 1786. Carlisle. 1796. 32 pp.
Nisbet's educational views.

Ouviere, Felix Pascalis. An account of the contagious yellow fever, which prevailed in Philadelphia in the summer and autumn of 1797, comprising the questions of its causes and domestic origin, characters, medical treatment, and preventives. Phila. 1798. 180 pp.

Parsons, Jacob Cox, ed. Extracts from the Diary of Jacob Hiltzheimer of Philadelphia 1765–98. Phila. 1893. 270 pp.
Betsy Hiltzheimer suffered from yellow fever in 1793 and was treated by Rush.

Pettigrew, Thomas J., ed. Selections from the medical papers and correspondence of the late John Coakley Lettsom. London. 1817. 464 pp.
Contains ten letters written by Rush to Lettsom between 1783 and 1810.

Philadelphia Society for the establishment and support of charity schools. Constitution and Laws of the Philadelphia Society for the Establishment and Support of Charity Schools. Phila. 1860. 85 pp.
Contains Rush's biographical sketch of Christopher Ludwick.

Portfolio, The. II, No. 4, Third Series, October 1813.
Contains a Tribute to the Memory of Dr. Rush.

Price Letters. Massachusetts Historical Society. Proceedings. 1903. Second Series, XVII.
Rev. Dr. Richard Price was a Unitarian minister in England. Contains several letters from Rush to Price on current events, 1786–87.

Proofs of the origin of the yellow fever in Philadelphia & Kensington, in the year 1797, from domestic exhalation; and from the foul air of the Snow Navigation, from Marseilles: and from that of the ship Huldah, from Hamburgh, in two letters addressed to the Governor of the Commonwealth of Pennsylvania, by the Academy of Medicine of Philadelphia. Phila. 1798. 49 pp.
Arguments for and against domestic origin of yellow fever.

Ramsay, David. An eulogium upon Benjamin Rush. Philadelphia. 1813.
Written at the request of the Medical Society of South Carolina. Ramsay knew Rush for thirty-five years.

Redman, John. An account of the yellow fever, as it prevailed in Philadelphia in the autumn of 1762. Phila. 1865. 44 pp.
This paper was presented to the College of Physicians, September 7, 1793. General and detailed account.

Rees, John T. Remarks on the medical theories of Brown, Cullen, Darwin, and Rush. Phila. 1805. 74 pp.
A doctoral dissertation. Discusses Rush's theory of fever.

Sanders, James. Critical remarks on the opinions of Dr. Rush, concerning the uses of the spleen, liver, pancreas and thyroid gland. Edinburgh. 1806. 24 pp.
Sanders was one of the presidents of the Royal Medical Society of Edinburgh.

Smyth, Albert Henry. The writings of Benjamin Franklin. 10 vols. New York. 1905-7.

Staughton, William. An eulogium in memory of the late Dr. Benjamin Rush. Phila. 1813. 32 pp.
Delivered in the Second Presbyterian Church, July 8, 1813.
Staughton was intimately acquainted with Rush for many years.

Thacher, James. A military journal during the American Revolutionary War, from 1775 to 1783; describing interesting events and transactions of this period; with numerous historical facts and anecdotes, from the original manuscript. Second ed. Boston. 1827. 487 pp.
First published in 1823.
Thacher was the first American medical biographer. He was an army surgeon during the War for Independence.

Tilton, James. Economical observations on military hospitals; and the prevention and cure of diseases incident to an army. Wilmington. 1813. 64 pp.
Tilton was a physician and surgeon in the Continental Army.

Warner, Harriet W. Autobiography of Charles Caldwell. Philadelphia. 1855. 454 pp.
Caldwell was one of Rush's students in 1792. Interesting anecdotes about Rush.

Watson, Edward W. A Medical Lecturer of 1804. *International Medical Magazine*, VI, 120–30. Phila. 1897–98.
Abstract of notes taken by Benj. Archer, one of Rush's students in 1802.

Watts, Washington. An inquiry into the causes and nature of the yellow fever. Phila. 1799. 42 pp.
A doctoral dissertation.
An attempt to prove that "the yellow fever possesses none of the essential characters of a strictly contagious disease."

Webster, Noah. A brief history of epidemic and pestilential diseases; with the principal phenomena of the physical world, which precede and accompany them, and observations deduced from the facts stated. 2 vols. Hartford. 1799.
Rush's own copy of this work, with marginal notes, is in the Ridgway Library. An interesting old volume containing many curious facts and statistics.

Yates, William, and Maclean, Charles. A view of the science of life on the principles established in the elements of medicine of the late celebrated John Brown, M.D. with an attempt to correct some important errors in that work. Phila. 1797. 231 pp.
This volume also contains Rush's *Three Lectures Upon Animal Life*.

V. SECONDARY WORKS

Abbe, Robert. Custodianship of the watch and bible of Dr. Benjamin Rush. *Medical Record*, vol. 78, 805–07, 1910.
Abbe's speech before the Practitioners' Society, making S. Weir Mitchell the custodian of the watch and bible.

Abbott, A. C. The development of public health work in Philadelphia. *Univ. of Penna. Medical Bulletin*. September and October, 1909.
The epidemic of 1793 is said to have been "the most devastating outbreak of yellow fever that has ever been seen in a city of the United States."

Alexander, A. Biographical sketches of the founder, and principal alumni of the Log College. Princeton. 1845. 369 pp.
Chapter on Rev. Samuel Finley, Rush's teacher.

American Medical Association. Rush Monument Committee. To the members of the profession of medicine in the United States. 3 pp. n.d.
This circular calls on every physician in the country to contribute one dollar to a fund for a monument of Rush in Washington, D. C.

Ashburn, Percy M. A history of the medical department of the United States Army. Boston. 1929. 448 pp.

Bancroft, George. Joseph Reed, an historical essay. New York. 1867. 64 pp.

Beveridge, Albert L. Life of John Marshall. 4 vols. Boston. 1919–22.
Of the Conway Cabal, Beveridge says: "Gates was its figurehead, Conway its brain, Wilkinson its tool, Rush its amanuensis, and certain members of Congress its accessories before the fact."

Billings, Frank. Chronic focal infections and their etiologic relations to arthritis and nephritis. *Archives of Internal Medicine*, IX, 484. 1912.
A verification of Rush's observations on focal infection.

Blanton, Wyndham B. Medicine in Virginia in the eighteenth century. Richmond. 1931, 449 pp.
An excellent survey.

Brasch, Frederick E. The Royal Society of London and its influence upon scientific thought in the American colonies. *Scientific Monthly*, October and November, 1931, 336–55; 448–69.
A splendid, comprehensive review.

Brown, Charles Brockden. Arthur Mervyn; or Memoirs of the Year 1793. 3 vols. Boston. 1827.
Arthur Mervyn was a country boy who came to Philadelphia penniless. This old-fashioned novel deals with his adventures in the city during the epidemic of 1793. There are some graphic and lurid descriptions of the Philadelphia scene. Important.

Brown, Harvey E. The medical department of the United States Army from 1775 to 1873. Washington. 1873. 314 pp.

Bryan, Wilhelmus B. A history of the National Capital. 2 vols. New York. 1914.

Camac, C. N. B. A modern and his times. *Proceedings of the Charaka Club*, N. Y., III, 131–49, 1910.
A sketch of Rush's life and work. Says that "Rush was a thinker, whose thoughts combined the practical with the imaginative."

Carrier, Lyman. Dr. John Mitchell, naturalist, cartographer, and historian. Annual Report of the American Historical Association, 1918. I, 201–19.
Rush was directly influenced by Mitchell's report on the yellow fever epidemics in Virginia in the 1730's and 1740's in his treatment of the fever in 1793.

Carson, Joseph. A history of the medical department of the University of Pennsylvania. From its foundation in 1765. With sketches of the lives of the deceased professors. Phila. 1869. 227 pp.

Chance, Burton. Benjamin Rush, a summary of an address delivered before the William Pepper Medical Society, December 4, 1903. Phila. 10 pp. Praises Rush as a physician and man of affairs. "As a sanitarian, Rush shines cloudless altogether."

Clarkson, Thomas. The history of the rise, progress and accomplishment of the abolition of the African slave-trade by the British Parliament. 2 vols. London. 1808.
Notes Rush's connection with the first American anti-slavery society.

Clymer, Meredith. Annual address before the society of the Alumni of the Medical Department of the University of Pennsylvania. Phila. 1876. 34 pp. There are many errors of fact in this address.

Cohen, H. M. Benjamin Rush and early American medicine.
Maryland Medical Journal. Baltimore. 1910. LIII, 341–46.

Collins, Thomas L. The Continental Congress at Princeton. Princeton. 1908. 295 pp.
In 1779 Rush hinted that the Federal capital might be moved to Princeton.

Conway, Moncure D. The Life of Thomas Paine with a history of his literary, political and religious career in America, France and England. 2 vols. New York. 1892.
Discusses Rush's connection with Paine's *Common Sense*.

Crooks, George R. Dickinson College. The History of a hundred years. 1883. 21 pp.
Calls Rush the "Father of Dickinson College."

Cummins, Ebenezer H. Biographical Memorial of Dr. Benjamin Rush.
Evangelical Repository. Phila. 1816. I, No. 2.
Brief outline of Rush's achievements.

Cumston, C. G. An introduction to the history of medicine. New York. 1927. 390 pp.

de Forest, Pelouze. Benjamin Rush's directions for preserving the health of soldiers, with a note upon Surgeon Ebenezer Alden.
Military Surgeon, XXII, 182–95.
Alden was one of Rush's medical students.

Delaplaine, Joseph. Delaplaine's repository of the lives and portraits of distinguished American characters. Phila. 1815. 223 pp.
Contains a short chapter on Rush.

The Doctrine of diseases as expounded by Benjamin Rush.
Medical Journal and Record. CXXVI, 572–73; 609–10. 1927.

Dubbs, Joseph H. The Reformed Church in Pennsylvania. Lancaster. 1902. 387 pp.
Indicates that Rush lent his support to Franklin and Marshall College.

Duncan, Louis C. Medical Men in the American Revolution, 1775–83.
Army Medical Bulletin, No. 25. Carlisle. 1931. 414 pp.
Calls Rush "the ablest medical man of his time in America."

Eddy, Richard. Alcohol in history, an account of intemperance in all ages; together with a history of the various methods employed for its removal. New York. 1887.

Eddy, Richard. Benjamin Rush's religious principles. *The Christian Leader*. October 1, 1885.

Egle, Wm. H. The Federal Constitution of 1787. Sketches of the members of the Pennsylvania Convention. *Penna. Magazine of History and Biography*, XI, 262–63.
Brief sketch of Rush.

Evans, George G. Illustrated history of the United States mint. Phila. 1886. 162 pp.

Exercises on the occasion of the dedication of the New Hall of the College of Physicians of Philadelphia. November 10, 11, 1909. n.p. n.d. Many historical references are found in these addresses.

Garrison, Fielding H. An introduction to the history of medicine. Second ed. Phila. 1917. 905 pp.
Refers to Rush as the "ablest clinician of his time."

Gates, Nathaniel. Benjamin Rush. *Grace Hospital Bulletin*, X, No. 2, 1–9. 1926.

Ghent, W. J. The early far west. New York. 1931. 411 pp.
In the spring of 1803, as a preliminary to his expedition to the Pacific, Meriwether Lewis consulted various scientific men in Philadelphia "and apparently learned something about medicine from the eminent Dr. Benjamin Rush."

Gilpin, Henry D. Benjamin Rush. n.p. n.d. 30 pp.

Good, Harry G. Benjamin Rush and his services to American education. Berne. 1918. 283 pp.
A Ph.D. thesis based on sources and carefully compiled.

Graves, Frank P. A history of education. 3 vols. New York. 1917. See especially the chapter on the rise of the common school in America.

Harvey, Thomas W. Benjamin Rush. International Clinics. Phila. 1912. 22nd series. IV, 232–43.
An address read before the Orange Mountain Medical Society.

Himes, Charles F. A sketch of Dickinson College, Carlisle. Harrisburg. 1879. 155 pp.

Hinsdale, G. Contributions to medical and biological research. Dedicated to Sir William Osler by his pupils and co-workers. 2 vols. New York. 1919. Hinsdale's chapter is on the "Epidemics of influenza in 1647, 1789–90, and 1807, as recorded by Noah Webster, Benjamin Rush and Daniel Drake." He notes a "very remarkable parallel between the course of the epidemic of 1789 and 1790 and that of 1918 and 1919. In the account presented to us by Benjamin Rush there are many of the familiar symptoms so noticeable in the last epidemic."

Hodge, Charles. The constitutional history of the Presbyterian Church in the United States of America. 2 vols. Phila. 1840.

Howe, M. A. de Wolfe. The life and letters of George Bancroft. 2 vols. New York. 1908.

Hughes, Rupert. George Washington. 3 vols. New York. 1926–1931. See references to Rush in volumes II and III.

Hunter, Robert J. The activities of members of the American Philosophical Society in the early history of the Philadelphia Almshouse (the Philadelphia General Hospital). *Proceedings of the American Philosophical Society*, LXXI, No. 6, 309–19. 1932.

Hunter, Robert J. The origin of the Philadelphia General Hospital.
Penna. Magazine of History and Biography, LVII, 32–57.
Hunter believes that this institution is older than the Pennsylvania Hospital.

James, Mrs. Thomas Potts. Memorial of Thomas Potts, Junior, who settled in Pennsylvania. Cambridge. 1874. 416 pp.
Jonathan Potts studied medicine with Rush at Edinburgh.

Jenkins, Howard M. Pennsylvania Colonial and Federal. A History, 1608–1903. 3 vols. Phila. 1903.

Johnson, John G. A criticism of Mr. Wm. B. Reed's aspersions on the character of Dr. Benjamin Rush, with an incidental consideration of General Joseph Reed's character. By a member of the Philadelphia Bar. Phila. 1867. 61 pp.
Defends Rush's character.

Journal of Health and Recreation. IV, No. 5, 129–34. New Series. Phila. 1833.
An outline of Rush's work.

Kiernan, James G. The physician as a revolutionist. *Medical Pickwick*, VI, 16–18.
Comment on Rush's life.

Knox, Katharine McC. The Sharples. Their portraits of George Washington and his contemporaries. New Haven. 1930. 133 pp.
James and Ellen Sharples painted several portraits of Rush. There is a pastel portrait in Independence Hall, another in the Bristol, England, Art Gallery, and a head of Rush in the Royal West of England Academy, Bristol.

Konkle, Burton A. Joseph Hopkinson, 1770–1842. Phila. 1931. 361 pp. A chapter is devoted to the Rush-Cobbett trial.

Lambert, Samuel W., and Goodwin, George M. Medical leaders from Hippocrates to Osler. Indianapolis. 1929.

Lettsom, John Coakley. Recollections of Dr. Rush. London. 1815. 16 pp. In this paper Rush was given the title of "The Sydenham of America" perhaps for the first time.

Liggett, Eliza Seaman. Journal. MSS.
Mrs. Liggett's father, Dr. Valentine Seaman, studied under Rush.

Lloyd, James H. Benjamin Rush and his critics. *Annals of Medical History*, II, 470–75. 1931.
A defense of Rush's work, particularly his study of the diseases of the mind.

Longacre, James B. The national portrait gallery of distinguished Americans. 4 vols. Phila. 1836.
Brief note on Rush's life.

Major, Ralph H. Classic descriptions of disease, with biographical sketches of the authors. Springfield. 1932. 630 pp.
Includes Rush's account of focal infection.

Marcy, Henry O. Dr. Benjamin Rush, the pioneer investigator of the effects of alcohol and tobacco on man. *Penna. Medical Journal*, XVI, 513–20.

Martindale, Joseph C. A history of the townships of Byberry and Moreland, in Philadelphia. rev. ed. Phila. n.d. 416 pp.

McFarland, Joseph. The epidemic of yellow fever in Philadelphia in 1793 and its influence upon Dr. Benjamin Rush. *Medical Life*, XXXVI, 449–96. A critical study of Rush's status as a physician.

McLaughlin, A. C. The Confederation and the Constitution. New York. 1905. 348 pp.

McMaster, John Bach. History of the people of the United States. 8 vols. New York. 1883–1913.

McMaster, John B., and Stone, Frederick D. Pennsylvania and the Federal Constitution, 1787–1788. Phila. 1888. 803 pp.
Rush took an active part in the Penna. Convention for the ratification of the federal constitution.

Melville, Lewis. The life and letters of William Cobbett in England and America. 2 vols. London, 1913.

Mills, Charles K. Benjamin Rush and American psychiatry. New York. 1886. 36 pp.

Mitchell, S. Weir. Commemorative Address. Centennial anniversary of the College of Physicians of Philadelphia. Transactions of the College of Physicians. Phila. 1887. See pages 305–34.
Calls Rush "the greatest physician this country has produced."

Mitchell, S. Weir. The Red City, a novel of the second administration of President Washington. New York. 1908. 421 pp.
Rush is one of the characters in this story.

Mitchell, T. D. The charge of falsehood against Dr. Rush, refuted. Phila. 1833. 34 pp. MSS. in College of Physicians.
The author vigorously defends the honesty of Rush's statements on the success of his treatment of yellow fever in 1793.

Mitchell, Thomas D. The character of Rush, an introductory to the course on the theory and practice of medicine in the Philadelphia College of Medicine. Phila. 1848. 23 pp.

Morton, Thomas G. The history of the Pennsylvania Hospital, 1751–1895. Phila. 1895. 575 pp.

Murphy, Thomas. The Presbytery, of the Log College, or the cradle of the Presbyterian Church in America. Phila. 1889. 526 pp.
Notes on Samuel Finley, Rush's uncle and teacher at Nottingham.

Musser, J. H. Memoranda of the life and works of Benjamin Rush. Phila. 1888. 7 pp.

Nevins, Allan. The American States during and after the Revolution, 1775–1789. New York. 1924. 728 pp.

Newell, Lyman C. Chemical education in America from the earliest days to 1820. Journal of Chemical Education, IV, No. 4, 677–695.

Norris, George W. The early history of medicine in Philadelphia. Phila. 1886. 232 pp.
A survey of the leading physicians, hospitals, and institutions.

Oberholtzer, Ellis P. The literary history of Philadelphia. Phila. 1906. 433 pp. Praises Rush's literary style.

Packard, Francis R. The history of medicine in the United States. Phila. 1901. 542 pp.
This book was revised and enlarged in 1932.

Packard, Francis R. How London and Edinburgh influenced medicine in Philadelphia in the eighteenth century. Transactions of the College of Physicians of Philadelphia. Third Series. LIII, 151–81.
Sketches of Rush's contemporaries.

Park, Roswell. An epitome of the history of medicine. Phila. 1897. 348 pp.
Calls Rush the leading American medical man in the eighteenth century.

Parker, William; and Cutler, Julia P. Life, Journals and Correspondence of Rev. Manasseh Cutler. 2 vols. Cincinnati. 1881.
Cutler was an agent of the Ohio Company. In 1787 he visited Philadelphia and observed Rush at work in the Pennsylvania Hospital.

Pennypacker, Samuel W. Pennsylvania in American History. Phila. 1910. 493 pp.

Pepper, William. Benjamin Rush. *Journal of the American Medical Association*, April 26, 1890, 24 pp.

Pepper, William. The medical side of Benjamin Franklin. Phila. 1911. 122 pp.

Pettigrew, Thomas J. Memoirs of the life and writings of the late John Coakley Lettsom. 2 vols. London. 1817.
Contains letters from Rush to Lettsom.

Pickering, Octavius; and Upham, Charles W. The life of Timothy Pickering. 4 vols. Boston. 1867–73.
Pickering was one of Rush's close friends.

Pleadwell, F. L. An early reference in medical literature to the relation between focal infection and arthritis. *Journal of the American Medical Association*, LXXII, No. 11, 819.
Refers to Rush's account of focal infection.

Pollock, Thomas C. The Philadelphia theatre in the eighteenth century. Phila. 1933. 445 pp.
Interesting background material.

Pryor, Abraham. Serious poems on several occasions. Lancaster. 1818. 20 pp.
Contains an "elegy to the memory of the excellent Benjamin Rush." Pryor studied under Rush in 1791–92.

Reed, William B. A rejoinder to Mr. Bancroft's historical essay on President Reed. Phila. 1867. 114 pp.

Reed, William B. President Reed of Pennsylvania. A Reply to Mr. George Bancroft and Others. Phila. 1867. 132 pp.
Denounces Rush as a "tattler."

Richardson, Benj. The Asclepiad. A book of original research and observation in the science, art, and literature of medicine, preventive and curative. London. 1885.
See volume II, 38–57.

Richardson, Benj. Disciples of Aesculapius. 2 vols. London. 827 pp. Praises Rush in his various capacities as physician, political leader, man of letters.

Roof, Katherine Metcalf. Colonel William Smith and Lady. Boston. 1929. 347 pp.
Colonel Smith married John Adams' daughter, Abigail.

Rurah, John. Pediatrics of the Past. New York. 1925. 592 pp.
Says that Rush's "description of cholera infantum places him among those who contributed to pediatrics in the early years," and that Rush was the first to connect the disease with hot weather.

Ruschenberger, W. S. W. An account of the institution and progress of the College of Physicians of Philadelphia during a hundred years, from January, 1787. Phila. 1887. 308 pp.

Rush, Benjamin. Wm. B. Reed expert in the art of exhumation of the dead. London. 1867. 15 pp.
A reply to *President Reed of Pennsylvania*.

Sanderson, John et al. Biographies of the signers to the Declaration of Independence. 3 vols. Phila. 1828.
The chapter on Rush is drawn largely from Ramsay's *Eulogium*.

Scharf, J. T., and Westcott, T. History of Philadelphia. 3 vols. Phila. 1884.

Smith, Edgar Fahs. Old chemistries. New York. 1927. 89 pp. Refers to Rush's *Syllabus of a Course of Lectures on Chemistry*, "the first textual contribution in chemistry from the hand of an American."

Smith, Horace W. Life of Rev. William Smith, first Provost of the College of Philadelphia. 2 vols. Phila. 1879.

Steiner, Bernard C. The life and correspondence of James McHenry, Secretary of War under Washington and Adams. Cleveland. 1907. 640 pp.
McHenry studied under Rush before the Revolution.

Stephenson, G. W. Benjamin Rush. Proceedings of the staff meetings of the Mayo Clinic. VII, No. 36, 524–27.
Calls Rush "one of the most famous of early American physicians."

Stille, Charles J. The Life and times of John Dickinson, 1732–1808. Phila. 1891.

Stoll, Henry F. Benjamin Rush as a phthisiotherapist. *Medical Record*, February 8, 1908.
Calls Rush a pioneer in phthisiotheraphy.

Strecker, Edward A. Reminiscences from the early days of the Pennsylvania Hospital. *Annals of Medical History*, July 1929, 429–34.
Calls attention to Rush's important work in the insane department.

Thacher, James. American medical biography, or, memoirs of eminent physicians who have flourished in America. 2 vols. Boston. 1828.
The sketch of Rush's life is excellent, even if uncritical.

Thorpe, Edward S. An inquiry into educational experiments. *The General Magazine and Historical Chronicle*, July 1931, 486–92.
Points out that in his essays on education, Rush covered practically every aspect of education, colonial and modern.

Toner, Joseph M. Contributions to the annals of medical progress and medical education in the United States, before and during the War of Independence. Washington. 1874. 118 pp.

Toner, Joseph M. The medical men of the Revolution with a brief history of the medical department of the Continental Army. Phila. 1876. 140 pp.

Tuke, Hack. The insane in the United States and Canada. London. 1885. 242 pp.

Tyler, Moses Coit. The literary history of the American Revolution, 1763–83. 2 vols. New York. 1897.

Tyler, Samuel. Memoir of Roger Brooke Taney. Baltimore. 1872. 659 pp.

Van Tyne, Claude H. The War of Independence, American phase. Boston. 1929. 518 pp.
Contains an excellent survey of conditions in the military hospitals.

Warren, Charles. The Making of the Constitution. Boston. 1929. 832 pp.

Watson, Edward W. The voice of Benjamin Rush from the medical past; with a biographical sketch of the life of Dr. Constans Curtin. International Clinics. Phila. XXXIV, Third Series, 261–67. 1924.
Curtin studied under Rush in 1807.

Watson, John F. Annals of Philadelphia and Pennsylvania in the Olden Time. 3 vols. Phila. 1899.

Wharton, Anne H. Salons, colonial and republican. Phila. 1900. 286 pp.

Wharton, Anne H. Social Life in the early republic. Phila. 1902. 346 pp.

Wilson, James C. An address delivered at the unveiling of a monument erected by the American Medical Association to the memory of Benjamin Rush in Washington, June 11, 1904. Phila. 1904. 20 pp.

Wood, George B. Early history of the University of Pennsylvania. Phila. n.d. 112 pp.

Woodbury, Frank. Benjamin Rush, patriot, physician and psychiator.
Transactions of the American Medico-Psychological Association. Proceedings for 1913. XX, 427–30.
Stresses Rush's pioneer work in mental diseases.

Woody, Thomas. A history of women's education in the United States. 2 vols. Lancaster. 1929.

INDEX

Index